THE FUTURE OF
THE INTERNATIONAL LEGAL ORDER
VOLUME III

Conflict Management

THE FUTURE OF THE
INTERNATIONAL LEGAL ORDER

EDITED BY CYRIL E. BLACK
AND RICHARD A. FALK

Volume I. *Trends and Patterns.* 1969.
Volume II. *Wealth and Resources.* 1970.
Volume III. *Conflict Management.* 1971.
Volume IV. *The Structure of the International Environment.* 1972.
Volume V. *Toward an International Consensus.* Forthcoming.

Written under the auspices of the
Center of International Studies,
Princeton University

THE FUTURE
OF THE INTERNATIONAL
LEGAL ORDER

VOLUME III

Conflict Management

EDITED BY CYRIL E. BLACK
AND RICHARD A. FALK

PRINCETON UNIVERSITY PRESS
PRINCETON, NEW JERSEY, 1971

Foreword

THIS SERIES has been organized and edited under the auspices of the Center of International Studies, Princeton University, with the assistance of a grant from the Ford Foundation. The views presented in these volumes are those of the authors of the individual chapters, and do not necessarily represent those of the contributors as a group, of the Center of International Studies, or of the Ford Foundation.

Volume IV, *The Structure of the International Environment*, is being prepared for publication, and plans are being made for the international assessment of the interpretations set forth in Volumes I-IV. This assessment will be the subject of Volume V.

The editors wish to thank Marjorie Putney of the Princeton University Press and Jane G. McDowall, June Traube, and Mary Merrick of the staff of the Center of International Studies at Princeton University for the careful attention that they have given to the preparation of this manuscript.

CYRIL E. BLACK
RICHARD A. FALK

Introduction

CONFLICT MANAGEMENT is the central problem of the international legal order, the fundamental yardstick by which the adequacy of the system as a whole must be measured. Indeed, the concerns of the twentieth century have gradually crystallized around the issue of whether general warfare can be avoided in the future. The management of conflict has always been a matter for concern, but until recently not even the most destructive of wars could retard the evolution of human societies by more than a few years. The development of nuclear weapons capable of inflicting awesome destruction has now added an apocalyptic dimension to this preexisting concern. Under these circumstances, the minimal undertaking of the international legal order is to prevent any recurrence of general warfare and, if possible, any recourse whatsoever to nuclear weapons.

The major responsibility for conflict management remains on a national level. Governments of powerful states possess the discretion and capability to initiate a nuclear war in less than an hour from the moment of decision. The most important limitations on these potentialities for general warfare derive from internal checks that operate to discourage the initiation of general war, a set of internal checks made more secure by the prospect of retaliation on the part of "the enemy," by the creation of a reliable technology of "command and control" to prevent unauthorized or accidental actions, and by the establishment of direct communications links between Washington and Moscow—the so-called hot line—to diminish risks of miscalculation and misunderstanding of adversary intentions. It is evident that in the nuclear age, more than ever, the international legal order depends on the values and actions of national leaders and bureaucracies.

Governments have also been persuaded to establish international institutions on a global and regional level to assist with the shared goals of conflict management. The League of Nations and the United Nations were both established in response to the widely held belief that world peace needs to be safeguarded by central institutions operating on behalf of international society as a whole. The member states have not, however, allowed either the League or the United Nations to develop the police or financial capabilities that would be needed if the mission of safeguarding world peace is to have any major hope of fulfillment. The League of Nations seemed helpless to halt the drift of international forces that culminated in World War II. The United Nations, designed in theory to be an improvement upon its predecessor, offers little in the way of assurance that its instrumentalities will significantly enhance the efforts of member states to prevent crises from developing into wars. It seems important to acknowledge that these institutional innovations, although useful in certain limited settings involving smaller states, have almost no discernible impact on the central directions of foreign policy embarked upon by either the United States or the Soviet Union. Even governments of lesser capability, including France, South Africa, Portugal, and Israel, have been singularly irresponsive to the decisions of the United Nations.

At this stage in the development of international society, international organizations can rarely do more than facilitate a consensus among national governments and, under limited circumstances (e.g. response to the Suez Campaign of 1956), impose a dominant consensus of governments upon a dissenting government or minority group of governments. Nevertheless, it is important to note that there was no substantial doubt among the governments victorious in World War II that, despite the failures of the League, it was essential to reconstitute a world organization with a central mandate in the area of peace and security. It is also noteworthy that, despite the severe cleavages in international society, virtually every government seems to agree upon the usefulness of membership in the United Nations and participation in its numerous specialized organs and activities. Members have neither withdrawn from the organization to express disappointment or opposition, nor has there been any swing of sentiment against the existence of the United Nations.

The menacing prospect of nuclear war has had its impacts upon the ways in which international conflict proceeds. These impacts have been, in turn, conditioned by certain other variables, especially the instabilities associated with the process of modernization in the countries of Asia, Africa, and Latin America. Dominant rivalries among governments have tended to focus upon efforts—ideological, economic, and military—to influence, and if possible to determine, the outcome of internal struggles for political control in foreign societies. Civil strife has been common in ex-colonial countries where national elites adhering to diverse ideological positions compete—violently and nonviolently—for national dominance. This kind of competition tends to become coupled with the rivalries going on among the most powerful governments. The most dangerous situations of conflict tend to be those in which American and Soviet interests are involved and where the territorial separation is artificial or unacceptable to the peoples living in the area. Not surprisingly, the four divided countries— Germany, China, Vietnam, and Korea—have provided the arenas where risks and actualities of major warfare have been raised to the highest magnitudes. The conflict in the Middle East has also assumed this character gradually since 1956, as the externally situated Palestinians and the internally situated Israelis maintain contradictory sacred claims to the land, each with backing that greatly amplifies its conflict potential. In these sorts of circumstances the role of the international legal order is more to provide constraints upon the expansion of conflict and facilities for the contraction of conflict. The persistence of violent conflict is almost inevitable given the prerogatives and capabilities of governments, the stakes of conflict, and the absence of traditions and alternatives inducing nonviolent strategies.

The choice of the term "conflict management" expresses an editorial judgment that needs to be made clear. First of all, we are agreed that it is a desirable normative objective to curtail large-scale violence as much as possible in international society. Secondly, we are convinced that no scheme of "war prevention" has any realistic hope of success in the near future and that, hence, the focus should be on "management."

Hannah Arendt has written with customary vigor that "the chief reason warfare is still with us is neither a secret death wish of the human species, nor an irrepressible instinct of aggression, nor, finally and more plausibly, the serious economic and social dangers inherent in disarmament, but the simple fact that no substitute for this final arbiter in international affairs has yet appeared on the political scene." [*On Violence*, p. 5.] By and large, we accept this account of the persistence of violence in international affairs, especially its stress upon the causal link between the organization of international society and the persistence of warfare. However, violence also persists in domestic society where a final arbiter has appeared on the scene. The emergence of a central institutional structure in the form of a government is no assurance of domestic peace. In fact, because of the risks and costs of warfare as an external policy, there has been a relative decline in the incidence of international warfare as compared with internal warfare.

The present volume has been conceived and organized in light of this basic line of interpretation. Hence, in the opening chapters by Cyril E. Black and Tom J. Farer an effort is made to establish a framework within which processes of conflict management can operate successfully. As with earlier volumes, our conception of the international legal order involved a focus on the interface between the international setting (Chapter 1) and the impact of formal norms and procedures (Chapter 2). We will deal more explicitly with the structure of conflict management in Volume IV, in the section devoted to international institutions.

In Part II of this volume we focus upon the *special problem areas* of international relations where the need for creative development of conflict management techniques seems most critical. Chapter 3 by Rosalyn Higgins examines the ways in which international law might develop to curtail external participation in internal wars, thereby moderating the impact of these wars upon international relations as a whole. In Chapter 4 John Norton Moore, building on his own concerns with the subject matter of Chapter 3, explores the extent to which regional actors might contribute positively to the job of conflict management by operating on an intermediate level of community action between the nation-state and the global actor. In part, the potentiality of international law and of regional actors involves their capacity to decouple—either by ground rules or institutional arrangements—geographically confined conflicts from the central strategic rivalries of world politics.

In Chapter 5 Daniel Wilkes accords creative attention to the special category of issues involving disputes among governments that have an important territorial component. This focus is fully justified by the extent governments crystallize their opposition to one another in terms of territorial grievances. Professor Wilkes' chapter explores some techniques by which these disputes may be resolved short of war and by which the delimitation of boundaries might occur in more authoritative fashion.

In Chapters 6 and 7 William B. Bader and Arnold Kramish examine trends and policies that underlie the transfer (or "proliferation") of weaponry from more powerful to less powerful governments. The transfer process goes to the heart of the capacity to insulate areas of high conflict potential from the infusion of weaponry in quantities and varieties that induce arms races and more dangerous and costly types of war. The subject matter of proliferation is complicated by the interplay of economic considerations (balance of payments) and political considerations (arms suppliers acquire leverage via training, spare parts), with considerations of conflict management. The problems of proliferation have been generally examined only in relation to nuclear weapons, but we feel that there are distinct issues of great world-order importance arising from the proliferation of conventional weapons. We also have included a chapter by Mason Willrich on the world-order implications of civil nuclear power. The concerns of Chapter 8 grow out of Kramish's concern with proliferation of nuclear weapons as plans under way make it clear that the proliferation of civil nuclear energy will be a global phenomenon by the end of the decade, and this type of supposedly benign proliferation contains some ominous potentialities for weaponry. In other words, the very dynamics of bargaining between nuclear and nonnuclear governments may cause *de facto* proliferation of weapons capability while international attention focuses upon the nonproliferation treaty system. At the same time, the availability of nuclear energy for poor countries may help these societies achieve domestic goals and diminish prospects of destructive local and regional conflict.

The chapters in Part II deal with an array of critical problem areas from the perspective of the international legal order. It will be in these areas that we anticipate some of the major tests of the conflict management potential of the present to take place in the 1970's and 1980's. The outcome of these tests is likely to determine the extent of risk of general war in this century, as well as the degree to which drastic revisions of the world-order system are perceived as necessary and desirable.

In Part III, the emphasis shifts from salient problems confronting conflict managers to the structural issues bearing on conflict management as an enterprise. These structural issues are a consequence of a world political system constituted by sovereign states and reflect the continuing importance of decentralization of power and authority. Michael Reisman's Chapter 9 examines the prospects for sanctions and enforcement in international society. This concern with sanctions and enforcement revives in creative fashion the traditional effort of international lawyers to explain how valid and effective law can be sustained without a central governmental presence. Reisman argues that "the challenge of international law in the future is . . . less one of construction of a highly effective enforcement system than one involving the inculcation of a generally sanctioned system of public order prescriptions." [p. 534.] The point here is that decentralized processes— rather than structural change via centralization—are relied upon to improve the compliance record of international law. In Chapter 10 the focus shifts from making the rules and standards effective to regulating the capabilities of national governments to wage war against one another. Harold Feiveson's concern with arms control and disarmament— and his explanation for the limited results attained so far—bears on the extent to which the magnitudes of threatened and actual violence can be reversed by negotiated agreements. This subject matter relates to Reisman's chapter because of the connection between expectations about effective compliance and responses to possible violations in the framework of arms control and disarmament. These issues are dealt with in even more general terms by Richard Barnet in the concluding chapter which considers the limits of legal control over bureaucratic behavior. This chapter raises the overall question as to whether basic problems of world order can be solved by legal means within the existing structure of international society.

The volume as a whole emphasizes analysis of existing tendencies of international relations that are significantly related to conflict management. Not much explicit or systematic attention is devoted to predictions about the future, except in very general terms. In almost every chapter the future is envisioned as an intensification of the present, accentuating existing features, but introducing no major discontinuities or surprises. Whether this attitude reflects a kind of methodological caution characteristic of students of the international legal order or represents a realistic assessment of a future that is stable in structural respects remains uncertain. This uncertainty will be the focus of the final volume in our collaborative enterprise where we will raise this issue with contributors to Volumes I-IV and with a group of foreign critics.

The Editors
C. E. BLACK
R. A. FALK

Contents

Part I
A Framework

CHAPTER 1

Conflict Management and World Order

CYRIL E. BLACK

I. THE PROBLEM

HUMAN BEINGS, like most other living organisms, are social creatures. Many considerations of self-preservation and development require them to live in groups. The size and organization of these groups depend on how they perceive the tasks of self-preservation, and this in turn depends upon the level of their knowledge of the resources necessary for these tasks. In an era of primitive farming, hunting, and fishing, small communities of only a few families may be adequate for self-preservation. Since the establishment some seven thousand years ago of more civilized societies, however, larger and more complex forms of organization have been necessary. Today most human beings live in one or another of 130 or more sovereign nation-states, with increasingly specialized domestic and international institutions.

The forms of organization change, but the problem remains the same: How to relate individuals and resources in such a way as to provide for their preservation and development in a manner commensurate with the prevailing level of knowledge. It is the changes in the level of knowledge that account for the different forms taken by the organizational problems of humankind since the time when a few families could manage the problems of survival by banding together. The scientific and technological revolution offers incalculably greater possibilities both for the advancement of human welfare and for universal destruction than have ever before been available. The problems inherent in directing the employment of this knowledge both for welfare and for conflict management with a view to minimizing destruction, are of a magnitude far surpassing all previous experience.

The prevalence of organization implies the existence of needs, and these needs include both the ability to utilize the available resources for food and shelter, and protection against other species and against other members of one's own species. In the animal world aggression toward others of the same species is an essentially species-preserving instinct in a natural environment, for it is employed not to exterminate others of the same species but to prevent them from gaining access to the resources of a given territory. What is a species-preserving instinct in a natural environment with adequate resources, however, becomes a destructive instinct under conditions of unnatural confinement. When the balance that is viable for a given species is upset, whether in regard to the distribution of individuals by sex or age within the group or the isolation of the group from its territory and other resources, then the members of the group turn on each other.[1]

A large gap, in terms of their ability to control their environment, separates human beings from even the animals that resemble them most, and similarities in behavior with regard to common basic problems must take into account the vast difference between the capacities of human and nonhuman individuals. The relative respect of nonhuman living creatures for others of the same species is conditioned by the assumption of adequate resources in the natural environment, as already noted, but under conditions of scarcity animals appear to be no more respectful than humans of the lives of fellow members of their species. What differentiates human beings is not only the apparently permanent crisis in which they live in regard to the scarcity and unequal distribution of resources, but also their soaring conception of what constitute adequate resources. Whereas a fish or a bird, and even our distant cousins the baboons, are satisfied with a relatively modest diet normally available in a territory that they can defend with reasonable success against others of their species and against more dangerous predators of other species, human beings demand the enormously more complex aggregate of resources required for modern industrial societies.

II. CONTINUING DIMENSIONS OF CONFLICT

In contrast to the relative balance between resources and needs in the animal world, and the consequently rather modest problems of conflict management that they face in defending their various territories, human beings face problems of gigantic proportions. To take only the simple dichotomy of the poorest half and the richest half of the world's population today, it has been estimated that the average per capita gross national product of the former is $100, and of the latter, $1,300. To equalize the wealth of the world's population at $750 per capita would require a sacrifice of almost three-quarters of the U.S. gross national product, and lesser but still enormous proportions of the wealth of other more prosperous countries. Even to raise the average gross national product of the poorer half of the world's population from $100 to $250 per capita would require a contribution of some 10 percent of the American gross national product, amounting to not much less than $100,000,000,000.[2]

The citation of such figures does not imply that the form of wealth

[1] Konrad Lorenz, *On Aggression* (New York 1967), 43-49.
[2] Richard A. Musgrave, *Fiscal Systems* (New Haven 1969), 313-20.

that goes into the calculation of gross national product is the only re-source worth striving for, or that a war of the poor nations against the rich nations is the necessary outcome of these disparities, for economic resources are only one of the issues that set nation against nation. At very least, however, these disparities illustrate the limited extent to which most societies of the world have been able to take advantage of the opportunities for advancement offered by the scientific and tech-nological revolution, and the problems of political, economic, and so-cial development that these societies still face. We know only too well the magnitude of domestic and international dislocation and conflict that has accompanied the modern development of the more affluent nations, and it may be assumed that comparable challenges to world order are likely to arise in the generation ahead.

There were only 25 nation-states in 1815. The number grew to 40 in 1900 and 60 in 1920, and there are about 130 today. The nation-state is thus a relatively modern phenomenon, and the organization of the whole world into nation-states is a contemporary development.

There are very few states today that existed in more or less their present form in 1800. England, France, the United States, Russia, Tur-key, China, and Japan are about the only ones. The other states of Europe and the New World assumed their present form after 1815, and most other states in other parts of the world are of even more re-cent origin. The fact that the contemporary system of nation-states is of such recent origin reflects the fact that all forms of human organ-ization are relatively transitory structures that represent institutional responses to the ever-changing challenges of the human environment.

For the leaders of any one of the myriad groupings that form hu-mankind, the struggle for self-preservation may be seen as a species-preserving effort "to preserve a status quo or to establish a better future one to endure for his children."[3] When these many local strug-gles for self-preservation are expressed as national interests, however, they have led to the world wars that have characterized the first half of the twentieth century. When these nationalist aspirations are backed by nuclear weapons, they can bring the whole of humankind to the point of self-destruction.

In seeking to understand the changes in the world political order that are likely to present challenges to conflict management, it is useful to take stock of the characteristics of that order in the period since the Second World War.

One such characteristic is the diversity of the nation-states. Mention has already been made of the great discrepancy in per capita wealth between the richest and poorest half of the world's population. If the levels of political, economic, and social development of each of the in-

[3] William Faulkner, "The Bear," in *Go Down, Moses* (New York 1942), 190.

dividual countries were examined more closely, the range of levels would be even more striking. Only fifteen or twenty countries, with less than a third of the world's population, can be said to be well advanced toward a reasonably effective application of modern knowledge to human needs. A hundred or more countries, including some of the most populous, are very far from reaching the halfway point in measurable indices of the level reached by the most advanced.

The significance of this relatively low level of development for the maintenance of world order, is that the forms of political, economic, and social change are inherently unsettling to existing orderly institutions at any level. One would like to think that the late modernizers could learn from the early modernizers, and in certain specialized fields they certainly can without repeating the mistakes of their predecessors. New states can take over ready-made the jet-powered airplanes of the technically advanced countries, without repeating the process of research and development that started with the invention of the steam engine. The borrowing of technical devices requires the training of no more than a few thousand specialists, and a relatively small per capita investment. When it comes to changing the deeply ingrained values and habits of many millions of people in a few years, however, the task is well beyond the capability of any society. One must assume that in the fundamental transition from an agrarian to an industrial way of life, with all that this implies in the sphere of intellectual and institutional adaptation, the less-developed countries of the world will not to any significant degree evolve with greater rationality or with less conflict than those that developed earlier.

To say this is to say that one must expect a relatively high incidence of violence within and among most of the countries of the world for several generations. One would like to think, and in 1971 it seems quite credible, that the degree of order that exists within and among the members of the European Economic Community and their immediate neighbors represents a type of order that is a relatively stable outcome of the profound conflicts that characterized these countries only a generation ago. Even taking this European achievement at its face value as a possible level of human achievement, there is little reason to believe that most of the rest of the world can attain this degree of organization and conflict management in thirty or fifty years. There are in fact many respected authorities who believe that few if any of the less-developed countries, as presently organized, can ever catch up with the more advanced countries.

The processes of change characteristic of the modern era have been discussed in an earlier chapter in this series,[4] and we are now more

---

[4] Cyril E. Black, "Challenges to an Evolving Legal Order," in Richard A. Falk and Cyril E. Black, eds., *The Future of the International Legal Order*, Vol. I, *Trends and Patterns* (Princeton 1969), 3-31.

specifically concerned with those changes that are likely to give rise to international conflict in the next twenty or thirty years with which we are particularly concerned.

The best starting point for such an analysis is a review of the nature of conflict during the past generation with a view to determining which types of conflict are likely to continue, and the extent that they may change in dimension and character. There is the further problem that new forms of conflict, unknown in the most recent past, may also appear in the years immediately ahead. We must also be concerned with the development of institutions for the management of conflict in the recent past and with the prospect for survival and change in the years ahead.

The contemporary era remains under the shadow of the two world wars that dominated the first half of the twentieth century. When in the spring of 1966 the period of general peace since the end of the Second World War concluded its twenty-first year—a period equal to the era of relative peace (1918-1939) between the two world wars—there was widespread and justifiable satisfaction that at least that record of peace had been broken. Now that the quarter of a century mark since 1945 has also passed, there is evidence that the particular forms of great power conflict that led to the two great wars in the first half of the century are now being more rationally managed than they were in the 1930's. At the same time, this relative stability is being maintained by a system of nuclear deterrence by the Soviet Union and the United States at a very great expenditure of resources that might otherwise be more directly applied to the advancement of human welfare. Moreover, this system of deterrence rests on a rather narrow margin of rational control. There have already been international crises in which the employment of nuclear weapons has been threatened, at least by implication, and the possibility cannot be ruled out that in a future crisis situation the misunderstanding of a diplomatic bluff or even a pure accident might unleash the full destructive power of nuclear war.

The incidence of local wars, as distinct from major international conflicts, has been greater since 1945 than between 1918 and 1939. Without entering into a detailed calculation of the number of people or size of territories involved, it is clear that more lives have been lost and more countries have been involved in the relatively restricted local wars in the Middle East, in South Asia, and in Southeast Asia in the past quarter of a century than in the earlier interwar period. No less than the European countries in the century after 1815, the newer countries of the world have conflicts arising from problems of frontiers, of national claims, and of ideology that to each of the peoples concerned justifies the use of force.

Even more prevalent than the local wars since 1945 have been the various types of domestic revolution, coups d'état, and other forms of civil strife, which we may refer to collectively as internal war. There are now twice as many countries as there were fifty years ago, and these newer countries are on the whole at a less advanced stage of political, economic, and social development than those that were established earlier. To say this is not to reflect either on the personal capacities of the leadership of the new countries or on the inherent capabilities of their peoples for attaining the levels of development that other countries have already achieved. It is to say rather that, for a variety of complex reasons, they are still at an early stage of applying the benefits of modern knowledge to the problems that confront them. The mechanization of agriculture lags, and the production of food is still barely able to keep up with the growing population. The education of many millions of people to the skills and habits of urban industrial life, the construction of the cities, factories, schools, hospitals, and other modern facilities needed for an entire nation—these are tasks that took generations in the countries that were the first to modernize, and in the newer countries the pace cannot be greatly accelerated. One could doubtless transform societies more rapidly today than fifty or a hundred years ago with a great per capita investment of capital. Perhaps Kuwait, with its great resources and small population, may accomplish this. In the case of most of the less-developed countries, the race between population and resources is a close one, and they are doing well to achieve even a small per capita growth with each year.

The significance of this situation for the prevalence of internal war is that these countries still face most of the adjustments in the changing allocation of political authority, economic wealth, and social status that accompanies the transformation of societies. One has only to recall the turmoil that marked the development of a France or a Germany from the mid-eighteenth to the mid-twentieth centuries, to imagine what lies ahead for the newer countries that still have to confront and solve similar problems. The link between internal and international war is a clear one, and it is normal for rivals in a closely fought domestic conflict to seek foreign allies. It is also normal for the great powers, seeking to broaden their own alliance systems, and to reduce those of other great powers, to take advantage of domestic conflicts for their own long-run strategic purposes. At a time when the strongest bulwark of their security, as they see it, is an alliance system, a change in regime on the part of a single ally or potential ally may be enough to dislodge an avalanche of international conflict.

Under these circumstances it takes only a modest degree of prescience to foresee that the incidence of conflict in the next twenty or thirty years will be no less, and probably greater, than in the quarter of a century since the Second World War. Even assuming that the level of conflict remains the same, the development and proliferation of nuclear weapons greatly enhances the dangers to humankind inherent in domestic and international conflict. The problems confronting conflict management are therefore likely to be comparatively greater.

III. PATTERNS OF INTERNATIONAL INTEGRATION

Since the world is constantly changing, one must look at the challenges to conflict management not only by projecting into the future patterns of the recent past, but also by seeking to imagine systemic changes that are likely to affect existing trends. It is not difficult to demonstrate from a purely abstract and theoretical point of view that the human community is moving in the direction of worldwide integration. Even though this process may not proceed very rapidly in the next twenty or thirty years, it is important in anticipating challenges in the level of conflict management to determine which of several alternative courses it is likely to take.

It seems reasonably clear that underdeveloped nation-states as presently organized are not at all likely in the near future to catch up with those that are now advanced. One sometimes thinks of them as being like separate trains on 130 parallel railroad tracks all headed together toward a station called "Modernity," or "The Postindustrial Society," with some trains arriving earlier and others later but all of them getting there eventually. There is in fact no foreseeable final station in the process of modernization, and so long as knowledge continues to advance societies will continue to be transformed. In this process the gap between the more advanced and the less advanced is widening in most respects, and most of the latter will have difficulty in reaching by the year 2000 the per capita levels of development that the more advanced have already achieved.

It is also apparent that in the near future of one or two generations the societies of the world will not converge in the sense that traditional institutions and values will be dissolved by the tasks of the modern era. No doubt at the level of applied technology, most countries already have industrial plants and transportation systems that do not differ very substantially in the level of knowledge that they reflect. When it comes to political, economic, and social institutions, however, the profound differences that characterize traditional cultures in the societies of the world are likely to persist for a long time. The essence of the process of transformation is the adaptation of the diverse traditional systems to the functions characteristic of the modern era, and there appear to be almost as many roads to modernization as there are traditional cultures.

For similar reasons it seems most unlikely that either the "Western" or "Marxist-Leninist" institutional systems will prevail in large areas of the world even if backed by extensive political force. It is by now quite apparent that there are within both the Western and the Marxist-Leninist orbits wide differences even among countries at a relatively similar level of development, and it takes more than an army of occupation to obliterate these differences. The "East-West" confrontation has tended to dominate thinking about international relations since 1945 and to distort the discussions regarding future alternatives. The confrontation is no doubt a real one in terms of military technology, but it is not of comparable significance in its influence on the development of the diverse countries of the world.

In considering alternative forms of international integration to those that are usually advanced, it is important to stress the ways in which international integration represents a continuation of domestic integration. The modernization of most forms of human activity requires increasing specialization, and this in turn leads to an ever-widening of the areas within which goods and services are produced and exchanged in order to take advantage of economies of scale. Just as the multitude of local barriers to trade have given way to national customs unions and to international trade agreements; local systems of exchange have given way to national currencies with international convertibility; local and national systems of weights and measures have given way to international units of measurement; and municipal and county governments are giving up their various authorities in favor of national systems of taxation, legislation, and social security—so it appears to be ineluctable that these and other institutions have functions that will gradually assume an international character.

This line of reasoning suggests a pattern of international development that may resemble that which has taken place in the recent past within the larger federally organized national political systems. Although such systems normally allocate specific functions to the constituent states and republics, which at earlier times may have had a relatively autonomous existence as politically organized societies, the contemporary trend has been toward a reallocation of all functions to larger entities than the constituent political units. In every case certain functions, such as those associated with fiscal systems, currencies, defense, and similar activities, have been allocated to an increasingly powerful central government. The reallocation of other functions, such as education, social legislation, and public health, has depended on the political culture of the countries concerned. In every case, however, the most significant functions involving large movements of population, such as industry and the diverse activities requiring the close proximity of many resources and skills, have tended to center in great urban complexes that bear no necessary relationship to the administrative divisions of the country established in earlier times. The essence of this process is the integration of functions in those geographical and institutional centers that can perform them most effectively, and the gradual decline in the relevance of internal political and administrative borders.

If international integration proceeds along lines such as these, one may expect to see a further concentration of many economic and social activities in the hands of various public and private international bodies, and also the increasing migration of skilled individuals from their country of origin to those world metropolitan centers where their skills can be most effectively employed. Although this latter process may be decried as a "brain drain" by the countries of origin, it is no more to be deplored from a long-run perspective than the movement of talented and ambitious individuals from the villages and small towns of a given country to its cities. Under this form of international integration, the existing national frontiers would for many purposes become as irrelevant as administrative frontiers within countries.

The United Nations may well play a central role in such a development, although it is a very different one from that which its founders had in mind. The original conception of the United Nations was essentially federal in the sense that the member states were regarded as discrete and equal entities. This conception implied that the political authority of the member states would be the first functions that would be reallocated to the United Nations, and that among its early tasks would be that of managing international conflicts.

Under the alternative process suggested here, the outlines of which can already be seen in practical developments, the member states have been most jealous to retain their political authority. Such conflict management as the United Nations has undertaken has been by means of authority and resources only temporarily assigned to the United Nations. The capacity of the Secretary-General to take action on the basis of resources independent of the control of the member states is no greater now than it was a quarter of a century ago. In the economic and social spheres, however, a considerable variety of international organs have developed relatively independent regulatory and other powers on the basis of authority specifically allocated to them by member states through international agreements. Many of these agencies come under the framework of the United Nations, and it is in this sphere rather than in the political that the initial forms of a possible future international government are beginning to emerge.

IV. Changing Patterns of Conflict Management

The anticipation of problems of conflict management in the near future should be based on the assumption that the sources of international conflict that the world has experienced in the past quarter of a century are likely to persist in the near future, and that they may well represent an increasing danger to humankind because of the development of military technology. It should also be recognized that, although the processes that in the more developed states have already led to a significant degree of domestic integration are likely in the long run to create an environment favorable to international integration, this trend is not likely to affect patterns of conflict management in the near future of twenty or thirty years. The predominance of the nation-state as the almost exclusive locus of sovereignty is a relatively new phenomenon in international relations, and already actors other than the nation-state are gaining in importance. It is quite possible that, even before the end of this century, not only the United Nations but also a considerable range of public and private international and trans-national organizations, regional as well as worldwide, will assume many of the functions now reserved exclusively for the nation-state. Even the individual human being, in whose interest all other institutions have supposedly been organized, may gain new influence in international affairs through direct recourse to international legal agencies.[5]

For reasons already sketched out above, however, this reallocation of functions from the nation-state to other institutions will in all likelihood be limited to the economic and social sphere in the next generation or two, and the political control over instruments of force will remain in the hands of the nation-state. The state-centric world view is beginning to crumble, but this is the type of long-term transition that goes on for many decades. Most of the world's nation-states are still in a relatively early stage of political development, and they are not likely to give up in the near future their exercise of the use of force for national defense even though they may defer to international and trans-national institutions in matters relating to economic growth and social transformation.

The system of conflict management that exists today is based on the sovereign power of the nation-state, and includes the older procedures for arbitration and judicial settlement, as well as methods of collective conciliation and peace-keeping developed by the Security Council and General Assembly of the United Nations since 1945.[6] The changes in patterns of conflict management proposed by the contributors to this volume represent extensions of the present system designed to develop existing instrumentalities to meet the critical challenges to interna-

[5] Oran R. Young, "The Actors in World Politics," in James N. Rosenau, Vincent Davis, and Maurice East, eds., *The Analysis of International Politics* (forthcoming).

[6] Julius Stone, *Legal Controls of International Conflict* (rev. edn., New York 1959); Myres S. McDougal and Florentino P. Feliciano, *Law and Minimum World Public Order: The Legal Regulation of International Coercion* (New Haven 1961); and Rosalyn Higgins, *United Nations Peacekeeping, 1946-1967: Documents and Commentary* (London 1969).

tional security that can be anticipated in the near future. These proposals may be described in terms of three main categories: international conventions designed to limit by mutual agreement the actions of individual states in regard to strategic weapons; monitoring measures designed to bring to the attention of world opinion information about conflict-engendering situations that might otherwise develop to menacing proportions without a parallel appreciation of the need for countermeasures; and a formal and systematic review of norms of international law that no longer conform to the realities of modern life.

The central issue of international security is the control of nuclear weapons, and the extent to which agreement has already been reached on such instruments as reflects a significant degree of international consensus. In the fundamental area of strategic arms limitation only a very modest beginning has been made. Although the initiation of formal negotiation on this subject between the Soviet Union and the United States is no doubt a hopeful sign, division within the two countries on this question is so great and the international environment in which the talks are being held is so fragile that strategic arms limitation must be regarded as essentially a matter for the future. Similarly the Nonproliferation Treaty and the related safeguards established by the International Atomic Energy Commission and Euratom are still at an early stage of implementation, and much remains to be done to ensure development into fully reliable instruments of control.

The monitoring of certain types of domestic activity that is not at present subject to direct international regulation, also commends itself as a means of bringing such activities to international attention. Particularly relevant applications of such monitoring concern the international traffic in conventional arms and the production and separation of plutonium in connection with nuclear power programs. Although the process of monitoring and verification in these cases represents a relatively limited safeguard against abuses that may endanger international security, such measures may be adequate to deter abuses by posing the threat of new international controls when existing regulations prove to be inadequate.

The elaboration of new norms of international law represents the most important task that lies ahead in the field of conflict management. It is by the establishment of new areas of international consensus, in the form of agreed extensions of existing international norms that eventually gain acceptance on the part of individuals through the normal process of national legislation, that the challenges of the future must eventually be met. Such legal concepts include national interest, the right of self-defense, the limits within which the intervention of one state in the affairs of another is permissible, the proper role of regional organizations as international agencies of conflict management, the attribution of a more effective status to current practices relating to cease-fire and armistice boundaries and the rules of the sea, and the refinement of currently accepted norms of sanctions and enforcement.

International conventions and related safeguards are essential elements of a system of conflict management, but they rest essentially on existing norms of international law. An extension of the existing system to meet the problems of the nuclear age is an important challenge to negotiators, because it involves compromises with regard to issues that each of the member states considers central to its national existence. The more difficult task confronting international law is the further elaboration of the basis of law itself, from conceptions which have had their center of gravity in the sovereignty of nation-states as the sole actors in international relations to conceptions which take into account the fact that the very survival of these nation-states and their inhabitants depends on their acceptance of norms based on the welfare of humankind rather than on the security of nation-states.

CHAPTER 2

Law and War

TOM J. FARER

I. A NOTE ON SCOPE, PURPOSE, AND JURISPRUDENTIAL PERSPECTIVE

"WAR," SAYS Lord McNair, "is a state or condition of affairs, not a mere series of acts of force. . . . Moreover, Peace and War are mutually exclusive; there is no half-way house."[1] He thus expresses succinctly one of the dominating perspectives of classical international law.[2] For the cognoscenti in the ministries of foreign affairs and the legal mandarins, the juridical term "war" was not a summary description of the objective phenomenon of armed conflict. Its central function was to signify a state's choice of the laws that were to govern its relations with other states: By declaring war, the national leadership activated a different body of rights and obligations than that which governed its international relations in times of "peace."[3] In the nineteenth and twentieth centuries there have been many cases of armed conflict between recognized states which the parties thereto chose not to characterize as war.[4] And there have even been cases of declared war where armies never clashed.[5]

A legal dichotomy largely insulated from the immensely varied objective features of conflict—such as its causes, temporal and spatial

---

[1] "The Legal Meaning of War and the Relation of War to Reprisals," Transactions of the Grotius Society, XI (1926), 29, 33. See also Ian Brownlie, *International Law and the Use of Force by States* (Oxford 1963), 38-39; Charles C. Hyde, *International Law*, 2nd rev. edn. (Boston 1945), III, 1686; and Robert W. Tucker, *The Law of War and Neutrality at Sea* (Washington, D. C. 1957), 9.

[2] For a brilliant and compact summary of the conceptual evolution of this rudimentary legal system, see Leo Gross, "The Peace of Westphalia, 1648-1948," in Leo Gross, ed., *International Law in the Twentieth Century* (New York 1969), 25. A longer and also estimable summary is Arthur Nussbaum's *A Concise History of the Law of Nations* (New York 1947).

[3] See Julius Stone, *Legal Controls of International Conflicts* (London 1954), 297-98. On the law of peace, see generally Vol. I, Hersch Lauterpacht-Lassa Oppenheim, *International Law*, 8th edn. (London 1955), 4; on the law of war, see, in addition to Stone, Lauterpacht-Oppenheim, same, Vol. II, Pt. II, 7th edn., and Georg Schwarzenberger, "The Law of Armed Conflict," in *International Law as Applied by International Courts and Tribunals*, Vol. II (London 1968).

[4] The cases are summarized by Brownlie (fn. 1) at 28-37, 384-92.

[5] Brownlie, same, 384, notes that "after the occupation of Vilna in October 1920 Lithuania maintained that a 'state of war' existed with Poland for seven years although no hostilities occurred and the Lithuanian government admitted that the forcible retaking of Vilna was out of the question." Other examples are those Latin American states which during World War II declared war against the Axis powers but did not actually participate in the conflict.

range and its destruction of values—served several purposes. In the first place it facilitated transnational commercial activity. If neither of the belligerents opted for suspension of the "Law of Peace," the exporters of nonbelligerent states were protected from harassment. Furthermore, since commercial relationships between the belligerents were not severed automatically by the onset of armed conflict, their own businessmen might be able to sustain operations involving both countries. Where the antagonists opted for war, neutral commercial interests still received significant protection and, in any event, had reasonably clear standards for determining the vulnerability of their operations to belligerent intervention.

The net influence of the subjective war-peace dichotomy on interstate violence is highly problematic. On the one hand, it tended to contain violence by reducing the opportunities for abrasive interaction between belligerents and initially neutral states. On the other hand, as elite foreign policies were subjected to evaluation by an increasingly broad constituency and as the term "war" began to evoke a negative psychological response, the freedom of states to eschew the state of war may have facilitated the continued employment of military instrumentalities for the promotion of national policy. Governments engaged in limited conflicts might shield themselves from antiwar feeling (and in certain cases constitutional encumbrances) without resorting to intense jingoistic appeals which could stir emotions that might subsequently limit strategic alternatives.[6]

Today the dichotomy is unresponsive to the principal issues generated by the phenomenon of organized violence. The main issue is the legality of recourse to force, an objective phenomenon of bullets and bombs. Related issues include the status of neutrality in a world where belligerency may be illegal and ways of minimizing value destruction in the course of armed conflict.[7] Prompted largely by humanitarian sympathies, this latter concern rejects juridical boundaries unrelated to the real dimensions of human suffering.[8]

[6] Cf. Brownlie, same, 39-40: "In most of the cases of resort to force which have been discussed considerations of internal and external policy have played a major role in determining whether or not a 'state of war' should be admitted to exist." He goes on, however, to defend the concept's utility as a means for limiting violent conflict at a time "when legal controls of the use of force were not conspicuous." As an example he cites its potential efficacy in cases where an initial act of violence results from inadvertence or is unauthorized.

[7] Limitations of space preclude discussion of the related issues. On neutrality, see, e.g., Derek Bowett, *Self-Defense in International Law* (Manchester 1958), 79-181; Brownlie (fn. 1), 402-04; Lauterpacht-Oppenheim, II (fn. 3), 623-830, with particular reference for contemporary relevance to 642-52, and Schwarzenberger (fn. 3), 549-664.

On the law of war, see, e.g., Morris Greenspan, *The Modern Law of Land Warfare* (Berkeley 1959); Lauterpacht-Oppenheim, II, 201-594; Schwarzenberger, 109-544.

[8] Article 2 of the Geneva Conventions of 1949 declares that "the present Convention shall apply to all cases of declared war or of any other armed conflict which

There is in addition the difficulty that hardly anyone[9] seems to declare war any more.[10] Conflict wears other verbal habiliments: "confrontation," "aggression," "threats to the peace," and so on. Hence a study of war in its classical legal sense must solicit an audience primarily among antiquarians.[11] It would find an uncongenial home in a volume devoted to *The Future of the International Legal Order*. Since the author, like the general editors, aspires to some influence, however Lilliputian, on contemporary affairs, he has addressed himself to the issue of the legality of recourse to force in all its verbal garments. While this chapter could, then, have unfolded under the rubric "Law and Armed Conflict," appropriation of the word "war" for purposes of a study of contemporary armed conflict seems a desirable way of protecting from obsolescence a powerfully affective verbal symbol.

Under any title and with respect to every variety of subject matter, a useful legal study ultimately requires performance of the following intellectual tasks:

(1) Identification of the main lines of controversy (competing prescriptive claims) and the underlying policy preferences;
(2) Clarification of existing patterns of authoritative decision and attendant conditioning factors;
(3) Projection of decisional trends and clarification of their implications for policy realization.[12]

Both the importance and difficulty of these intellectual operations is heightened in a time of acute controversy about the substance or

---

may arise between two or more of the High Contracting Parties, even if the state of war is not recognized by one of them." International Committee of the Red Cross, *The Geneva Conventions of August 12, 1949*, 2nd rev. edn. (Geneva 1950).

[9] One post-World War II exception was the Arab states' declaration of war against Israel in 1948.

[10] This phenomenon is presumably attributable, at least in part, to the explicit outlawry of war as an instrument of national policy. See pp. 26-27.

[11] The two most recent major studies, Brownlie's (fn. 1), and Schwarzenberger's (fn. 3), identify their subject respectively as "The Use of Force by States" and "Armed Conflict."

[12] See Myres McDougal and Florentino Feliciano, *Law and Minimum World Public Order* (New Haven 1961), 10. See also Harold Lasswell, "The Political Science of Science," *American Political Science Review*, L (December 1956), 961, 977-78; Lasswell and McDougal, "Legal Education and Public Policy: Professional Training in the Public Interest," *Yale Law Journal*, 52 (March 1943), 203.

My intellectual debt to Professors Lasswell, McDougal, and Feliciano is immense. Although, as will be apparent shortly, I disagree with Professor McDougal and Dr. Feliciano on certain issues, this in no way hinders my recognition of the immense contribution they have made, in conjunction with Professor Lasswell, to the study of international law.

For a recent statement of the jurisprudential perspective of the "Yale School," see McDougal, Lasswell, and W. Michael Reisman, "Theories about International Law: Prologue to a Configurative Jurisprudence," *Virginia Journal of International Law*, 8 (April 1968), 188.

applicability of the policies, principles and rules allegedly governing recourse to force. Of course, because of the rigidity and ultimately the ambiguity of its "Rules of Change"[13] coupled with the absence of consistently effective centralized organs for prescribing and applying standards, international society has necessarily been subject to a considerable degree of normative uncertainty. Obligations created by treaty are deemed susceptible to legitimate unilateral termination only in the concededly exceptional case where there have been "vital changes in circumstances,"[14] a concept which by its vagueness seems almost to solicit adversary application. The occasion for modifying or dissolving customary obligations is even less clearly specified. As a practical matter such obligations were not really imposed by a con-

---

[13] The term was coined by Professor H.L.A. Hart and used in constructing the imposing jurisprudential edifice which he reveals in *The Concept of Law* (Oxford 1961). His thesis, in essence, is that much of what we mean by reference to "law" or a "legal system" can be usefully expressed in terms of the interplay of primary and secondary rules. Primary rules require human beings "to do or abstain from certain actions, whether they wish or not," (78-79). Secondary rules "provide that human beings may by doing or saying certain things introduce new rules of the primary type, extinguish or modify old ones, or in various ways determine their incidence or control their operations." (79).

There are three omnibus secondary rules, each of which responds to a particular defect in a primitive social structure which operates only with primary rules of obligation. The first defect is the inability to resolve *uncertainty* about "what the rules are or as to the proper scope of some given rule. . . . A second defect is the *static* character of the rules." (90). "The third defect . . . is the *inefficiency* of the diffuse social pressure by which the rules are maintained," and this results primarily from "the lack of official agencies to determine authoritatively the fact of violation of the rules. . . ." (91).

The " 'rule of recognition' . . . will specify some feature or features possession of which by a suggested rule is taken as a conclusive affirmative indication that it is a rule of the group to be supported by the social pressure it exerts." (92). "The simplest form of . . . 'rules of change' . . . is that which empowers an individual or body of persons to introduce new primary rules for the conduct of the life of the group, or of some class within it, and to eliminate old rules." (93). Finally, "rules of adjudication" empower individuals "to make authoritative determinations of the question whether, on a particular occasion, a primary rule has been broken." They also "define the procedure to be followed" in making such determinations. (94).

For persuasive criticism of Professor Hart's schema see, inter alia, Gidon Gottlieb, *The Logic of Choice* (New York 1968); Ronald Dworkin, "The Model of Rules" and Graham Hughes, "Rules, Policy and Decision-Making," in *Law, Reason and Justice*, Graham Hughes, ed. (New York 1969), 3 and 101, respectively; and McDougal, Lasswell, and Reisman (fn. 12), 243-60.

[14] Then unilateral repudiation or modification of commitments is allowed under the doctrine of *rebus sic stantibus*. Professor Lauterpacht notes that "in almost all cases in which the doctrine . . . has been invoked before an international tribunal, the latter while not rejecting it in principle, has refused to admit that it could be applied to the case before it." Lauterpacht-Oppenheim, II (fn. 3), 940. Professor Wolfgang Friedmann, *The Changing Structure of International Law* (New York 1967), 301, suggests it has been operative in certain informal arenas. In *The Political Foundations of International Law* (New York 1961), Morton A. Kaplan and Nicholas deB. Katzenbach state that while the doctrine is "occasionally invoked . . . it is never a mutually satisfactory basis for termination" and conclude that "Unilateral termination is not generally acknowledged as legally proper." (24).

scious unilateral decision. Rather the requisite *opinio juris*[15] was implied from the consistent practice of all the leading Western states.[16] The plausible underlying assumption was that a powerful state would not intentionally impose limitations on its freedom of action which were not accepted by all its peers. An apparent corollary assumption was that state acceptance of customary obligations was conditioned on reciprocal behavior by other leading states. The obligation terminated when reciprocity ceased. This left, of course, a very large area of uncertainty about the extent and intensity of deviation which would activate the condition. At some point the custom became obsolete and deviations were metamorphosed from violations to precedents.[17]

A comparable phenomenon does, of course, occur in fully developed domestic legal systems,[18] most perceptibly in societies where the courts openly shape a body of customary law or apply Constitutional language without the inhibition of an inflexible rule of *stare decisis*. A dispenser of birth control information in Connecticut, for instance, was prima facie in violation of the law until the Supreme Court declared the law unconstitutional.[19]

In stable domestic societies, however, the uncertainties and hence tensions generated by the possibility of retroactive legitimation are relatively confined. In the first place, the bulk of legal change is prospective, engineered by specialized institutions of law reform. By definition the stable society has the capacity to liquidate new demands or to satisfy them, rather than allowing them to accumulate and intensify until they reach revolutionary proportions.

A second stabilizing factor is the normally effective monopoly of force enjoyed by the society's specialized sanctioning institutions. Challenge to public order precedents is restrained by the assurance of imposition of deprivations by the sanctioning institutions if the challenger should fail in his effort to create a precedent for doctrinal change.

The comparable cushioning forces in international society are feeble. The United Nations is at best a rudimentary legislative institution. Its one organ with an arguable mandate to effect legal change is emasculated by the veto. And despite the promise of Article 43 of the Charter, it has been unable to marshal any regular force, much less one of a dominant character, for sanctioning purposes.

In the eighteenth and nineteenth centuries the inherent instability

[15] See Lauterpacht-Oppenheim, I (fn. 3), 23-28.
[16] See Friedmann (fn. 14), 121.
[17] Cf. Kaplan and Katzenbach (fn. 14), 6-7, 21-22 and Hart (fn. 13), 90.
[18] For an illuminating and compact discussion, see Ronald Dworkin, "On Not Prosecuting Civil Disobedience," *The New York Review of Books,* x (June 6, 1968), 14.
[19] *Griswold v. Connecticut,* 381, U.S. 479 (1964).

of the international legal order as it was then conceived was offset by the fact that decision-making elites in the more powerful states shared similar values and perceptions. On the one hand, this contributed to restraint among participants. Basically satisfied with the allocation of values in international society, accepting each other as permanent, legitimate actors in the international arena, they had small incentives for precipitous and recurrent deviation from established doctrine. On the other hand, the relative homogeneity of the actors permitted a body of uniformly applicable though often vague rules and principles to express with rough adequacy their needs and preferences.[20] Law assumed the modest vocation of stabilizing and legitimizing the widely preferred structure of international society. Significantly it did not aspire to constrain resort to war for the promotion of national policy.[21] Rather war was kept limited by the mutual interest of the parties in the preservation of major actors as well as by a considerable degree of transnational sympathy among elites. Presumably, the prevailing expectation that force could be employed without serious risk of igniting a conflagration probably lent it a certain cachet of prudence as a means for promoting the interests of the state.

In our own time we are confronted with the paradox of attribution of a wider ambition to law simultaneous with collapse of the traditional socio-political bases of legal efficacy. The forceful promotion of national policy is widely claimed to be outlawed[22] at a time when international society, through the admission of new members and changes within certain older ones, has lost the congruence of perspectives and preferences which both restrained doctrinal deviation and made major deviation unnecessary for the achievement of strongly preferred values.

The concept of a "universal law" hardly seemed audacious when its subjects were a handful of states governed by like-minded elites. But a universal law which aspires to regulate by large and deceptively simple generalities the relation of dozens of states (some of them bitterly dissatisfied with the very arrangements confirmed by traditional doctrine) must stagger under the weight of its ambitions. Naturally, these strains sometimes produce vertiginous deviations from presumed orthodoxy, and this stimulates scholarly effort to organize the new precedents (violations?) into new rules of universal applicability. The

---

[20] Cf. William D. Coplin, "International Law and Assumptions about the State System," *World Politics*, xvii (July 1965), 615, 633: "To conclude that international law must adjust to political reality, therefore, is to miss the point, since international law is part of political reality and serves as an institutional means of developing and reflecting a general consensus on the nature of international reality."

[21] See Lauterpacht-Oppenheim, ii (fn. 3), 177-78; Stone (fn. 3), 297-98; Gerhard von Glahn, *Law Among Nations* (New York 1965), 519.

[22] See, e.g., Brownlie (fn. 1), 110-11; Lauterpacht-Oppenheim, ii (fn. 3), 196-97, 223.

tormenting riddle is how the body of customary rules can assimilate behavior which has no articulate pretension to multilateral applicability without undermining the perspective of interdependence crystallized in the United Nations Charter and, for that matter, without experiencing a fundamental alteration of its own character.

There is here a Scylla-Charybdis problem. On one side there is the danger of normlessness resulting from the failure to stabilize patterns of behavior. On the other the danger of eroding the affective power of international law by associating this powerful verbal symbol with the merely systematic exercise of power.[23] The international lawyer must never forget that law involves perspectives of authority, as well as efficacy.[24]

My critical assumption is that under the existing constitutive rules of international relations, state practice can be norm-generating only where it reflects acceptance of the principle of reciprocity. It follows that one distinctive function of the legal scholar sifting state practice is identification and clarification of latent reciprocities by means of which states may promote their preferred values.[25] In performing this function he helps to guide international society through a perilous revolutionary epoch.

II. LIMITING INTERSTATE VIOLENCE: THE HISTORICAL CONTEXT

The idea that a political entity requires some justification, other than the delectations of aggrandizement, for resort to force appears to have made its first Western appearance in pre-Republican Rome.[26] A necessary prelude to the initiation of hostilities was a finding by a special group of priests, the *fetiales*, that a foreign nation had violated its duties towards the Romans.[27] Following this determination, as Professor Nussbaum describes the process,

> the delegate of the *fetiales*, under oath by the Roman gods as to the justice of his assertion, would demand satisfaction of the foreign nation. The oath culminated in self-execration condemning the whole Roman people should the delegate's assertion be wrong. In case the foreign nation wanted time for deliberation, thirty or thirty-three days would be granted. In the days of the Republic, if the period terminated without result, the *fetiales* would certify to the

[23] The source of the danger is the extreme realist position that "law" is what officials actually do. In the international arena, the logically relevant officials are those who serve the most powerful states; or perhaps the states themselves as reifications would be, for purposes of the theory, the international law analogue of domestic officials.

[24] See McDougal, Lasswell, and Reisman (fn. 12), 195.

[25] See Kaplan and Katzenbach (fn. 14), 21-22.

[26] See Nussbaum (fn. 2), 16-17.

[27] Same.

senate the existence of a just cause of war; the ultimate political decision was left with the senate and the people.[28]

This potentially inhibiting procedure was discarded in the mature years of the Republic,[29] but its doctrinal substance was disinterred and clad in Christian vestments by St. Augustine who found in it an effective means for mediating between the demands of Caesar and Christ. The specific occasion for the doctrine's reappearance in respectable society was a response to continuing concern within the Church over the propriety of Christian participation in military service. St. Augustine concluded that Christian principles allowed participation if the war were just. The primary requisite of justice was a prior injury to which the war was a response.[30]

St. Augustine's conception was elaborated by Thomas Aquinas whose formulation became the cornerstone of Roman Catholic doctrine on war. He listed three criteria of justness:

(1) that the prince has authorized the war (that there is *auctoritas principis*);

(2) that there is a *justa causa*, to wit, that the adverse party deserves to be fought against because of some guilt of his own (*propter aliquam culpam*);

(3) that the belligerent is possessed of a *recta intentio*, namely, the intention to promote the good or to avoid the evil.[31]

As one would anticipate, the progressive enfeeblement of the just-war doctrine began on the eve of the epoch of national consolidation. Writing on the conflict between the Conquistadores and the American Indians, the Spanish Dominican scholar, Vitoria, distinguished objective and subjective justness, the latter being the result of "invincible ignorance."[32] By blurring the just-war doctrine's pristine clarity, Vitoria appears to augur, however faintly, its eclipse.

---

[28] Same.   [29] Same.   [30] Same, 40-41.   [31] Same, 42.

[32] Same, 61. Professor Nussbaum disparages the distinction as a contribution to juristic theory "which must by all means keep asunder the objective criterion of good faith." This cursory dismissal of the distinction's utility may be unwarranted. As Professor Nussbaum himself points out, the distinction was proffered in the course of an analysis of the moral situation at the end of a war when the victor is judging his adversary. A differential response at that point to an objective delinquency committed in good faith would be analogous to a not uncommon domestic law distinction between a tort-feasor and a criminal. "Invincible ignorance" might be analogized to that degree of negligence which requires compensation but does not elicit criminal sanctions. It would seem that this kind of distinction could facilitate termination of conflict through compromise and the restoration of amity. If prospectively different severities of post-defeat deprivations were likely to influence the calculations of potential aggressors, the proposed distinction might weaken the just-war doctrine's prophylactic value in that it creates the opportunity to prove good faith and thus win the lesser punishment (for example, money damages imposed on the defeated state as distinguished from physical sanctions imposed on its leaders).

While Vitoria was a sign of impending change, Vattel was the confirmation of its occurrence. He did not reject the notion of the just-war as a moral doctrine, but, as Wolfgang Friedmann has noted, he swept away its claim to practical relevance by effecting "the decisive break with . . . natural law philosophy. [While paying] lip service to natural law [Vattel relegated it] to the unfathomable depths of the inner conscience of a state, while the only international law that counts for practical purposes is derived from the will of the nations whose presumed consent expresses itself in treaties and customs."[33]

If the narrator is concerned solely with the particular doctrinal form wrought by Aquinas, one could describe the subsequent history of the doctrine in terms of a gradual but perceptible decline into desuetude.[34] But the particular form enclosed a Protean idea which does appear in the nineteenth century system of law erected by scholarly zeal out of the bits and pieces of theory and state practice which had been accumulating for the two prior centuries.[35]

As indicated earlier,[36] the fully emergent system contained two parallel bodies of law: a more elaborate one functioning in time of peace; another which became operative following a declaration of war. Aquinas's central criterion, the *justa causa*, played a rather paradoxical and at least partially theoretical role in retarding movement across the line from peace to war, though not necessarily in reducing the incidence of organized violence. International law provided no real obstacles to passage; but there were certain psychological, commercial and constitutional inhibitions. Moreover, the complex of rights and obligations attendant on the state of war must have seemed largely irrelevant to the short, decisive little struggles with indigenous groups which in the nineteenth century were the most common occasion for the employment of force.

Responding to the real needs of the Western states, the "Law of Peace" legitimized recourse to force for such laudable purposes as "reprisal," "self-preservation," "self-defense," "necessity," and "humani-

---

But the underlying assumption that men would initiate wars even if they regarded the risk of defeat to be substantial enough to require a careful weighing of its personal consequences would appear on historical grounds rather doubtful. At least I know of no evidence that the precedent of Allied efforts after World War I to extradite the Kaiser for trial ever engaged the concerned attention of Hitler, Mussolini, or their Japanese counterparts.

[33] Friedmann (fn. 14), 76.

[34] For a fuller treatment of the doctrine's development from the Middle Ages through the eighteenth century, see Feliciano and McDougal (fn. 12), 131-35 and authorities cited therein. With respect to the doctrine's contemporary applicability, see Paul Ramsey, *The Just War* (New York 1968).

[35] See Lauterpacht-Oppenheim, II (fn. 3), 177-78, and von Glahn (fn. 21), 562. See also C. A. Pompe, *Aggressive War: An International Crime* (The Hague 1953), 138-39.

[36] See pp. 15-16.

tarian intervention."[37] The modest price of this opportunity to employ force and remain quite at peace was compliance with certain criteria and the consequent theoretical subjection of national behavior to external appreciation of its propriety to the extent that other states—most of whom lived in similar glass houses—might have any interest in the legitimacy of behavior which did not intrude on their own colonial preserves.

The varied justifications for resort to force in time of peace had three broad criteria in common.[38] One was that before resorting to force, alternative means of settlement had to be exhausted, except where action was required to prevent imminent or continued value destruction. A second criterion was that force could not be employed for sheer aggrandizement; there had to be a *justa causa*. The third requirement was that the quantum of force had to be proportional to the cause.

The ambiguities clustering around the word "proportional" will be examined more fully later. For purposes of foreshadowing, I would simply call attention to the fact that on linguistic grounds alone the term might refer either to the magnitude of the *causa* or the minimum coercion required to achieve satisfaction even if it necessitates inflicting far greater injury than that caused by the precipitating delinquency.

Given the realities of nineteenth-century practice, it seems fair to say that the definitions of delinquencies were sufficiently vague and the delinquencies themselves sufficiently numerous to provide a legal cloak for any state with the slightest desire to secure one. Lauterpacht's most recent edition of Oppenheim's prestigious treatise, for instance, refers blandly to "The right of protection over citizens abroad, which a state holds, and which may cause an intervention by right to which the other party is legally bound to submit. And it matters not whether protection of the life, security, *honour*, or property of a citizen abroad is concerned."[39] (Emphasis added.) The term "property" included contract debts of all kinds. Since citizens of the principal powers were likely in this era to be found in every corner of the globe spreading the benefits of commerce or Faith, and since failure to protect their activities (as well as positive interference), was itself an international delinquency, and since their citizens could through purchase of foreign bonds obtain protected contract rights without moving from the benign Western hearthside to rigorous tropical climes, and since, in addition, national bankruptcy was not re-

---

[37] On the various "Coercive Methods Short of War for Settling Differences Between States," see Brownlie (fn. 1), 44-46, 219-26, 281-301 and 338-49; Lauterpacht-Oppenheim, II (fn. 3), 132-51; Stone (fn. 3), 285-93; von Glahn (fn. 21), 498-516.
[38] Same. [39] Vol. I, 309.

garded as a defense of nonpayment, the opportunities for legitimate intervention were not infrequent. And their number was augmented still further by a doctrine of humanitarian intervention[40] which permitted the application of force to protect citizens of other states—who were almost invariably white and Christian—from uncivilized behavior by the target government or its subjects. Examples of this principle in action were the dispatch of troops to China during the Boxer Rebellion and intervention by Great Britain, France, and Russia in 1827 during the conflict between the Ottoman Empire and its Greek subjects.

As Ian Brownlie notes in his penetrating work, *International Law and the Use of Force by States*, "modern writers refer to [the various forceful measures short of war] as though they were highly formalized and well defined."[41] In fact, state practice was complacently casual,[42] at least where the target was comparatively weak, as was normally the case. With an abandon seemingly restrained only by the moment's political sensitivities, governments wrapped their coercive policies in established legal terminology or improvised new language which was dutifully added by zealous scholars to the heap of available syntactical alternatives. Despite assiduous efforts to achieve systematic categorization of state practice, the politicians' indifference to the nuance of relationship between fact and doctrine stimulated scholarly cacophony. Brownlie notes, for instance, that "some works discuss self-preservation and necessity without mentioning a separate category of 'intervention.' In other works and in monographs on intervention there is an untidy enumeration of grounds of intervention which overlaps the customary law developing on hostile measures short of war and does not reserve the term 'intervention' for cases in which no formal state of war is created."[43] At the base of this open-textured system was the opportunity to leave it whenever its standards inhibited state policy. Surely a system which did not regard war as the fundamental right of every sovereign state would not have tolerated the amplitude of discretionary behavior legitimized by its fluid doctrinal referents.

Although one may reasonably regard the nineteenth century's legal schema for the restraint of armed conflict with a moderate cynicism, it should not obscure recognition of a certain unease on the part of authoritative decision-makers about the use of force to aggrandize the state.[44] One minor manifestation of this unease was the gradual acceptance of the doctrine that resort to war, as well as lesser policies of force, without prior efforts to achieve a negotiated settlement of differ-

[40] See generally Brownlie (fn. 1), 339-42.
[41] Same, 47.
[42] Same.   [43] Same, 41.
[44] Same, 47, and Lauterpacht-Oppenheim, II (fn. 3), 177-78.

ences, was a "violation of the Law of Nations."[45] An obvious corollary was the necessity of a preexisting conflict requiring resolution. There is little evidence that up to the First World War this was in any sense a substantive limitation. The genesis and equities of the disputed issue were irrelevant. If State *A* demanded of State *B* surrender of one-half of *B*'s territory and *B* failed to respond with an enthusiastic affirmative, the requisite dispute existed. In practice, however, war or lesser coercive means were always accompanied by appeals to legal or moral rights which had in some way been injured.[46] Here was evidence of residual just-law conceptions, of attitudes which could serve as the springboard to significant legal control of armed conflict.

Widespread condemnation of Britain for its role in the Boer War evidenced more dramatically an intensifying sentiment against the right of might. The Convention respecting the Limitation of the Employment of Force for the Recovery of Contract Debts ("Porter Convention") adopted at the Second Hague Peace Conference in 1907 may have been a modest obeisance to that sentiment. Its impact was limited, however, by the conditions that the debtor state had to accept arbitration and honor the arbiter's award. Failure of either condition released a party from his no-force commitment.

The uneven but persistent process through which antiwar sentiment grew and achieved rudimentary legal expression during the period extending from the First World War to the conclusion of its successor conflagration and the adoption of the United Nations Charter has received ample treatment in many standard works.[47] Its monuments were the Covenant of the League of Nations which may be seen as a codification of the emergent customary obligation to exhaust peaceful means of settling disputes before resorting to war,[48] the Treaty of Paris which supplemented the Covenant by precluding resort to war for purposes of national aggrandizement, and the Nuremberg Trials which confirmed the demise of the conception that justifications for resort to war are not susceptible to evaluation by third parties.[49]

Since 1945, debate about armed conflict has occurred almost entirely within the broad normative framework established by the Charter. At a minimum it has largely determined the debaters' vocabulary. The extent to which it has influenced nonverbal behavior is a principal con-

---

[45] Same, Brownlie, 43 and Lauterpacht-Oppenheim, II, 291.

[46] Lauterpacht-Oppenheim, same.

[47] See, e.g., Brownlie (fn. 1), 55-101, 216-50, and Stone (fn. 3), 165-84.

[48] See Stone, same, 175.

[49] At Nuremberg, Professor Jahrreiss for the defense argued that "every state is sole judge of whether in a given case it is waging a war of self-defense." (Trial of Major War Criminals, Nuremberg, 1948, Vol. XVII, 469.) When it was alleged specifically that the invasion of Norway was an act of self-defense, the Tribunal treated this as raising a question of fact and concluded that the criterion of immediate necessity was not satisfied. *American Journal of International Law*, 41 (1947), 206.

cern of this chapter. An appropriate point of departure would seem to be the relevant Charter language examined with an eye to determining the range of behavioral options consistent with its syntax and legislative history.

III. THE REGIME OF THE CHARTER

A. Optional Interpretations

The assertion that Paragraph 4 of Article 2 embodies the Charter's principal substantive restraint on the use of force seems uncontroversial. For purposes of the subsequent discussion it may be useful to recall its exact language.

> 4. All Members shall refrain in their international relations from the threat or use of force against the territorial integrity or political independence of any state, or in any other manner inconsistent with the Purposes of the United Nations.

In the context of debate over the use of force, frequent reference is also made to the Article 51 provision that "nothing in the present Charter shall impair the inherent right of individual or collective self-defense if an armed attack occurs against a Member of the United Nations."

There is substantial scholarly support for the proposition that these provisions in conjunction with the provisions authorizing collective action divide the world of force into three parts: delict, self-defense, and sanction.[50] All acts of force undertaken or authorized by the Security Council fall into the realm of sanction. All other such acts other than those required for self-defense may be analogized to the private violence against which Aquinas hurled the first of his just-war criteria.

Study of the practice of states and the writings of prestigious publicists makes it difficult to avoid Julius Stone's acid conclusion that the "right of self-defense under general international law is as vague as it is unquestioned."[51] As Ian Brownlie has pointed out, "the doctrine's

---

[50] See, e.g., McDougal and Feliciano (fn. 12), 126; Lauterpacht-Oppenheim, II (fn. 3), 154; George Scelle, "Quelques réflexions sur l'Abolition de la Compétence de Guerre," *Revue Générale de Droit International Public*, LVIII (1954), 5, 13, quoted in Julius Stone, *Aggression and World Order* (Berkeley 1958), 5. See also Article 2 (i) of the Draft Code of Offenses against the Peace and Security of Mankind, Report of the International Law Commission, Third Sess. (1951), U.N. Doc. A/1858. Cf. Bowett (fn. 7), 11-13. But see Stone (fn. 3), 43. In addition, there is, of course, the theoretical possibility of military action against "enemy states" (the World War II Axis powers and their allies) under Articles 53 (1) or 107 of the Charter, or joint action of the five permanent members of the Security Council under Article 106. Expectations about the possibility of such action would appear to be very low. The relevant provisions might reasonably be characterized as the Charter analogue of the vermiform appendix.

[51] Stone (fn. 50), 243.

diffuse character . . . reflects the lack of legal regulations of the use of force in the Nineteenth Century."[52] Even in the decade following adoption of the League Covenant, he notes, "many writers . . . did not introduce the category since it was superfluous if a broad right of self-preservation or right to resort to war as a means of settlement were asserted."[53]

Through the mist of erratic state behavior and varying scholarly assessments at least one specific requirement can be observed: The precipitating event must consist of a breach of legal duty owed to the state claiming a right of self-defense. Beyond that point nothing is wholly clear. Professor Bowett, who has devoted an entire book to the concept's clarification, lists these additional criteria.[54] The injury must not have been consummated. In other words, self-defense must not be "punitive in character"; it is thus distinguishable from reprisal where "the object is to compel the offending state to make reparation for the injury or to return to legality, by avoiding further offenses."[55] The rights being protected must be "essential," the harm to them "irreparable" and "imminent," and there must not be "alternative means of protection."[56] Finally, the reaction to threatened or actual injury must be "proportional."[57]

Proportional to what: the importance of the jeopardized right or the obstacles which hinder its vindication? On that point Professor Bowett is less than limpid. Since the right must, in the first place, be "essential" and Professor Bowett equates "essential" with "the security of the state,"[58] one might assume that proportional means reasonably necessary, for the security of the state is treated by most people as virtually an absolute value.[59] However, Professor Bowett's initial identification of self-defense with security seems a little misleading when one comes to appreciate the multitudinous rights he associates with it. They include protection of the person and, in appropriate cases, even the property of nationals.[60] When the concept of security houses such a

---

[52] Brownlie (fn. 1), 251.

[53] Same, 231.   [54] Bowett (fn. 7).   [55] Same, 11-12.

[56] Same, 11.   [57] Same, 24.   [58] Same, 101.

[59] See Coplin (fn. 20), 618: "Before analyzing the way in which international law has in the past and continues today to reflect common attitudes about the nature of the state system, let us discuss briefly the three basic assumptions which have generally structured those attitudes. First, has been assumed that the state is an absolute institutional value and that its security is the one immutable imperative for state action."

[60] Same, 104: "In conclusion, therefore, it is submitted that, in the absence of international guarantees of the protection of the lives and property of aliens, the state may exercise its right of self-defense to protect the lives, and in exceptional cases the property, of its subjects. For, '. . . the price of inviolability of any territory is the maintenance of justice therein. Accordingly, when the price is not paid in relation to foreign life and property, the landing of forces for their protection is to be anticipated,'" quoting Charles C. Hyde, *International Law*, 1 (New York 1945),

lush variety of interests, it no longer is implausible to assume an intention to distinguish among them for purposes of deciding whether the minimum response required for their protection in particular cases is disproportional to the predictable magnitude of value destruction which that response will occasion. If, for example, the only way to protect the property of a citizen is to invade a neighboring state, bombard its cities and smash its armed forces, would the rule of proportionality preclude resort to force even if the property in question is a valuable oil refinery? The following statement, standing alone, suggests the author's preference for an interpretation of proportionality which would require discrimination among interests:

> The principle of relativity of rights and the notion of proportionality involve a strict adherence to the measure of proportionality which the occasion demands, so that a state may not lightly violate the independence and integrity of another state in defense of its own right to the treatment of its nationals according to established standards.
>
> This would mean in practice that a large-scale naval demonstration or military landing could never be justified as action in the defense of a single national; to undertake such action would be to totally disregard the rights of the territorial state by the disproportionate enforcement of the protecting state. On the other hand the use or threat of force by the protecting state would be justified where the magnitude of the danger of its nationals satisfied the requirement of proportionality, for the relativity of rights would have been properly assessed.[61]

But an instant earlier he approvingly quotes Webster's statement of criteria which requires simply that the amount of force be "limited . . . by the necessity of self-defense . . . and kept clearly within it."[62] Equivalent language is endorsed by most scholars regardless of their views concerning the scope of rights included in the concept of self-defense.[63]

As a practical matter, protection of nationals and their property will require highly destructive coercion only where the target state resists. Since self-defense is really a "privilege"[64] to effect a prima facie viola-

---

64[9]. Before reaching this conclusion, Dr. Bowett's argument undergoes certain modulations which left this reader breathless as he attempted to determine Dr. Bowett's precise position. Cf. 94, 98, 101, 103.

61 Same, 94.   62 Same, 93-94.

63 See, e.g., Rosalyn Higgins, *The Development of International Law through the Political Organs of the United Nations* (London 1963), 198-99 and Sir Humphrey Waldock, "The Regulation of the Use of Force by Individual States in International Law," *Hague Recueil*, LXXXI (1952), 455-63.

64 For the distinction between a "privilege" and a "right," see generally Wesley Hohfeld, *Fundamental Legal Conceptions* (New Haven 1963).

tion of the rights of the target state activated by a prior threatened or persisting violation of the actor's rights, efforts to obstruct exercise of the privilege would appear to constitute a distinct, additional delict and one involving the use of force. Hence even if force must be proportional to the interest threatened, an escalation of force can be justified because an extremely important interest is jeopardized when the armed forces of the state are attacked. If the attacks intensify, the right of the intervening state to intensify his coercive behavior will increase proportionately, and so on ad infinitum.

The apparently uniform indifference to the latent complexities of the notion of proportionality is probably explained by the ease with which the privilege to protect nationals and their property was exercised against non-European states by the Western powers. A few marines or a brief blockade would generally suffice. Today, when any use of force is so much more likely to send ripples of apprehension around the world and when even weak states may resist vigorously the intrusion of the strong, there is bound to be a more studied assessment of the importance of the threatened right.

Some scholars now argue that Paragraph 4 of Article 2 alone, or in conjunction with Article 51, limits legitimate self-defense to defense against an armed attack.[65] It is argued, in other words, either that Paragraph 4 constitutes a preclusion of all force qualified only by a single exception contained in Article 51 or that Article 51 operates to limit the right of self-defense left unimpaired by Paragraph 4. Advocates of this interpretation tend to deny the legitimacy of anticipatory military initiatives even in the face of a presumably imminent attack.[66] Precisely what behavior constitutes an "armed attack," whether, for example, it includes assistance to guerrillas who are indigenous to the state in which they are operating, is not terribly clear.[67]

Other scholars insist that the term self-defense embraces a greater variety of contexts.[68] Professor Derek Bowett, for instance, appears to

[65] See Louis Henkin, "Force, Intervention and Neutrality in Contemporary International Law," *Proceedings of the American Society of International Law, 1963*, 147, 149, 165; Philip Jessup, *A Modern Law of Nations* (New York 1948), 166; Hans Kelsen, *The Law of the United Nations* (New York 1950), 797-98; Josef Kunz, "Individual and Collective Self-Defense in Article 51 of the Charter of the United Nations," *American Journal of International Law*, 41 (October 1947), 872, 878; Dr. Djura Nińcié, in Georg Schwarzenberger, "Report on Some Aspects of the Principle of Self-Defense in the Charter of the United Nations and the Topics Covered by the Dubrovnic Resolution" (International Law Association 1958), 617; Lauterpacht-Oppenheim, II (fn. 3), 156; cf. Stone (fn. 3), 244. But cf. Stone (fn. 50), 43-44.

[66] See, e.g., Jessup, same; Kelsen, same, 797; Kunz, same; Nińcié, same; Lauterpacht-Oppenheim, II, same. But see Stone (fn. 3), n.8.

[67] See the discussion in Brownlie (fn. 1), 278-79.

[68] See Bowett (fn. 7), 24-25; Leland Goodrich and Edvard Hambro, *Charter of the United Nations* (Boston 1949), 107; McDougal and Feliciano (fn. 12), 232-41; Waldock (fn. 63), 455, 498.

argue that any illegal act, regardless of its form, which threatens major security interests of the target state legitimates a forceful response.[69] A variety of techniques are marshaled to avoid the strictures of the "armed attack" reference. All of them begin with the premise that Paragraph 4 does not itself restrict the right of self-defense.[70] This fundamental premise is generally defended on the grounds that a momentous change in international law requires explicit language.[71] It is also argued that the exercise of rights of self-defense cannot by definition threaten the territorial integrity or political independence of any state, or be inconsistent with any of the enumerated "Purposes of the United Nations."[72]

When uttered by scholars urging a broad conception of self-defense, the latter proposition is not terribly persuasive. But even if the right of self-defense were limited to cases of armed attack against the territory of a state, conflict is possible if the right may be exercised preemptively; surely cases where each state believes the other is about to attack are not inconceivable. "Invincible ignorance" can be bilateral, because it may be reciprocally induced. One may also imagine a scenario in which one state attacks another in order to promote self-determination or protect human rights. It could be argued, of course, that the promotion of self-determination and the protection of human rights are "Purposes of the United Nations" which are permanently subordinated to the dominant purpose of maintaining international peace and security. Hence, no state can claim to be advancing these "Purposes" when it breaches the peace to promote other interests, for they simply have no legitimate independent existence outside the context of international peace. This certainly is a possible interpretation. Perhaps, measured by syntactical practice and the intent of the drafters, it is easily the most plausible construction. Still it is not the only possible one. The Afro-Asian and Communist states would, I think, deny that force may never be used against colonial regimes or regimes which discriminate openly on the basis of race.[73] The views of repre-

---

[69] Waldock, same, 20, 24, 101.

[70] There is substantial reliance on the fact that Charter drafting Committee 1/I stated in its report that the "use of arms in legitimate self-defense remains admitted and unimpaired." Report of Rapporteur of Committee 1 to Commission I, as adopted by Committee 1/I, U.N.C.I.O., Vol. vi, 446, 459. The report was approved by both Commission I and the Plenary Conference. See Verbatim Minutes of Fifth meeting of Commission I, U.N.C.I.O., Vol. vi, 202, 204; Report of Rapporteur of Commission I to Plenary Session, same, 245, 247. For approval of Report by Plenary Conference, see Verbatim Minutes of the Ninth Plenary Session, 1 same, 612, 620.

[71] See, e.g., Bowett (fn. 7), 188.

[72] Same, 185-86.

[73] See Richard Falk, *Legal Order in a Violent World* (Princeton 1968), 111-13.

In the deliberations of the Special Committee established by the General Assembly (G.A. Res. 1966 [XVIII]) to study and report on the "Principles of International Law Concerning Friendly Relations and Co-operation Among States," both

sentatives of well over half the human race cannot be casually dismissed, even by legal scholars. It seems fair, then, to suggest that a narrowly defined self-defense is not necessarily compatible in every context with territorial integrity, political independence, *and* all "Purposes of the Charter" unrelated to those values. When one accepts broader definitions, when self-defense is, for instance, extended to embrace property interests,[74] the possibility of actual conflict between the right of self-defense and, for example, political independence is evident. With virtual unanimity, the General Assembly has recognized a nation's control over its natural resources to be a fundamental right.[75] But exercise of that right may be seen by a foreign state as a grave threat to its security. Suppose, for instance, that all the African and Arab states expropriated the resident oil companies and declared their intention of withholding oil from the United Kingdom until it severed relations with the Union of South Africa. This act might appear to authoritative decision-makers in the United Kingdom as a most serious threat to the state's security which justified a forceful response.

In light of the difficulties outlined above, the proposition that self-defense is necessarily compatible with Paragraph 4 seems to fall well short of being a truism, even if one construes the reference to territorial integrity, etc. as limiting the initial flat prohibition: "All Members shall refrain in their international relations from the threat or use of force." That construction is itself not inevitable. From the Travaux Préparatoires it appears that the apparently qualifying language was added at the specific request of smaller states laboring to close every

---

Soviet bloc and uncommitted Afro-Asian states insisted that the prohibition of the use of force was not to affect "self-defense of nations against colonial domination in the exercise of the right to self-determination." (Czechoslovakian Proposal, Doc. A/AC. 119/L.6; Report of Special Committee, Doc. A/5746, p. 19.) See Edward McWhinney, "The 'New' Countries and the 'New' International Law: The United Nations Special Conference on Friendly Relations and Co-operation Among States." *American Journal of International Law*, 60 (January 1966), 12.

In defending India's occupation of Goa, the Indian spokesman at the Security Council characterized Portugal's 300-year presence on the Asian subcontinent as a continuing aggression. The Portuguese effort to obtain Security Council action was blocked by the Soviet Union which was joined in opposition by Ceylon, Liberia, and the United Arab Republic. See SCOR, 918-919th Meetings, December 18-19, 1961. The incident is ably discussed in Richard A. Falk, *The New States and International Legal Order* (Leyden 1966), 53-57.

74 See, e.g., the statement of the Lord Chancellor and principal Law Officer of the Crown, Viscount Kilmuir, during the Suez crisis. *Parliamentary Debates*, House of Lords, Vol. 199, Col. 1349, November 1, 1956. See also Bowett (fn. 7), 103.

75 Resolution on Permanent Sovereignty Over Natural Resources, U.N. Doc. A/PV. 1193, December 14, 1962. The resolution both affirmed the rights of all states "freely to dispose of their natural wealth and resources" and required, in case of expropriation, "appropriate compensation, in accordance with the rules in force in the [expropriating] state . . . and in accordance with international law." Whether exercise of the right is dependent on fulfillment of the obligation and the nature of the obligation imposed by international law were issues left unresolved.

verbal loophole through which might slip a threat to their territorial integrity or political independence.[76] Thus we are confronted with the splendid irony of a myopic search for specificity culminating in dangerous ambiguity. Although an ardent advocate of a capacious definition of self-defense, Professor Bowett in his useful study, *Self-Defense in International Law*, concludes flatly that "the introduction of the specific references at San Francisco had not, as its purpose, the qualifying of the obligation."[77] Bowett goes on to adduce considerations of policy for not finding a negative pregnant in the reference to the consequences or objectives of a policy of force: "Secondly, to introduce the subjective element of 'intent' seems anomalous once 'war' had been replaced by the more objective phrase 'threat or use of force.' Moreover, in the initial stages at least, it may be extremely difficult to ascertain the intention of a state, and even the most obvious aggression may be accompanied by statements to show a lack of any such specific intent."[78] Finally he approvingly quotes Lauterpacht who argues that "territorial integrity especially where coupled with 'political independence' is synonymous with territorial inviolability."[79]

From this carefully constructed platform of argumentation Professor Bowett then executes a surprising backflip to the obscurantist *ipse dixit* that "the phrase having been included, it must be given its plain meaning."[80] While appearing to regard obeisance to "plain meaning" as a good in itself, he adds, "Moreover to give it its plain meaning coincides with the limitations on the obligation of nonintervention which traditional international law recognizes."[81] The formal virtue of this result is its congruence with the first argument in favor of a narrow reading of Paragraph 4 mentioned above—the plea against implying surrender of important traditional rights. This might well be an acceptable guide to the interpretation of an ordinary international agreement. Its implicit assumptions about the intentions of states are considerably less compelling when applied to what might reasonably be regarded as the twentieth century's most important treaty, a treaty which among other things, unequivocally delegates novel powers to a centralized authority and converts the treatment of colonial peoples into a matter of international concern. Implying certain diminutions in the range of state discretion from the ambiguous language of an agreement which was reached at the end of a staggering human disaster, and riding the crest of hopes for the inauguration of a new and more humane international system, does not seem anomalous.

[76] U.N.C.I.O., Vol. VI, 69, 346, 557, 720. See Goodrich and Hambro (fn. 68), 103.
[77] Bowett (fn. 7), 151.   [78] Same.
[79] Same, 152.
[80] Same.
[81] Same. For a persuasive account of the uncertainty of traditional international law in this connection see Brownlie (fn. 1), 231ff.

To this point we have explored divisions concerning the meaning of Paragraph 4 which exist among those who at least agree that self-defense is the only contemporary legal justification for recourse to force. This view does not command unanimous support. There are those who conclude that additional justifications are and ought to be available. Professor Julius Stone, for example has argued in favor of taking "seriously" the qualification on Article 2 (4)'s prohibitions.[82]

> What it prohibits is not use of force as such, but as used against the "territorial integrity or political independence of any State," or "in any other manner inconsistent with the Purposes of the United Nations." These "purposes" may properly extend beyond Article 1 (devoted to "the Purposes of the United Nations"), to include (inter alia) the preambulatory references to the saving of the world from the scourge of war, to fundamental human rights, and maintenance of the conditions assuring justice, respect for the obligations arising from treaties, and general international law. The purposes expressed in Article 1 itself, moreover, embrace not only collective measures against threats to the peace, breaches of the peace and acts of aggression, but also (and coordinately) the bringing about "by peaceful means, and in conformity with the principles of justice and international law, adjustment or settlement" of peace-endangering disputes.
>
> It is, we shall submit, far from impossible to argue that a threat or use of force employed consistently with these purposes, and not directed against the "territorial integrity or political independence of any state," may be commendable rather than necessarily forbidden by the Charter. Nor is it inconceivable that situations may arise in which attempts to settle disputes by peaceful means may be so delayed, and prospects of success so fantastically remote, that a minimal regard for law and justice in inter-State relations might require the use of force in due time to vindicate these standards, and avoid even more catastrophic resort to force at a later stage.

Sir Eric Beckett, the United Kingdom Agent in the *Corfu Channel Case,* used equivalent language in defending the British mine-sweeping operation in Albanian territorial waters: "Our action . . . threatened neither the territorial integrity nor the political independence of Albania. Albania suffered thereby neither territorial loss nor any part of its political independence."[83]

Neither those like Dr. Bowett who recognize self-defense as the only justification for recourse to force but interpret it broadly, nor men like Professor Stone who would accept additional justifications, appear to

---

[82] Stone (fn. 50), 43.
[83] *I.C.J. Pleadings*, Vol. III, 295-96. For discussion of the case see note 136.

regard the Article 51 reference to "armed attack" as a serious objection to their respective interpretations of the Charter. Professor McDougal and Dr. Feliciano who have the most developed and persuasive set of arguments on this point begin by disparaging the notion that a "word formula can have, apart from context, any single 'clear and unambiguous' or 'popular, natural and ordinary' meaning that predetermines decision in infinitely varying particular controversies."[84] But just in case anyone is witless enough to impute "some mystical preexistent, reified meaning"[85] to words, they pause to note that Article 51 does not say "if, *and only if*, an armed attack occurs."[86] (Emphasis added.)

They point also to the absence in the provision's "legislative history" of any evidence of an intent to narrow the scope of self-defense.[87] Like the qualifying language of Paragraph 4, Article 51 appears not as one carefully placed arch in a grand architectural design, but a clumsy ad-hoc response to the special concerns of a limited constituency, in this case the Pan-American states—and, to a much lesser degree, the Arab League states. They apparently feared that the veto power might be employed to block regional measures of collective self-defense.[88] This much about the origins of Article 51 is clear. What is wholly obscure is the motive which prompted inclusion of the phrase "armed attack." Whatever the motive for its employment, it stands there solid and sphinx-like, demanding (particularly from those who believe that language has a residuum of denotation which cannot be avoided by contextual fact-grabbing) the attribution to it of operational significance. In the end, McDougal and Feliciano eschew that task, preferring to treat the phrase as accidental in origin and functionally non-existent, a form of words without substance.

Professor Stone, who shares their desire to preserve inviolate the customary-law conception of self-defense, tries a different approach. He concludes that:

> In reserving a licence limited to the case of "armed attack against a Member" the draftsmen were delimiting the reserved powers of Members as against United Nations organs. For other purposes, for instance where the Security Council is not acting, the broader licence of self-defense and self-redress under customary international law must surely continue to exist so far as the postive prohibitions of the Charter do not exclude it. Article 51 itself, in reserving as against the Security Council's powers a narrow range of self-defense, can surely not have destroyed the broader area of the licence of self-defense and self-redress where the Security Council

---

[84] Fn. 12, 234.   [85] Same.   [86] Same, 237n.   [87] Same, 235.
[88] See U.N.C.I.O., Vol. XII, 680-82; same, Vol. XI, 52-59. See also Bowett (fn. 7), 182-84; Goodrich and Hambro (fn. 68), 297-99.

is not acting, and there is no inconsistency with the purposes of the United Nations.[89]

No one is likely to attribute the varying interpretations of Article 51 and Paragraph 4 primarily to different methods and capacities for exegesis. There is nothing cynical in the judgment that they reflect major differences in value preferences or in calculations of the efficacy of alternative strategies for promoting values. Scholars and elite decision-makers openly concede this by invariably citing policy-rooted justifications for preferring one construction over another. There are, of course, times when policy preference degrades law by stretching language to the point of inelasticity and ignoring or distorting legislative history. But within the bounds established by the raw data which the interpreter processes, the rejection of policy guidance would be an act of existential absurdity.

B. Charter Interpretation in Policy Perspective

1. ANTICIPATORY ATTACK

Nuclear weapons appear to have a numbing effect on distinguished scholars, as well as ordinary folk. At least that is one conceivable explanation for the failure of some of international law's most creative and inquisitive minds to examine with wonted care the consequences of a ban on preemptive strikes in the nuclear age.

There is no dearth of reference to nuclear weapons. Indeed, their existence in conjunction with missile delivery systems is sometimes seen as the clinching argument against treating the phrase "armed attack" as a comprehensive restraint on state policy. McDougal and Feliciano, for example, argue that:

> In case of delivery by ballistic (as distinguished from guided) missiles, whose trajectory is traversed in a matter of minutes and against which effective repulsion measures have yet to be devised, it should be even clearer that to require postponement of response until after the "last irrevocable act" is in effect to reduce self-defense to the possible infliction, if enough defenders survive, of retaliatory damage upon the enemy. It is precisely this probable effect that gives to the narrowly restrictive construction of Article 51, when appraised for future application, a strong air of romanticism.[90]

To some that may sound more like an exercise in terrorization than analysis. Analysis would identify far more ambiguous consequences flowing from the availability of nuclear weapons. At least one proposition ought to be uncontroversial, namely that when nuclear weapons

[89] Fn. 50, 43-44.   [90] Fn. 12, 240.

are involved, mistakes are irremediable. At best they would result merely in the murder of a substantial proportion of the inhabitants of the country erroneously perceived to have been preparing an attack At worst the launching of a preemptive strike would catalyze retaliation and thus end in the devastation of both societies with possible severe side effects on adjoining neutrals.

For those who believe that the concept of "victory" would remain relevant despite the massive hemorrhage of both societies, it should be noted that if the states involved have a rough parity in nuclear weapons and they are hardened, mobile, or concealed, the state which absorbs an all-out preemptive strike (the "spasm") would be left with some part of its nuclear force intact, since there is no present capability to achieve a one-to-one kill ratio against missiles which have been protected by sophisticated techniques.[91] Therefore, if victory is defined as the destruction of the enemy's forces (in this case self-destruction) so that one's will can be imposed on the defenseless civilian society[92] (this assumes, plausibly under contemporaneous conditions, that the kill ratio would be sufficiently poor so that the surviving force could penetrate whatever primitive defense systems might be available and impose dreadful antipopulation damage),[93] the devastated target will have "won" without firing a shot either in sadness or in anger. On the other hand, if the national priority is minimizing damage to itself rather than creating the opportunity to impose its will, a first strike might seem rational if one could only be certain that the other side was about to attack, a state of mind singularly difficult to

[91] This is implicit in two juxtaposed statements of Robert McNamara made when he was Secretary of Defense:

> By using the realistic measurement of the number of warheads available, those which could be delivered with accuracy and effectiveness on appropriate targets in the United States or Soviet Union, the United States currently possesses a superiority over the Soviet Union of at least three or four to one.

> The blunt, inescapable fact remains that the Soviet Union, with its present forces, could still effectively destroy the United States, even after absorbing the full weight of an American first Strike.

Robert McNamara, *The Essence of Security* (New York 1968), 57. See also Curtis LeMay, *America IS in Danger* (New York 1968), 269.

[92] See J. M. Spaight, *Air Power and War Rights*, 3rd edn. (London 1947), 2-3:

> ... the purpose for which either party fights is to impose its will upon the other party, that is, to force the other party to recognize the validity of the claims which it has hitherto declined to admit. ... It is necessary to bear in mind, that these preliminary stages, the slaughter of armies, the destruction . . . of fleets, are *not* the end of war but only a means to an end. The real end is a purely mental one. From the first disagreement in council to the last ball-cartridge that is fired in action, it is entirely a question of persuading minds and nothing else. It is the survivors, not the dead, who make peace. Victory or defeat is a state of mind.

See also J. F. C. Fuller, *Reformation of War* (London 1922), 148.

[93] McNamara (fn. 91).

achieve when, under the conditions stipulated, an attack by the other side would itself seem "rational" only to preempt an anticipated attack by you.

Even if the aggressor holds a portion of its force in reserve, as long as its anticipated kill ratio is less favorable than one-to-one, the odds would favor the state absorbing the first strike. Imagine, for example, two states, *A* and *D*, each armed with ten hardened and dispersed missiles. Assume that because of the manner in which the missiles are deployed, each state can be confident of destroying one of the other's missiles only by firing two of its own. *A* attacks three times with a two-missile barrage. Following each attack *D* responds with two of its missiles. As a result of this series of exchanges, each state would retain one missile. Obviously, if *A* now fires its last missile, the best outcome it can hope to achieve is stalemate. But there is a very substantial chance that it will miss, thus leaving *D* in a militarily superior position.

The case for preemption assumes imposing dimensions when each state develops the capacity to destroy the other's forces by a surprise strike. That is why the prospective deployment of MIRV's (Multiple Reentry Vehicles) appears dangerously destabilizing.[94] Missiles carrying multiple warheads might achieve one-to-one kill ratios against their fixed, hardened counterparts on the other side.[95] For the immediate future, however, the danger is reduced by the continuing practical invulnerability of submarine-launched missiles. During the Senate debate over the antiballistic missile system, it was intimated that within the next decade even submarines might become highly vulnerable.[96] This hint was fashioned, of course, as a justification not for despair but rather for the deployment of new hardware. No one now appears to deny the theoretical capacity of the principal nuclear powers to retain effective second-strike forces.

The model of maximum instability is most likely to be approximated by hostilely juxtaposed states which develop a handful of nuclear weapons carried by primitive and vulnerable delivery systems. Since mutual deployment of weapons systems with marginal capability to survive first-strike strategies available to both sides is blatantly irrational and, in this sophisticated era, is likely to appear so to authoritative decision-makers, it seems reasonable to assume that states will not deploy vulnerable systems unless they have insurance in the form of

[94] I. F. Stone, "Nixon: How Many Missiles?" *The New York Review of Books*, XII (March 27, 1969), 17-18.

[95] Same.

[96] See *New York Times*, October 15, 1968, p. 14, cols. 5-6. For a compact summary of the arguments and a persuasive reaffirmation of the continuing deterrent capability of U.S. missile-bearing submarines see McGeorge Bundy, "How to Wind Down the Nuclear Arms Race," the *New York Times Magazine*, November 16, 1969, p. 46, at 159-60.

great-power guarantees of retaliation[97] or alternative strategic capabilities, for instance pre-placed biological or even chemical weapons.[98]

The contention here is not that a preemptive strike is necessarily and invariably irrational. It is conceivable that members of the various national security bureaucracies while wandering through the dozens of scenarios thrown up by the macabre imagination of a man like Herman Kahn[99] would conclude in certain instances that a preemptive strike offered an attractive option. But, as a general proposition, this is hardly self-evident.

One can, of course, take the position that because in certain conceivable cases a preemptive strike might appear overwhelmingly attractive, even "just," to authoritative decision-makers, it is undesirable to create—by implication or otherwise—a general rule prohibiting it. Those who adhere to the configurative approach so eloquently championed by Professor McDougal would contend, I take it, that a checklist of factors the relative weights of which will vary from context to context is superior here, as elsewhere, to a rigid formula which seeks to impose one standard on a universe of diverse intentions, capacities, expectations and participants.[100] Such formulae are deemed indefensible, as well as illusory, because of a supposed lack of policy sensitivity. Moreover, if they command behavior which from a national decision-making perspective is irrational, they will be ignored. Law should not be an abstract exercise in futility or a summary of bad advice.

The persuasive force of this argument will itself vary in different contexts. Occasionally one or a very few factors may dwarf their surrounding contextual features. Nuclear weapons might reasonably be deemed to possess such overwhelming significance. Reasonable men might conclude that the balance of risks would almost never favor a preemptive strike and might then also conclude that the most effica-

[97] Herman Kahn has argued that such guarantees may be required to *prevent* further proliferation: "Nuclear Proliferation and Rules of Retaliation," *Yale Law Journal*, 76 (November 1966), 77. That is, of course, the most plausible condition for superpower extension of retaliation insurance.

[98] For a discussion of the possibilities, see Marcel Fetizon and Michel Magat, "The Toxic Arsenal" and Carl-Goran Hedén, "Microbiological Weapons," in Nigel Calder, ed., *Unless Peace Comes* (New York 1968), 128, 147. See also "Chemical and Bacteriological (Biological) Weapons and the Effects of Their Possible Use," *Report of the Secretary-General*, United Nations (New York 1969), 12, A/7575/Rev. 1, S/9292/Rev. 1.

On chemical and biological warfare generally see Seymour M. Hersh, *Chemical and Biological Warfare* (Garden City, New York 1969), and *CBW: Chemical and Biological Warfare*, Steven Rose, ed. (Boston 1968).

[99] See, e.g., Herman Kahn, *On Escalation: Metaphors and Scenarios* (New York 1965); *Thinking About the Unthinkable* (New York 1962); *On Thermonuclear War* (Princeton 1961).

[100] See, e.g., McDougal and Feliciano (fn. 12), 158.

cious means for codifying this prudential judgment would be a flat prohibition.[101] The rigor of its language, its manifest insensitivity to context, might help to remind authoritative decision-makers, isolated and tense in the maelstrom of crisis, of the collective judgment which the rule embodies. A rule which requires the decision-maker to assess with his tension-distorted faculties a host of factors, tangible and intangible, concerning which he will normally possess fragmentary information, may deprive him of the community's studied judgment.[102]

Nonnuclear conflicts raise their own set of problems. In the first place, the consequences of a "mistake" seem considerably less catastrophic. Since conventional armament for strategic bombardment is far more discriminating than strategic and even most tactical nuclear weapons, a preemptive strike against weapons systems—usually airfields—is far less likely to cause substantial ancillary damage. And what damage is caused to military or civilian installations can be repaired more easily where there have been no radioactive emissions.

Militarily the *status quo ante* can probably be restored fairly quickly if funds are available for the purchase of new weapons and other states are willing to train replacements for the officers and technicians killed in the preemptive assault. That, of course, is a point worth remembering. Men who in fact were not about to launch an attack have

[101] Cf. Henkin (fn. 65), 150-51:

Proponents of anticipatory self-defense raise the spectre of the all-out nuclear attack and of the obvious need to anticipate it. . . . A nation planning all-out attack will not be deterred by the Charter, though it may well talk "anticipatory self-defense" in its justification. Nor does one prescribe rules for the nation threatened with such an attack. If a nation is satisfied that another is about to obliterate it, it will not wait. But it has to make that decision on its own awesome responsibility. Anticipation in that case may have to be practiced; it need not be preached. The Charter need not make a principle of it; the law need not authorize or encourage it.

[102] Cf. Henkin, same, 168-69:

Professor McDougal seems to think of law principally in retrospect, as if by applying (sic) here the old dictum that law is what the judge or the United Nations, or God, or history says it is, *later*. If one is to sit in judgment on the past conduct of a nation, differences of context, degree, detail, may be critical, and the more factors recognized as relevant and the greater the care with which they are weighed, the wiser and sounder the judgment. . . .

Unfortunately, there is no court available to make such judgments, and, if there were, one might yet hesitate to be confident of its wisdom. . . .

To me, a major purpose of international law, and most particularly of the rule against unilateral force, is to influence the behavior of nations. However one may sympathize with Mr. McDougal's quest for just and reasonable order in many areas of international law, international society cannot afford to pursue it with his refinements in regard to the use of external force. I insist on the rule and its validity because I believe that international law and the fate of international society, especially in the days of new weapons, may depend on whether or not this rule is strictly observed.

If the purpose is to influence behavior, there must be a rule, and the rule must be as clear and unambiguous as possible.

been killed. For the dead and those who identify with them, the "mistake" is irremediable. Apologies and offers of compensation are, in the face of this irreducible fact, not likely to restore the psychological *status quo ante*. However uneasy relations between the states involved may have been, tension will probably be far greater after the mistake, even if the parties are quickly separated.

Effecting separation may itself be terribly difficult. Preemptive strikes will occur only where there already exists a high level of tension and animosity with concomitant expectations of violence between the states concerned. In these circumstances the preemptor is not likely to feel contrite when he discovers his error, assuming such an error can ever be established to his satisfaction. Indeed, if preemption is regarded as legitimate under the Charter, the incentives to "erroneous" judgment should be augmented. Even when he acted in a "good faith" belief that an attack was imminent, the preemptor may not be disposed to surrender the fruits of his error—for which he himself may have paid some price in blood and equipment—despite being convinced that the other side had not been planning an attack. If the facts are unclear he may be tempted by the prospect of convincing authoritative decision-makers in third states that preemption had been justified and that the resulting reallocation of values should in some measure be accepted in order to avert a new threat to the peace by the defeated state. At a minimum, then, the preemptor will be reluctant to pay compensation. And he may be tempted to seek favorable adjustments of the prewar situation.

On the other side, the normal hostility toward the preemptor will be intensified by a sense of outrageous injustice. The victim of preemption is unlikely to impute good faith to the other party. If the preemptor has thereby obtained a commanding advantage, the cessation of hostilities may be accepted, but planning for the "next round" will begin immediately.

The 1967 Arab-Israeli War lends rather substantial credibility to this scenario. On the other hand, it may be interpreted as an illustration of why countries cannot wait to achieve certainty. By striking first and eliminating the Arab air capability, Israel obtained a dominating advantage which it exploited effectively. But it seems clear in retrospect that Arab vulnerability was a consequence of very bad planning rather than the inherent efficacy of a first strike. Arab air commanders simply failed to exploit available options for protecting their forces, such as dispersal, underground hangars and concrete shields. Deployment of planes was optimal for purposes of their destruction.[103]

On the ground, the presumptive advantage of a first strike is the

---

[103] See W. Byford-Jones, *The Lightning War* (London 1967), 72-73; S.L.A. Marshall, *Swift Sword* (New York 1967), 26.

capacity to concentrate forces at one point of the other side's defenses and thus achieve penetration. It is possible to imagine a case where one state learns of a surreptitious concentration on its borders but not in time to shift its own ground forces. In that event, there certainly would be a great temptation to strike the concentration and its logistical bases with air power or a highly mobile armored force which could disrupt the prospective attacker's schedule sufficiently to permit necessary strengthening of defensive positions.

It is useful to recall, however, that in conventional warfare between fairly evenly matched opponents, the defense is thought to retain a very substantial advantage over the offense.[104] Ratios of two or three to one are sometimes cited as requisite for penetration.[105] Given modern surveillance techniques, it does seem somewhat improbable that a hostile state could surreptitiously achieve the requisite buildup without being detected in time to permit the strengthening of defensive positions.

2. RESPONSES TO LOWER-ORDER THREATS

Today, overt sustained armed attack is a relatively uncommon threat to incumbent elites. It is hardly surprising, therefore, that preemption has not been the primary focus of debate over the existing boundaries of legitimate force. Both decision-makers and scholars have been concerned principally with the legality of recourse to force in response to stimuli other than the actual or apparently imminent movement of armed forces across recognized boundaries. The following are archetypical contexts for the assertion of antagonistic claims relating to the use of force:

(1) One state threatens important security interests of another

    (a) by military behavior short of preparation for an armed attack

    (b) by assistance to counterelites using force to revise the structure of authority in their society, such assistance consisting of

        (i) covert operational support (e.g. advisors attached to combat units)

        (ii) political direction

        (iii) training, materiel, financial aid

        (iv) sanctuary

        (v) "propaganda";

    (c) by manipulation of nonmilitary modalities including economic policies and abuse of jurisdictional authority.

---

[104] Cf. Paul-Henri Spaak, *Why NATO* (Baltimore 1959), 21.

[105] See Samuel H. Ordway, "An Analysis of Soviet Military Doctrine and Its Application," in W. Barton Leach, ed., *Defense Policy Seminar* (Cambridge 1954-55), 207.

(2) One state threatens less central values of another, for example by seizure of property of its citizens or an isolated attack against an inconsequential unit of its armed forces.

For purposes of highly nuanced policy prescription, each of these complex cases might usefully be broken down into such constituents as participants, modalities, objectives, consequentiality of objectives and the prevailing socio-political and technological environment.[106] Scholars differ in their evaluation of the salience of different factors. Some like Bowett[107] and McDougal and Feliciano[108] seem to emphasize objectives and consequences. They would apparently recognize a right of recourse to force in response to major threats to national security regardless of the modalities employed to project such threats.

The assumption which underlies the permission of lawful coercion is . . . that the value distribution map and the particular configuration of the international arena existent at any given time should not be reconstructed through intense coercion *or* violence. . . . Beyond cavil, political and economic pressures may, in some particular contexts, endanger "international peace and security and justice" when they assume such proportions and intensity as to generate a substantial likelihood of or need for a military response. . . . [Modality] may be useful as a quick index to intensity and scope [of coercion, but does not allow one to] dispense with more detailed inquiry into the consequentiality of coercion.[109] (Emphasis added.)

As noted earlier,[110] this view is contraposed against the claim that unless the modality of coercion is military force, a forceful response cannot be justified under the Charter, and both conflict with the claim that the ambit of values subject to forceful protection extends beyond political independence and territorial integrity to include protection of the person or property of citizens from abuse by alien political elites.

The linguistic references employed in the claiming process frequently are drawn from the corpus of classical international law. Thus controversy centers on the contemporary legitimacy of "reprisal" and "humanitarian intervention" and "self-preservation," as well as the occasion for and breadth of "self-defense." What are the real policy issues which underlie these conflicting assertions?

---

106 Cf. McDougal and Feliciano (fn. 12), 159.

107 Bowett (fn. 7), 24: "When the delict does not involve force or the threat of force, it would similarly seem arbitrary to deny to the defending state the right to use force in defense of its rights as a matter of fixed principle. As we shall see, there is something to be said for the view that economic or ideological aggression can be as detrimental to a state's security and, if illegal, as dangerous a violation of the state's essential rights as the use or threat of force.

108 Fn. 12, 125, 130.

109 Same.   110 See pp. 28-31.

The optimal rule for each of the superpowers would be one which maximized discretionary use of force for one while minimizing it for the other. In practice each has attempted to achieve this happy asymmetry through elaboration of special exceptions to a nominally recognized neutral preclusion of violence: In the case of the Soviet Union, the exception is an alleged special relationship of socialist states; in the case of the United States, the exception is the alleged norm-creating powers of the Organization of American States.

One might argue that a restrictive interpretation of the Charter which emphasizes unilateral appreciation of the need for forceful response is more beneficial to American than Russian interests. The argument would be premised on the assumption that the costs of behavior apparently inconsistent with Charter requirements are greater for the United States, because of its more modest control over the flow of information to constituencies in its own and allied societies and the sensitivity of those constituencies to violations of the "law." Published reports of the phlegmatic reaction of Soviet citizens to news of the invasion of Czechoslovakia including admissions of widespread opposition by the Czech people may seem to confirm this speculation.[111] On the other hand, any assessment of its probable validity must

[111] See, e.g., Vera S. Dunham's review of *Message from Moscow* (New York 1969) in the *New York Times Book Review*, November 23, 1969, p. 3.

The contrasting attitudes of the Soviet Union and the United States in connection with the effort at the United Nations to achieve agreement on a definition of "aggression" may appear consistent with this hypothesis. The Soviet Union has generally urged adoption of an enumerative definition, i.e., a definition under which the state first committing one of certain specified acts will be declared the aggressor. (See e.g., the Soviet Union's proposed definition submitted to the 1956 Special Committee on the Question of Defining Aggression. U.N. Doc. No. A/AC. 77/L. 4 [1956] or Report of the 1956 Special Committee on the Question of Defining Aggression, G.A., *U.N. Official Records*, 12th Sess., Supp. No. 16 [A/3574], 1957 30-31.) By 1968, however, the Soviet position had become a little more ambiguous. In the deliberations of the 1968 Special Committee on the Question of Defining Aggression, the Soviet representative noted that military techniques were developing so rapidly that any lists of forms of aggression would soon be out of date. However, he went on to say that a draft definition should contain a list of the most typical and most dangerous acts of aggression. A/AC. 134/SR. 8, 175. Pre-Charter Soviet positions varied far more widely. In 1933, the Soviet Union formulated an enumerative definition which was incorporated in the 1933 London Conventions for the Definition of Aggression. *147 League of Nations Treaty Series*, 66, 69 n2 (1933); 148, same, 211; *American Journal of International Law Supp.*, 27 (1933), 192-24. But at the 1945 London Conference on war crimes, it opposed the United States proposal to include an enumerative definition in the Charter of the International Military Tribunal. See Report of Robert H. Jackson, U.S. Representative to the International Conference on Military Trials, U.S. Department of State, Pub. No. 3080 (1949), 328.

The Soviet Union's continuing support for some kind of an enumerative definition is, of course, consistent with the hypothesis that the Soviet Union is essentially defensive in its orientation and genuinely fears attack from the West. See sources cited below (fn. 192).

Since the founding of the U.N. (and the inception of the cold war) the United States has consistently opposed not only an enumerative definition (see, e.g., the

take into account the limited and essentially transient negative reaction to certain well-known violations by the United States of its own conception of Charter obligations, most notably in the assistance extended to rebel expeditions against the recognized governments of Guatemala and Cuba. Still, one might contend that the failure to provide unequivocal air cover for the Bay of Pigs invaders or otherwise to engage regular units of the armed forces does evidence greater United States concern for compliance with Charter restraints, particularly in light of the fervid desire of powerful constituencies in the United States for the elimination of the Castro government. Probably the only proposition on this score which can be uttered with confidence is that the role of law in national decision-making requires additional research.[112]

Western states with substantial residual interests in ex-colonial territories might prefer a Charter interpretation which permits recourse to force for the vindication of a wide range of legally protected interests. Lounging under the United States nuclear umbrella, they seem insulated from the threat of overt Soviet force, and the relative stability of their political institutions minimizes the threat from covertly mounted violence. Nor do they appear to fear military intrusion by the United States. Since they still have sufficient force to intervene quickly and decisively in many ex-colonial states, and since their property interest in those states have legally protected status under the traditional doctrines of international law, the incentives to claim a continuing right of intervention under such rubrics as "self-defense," "self-help," and "humanitarian intervention" are incontestable.[113]

In the ex-colonial areas, a broad reading of Charter restraints on the use of force seems to promote the interests of most states because the

---

comments of the U.S. Representative to the 1968 Special Committee, Summary Records, A/AC. 134/SR. 1-24, 195-96), but in effect any definition which would inhibit ad hoc appreciation of individual cases. See McDougal and Feliciano (fn. 12), 62.

[112] The American Society of International Law's Panel on The Role of International Law in Government Decision-Making in War-Peace Crises is currently engaged in such research under the chairmanship of Professor Roger Fisher. To date, the best work on the subject is Professor Louis Henkin's study: *How Nations Behave* (New York 1968). Another very useful book is *International Law and Political Crisis*, Lawrence Scheinman and David Wilkinson, eds. (Boston 1968).

[113] British claiming behavior is consistent with this hypothesis. Fitzmaurice, the United Kingdom delegate to the Sixth Committee of the General Assembly in 1952, commenting on a Soviet proposal for an enumerative definition of aggression which excluded mistreatment of foreigners as a justification for *prima facie* aggression, stated: "by mistreating foreigners on its own territory, a state committed an act of aggression against the country of which the foreigners were nationals: and in defending itself, the State concerned was exercising its right of self-defense." G.A., *U.N. Official Records* Sixth Committee, Sixth Sess., 292nd Mtg. See also fn. 141 and ft. 142 and accompanying text.

majority have accepted the vagaries of colonial boundaries and, in any event, lack the resources and internal cohesion requisite for the application of force beyond national boundaries. Indeed, many governments have quite limited capacities to impose their will even on the domestic society. Hence, from their perspective discretionary recourse to force in the international arena is far more of a threat than an opportunity.[114] Unfortunately, a broad reading of the Charter that might have the beneficial effect of inhibiting Western intervention might also interfere with African efforts to terminate white domination in the southern part of the continent. However, in view of their ability to command large General Assembly majorities for anticolonial resolutions including those authorizing aid to the black majority[115]—an ability based both on their own numbers and the almost universal repudiation of systematic, government-enforced racial discrimination —the African states may continue to surround "liberation" efforts with an aura of moral and political respectability, which may well be ripening into juridical significance. The ultimate result of this continuing effort to legitimate the transnational coercion of racist regimes could be open acceptance of a special exception to the no-force principle.[116]

The Middle East may offer a special set of problems. As a "satisfied" power with regional military preeminence, Israel has two complementary desires: to ban all efforts to change the status quo by force and to legitimatize overt force used in response to covert force. In other words, Israeli interests are served best by interpreting Article 2, Paragraph 4 as a ban on all forceful initiatives across de facto national boundaries and Article 51 as permission for a forceful response to the *threat* of a major military intrusion or sustained guerrilla raids. Arab interests vis-à-vis Israel are served by a converse approach.

That conflicts of interest between different states obstruct the shap-

---

[114] See McDougal and Feliciano (fn. 12), 187n.

[115] See, e.g., G.A. Res. 2465, 23rd Sess., 1968; G.A. Res. 2151, 21st Sess., 1966; G.A. Res. 2107, 20th Sess., 1965.

[116] Cf. Higgins (fn. 63), 5-6:

While there seems to be every reason for examining the law-developing role of political organs, it must be admitted that this entails a quantitative problem of some magnitude. That is to say it is often far from easy to see, when analysing the practice of states, the point at which a repeated practice has hardened into a rule of law. . . .

The only possible answer to the problem of at what stage a usage becomes law must be *at that point at which states regard themselves as legally bound by the practice*—a point which can only be ascertained by the close examination of states' attitudes and public statements.

There may well exist a period during which a resolution or resolutions of the Assembly may command considerable moral force without yet constituting new law. . . .

It may well be that . . . the "waiting-period" during which a new custom must be proved will be considerably shorter than in the past. (Emphasis added.)

ing of universally applicable restraints is a proposition that hardly requires further underscoring. The obstructions erected by conflicts between values which transcend the various regional, ideological and ethnic groupings seem to experience greater difficulty in securing recognition. An important illustration of this phenomenon is McDougal and Feliciano's landmark study of the legal regulation of international coercion.[117] They identify as the linchpin of international legal order "the minimum policy which demands that no change shall be effected through intense coercion and violence."[118] Coercion reaches a level of intensity justifying recourse to force when it engenders "reasonable expectations" in the governing elite of the target state "that it must forthwith respond with exercises of military force if it is to maintain its primary values, customarily described as 'territorial integrity and political independence.' "[119] More specifically, a violent response is deemed legitimate where

> the claimant shows that particular "rights" or values or interest threatened or attacked to be indispensable components of its "territorial integrity" and "political independence." . . . the primary reference of the words "territorial integrity" and "political independence" is to the more important bases of community power. These bases are comprised of a community's continuing, comprehensive control over its geographical base and physical resources, over its people, and over its institutions. This control over institutions extends to both the integrity and continuity of the community's internal arrangements of authority and effective power and its freedom of self-direction and self-commitment in customary interaction with other communities.[120]

The minimum policy (i.e., no recourse to force) announced by McDougal and Feliciano cannot be an end in itself except, perhaps, for pacifists, and the authors quite clearly do not share that particular value orientation. Rather it is a necessary means for advancing towards "the overriding conception of human dignity,"[121] which the authors seem to equate with "the richest production and widest sharing of all values,"[122] and which includes freedom of choice[123] among its central features.

The utility of the authors' essentially procedural prescription must be a function of its capacity to promote the ultimate goals which they postulate. To the extent that it reflects the present and prospective preferences of all important actors, a prescription which outlaws intense coercion or violence as a means of reallocating important

[117] See fn. 12.
[118] Same, 170.   [119] Same, 200.   [120] Same, 227-28.
[121] Same, 188.   [122] Same, 121-33.   [123] Same, 122.

values[124] among discrete political entities serves the goal of minimizing the risk of serious violence that might conceivably culminate in nuclear war. Parenthetically it may be useful to note, however, that where it fails to reflect the priorities of significant actors, the prescription can produce an escalation of conflict by distorting mutual assessments of objectives and consequences.[125]

In certain contexts the prescription may also appear to promote freedom of choice, i.e., self-determination. Here the relationship between value and prescription is uncertain initially because of conflicting claims about the value's essential features. These claims are muted in the case of societies which provide effective institutional means for value reallocation. But where societies with authority structures which are unresponsive to the value preferences of significant social groups are at the focus of attention, one may be compelled to choose between a definition of self-determination which emphasizes freedom from external constraint and one which emphasizes internal constraints on value realization. One view focuses on the freedom of recognized but not necessarily representative political authorities, the other is concerned equally with freedom for domestic groups other than governing elites. In the work of McDougal and Feliciano, there is implicit but unmistakable subordination of the latter conception of self-determination.

While they claim that the "basic policy at stake is . . . the preservation of the genuine self-direction of territorial communities and not the restraining of peoples from changing their governments,"[126] McDougal and Feliciano operationalize their prescription in such a way as to eviscerate the putative right of internal self-determination. To begin with, the authors appear to reaffirm the alleged rule of traditional international law which permitted foreign states to aid the incumbent regime in "quelling internal disturbances."[127] If rebels nevertheless succeed in maintaining "prolonged civil strife, waging general hostilities, and occupying substantial territory," McDougal and Feliciano conclude that it might then be appropriate to require foreign states to assume the posture of neutrality.[128] This assumes, of course, that "the rebellion is of indigenous *stimulation* and genuine internal direction."[129] (Emphasis added.) If the rebellion fails to meet that test, it

[124] Use of the word "intense" is, of course, tautological, since coercion is by definition "intense" if it results in a risk of major value reallocation.

[125] See Farer, "Harnessing Rogue Elephants: A Short Discourse on Foreign Intervention in Civil Strife," *Harvard Law Review*, 72 (January 1969), 523-24, 529-30.

[126] McDougal and Feliciano (fn. 12), 194n.

[127] Same.

[128] Same.

[129] Same, 192. Reference to the rigorous criterion of foreign stimulation is suggestive of the perspective manifested by Dean Rusk when he claimed in a speech delivered two years after the Chinese Revolution that Mao Tse-Tung was a Russian

is presumed to be a mere guise for "indirect aggression" in which case the target elite and its allies are free to employ military measures of whatever scope and intensity may be required to assure the conservation of values threatened by the rebels and their covert allies.[130] For purposes of protecting the right of free choice of groups other than governing elites the critical question is what the standards are for determining whether in a given case we are faced with rebellion or aggression. And it is precisely at the moment when the authors' clarify their preferred standards, that the rabbit levitates out of their hat.

The fact that the rebels are nationals of the "target" state by no means concludes the issue, for they may still be "directed" by a foreign state. Even if they are only "stimulated" from afar—perhaps, one imagines, by reading Marx in the library of the British Council—they apparently will lack the requisite authentic indigenousness. More concrete indices of indirect aggression may include the giving of aid and support in the form of military materiel and sanctuary to rebel groups.[131] It also appears possible under the proposed tests for rebels to be mere instruments of indirect aggression even where they receive no material support from abroad: "more subtle and covert factors" must be considered including "the relation, if any, of the internal disturbance to claimed world revolutionary movements; the differential allegiance of various internal groups to varying competing systems of world public order; the degree of sharing of power admitted in internal structures of public order; the degree to which internal practices, institutionalized or not, constitute 'provocative conditions' by denial of human rights to minorities or even whole populations; and so on."[132]

In the light cast by the authors' candor, it seems fair to describe their conception of the legitimate rebel as follows. He is a right-thinking patriot who feels no identity with groups outside his own state, with the possible exception, one may gather, of groups "in the half-world adhering to non-totalitarian systems of public order."[133] Although confronted with the imposing task of toppling an elite committed to its perpetuation through authoritarian controls and deploying organized military forces inevitably armed with automatic weapons and other implements of modern military technology, he

---

agent. Mao's regime was "a colonial Russian government—a slavic Manchuko on a larger scale—it is not the government of China. It does not pass the first test. It is not Chinese." Quoted in Ronald Steel, *Pax Americana* (New York 1967), 129.

[130] Same, 192n, 241-44. Until the rebels are destroyed, proportional force is more force.

[131] Same, 190-93.

[132] Same, 193n. For an assessment of multifactor analysis as a means of promoting self-determination in the context of civil strife, see Farer (fn. 125), 516-18, 522-23.

[133] McDougal and Feliciano (fn. 12), 188.

must not accept gifts of weapons from foreign states. Rather he must make his own or steal them or, perhaps, buy them in the commercial market, if he can obtain the necessary funds from indigenous sources and arrange for their importation. Assuming he passes through this initial barrier and becomes a serious threat, he may then be attacked by the forces of foreign governments hustling to the assistance of the embattled incumbents. This may seem provocative, but it is not illegal, so the good rebel must not submit to the temptation to break the rules and himself seek foreign assistance. If, despite the additional difficulty posed by foreign intervention, he succeeds in taking, holding and administering a substantial piece of territory, the foreigners presumably will go away. Of course, an effort to hold specific territory will expose his forces to destruction by the undoubtedly superior firepower of the reenforced elite, but those are the rules of the game. Of such fools as would comply with them are martyrs made.

One might argue, I suppose, that there is no conflict here between values. Everyone is for free choice. The question simply is how to distinguish free from coerced choice in a world where many national societies are considerably more permeable than a moist membrane and public authority, even where reasonably representative, is fragile. I agree, of course, that that is a profoundly important and difficult question, but it seems doubtful that McDougal and Feliciano are concerned primarily with providing an answer. Their principal concern appears to be either avoidance of any change in the allegiance of states which identify with the bloc led by the United States or avoidance of change in either direction because of its possible impact on "the balance of global power which teeters precariously between two poles."[134] By insisting on the isolation of the rebel, McDougal and Feliciano, living at a time when large numbers of states on both sides of the iron and bamboo curtains are ruled by unrepresentative elites, sacrifice freedom of choice for the values which they feel would be jeopardized if the delicate balance were threatened. They may also be moved by the proposition that the domestic costs of violent change almost always outweigh the benefits. This is the classical conservative judgment which has thus far resisted empirical confirmation or rejection. One may ask, however, whether the people who are actually paying the price of the status quo or cloistered scholars in far-off lands are the best judges of the putative costs and benefits of change.

The net effect of the proffered prescription may or may not promote human dignity. If it reduces the danger of general war, the case for sacrificing internal self-determination may be strong. Unfortunately for the case, one might plausibly argue that the proposed normative

134 Same, 193n.

scheme will actually exacerbate the risk of war. In the real world, many political and social groups do experience profound transnational identification. McDougal and Feliciano are peculiarly sensitive to a single source of political identification, namely Communist ideology. Yet they also recognize in a related context that political elites of all manner of ideological persuasion may feel a sufficient identity of interest to claim a right of collective self-defense.[135] As long as all the elites control a territorially defined unit, this phenomenon is applauded. It becomes insidious only when one of the actors is a counterelite (presumably with a Communist orientation) seeking to revise the structure of authority.

In fact, the ties which bind counterelites to the outside world are not invariably political or ideological. Ethnic and religious bonds may be equally effective. There is no evidence that these "illicit" transnational relationships are about to crumble. As in the past and present, they will in certain cases result in some degree of foreign support for rebels which under the McDougal-Feliciano scheme will constitute indirect aggression.

It is necessary to recall at this point their conception of the function of international law. Above all things it is a source of advice for decision-makers.[136] It informs their judgment about the appropriate response to a given stimulus. The alleged appropriate response to aggression, direct or indirect, is that measure of force required for secure return to the status quo.[137]

Thus the incumbent elite and its allies are given a ticket to widen the conflict geographically, a perfectly logical consequence of the division of rebellion into two categories: the pure essence of the indigenous, and "indirect aggression." An obvious alternative would be to recognize here the same vast spectrum of contexts which the authors so readily discover when investigating most other features of transnational interaction—at least to recognize a *status mixtus* wherein the rebels are their own masters but receive substantial assistance from outside sources. In such a case, zeal for freedom of choice would seemingly lead to a prescription legitimizing aid to incumbents roughly proportional to the external aid received by the rebels.[138] Such a policy would also tend to restrict the geographic and symbolic escalation of the conflict. While search for a perfect reconciliation of the values at stake in civil strife is utopian, it does not seem unlikely that a more ideologically neutral quest might stumble on a more felicitous formula than the one unearthed by Professor McDougal and Dr. Feliciano.

---

135 Same, 248-50.   136 Same, 158-59.
137 See text at fn. 112.
138 See Farer (fn. 125).

IV. IMPERMISSIBLE FORCE AND SELF-DEFENSE: PATTERNS OF BEHAVIOR

A. Defense of Property

Sir Humphrey Waldock has asserted on the basis of his reading of the Court's opinion in the Corfu Channel Case[139] that the nature of permissible self-defense is the forcible affirmation of legal rights which have been denied.[140]

For those wedded to the notion that "old law is good law," Professor Waldock's cocky insistence that the Charter has changed very little indeed is likely to draw kudos. Nor can it be dismissed as a trumpet in the ivory tower, since it reflects the views forcefully asserted by Her Majesty's Government in justification for the Suez expedition. The

[139] Dr. Bowett notes with classic British understatement that the "judgment is not, however, free from ambiguity" (fn. 7), 15. The ambiguity arises primarily from the fact that the Court reached different conclusions with respect to two distinct acts of self-help and made no perceptible effort to explain in operational language the reasons why it discriminated between the two events. One act was the passage of British warships with crews at action stations through the North Corfu Strait. Passage was effected to assert rights of innocent passage in the face of Albanian insistence on prior notification and permission, and, in the Court's own language, "to demonstrate such force that she would abstain from firing again on passing ships" (*I.C.J. Reports* 1949, 31). Nevertheless, it found that "having regard . . . to all the circumstances of the case," the naval demonstration did not amount to a breach of Albanian sovereignty. Same. The other act of "self-protection or self-help" (*Oral Argument*, Vol. III, 294-96, statement by Sir Eric Beckett) was a minesweeping operation conducted by British ships in Albanian territorial waters subsequent to the actual mining of two British destroyers. (The United Kingdom also justified the operation as "safeguarding evidence necessary for the purposes of justice" and as intervention to abate an international nuisance caused by the obstruction of the right of passage.) The Court rejected all of these arguments, stating that:

> The Court can only regard the alleged right of intervention as the manifestation of a policy of force, such as has in the past given rise to most serious abuses and such as cannot, whatever be the present defects in international organization, find a place in international law. Intervention is perhaps still less admissible in the particular form it would take here; for, from the nature of things, it would be reserved for the most powerful states, and might easily lead to preventing the administration of international justice itself.

(*I.C.J. Reports*, 1949, 35.) Specifically in response to the plea of self-help the Court said: "The Court cannot accept this defence either. Between independent states, respect for territorial sovereignty is an essential foundation of international relations." Same. Uncertainty about the precedental significance of the case is heightened by the failure of the majority to make, in Professor Schwarzenberger's delicate description, "any articulate reference to the potentially relevant Articles of the Charter of the United Nations, that is, Paragraph 4 of Article 2 and Article 51." (Fn. 3), 34. Hence to conclude on the basis of this case that as a general rule force remains a permissible means for the vindication of legal rights is to haul millstones with a paper chain (cf. McDougal and Feliciano [fn. 12], 225-26). One does find considerably greater plausibility in Rosalyn Higgins' interpretation: "What the Court's finding *does* show is that a threat, or demonstration of force, may be considered self-defensive, when it is in affirmation of rights which have been legally *and forcibly* denied." (fn. 63, 199n). (Emphasis added.)

[140] Sir Humphrey Waldock (fn. 63), 502.

Suez case represents a major test of claims to a continuing unilateral right to use force in defense of interests other than political independence and territorial integrity and therefore merits careful examination.

In various forums including the Houses of Parliament, the Security Council and the General Assembly, British spokesmen announced three justifications for the invasion of Egypt. First, protection of the lives of British nationals;[141] second, protection of "valuable . . . property . . . in danger of irreparable injury,"[142] and third the protection of the general interest in free passage through the Canal and the prevention of continued hostilities between Israel and Egypt which threatened such passage.[143] Since none of these justifications seemed related even haphazardly to the facts—the Anglo-French invasion being itself the source of any possible peril to British citizens and their property and the effort to separate the combatants being effected by an invasion behind the lines of one—the almost universal demand for withdrawal[144] need not necessarily be construed as a rejection of the justifications themselves.[145]

Such a construction is buttressed if Suez is placed in the larger context of claims and acts. Perhaps the single most significant aspect of the Suez affair in this connection is that it is just about the only case in point. Neither before nor since has any state used overt force to defend interests in property. And there certainly have been provocations of the kind calculated in the nineteenth century to catalyze intervention. One can cite, among others, Iranian nationalization of British oil properties, Cuba's discriminatory nationalization of all American-owned property and the recent Peruvian nationalization. In the latter two instances, no right of recourse to force was even suggested. With respect to Suez itself, it is noteworthy that when the United Kingdom and France finally resorted to force in response to the nationalization of the Canal, they did not rely on an alleged failure of legally required compensation or on Egyptian violation of putative treaty rights. In light of the chasm between the three articulated justifications and the facts, their failure to advance these somewhat more tenable claims for redress is impressive evidence of doubt about the survival in the post-

---

141 See, e.g., *Parliamentary Debates*, House of Commons, Vol. 558, col. 1277, October 30, 1956.

142 See, e.g., *Parliamentary Debates*, House of Lords, Vol. 199, cols. 1350-52, November 1, 1956.

143 See, e.g., GAOR, 563rd Mtg., 7, 73.

144 See G.A. Res. 1120 (XI), November 24, 1956. See also Wolfgang Friedmann and Lawrence Collins, "The Suez Canal Crisis of 1956," in Scheinman and Wilkinson (fn. 112), 91, 119.

145 See Brownlie (fn. 1), 297. Cf. Bowett (fn. 7), 15: "the view that intervention involving the threat or use of force otherwise than in self-defense is illegal finds some support in the condemnation by the General Assembly of the United Nations of the Joint British and French intervention in Egypt in October, 1956."

Charter era of a general right of self-help even in the guise of self-defense.

While expectations of overt intervention in defense of property interests seem low, the same cannot be said with equal confidence of covert operations. On two occasions—Guatemala in 1954, and the Bay of Pigs in 1961—the United States, acting primarily through the Central Intelligence Agency,[146] has supported anti-government forces in an effort to replace regimes which had recently nationalized American property. In both cases, however, United States action may be traceable primarily to national security concerns related to the cold war.[147] In any event, the covert nature of the operations may further evidence the recognition of the illegitimacy of force as a means of defending property interests.

B. Defense of Nationals

The status of expeditions for the protection of citizens carried out under the rubric of self-defense is more problematical. Like the privilege of intervention for the protection of property, in the nineteenth century it was exercised exclusively by the European powers and the United States at the expense of political entities in those areas of the world now characterized as "less-developed." It is possible, therefore, to doubt that the privilege can have survived the colonial era in which it matured.[148] One response to such skepticism has been to question the alleged symbiosis between the privilege and the complex of practices labeled "imperialism." On the basis of his examination of Foreign Office Records, Professor Richard Lillich appears to conclude that the privilege of intervention was not a mere cloak for coercive value reallocation. Rather, he argues, each case of alleged abuse was carefully evaluated on its merits and assistance was given only when the victim of foreign governmental harassment had not provoked his misfortunes by, for instance, dabbling in local politics.[149]

This conclusion may miss the real point. Even if military intrusions occurred in response to the plaintive appeals of only those nationals who could lay legitimate claim to a cherubic innocence, it could still be deemed imperialistic, since the substantive rights being defended

[146] See New York Times, April 27, 1966, p. 28, col. 5; Richard Barnet, Intervention and Revolution (New York 1968), 233-36. Roger Hilsman, To Move a Nation (Garden City 1967), 30-33.

[147] Cf. Barnet (fn. 146), 17-18.

[148] See Ian Brownlie, Principles of Public International Law (Oxford 1966), 458. See also Richard Falk, "Historical Tendencies, Modernizing and Revolutionary Nations, and the International Legal Order," Howard Law Journal, 8 (Spring 1962), 128, 133.

[149] "Forcible Self-Help by States to Protect Human Rights," Iowa Law Review, 53 (October 1967), 325, 328n.

and the means appropriate for their vindication were both defined in a body of law shaped by the imperatives felt by the intervening powers. Imperialism was hardly synonymous with illegality.

As noted earlier,[150] Professor Bowett has suggested at least two limitations of the privilege to intervene which, he appears to believe, will reconcile it with the altered conditions of international society. First, it should be exercised only prophylactically, not punitively. If the damage has been consummated, time is no longer of the essence and there must be recourse to modes of redress other than unilateral coercion. In addition, he makes some ambiguous references to a required proportionality between the number of lives threatened and the intensity of coercion required for their protection.

The doctrinal effort to combine defense of nationals with intervention for transnational humanitarian purposes is another response to the post-Charter world.[151] Unless it is authorized by the United Nations or, possibly, by a regional organization[152] or a recognized government,[153] intervention for humanitarian purposes can be reconciled with Charter language only if Paragraph 2 of Article 4 is narrowly construed. The narrow construction then leads to defense of intervention as consistent with the purposes of the United Nations (which include promotion of human rights).

These exercises in doctrinal manipulation are part of a continuing effort to rationalize state control operations and to reconcile the claims

[150] See pp. 28-31.

[151] Professor Lillich's article is one example of the effort.

In this connection, it may be significant that following the Stanleyville Operation of 1964, carried out by the United States and Belgium at the invitation of the shaky Tshombe government based in Leopoldville, over 20 states, most of them African, asked for an urgent meeting of the Security Council to consider the Operation which they alleged to be "an intervention in African affairs, a flagrant violation of the Charter of the United Nations and a threat to the peace and security of the African continent." See Falk (fn. 73), 325. And this occurred despite the fact that unlike certain other post-Charter humanitarian interventions (e.g., the Dominican Republic, see footnotes 155-58 and accompanying text), the primary, probably the exclusive, motive was humanitarian. Incidentally, however, the operation did drive rebel troops out of Stanleyville, thus permitting Tshombe's U.S.-supported forces to enter the rebel capital unopposed. See generally Falk, same, 324-35. After a long and acrimonious debate in the Security Council, an equivocal Resolution was adopted "deploring the recent events in the Democratic Republic of the Congo." S.C. Res. 199 (XIX), December 30, 1964. In view of the profusion of "recent events," antithetical appreciations of the Resolution's objective were thus expedited.

[152] Cf. Lillich (fn. 149), 343-44.

[153] Professor Lillich appears to recommend that a request from "the de jure government of a state [for] foreign troops to protect lives and property" should be regarded as bestowing at least prima facie legitimacy on an intervention. Same, 349. He thus appears to revert to the traditional view that states were free to assist incumbents against insurgents. One may easily doubt that this view reflects existing expectation and preferences. See Rosalyn Higgins, "Internal War and International Law," Chap. 3; cf. Brownlie (fn. 1), 321-27.

of authoritative decision-makers with their commitments under the Charter. United States occupation of the Dominican Republic,[154] the combined United States-Belgian operation at Stanleyville,[155] and El Salvador's invasion of Honduras[156] were all accompanied by assertions of authority to intervene for the protection of basic human rights.

The invasion of Honduras comes closest to a pure nineteenth-century case of overt military intrusion opposed by a recognized government and justified solely as a defense of the rights of nationals to treatment consistent with recognized international standards.[157] The reaction of authoritative decision-makers inevitably more concerned with dousing the flames than establishing clear precedents was, as usual, less than unambiguous. Although El Salvador was ordered to withdraw its forces from the territory of Honduras,[158] it was not declared an aggressor nor ordered to pay compensation for damage to persons and property in Honduras. Nevertheless, the flat insistence of the O.A.S., acting in the face of a report by one of its own committees confirming El Salvador's charges of severe abuse of its nationals,[159] on the withdrawal of El Salvador's forces without compensating guarantees is subject to the inference that in the Western Hemisphere, at least, unilateral armed intervention for the defense of nationals from harassment which stops short of an imminent threat to their lives is illegitimate if opposed by a recognized government.

3. DEFENSE OF "VITAL INTERESTS"

The opposition of a recognized government is one possible means of distinguishing the Salvador-Honduras case from the United States invasion of the Dominican Republic. But in this instance the possible and the plausible do not coincide. Treating the Dominican affair as just another case of intervention in defense of nationals[160] on the nineteenth-century pattern does violence both to the event's subsequently revealed factual and normative complexity, and to its larger context. Despite public expression of concern for the safety of nationals,[161] the assessments of non-governmental authorities, including eye wit-

---

[154] See President Johnson's statement in the *Department of State Bulletin*, LIII (July 5, 1965), 20.

[155] See President Johnson's statement in same, LI (December 14, 1964), 846.

[156] See *New York Times*, July 28, 1969, p. 12.

[157] A somewhat similar contemporary case is Turkey's aerial intervention in Cyprus in defense of the island's Turkish community. See *New York Times*, August 9, 1964, p. 1.

[158] See same, July 30, 1969, p. 1.

[159] See same, July 28, 1969, p. 12.

[160] On April 30, 1965, President Johnson announced: "For two days American forces have been in Santo Domingo in an effort to protect the lives of Americans and nationals of other countries in the face of increasing violence and disorder." *New York Times*, May 1, 1965, p. 6, col. 4.

[161] See fn. 154.

nesses,[162] coupled with public statements emerging at various times from policy-making levels of the United States government in defense of United States behavior as a response to Communist infiltration,[163] as well as the unabashed confessions of the President's special representative, John Bartlow Martin,[164] have convinced this writer that the defense-of-nationals justification is only slightly less flimsy here than it was at Suez. A second justification—prevention of the fratricidal slaughter of Dominicans,[165] with its aura of transcendence of ordinary considerations of national interest—is also somewhat reminiscent of the factually shabby Anglo-French claims to be acting as an arm of the international community to assure free passage through the Suez Canal. One is hard put to recall a pronounced concern for slaughter in the Caribbean unless one's own citizens were threatened or cold-war perspectives were engaged. It is possible, for instance, to cite relative indifference to the sustained barbarities of the Trujillo regime, including the massacre of thousands of Haitians.

The Dominican intervention bears a more credible resemblance to the Soviet invasion of Hungary than El Salvador's invasion of Honduras. In both cases great power intervention determined the outcome of violent domestic struggles for political control. Both intervening powers made justificatory reference to traditional legal doctrine: In the United States case, protection of nationals; in the Soviet case, the request of an established government for assistance.[166] Both responded to allegations of interference in domestic affairs and self-determination processes with countercharges of foreign support or direction for the groups whose success they sought to preclude. These are arresting similarities, yet the Soviet Union and not the United States was condemned by the General Assembly.[167]

The troubling question is whether the discriminatory reaction of the

---

[162] See, e.g., Theodore Draper, "The Dominican Crisis," *Commentary*, XL (December 1965), 33-68; Philip Geyelin, *Lyndon B. Johnson and the World* (New York 1966); Tad Szulc, *Dominican Diary* (New York 1965). Geyelin and Szulc had access to cables that passed between Washington and the embassy in Santo Domingo.

[163] On May 2, eight days after the beginning of the revolution President Johnson publicly declared that the revolution had taken a "tragic turn." "What began as a popular democratic revolution that was committed to democracy and social justice moved into the hands of a band of Communist conspirators." Quoted in Draper (fn. 162), 42.

[164] In his book *Overtaken by Events: The Dominican Crisis from the Fall of Trujillo to Civil War* (New York 1966), Martin quotes Ambassador Bennett to the effect that President Johnson asked for a written request from the military junta for U.S. military intervention, citing the danger to lives and property in order to provide the "juridical basis" of the action. (657).

[165] See Leonard Meeker, "The Dominican Situation in the Perspective of International Law," *Department of State Bulletin*, LIII (July 12, 1965), 60, 62.

[166] See, e.g., statement of the Soviet delegate (GAOR, 2nd Emergency Special Sess., 564th Mtg.).

[167] Res. 1004 (ES-II), November 4, 1956.

United Nations can be justified in terms of criteria susceptible of universal application or whether it evidences breakdown of the notion of a universal legal order.

The case for discrimination on neutral juridical grounds might rely on the willingness of the United States, in contradistinction to the Soviet Union, to permit general elections under the gaze of impartial observers.[168] While I believe that the elections were not and, indeed, could not have been impartial when United States forces were still the effective operating authority in the country and the United States government was resting on its claim that one of the contestants was under Communist influence, nevertheless victory for the Boschites, though unlikely, seemed possible.[169] If that is true, then the General Assembly could not with equal assurance condemn the United States, as it condemned the Soviet Union, for imposing a regime by "armed intervention."[170] A related basis for distinguishing the cases is United States acceptance of a United Nations observer in the Republic.[171] United Nations representatives were denied access to Hungary.[172]

A further distinction between the cases was the absence in the Dominican Republic of an effective government. At the time of the Russian attack in Hungary, Nagy was in control of the entire country and was supported by the regular armed forces. The self-determination process had come to rest. Although some reports indicate that the Dominican right-wing military group was on the point of collapse prior to United States intervention,[173] this has never been established conclusively.

A final possible distinction could rest on the implication of *ex post facto* O.A.S. ratification of United States action, arising from the Organization's willingness to assume responsibility for the occupation force.[174] The argument would be that the Dominican strife was a matter "relating to the maintenance of international peace and security,"

---

[168] See Barnet (fn. 146), 178.

[169] With the assistance of U.S. forces, the military junta eventually destroyed the Boschite military capability. Barnet, same, 173, 175. Hence in the months immediately preceding the election, the right-wing military group was the only indigenous public order authority, a de facto position it employed to intimidate the opposition. Juan Bosch was so fearful of his personal safety that he never left his residence during the campaign. In addition, the United States government, openly anti-Bosch, poured aid funds into the country. Indeed, in the year following the revolution the Dominican Republic received almost 300 percent more aid per capita than any other country in Latin America. See Barnet, same, 173-78.

[170] See Res. 1133 (II), September 14, 1957.

[171] See *New York Times*, May 15, 1965, p. 1, col. 5 and same, May 16, 1965, p. 62, cols. 4, 6, and 7; U.N. Docs. Nos. S/6365, S/6369, 1965; U.N. Doc. No. S/6358, 1965.

[172] See *New York Times*, November 13, 1956, p. 1, col. 8.

[173] See, e.g., Barnet (fn. 146), 170-71, and Juan de Onis in the *New York Times*, November 5, 1969, p. 8.

[174] But see Richard Bohan, "The Dominican Case: Unilateral Intervention," *American Journal of International Law*, 60 (October 1966), 809, 811-12.

that it was "appropriate for regional action," and that such action was "consistent with the Purposes and Principles of the United Nations" in that it was designed to minimize destruction and promote self-determination.[175] Allegations that the enterprise violated Article 53's prohibition of "enforcement action . . . without the authorization of the Security Council" have encountered the following responses: That "enforcement action" refers to regional action against an established government or it refers to compulsory collective action as distinguished from merely recommended behavior or, finally, that the silence of the Security Council can be construed as assent.[176] If the latter argument is applied to the case of silence induced by veto of the concerned great power, it emerges as a transparent assertion of great power freedom from Charter norms and hence its claim to juridical significance can be dismissed with contempt. On the other hand, if a Security Council Resolution under Chapter VI—and thus not subject to veto by "a party to [the] dispute"—recommending nonintervention is deemed a denial of authorization, the acquiescence argument may aspire to a modest respectability, although it hovers on the outer fringe of the syntactically plausible and, as a matter of policy, encourages decentralized appreciation of issues of war and peace even where they have transregional implications.

A similar tendency can be seen in the alternative juridical implication which might be drawn from the Dominican affair if it is seen not in isolation but as part of the continuing pattern of behavior by the United States in the Western Hemisphere. On the control side, one can point to Guatemala and the Bay of Pigs, both cases where United States involvement was inconsistent with the views of its own govern-

175 Art. 52, Par. 1 of the Charter of the United Nations. Cf. Meeker (fn. 165), 61-62. With a dauntless indifference to United Nations Charter obligations, Dr. Charles G. Fenwick has proclaimed that: "Had the Meeting of Consultation [of O.A.S.] been willing to justify its action on the ground of a *possible* take-over of the pro-Bosch rebels by Communist elements, *there would have been no legal basis of criticism*, assuming . . . that there was *reasonable* evidence of the fact. For the resolution taken (sic) at Caracas in 1954 clearly covered such a situation." (Emphasis added.) *American Journal of International Law*, 60 (January 1966), 64, 66.

Dr. Fenwick also argued that the United States could have acted alone to assure rebel failure on the grounds that prior experience with the Communist government of Cuba would justify "intervention in self-defense." Same, 65. In light of the balanced concern for relevant juridical data manifested by Dr. Fenwick, Richard Bohan's suggestion that Fenwick's piece "shows . . . the possibilities for the misuse of international law as an instrument for the self-righteous justification of illegal acts" does not seem unfair (fn. 174), 809.

176 See, e.g., statements of the United States representative in the Security Council, U.N. S.C. *Official Records*, 20th year 1220th Mtg. 17 (S/PV. 1220), 1965; same, 1219th Mtg. 5 (S/PV. 1219), 1965. And see Abram Chayes, "Law and the Quarantine of Cuba," *Foreign Affairs* (April 1963), 556. After the Cuban quarantine, the State Department Legal Advisor, Leonard Meeker, seemed to intimate that in the view of the United States, authorization simply is no longer necessary. "Defensive Quarantine and the Law," *American Journal of International Law*, 57 (July 1963), 515, 522.

ing elite that aid to rebel expeditions violates international law.[177] The sense of an emerging pattern is strengthened by undenied allegations of covert United States involvement in British Guiana to prevent the electoral success of Cheddi Jagan's left-wing party[178] and in Bolivia to assist in antiguerrilla operations.[179] On the authority side, one can point principally to the Punta del Este Resolution[180] which may be construed as a declaration of the inherent illegitimacy of Western Hemisphere regimes that espouse Marxist-Leninist principles of domestic public order. In this data one might discern an emerging regional norm allowing intervention pursuant to O.A.S. constitutional procedures, and possibly unilaterally as well, for the purpose of preventing the creation of Communist regimes or of eliminating those already established. If confirmed by future events, it would constitute the Western Hemisphere's analogue to the Brezhnev Doctrine, enunciated after the occupation of Czechoslovakia, which in effect declares that the national sovereignty of Socialist states is conditioned on governance by ideologically sanitized regimes.[181] While the Soviet claim has been rejected explicitly by two Communist governments within Eastern Europe[182] and by a substantial number of Communist par-

---

[177] This view is implicit in the Government's contention that North Vietnam's support of the Vietcong constituted an "armed attack" against the Saigon regime. See the Memorandum of the State Department on "The Legality of U.S. Participation in the Defense of Vietnam," submitted to the Senate Committee on Foreign Relations on March 8, 1966, reprinted in Richard A. Falk, ed., *The Vietnam War and International Law* (Princeton 1968), 583.

[178] See Barnet (fn. 146), 240-43, and sources cited there.

[179] See *New York Times*: September 11, 1967, p. 13; January 5, 1968, p. 18; August 18, 1968, p. 1; August 19, 1968, p. 8.

[180] The principles of communism are incompatible with the principles of the Inter-American system . . . (and) adherence by any member of the Organization of American States to Marxism-Leninism is incompatible with the inter-American system and the alignment of such a government with the communist block breaks the unity and solidarity of the hemisphere. . . . [The] member states [are therefore urged] to take those steps that they may consider appropriate for their individual or collective self-defense, and to cooperate, as may be necessary or desirable, to strengthen their capacity to counteract threats or acts of aggression, subversion, or other dangers to peace and security resulting from the continued intervention in this hemisphere of Sino-Soviet powers, in accordance with the obligations established in treaties and agreements such as the Charter of the Organization of American States and the Inter-American Treaty of Reciprocal Assistance.

State Department Bulletin (February 19, 1962), 278. See also the Declaration of the Caracas Inter-American Conference of 1954 (which was motivated by U.S. concern with the Arbenz government in Guatemala). Documents in *American Foreign Relations 1954* (1955), 412.

[181] The "Doctrine" is actually a composite of a number of pronouncements: See statement of Ambassador Malik addressing the Security Council, U.N. Doc. S/PV.-1441, August 21, 1968, 48-50; *Pravda* editorial, translation by the Soviet Press Agency reprinted in the *New York Times*, September 27, 1968, p. 3; statement of Foreign Minister Gromyko to the U.N. General Assembly, U.N. Doc. A/PV.1679, October 3, 1968, 26, 30-31.

[182] Rumania and Yugoslavia.

ties,[183] United States reaction has been restrained[184] and the United Nations accordingly acquiescent.

Neither the explicit Soviet claim nor its more ambiguous United States counterpart seems reconcilable with prevailing perceptions of the legal order established by the United Nations Charter. The keystone of that perceived order is the sovereign equality of states and the corollary inviolability of their respective authority structures except in those instances where the Security Council finds a threat to the peace, as it has done in the case of Southern Rhodesia.[185] The Charter is seen, in other words, as an effort to centralize peacekeeping and restrain "private violence." Regional organization plays a supplementary role in this scheme.

At their narrowest, explicit Soviet and muted United States assertions of an interventionary privilege in their respective regions constitute claims to treat certain domestic political phenomena as threats to their national security thus activating the privilege to engage in normally proscribed behavior, whether under the rubric of self-defense, or some less conventional fig leaf. Although each power's claim is phrased in terms which implicitly reject reciprocal application, in the context of events, including a low Soviet profile in the Western Hemisphere since the missile crisis, they may be construed as reflections of an emerging pattern of reciprocity, a kind of normative regime specialized to the self-defined requirements of the superpowers. Their toleration of the regional renegades—Yugoslavia and Cuba, respectively—may reflect a tacit agreement against retrospective application of their inter-

---

[183] See *New York Times*: August 22, 1968, p. 18; September 27, 1968, p. 3; October 22, 1968, p. 11.

[184] Conceptions of restraint assume meaning, of course, only within a specific context of expectations and possibilities. One certainly might argue that United States behavior should not be characterized as acquiescent. Washington did go beyond purely verbal condemnation. There were N.A.T.O. meetings and announcements of plans to bolster N.A.T.O.'s military capabilities. The White House's planned announcement of an agreement to enter into missile limitation talks with the Soviet Union was postponed. Under-Secretary of State Katzenbach was dispatched to Belgrade with assurances of support (assurances which did not appear to commit the United States to any concrete action in case of Soviet intervention). And Rumania, the only Warsaw Pact nonparticipant in the invasion was rewarded with new agreements relating to the peaceful uses of atomic energy and cultural exchanges, while prospective agreements with the other Pact states were placed in the freezer. (See Andrew J. Pierre, "Implications of the Western Response to the Soviet Intervention in Czechoslovakia," paper delivered at the Conference on "The Impact of the Czechoslovak Events on Current International Relations," Center for International Studies, New York University, December 6, 1968.) But there is no evidence of which I am aware that either the United States or the Soviet Union regarded these moves as more than formal gestures, largely occasioned by the requirements of domestic and N.A.T.O. politics. They were not costly either to Washington or Moscow. The latter capital did not treat them as provocative or threatening. They seemed to fall well within the ambit of a relatively unconcerned expectation concerning the probable Western response.

[185] S.C. Res. 232, December 16, 1966 and S.C. Res. 221, April 9, 1966.

ventionary doctrines or rational assessments of the costs of occupying countries which appear to possess the will and capacity to offer substantial resistance.

United States reaction to the emplacement of Soviet missiles in Cuba would be an *a fortiori* application of the norm, as well as confirmation of its operative force. The efforts to drape it with the venerable mantle of self-defense, without radical alteration of the concept encounters imposing obstructions. They require, of course, repudiation of the view that an actual or imminent armed attack is a necessary precondition for legitimate recourse to force or the threat of force. Descriptions of Soviet behavior as preparation for an armed attack[186] are wantonly unconvincing because they require imputation of psychotic, suicidal tendencies to the Soviet leadership. Secretary of Defense McNamara pointed out during the secret discussions which led to the quarantine that the missile buildup in Cuba did not give the Soviets anything resembling a first-strike capability.[187] Indeed, it could easily have been construed as a desperate defensive response to the missile gap which exposed the Soviet Union to the risk of an American first strike.[188] Authoritative and semi-authoritative accounts of the crisis agree that the decision to act was based on concern for the broad political and psychological consequences, both in the international arena and within the United States, of the Soviet gambit.[189]

It has been argued, sometimes with more noise than reason, that if nothing else, the Soviet move threatened the stable balance of power.[190] The factual predicate is doubtful. Given the dimensions of the missile gap which became apparent after Kennedy's election, any possible impact of the missile buildup would have been in the direction of

---

[186] See, e.g., Charles Fenwick, "The Quarantine Against Cuba: Legal or Illegal?" *American Journal of International Law*, 57 (July 1963), 588, 589-90.

[187] See Elie Abel, *The Missile Crisis* (New York 1966), 36, and Hilsman (fn. 146), 195. Hilsman, himself, takes the position that "what the Soviet increase in firepower did do was to give them enough to erode the American capacity to strike back—and hence to degrade the ultimate deterrent" (201). This turbid declaration leaves the reader in doubt about Hilsman's assessment of the significance of that degree of erosion which was threatened. Since today, when the Soviet Union is approaching parity with the U.S. in strategic weapons, even the Nixon administration appears to concede that the U.S. deterrent remains for the moment adequate and since the projected increase in Soviet strategic capabilities resulting from the buildup in Cuba would "still leave the U.S. with at least a 2 to 1 superiority in nuclear power" (Arthur Schlesinger, Jr., *A Thousand Days* [Boston 1965], 803), one may reasonably conclude that the erosion to which Hilsman refers was not significant. This conclusion finds support in Theodore Sorenson's subsequent statement that "the President was concerned less about the missiles' military implications than with their effect on the global political balance." (*Kennedy* [New York 1965], 683.)

[188] See Hilsman (fn. 146), 201. See also the speech delivered by Deputy Secretary of Defense Roswell Gilpatrick on October 21, 1961, quoted in Abel (fn. 187), 39.

[189] See Abel, same, 60; Schlesinger (fn. 187), 796-97; Sorenson (fn. 187), 683.

[190] See, e.g., Myres McDougal, "The Soviet-Cuban Quarantine and Self-Defense," *American Journal of International Law*, 53 (July 1963), 597, 601.

creating nuclear equilibrium between the superpowers.[191] It is arguable, however, that the creation of nuclear equilibrium might eventually have encouraged the Soviet Union to new adventures in areas such as Berlin where it enjoys conventional superiority. Speculations concerning Soviet reaction to the creation of a true nuclear standoff are inevitably guided by underlying assumptions about the essential thrust of Soviet foreign policy: Those who see the Soviet Union as an aggressive, expanding power, and view the cold war as a mere reflection of those characteristics, naturally read the emplacement of missiles in Cuba as a prelude to intensified coercive behavior.[192] But even if the postulation of disequilibrating consequences were true, they have no juridical significance if self-defense is the only justification for unilateral recourse to force, unless the criterion of imminent and irremediable injury to specific interests is rejected.

Perhaps it is just such a rejection which the impartial empiricist should record. From the tremors in Czechoslovakia and Cuba followed by little more than token opposition in the former case and large-scale support for the party defending his sphere in the latter, one might infer a change of state for self-defense from a solid cluster of criteria to a fluid prescription for maintenance of the prevailing relationship of force. Such an inference would, however, seem to require at least one important qualification. Where the behavior (other than

[191] See sources cited at footnote 188.

[192] See McDougal (fn. 190), 601-02. In his review of *Law and Minimum World Public Order*, Richard Falk suggests that

> McDougal and Feliciano apparently accept without question (at least they do not disclose any questioning) the image of the cold war put forward by Robert Strausz-Hupé and others in *Protracted Conflict*, New York, Harper and Brothers, 1959; see, e.g., p. 279, passim. I find this image to be an unacceptably self-serving interpretation of the cold war that overrigidifies "the enemy" and is *too clear* about his objectives. See note 57, pp. 86-7n.

Unfortunately, a not altogether dissimilar perspective may be found in Professor Falk's early writing. See, for example, the following ominous reference: "The Caracas Declaration of Solidarity is but an illustration of a coherent worldwide policy pursued by the United States since the close of World War II. It has, by necessity, manifested the interventionary character inevitable *in a world stalked by a potent aggressor*." (Emphasis added), same, 178. On the other hand, the guiding conception of world affairs manifested in such prose is balanced, to some degree at least, by insights such as the following: "As well as the Dulles version of the overthrow of Arbenz—patriots arose in Guatemala to challenge the Communist leadership—there are those who regard the revolution as an interventionary joint venture between the United Fruit Company and Ambassador Peurifoy." Same, 177.

For interpretation of Soviet behavior at variance with the one urged by Strausz-Hupé and company, see, inter alia, Gar Alperovitz, *Atomic Diplomacy: Hiroshima and Potsdam* (New York 1965); David Dallin, *Soviet Foreign Policy After Stalin* (New York 1961); D. F. Fleming, *The Cold War and Its Origins*, Vols. I and II (Garden City 1961); Louis Halle, *The Origins of the Cold War* (New York 1967); David Horowitz, *The Free World Colossus* (New York 1965); Marshall D. Shulman, *Stalin's Foreign Policy Reappraised* (New York 1963). See also, Arthur Schlesinger, "The Origins of the Cold War," *Foreign Affairs*, XLVI (October 1967).

preparation for an imminent attack) which threatens the existing relationship of force occurs within the territorial confines of one of the belligerently juxtaposed states—for example, by a dramatic increase in the defense budget—efforts to abort the development by threats of force would be precedent shattering and presumably would be regarded as impermissible. Looking ahead, a possible exception to that qualification would be the case where a change in domestic behavior violated treaty obligations relating to arms control or disarmament. In its first report, issued in 1946, the United Nations Atomic Energy Commission suggested that if the Members concluded an atomic arms control treaty, "a violation might be of so grave a character as to give rise to the inherent right of self-defense recognized in Article 51."[193] The limited Test Ban and the Nonproliferation Treaty can vastly increase the probability of such a contingency. And this would be true of any other significant arms control or disarmament agreements which may be negotiated. Such agreements are likely to create powerful expectations of an intensely coercive response to major violations.

Recourse to force in case of a violation of an important arms control or disarmament treaty could be justified as self-defense without severely straining the term's traditional connotations. One could reasonably presume that no state would violate such a treaty unless it anticipated important military gains and intended to exploit them to achieve major value reallocations. Since violation would inevitably be covert, once discovered it would be difficult to determine quickly how long violations had been occurring and hence how great an advantage had been secured. Under those circumstances, the requirements of an apparent need to act immediately for the protection of essential values would appear to be satisfied.

While the decline of a rigorous conception of self-defense is a conceivable inference from contemporary behavior, the alternative inferences of a merely regional relaxation of criteria or of the evolution of special criteria governing relations between the polar powers seems more in accord with both control and claiming behavior. President Kennedy's decision in the missile crisis, reportedly based in substantial measure on concern for the precedental implications of a self-defense claim,[194] to rely on regional processes and norms for defense of the quarantine rather than Article 51 of the Charter may evidence a desire to restrain the tendency to return to uninhibited unilateral appreciation of the need for recourse to force. The international community's reaction to Israel's initiation of hostilities in 1956 may also be interpreted as evidence that a rigorous conception of self-defense still enjoys wide support.

193 U.N. Doc. AEC/18/Rev. 1, 24.
194 See Abel (fn. 187), 155.

In 1956, Israel justified its movement of forces across the armistice lines both as a response to a continuing "armed attack" by *Fedayeen* commandos and as an anticipation of new encroachments on Israeli territory by Egyptian forces, as well as the *Fedayeen*.[195] The fact of continuing terrorist raids was indisputable. Allegations of an Egyptian plan to initiate large-scale conflict were never confirmed; in any event, there was little evidence of an imminent attack, as distinguished from a long-range program for the elimination of Israel. Although Israel was not formally censured, its behavior was condemned by authoritative spokesmen for almost all the major interest groups in the United Nations. Secretary Dulles, after reviewing past Egyptian behavior, stated:

> We have, however, come to the conclusion that these provocations —serious as they were—cannot justify the resort to armed force. If . . . we were to agree that the existence in the world of injustices which this Organization has so far been unable to cure means that the principle of the renunciation of force should no longer be respected, that whenever a nation feels that it has been subjected to injustice it should have the right to resort to force in an attempt to correct that injustice, then I fear that we should be tearing this Charter into shreds. . . . [T]he violent armed attack by three Members of the United Nations upon a fourth cannot be treated as anything but a grave error inconsistent with the principles and purposes of the Charter; an error which, if persisted in, would gravely undermine this Organization and its Charter.[196]

Summarizing the international community's views in response to Israeli demands for a guarantee against renewal of the U.A.R. blockade of the Gulf of Aqaba, the Secretary-General reported that the United Nations would not allow a change of status resulting from military action *contrary to the charter*.[197] This view was, of course, implicit in the categorical demand (embodied in a General Assembly Resolution commanding nearly unanimous support) for Israeli withdrawal behind the 1948 armistice lines.[198]

Two features capable of broad generalization may distinguish the Israeli case from the Cuban quarantine. First, Israel was not responding to a dramatic change in Egyptian behavior. Secondly, by apparently acting in concert with the United Kingdom and France, Israel in a sense associated itself with behavior that had a far more dubious claim to legitimacy. In 1967, when Israel again launched a major assault across the armistice lines, the Arab states were unable to secure from

195 U.N. G.A. *Records*, 1st Emergency Special Sess., 562nd Mtg., 23.
196 Same, 561st Mtg., 10-11.   197 U.N. Doc. A/3512.
198 Res. 997, 1002 and 1120 (XI) of 2, 7 and 24 November, 1956.

the United Nations an order for unconditional withdrawal.[199] In that case, the Israelis, acting alone, were responding to a dramatic increase in the magnitude of coercive behavior,[200] although there is still considerable doubt that the Egyptians were in fact planning a first-strike or even that the Israelis believed they were.[201]

Israel's 1956 claim of a right to treat repeated guerrilla incursions as an "armed attack" by the sanctuary state is identical in syntax and similar in substance to the United States claim of right[202] with respect to the sustained bombing of North Vietnam which succeeded the initial reprisal raids to be discussed below. Since the United States and certain of its allies in Vietnam[203] joined in condemning the Israeli action, one might cite this as another of those infuriating double-standard cases which lend international law a reputation for impotence and spread an aura of hypocrisy around the functioning of the United Nations.

Yet there are differences between the two cases which might permit justification of a differential response by reference to generally applicable criteria. The cardinal difference is United States reliance on air strikes allegedly against targets implicated in the infiltration process.[204] Unlike an invasion, such air strikes could not threaten the political independence of North Vietnam. This restraint on United States counter-insurgency behavior helped to keep the risk of further geographical escalation of the conflict below crisis levels. In addition, it tended to confirm the United States government's assertion that its objective was purely conservational, that it did not seek to enlarge the area where it exercised dominant influence.

On the other hand, Israel's case may seem stronger because the guerrillas were a theat to its very existence, while United States inter-

[199] All draft resolutions which condemned Israel were defeated. *Official Records of the Fifth Emergency Session Annexes*, 39-45. Israel was called upon to terminate any action which sought to alter the status quo in Jerusalem. There was no operational reference to the other occupied territories. *Official Records of the Fifth Emergency Special Session* Supp. No. 1, p. 4, Res. 2253 (ES-V).

[200] Most notably, the sudden demand for the withdrawal of the United Nations peace-keeping force.

[201] S.L.A. Marshall (fn. 103), 21-22. But cf. David Dayan, *Strike First* (Jerusalem 1967), 18-19.

[202] See the Memorandum of the State Department (fn. 177).

[203] Res. 1124 (XI) of the U.N. General Assembly which deplored Israel's non-compliance with previous resolutions (1002, 1123) calling for withdrawal, and once again called for withdrawal, was passed by a vote of 74-2-2. Israel and France opposed the resolution and Luxembourg and the Netherlands abstained. The Philippines, Thailand, and the U.S. voted for the Resolution. U.N. G.A. *Official Records*, 11th Sess., 1956-57.

[204] Eye witness reports by Harrison Salisbury, *Behind The Lines—Hanoi* (New York 1967) and Richard A. Falk, "A Vietnam Settlement: The View from Hanoi," Policy Memorandum No. 34, Center of International Studies, Princeton, 1968, 4, among others, have raised doubt about the U.S. Government's contention that the air strikes have carefully discriminated between civilian and military targets.

ests in Vietnam seem peripheral. In response, it might be alleged that the relevant interest to be compared is that of the Saigon government, not the United States. This in turn raises the lively controversy over the meaning of "collective self-defense." There appear to be essentially three positions: that all states which purport to exercise the right must have a valid independent claim;[205] that where an attack on one state threatens a substantial security interest of another, the latter may aid the former;[206] any group of states are free to treat an attack on one as an attack on all.[207] Since states almost invariably justify recourse to force as self-defense, the second and third positions endorse unilateral appreciation of the merits of these competing claims and thus encourage expansion of conflict while conversely reducing the incentives for recourse to collective judgment within the structure of the United Nations.

The seemingly permanent antagonism which convulses the Middle East has held at or near the center of international concern another important issue of normative policy—the status of reprisal as a response short of war to threats to territorial integrity or political independence. The most frequently cited definition of reprisal is contained in the award of the German-Portuguese Arbitration Tribunal on the Naulilaa claim.[208] The Tribunal declared:

Reprisals are acts of self-help by the injured State, acts in retaliation for unredressed acts contrary to international law on the part of the offending State. In consequence of such measures, the observation of this or that rule of international law is temporarily suspended. They are limited by considerations of humanity and the rules of good faith, applicable in the relations between States. They are illegal unless justified by a previous act contrary to international law. It is their object to impose on the offending State reparation for the offense or the return to legality, avoiding the commission of new offenses.[209]

On the basis of this declaration, Professor Schwarzenberger incorporates the essential requirements into three propositions:

205 See, e.g., Bowett (fn. 7), 206-07, 216; Stone (fn. 3), 245. Bowett's position is actually somewhat uncertain: compare the cited pages with 237-38 where he seems to incline toward the middle position.

206 See, e.g., McDougal and Feliciano (fn. 12), 252, and Lauterpacht-Oppenheim, II (fn. 3), 155.

207 This, for example, would appear to be the formal position of all the members of the O.A.S., since they have, under the Rio Treaty, individually assumed the obligation of assisting any member that is the victim of aggression. It is difficult to imagine how any substantive security interest of Ecuador, for instance, could be jeopardized by an attack launched by one Central American state against another.

208 U.N., *Reports of International Arbitral Awards*, 1948, II, 1011.

209 Same, 225-26.

(1) A prior illegal act must be the reason for the act of reprisal against the wrongdoer.

(2) The application of reprisals must be preceded by an unsuccessful attempt to obtain redress for the alleged international tort.

(3) The reprisals taken must not be patently excessive, that is, out of all proportion to the original wrong committed or run counter to the minimum requirements of the standard of civilisation.[210]

The distinction between reprisal and self-defense is relatively easy to state in the abstract but rather difficult in certain cases to apply. Professor Bowett finds these "two forms of self-help . . . properly distinguished by reference to their aim. . . . In contrast to self-defense, reprisals are 'punitive' in character; their object is 'to compel the offending state to make reparation for the injury or to return to legality, by avoiding further offenses.' "[211] But what if the injury consists of the tortious seizure of property of a foreign state or one of its nationals. In that case is the form of response controlling for purposes of characterization? Is it "self-defense" if troops are sent in to recapture the property, "reprisal" if some property of the tort-feasor is seized?[212] Does it make a difference whether the responsive seizure is compensatory in intent or designed to provide the basis for an exchange? To take another difficult case, is it "reprisal" or "self-defense" when a state's armed forces attack a commando or guerrilla group which has completed its mission and returned across the border? Does it depend on whether there is a reasonable expectation that this group will penetrate again as soon as it eludes the pursuing force?

These questions assume a certain importance because "reprisals," even in response to delictual behavior involving the use of force, have been condemned by the Security Council on several occasions. In 1953, responding to an Israeli attack at Qibya explicitly justified as a reprisal, the Security Council found "that the retaliatory actions at Qibya taken by armed forces of Israel constitute a violation of the cease-fire provisions . . . *and* are inconsistent with . . . the Charter."[213] (Emphasis added.) In 1956, the Security Council, while condemning the entry of Israeli forces into Syria at Lake Tiberias, noted that "the Council has already condemned military action in breach of the general armistice agreements, whether or not undertaken by way of retaliation."[214]

---

[210] Fn. 3, 50.   [211] Fn. 7, 13.

[212] Dr. Bowett might contend that neither act could be characterized as self-defense: "recaption is not self-defense" (18). But he does not discuss the problem of determining at what point a seizure may be deemed consummated. If U.S. ships had attacked the ships convoying the *Pueblo* toward a North Korean port, would it have been self-defense or recapture? Same.

[213] Res. S/3139/Rev. 2, November 24, 1953.

[214] Res. S/3538, January 19, 1956.

Again in 1962, the Security Council voted to censure Israel for military action against Syria "whether or not taken by way of retaliation."[215] Although there was no specific reference to reprisal in the Security Council's most recent condemnation of Israel for the Beirut airport raid,[216] it too may be construed as a reaffirmation of earlier declarations, since reprisal was the only strictly doctrinal justification available to Israel.[217]

Do these successive condemnations of Israeli behavior compel the inference that there is a generally applicable community policy against reprisals? An affirmative response would cite Council condemnation of a bombing raid carried out by the United Kingdom against a Yemeni village alleged to have been a base for guerrilla expeditions into Aden and its environs.[218] Anyone preferring to uphold the negative could cite in response the monumental indifference to United States raids against North Vietnam announced as retaliations for the attack at Pleiku and the alleged attacks in the Tonkin Gulf.[219] Not only were the United States raids acknowledged, indeed justified, as reprisals, they were also, at least in the case of those responding to the Tonkin Gulf event, grotesquely disproportional, since as the United States conceded, no damage either to personnel or property had been inflicted. The absence of formal United Nations action in the Tonkin Gulf case might be deemed insignificant simply on the ground that it had no jurisdiction over the case at the time of the reprisals. This lack of jurisdiction resulted from the disinclination of any of the principal actors to seek United Nations intervention. Just as courts cannot be criticized for failing to seek jurisdiction *sua sponte* and are expected to treat alike only similar cases which are brought before it, so the Security Council cannot be accused of hypocrisy for ignoring cases which the parties have seen fit to settle between themselves. What really provoked one's sense of a vivid asymmetry of reaction was the absence of a clamorous hue and cry in the unorganized arenas of international society or, for that matter, within the United States.[220] Whether this resulted from a feeling that United States behavior was legitimate—either because the superpowers have their own rules or

215 Res. S/5110 and Corr. 1.

216 Res. S/262, December 31, 1968.

217 See generally Richard A. Falk, "The Beirut Raid and the International Law of Retaliation," *American Journal of International Law*, 70 (July 1969), 415. Today the words "reprisal" and "retaliation" are used interchangeably.

218 Res. S/188, 1964.

219 See *New York Times*, August 5, 1964, p. 1.

220 Polls in the U.S. showed 85 percent approval. Barnet (fn. 146), 217. The Congress passed the Tonkin Gulf Resolution effectively endorsing the retaliatory raids and giving the President a blank check for escalation. Only two Senators voted against the Resolution.

because the bombing occurred in the context of an escalating struggle rapidly assuming the character of an international armed conflict—or from a sense of futility, one can only speculate.

The poignance of this asymmetrical reaction is heightened by one's realization that the Israelis were responding to attacks on the civilian population which thereby violate fundamental humanitarian rules of conflict, while in the Tonkin Gulf reprisal, the United States responded to an alleged attack[221] which destroyed nothing and, assuming it occurred, may itself have been a legitimate response to United States participation in a covert attack on North Vietnamese territory.[222] Moreover, as noted above, while the Arab attacks were part of a pattern of harassment threatening the political independence of the Israeli state, no comparable United States interests were jeopardized.

The United Nations apparent application of a double standard against Israel vis-à-vis the United States and, of course, vis-à-vis the Arab states (who were not concomitantly censured for participation in violations of the armistice agreements, the humanitarian rules of war, and the duty of settling disputes by peaceful means), might possibly submit to an explanation along these lines. From 1948 to 1967 there may well have been a feeling in the international community that the Arab-Israeli confrontation could be stabilized indefinitely at the level of mutual coercion short of war which existed after the armistice was concluded in 1948. Thus all the energies of the United Nations were focused on minimizing deviation from the equilibrium. Since Israeli responses to Arab incursions were on a far larger scale than any single Arab attack, they were seen as dangerously destabilizing events. In a real sense, Israel was being asked to accept a pattern of interaction which included sporadic, small-scale, and covert violations of its territorial integrity which did not appear to threaten its political independence. Perhaps this is just another way of suggesting that Israel was censured because its responses lacked an intimate proportionality with any single, identifiable delinquency, and that this requirement of precise proportionality was imposed in the interest of preventing the recrudescence of major armed conflict. In addition, the United Nations membership may have been influenced by the conviction that the fragility of the Arab governments precluded them from asserting fully effective controls over Palestinian guerrillas, and hence they should not be held fully responsible for guerrilla activities. Finally, Professor Richard Falk has suggested that in the Beirut airport incident, the Se-

---

[221] Evidence which raises doubts about the U.S. government's version of the episode is marshaled in three articles by I. F. Stone in the *New York Review of Books*: "Fulbright: From Hawk to Dove" (Pt 2), VII (January 12, 1967), 8; "Mc-Namara and Tonkin Bay: The Unanswered Questions," X (March 28, 1968), 5; "The Supineness of the Senate," XII (February 13, 1969), 3.

[222] See Stone, same, VII, 10.

curity Council's attitude may reflect a judgment that the Israelis have been unduly intransigent in responding to Arab claims for settlement of the overall dispute.[223]

The suggested bases for a differential international community assessment of Arab and Israeli behavior may be confirmed by developments since 1967. In 1967, unlike 1948 or even 1956, expectations of sharply reduced levels of coercion have not followed in the wake of a cease-fire agreement. The unsettled status of occupied territory, the rapid rebuilding of the Egyptian armed forces,[224] the increase in the military capability and autonomy of the Palestinian guerrillas[225] have all supported expectations of sustained violence well above pre-1967 levels. There remains, in other words, a virtual state of war in the Middle East. In this context, Arab attacks, both overt and covert, and Israeli responses no longer appear as discrete threats to an uneasy peace, but as integrally related events in a protracted, violent conflict. The corresponding response of the Security Council—and to a considerable degree of the Arab states themselves—has been to ignore most Israeli counterforce attacks which before 1967 would have been treated as illegal reprisals.[226]

The principal exception to the pattern of acquiescence was the Security Council's unanimous condemnation of the Israeli attack on the Beirut airport which resulted in the destruction of 13 planes belonging to various Arab airlines.[227] The airport raid was defended by Israeli spokesmen as a legitimate retaliation for an attack by two Arab guerrillas two days earlier upon an El Al passenger plane at the Athens airport, which resulted in the death of an Israeli citizen. In the background was an incident which occurred about six months earlier. On July 23, 1968, an El Al plane was hijacked by three Arab guerrillas and forced to land in Algiers. Non-Israeli passengers were released immediately; Israeli male passengers were held for over a month until they were finally exchanged for some Arab common-law criminals imprisoned in Israel. In his initial statement to the Security Council, the Israeli Ambassador referred specifically to this event as one of the factors precipitating and justifying the reprisal.[228]

---

[223] Fn. 217, 435-36.

[224] See article by James Feron, "Dayan Concedes Concern over Guerrillas but Says Israel Maintains Military Superiority over Arabs," *New York Times*, November 13, 1969, p. 1.

[225] Same; see also article by Dana Adams Schmidt, "Commandos Rule 14 Refugee Camps," same, 1.

[226] Cf. Falk, (fn. 217), 420. The one notable exception involved Israeli bombardment of the City of Suez in response to the sinking of the Israeli destroyer *Elath* by Egyptian rockets. A resolution in the Security Council condemned both acts of violence as violations of the cease-fire. Same, 430.

[227] See *New York Times*, January 5, 1969, p. 1.

[228] U.N. Doc. S/PV. 1460, 23.

Both the earlier incident and the Athens attack were, as Ambassador Rosenne went on to point out,[229] merely obtrusive ridges on top of the rapidly growing iceberg of terrorism with which Israel has had to contend since its birth in 1948. In its assessment of the Beirut attack, the Security Council ignored the larger context of sustained terrorism. Deprived of contextual support, the precipitating event could not begin to meet the traditional criteria. There was little, if any, evidence of the Lebanese government's involvement in the particular incident; no effort had been made to secure redress through peaceful means; and the response seemed grossly disproportionate, not because 13 planes are worth more than a life, but because of the open and large-scale military intrusion into the heart of the Lebanese state with all that entailed symbolically and psychologically.

In context, the Israeli case was considerably stronger. Although not apparently involved in this discrete event, the Lebanese government had for some time tolerated guerrilla activities, including recruitment in the refugee camps,[230] and had publicly endorsed the guerrillas' aims.[231] On the basis of prior behavior coupled with expressions of approval for the Athens attack by Lebanese leaders,[232] the Israeli government might reasonably have concluded that appeals for a return to legality through the imposition of restraints on guerrilla activities were doomed to ineffectuality. Finally, if the Athens attack is seen as a mere link in the chain of behavior which since 1967 has produced the death of 47 Israeli civilians and the wounding of 330,[233] the sense of disproportionality tends to evaporate, assuming one can lump the Lebanese with the principal guerrilla sanctuaries—Syria, Jordan, and the U.A.R. Since Lebanon did not join the fighting in either 1956 or 1967, had not been, until recently, a significant terrorist base, and appears to lack the means for eliminating the guerrillas if they are determined to use the country as a sanctuary, an effort to treat Lebanon as a co-delinquent lacks persuasive force. This may largely explain the disinclination even of the United States to moderate censure by reference to the contextual provocations cited by the Israelis.

The doctrine of reprisal, being like any of its normative siblings a summary of actual experience, inclines third-party perspectives away from contextual assessment. It reflects the behavior of nineteenth-century sovereigns responding to discrete delinquencies rather than protracted conflict. The rigorous criteria which emerge from the doc-

229 U.N. Doc. S/PV. 1460, 24-25.
230 See Falk (fn. 217), 420-21. The subsequent efforts by the Lebanese authorities to restrict guerrilla activities within the country have had a dubious impact. See, e.g., note 225.
231 See Falk, same, 421 and sources cited there.
232 See *New York Times*, January 5, 1969, p. 1.
233 See Falk (fn. 217), 440, citing Israeli sources.

trine's historical matrix impose severe inhibitions on comparatively strong states confronted with continuing guerrilla harassment.

As Professor Falk has pointed out, where the state which is the target of guerrilla attack from foreign sanctuaries is unwilling to satisfy the guerrillas' political demands, it has only two conceivably effective alternatives: seek out and destroy the guerrillas in their sanctuaries or convince the sanctuary state to do the job itself.[234] The former strategy assumes the form of a large-scale movement of forces across a national boundary. Particularly where ground forces are employed, expectations of community condemnation and coercive reaction by governments associated with the sanctuary seem high. Air strikes appear to evoke a more context-sensitive response but seem largely ineffectual in relation to the objective of eliminating the guerrillas as a serious threat. As long as only conventional ordnance is employed, camouflage, dispersion and shelter seem to prevent crippling damage from air attack.

The second main strategic option—retaliation against the sanctuary state to induce it to restrain the guerrillas—has yet to demonstrate its ultimate efficacy. It may fail, as in the case of North Vietnam, Syria, and perhaps the U.A.R., because of the sanctuary state's intimate identification with the guerrillas. It may fail as in Lebanon because the sanctuary government's public order capabilities are comparatively small, and important constituencies within the sanctuary state insist on continuing support for the guerrillas. But despite its seeming incapacity to terminate guerrilla conflict, reprisal, particularly where inflicted by a more powerful ally, may serve to sustain the morale of the government threatened by guerrilla action, as may have been the case in Vietnam where the reprisals were seen as expressions of United States determination to stay and preserve the Saigon government.[235] Reprisals also may reduce, at least temporarily, the demand of domestic constituencies for invasion of the sanctuary state, and thus serve as a kind of escape valve for pressures instinct with a passion for war. Finally, even though the sanctuary state may be unable or unwilling to put the guerrillas out of business, it may be convinced through reprisals to attempt to limit their freedom of movement. Where their freedom of movement is restrained, guerrillas undoubtedly encounter greater difficulty in penetrating the target state's border and in protecting their sanctuaries from air strikes. Moreover, if the guerrillas must struggle with the sanctuary state's government to achieve freedom of movement, the resources available for terrorist attack are necessarily reduced.

A third theoretically available option—covert commando raids

234 See same, 426.
235 See *New York Times*, August 9, 1964, Sec. IV, p. 3.

against the sanctuaries—does not appear to have been widely employed. Reasons are not hard to find. A covert operation by its nature prevents the more powerful state (or the state with more powerful allies) from exploiting its conventional military superiority to protect its men.[236] And protection with superior firepower may be exactly what they urgently need, because the conditions which make sustained guerrilla warfare possible—active or even passive support from the indigenous population—normally will not be available to the covert forces penetrating the sanctuary state.

If this analysis is accurate, then community refusal to take full account of context in applying the doctrine of reprisal deprives states of a means of self-help which, in certain cases, may have a meliorative effect. For the most part, however, such refusal merely aggravates the frustration generated by inhibitions on recourse to full-scale war. Community reaction to Israel's allegation in 1956 that cumulative guerrilla attacks can constitute an "armed attack" within the meaning of the Charter when compared with the reaction to the same claim used by the United States to justify only air strikes against the sanctuary state does permit the inference that one of those inhibitions, possibly the primary and ubiquitous one, is a generally held conviction that the attempted seizure of territory for an indeterminate period is an impermissible response to so-called "indirect aggression."

Presumably this conviction rests at least in part on fear of catalyzing a war between the superpowers. As Professor Falk has suggested, it may rest also on an ambivalent value judgment concerning the legitimacy of terrorist activity.

> The idea of national sovereignty, the sanctity of domestic jurisdiction, and the absence of central sanctioning procedures work against the non-violent implementation of the will of the international community on matters of social and political justice. The modern state often enjoys a great technological advantage over its population in a struggle for political control, especially if the struggle assumes a military form. To overcome this disadvantage, social forces favoring change have used techniques of coercion that give a maximum role to their distinctive capabilities. Recourse to terror and random violence has been a principal tactic of the dispossessed, insurgent, revolutionary faction seeking to gain control over the machinery of government of a state. The rise of Communism, the rapid collapse of colonialism, the formation of "liberation" movements to deal with racism and residual colonialism in southern Africa, and the predominance of the Afro-Asian outlook in the General Assembly are among

---

[236] Cf. Amnon Rubinstein, "'Damn Everybody' Sums up the Angry Mood of Israel," *New York Times Magazine*, February 9, 1969, p. 24, at 98.

the factors that have given prominence to terror as an instrument of political change and as a "legitimate" tactic of military struggle.[237]

This ambivalence is exemplified dramatically by juxtaposition of the Declaration on Inadmissibility of Intervention adopted by the General Assembly in 1965[238] with resolutions of the General Assembly[239] urging support for insurgents in southern Africa. Comparable juxtapositions appear at every level of international discourse.[240]

Judgments about political values which are the stakes in a guerrilla war undoubtedly influence the selection and application of legal doctrine by third parties. It hardly requires prophetic insight to predict universal outrage if Southern Rhodesia responds to Zambian support for Rhodesian guerrillas with a military foray of one kind or another. The community judgment is that insurgency is a legitimate weapon against white minority regimes in Africa. It is hard to envision any other context which might evoke a comparable consensus. In the absence of a uniform judgment, one must assume that for the reasons suggested above, reprisals will occur despite large doubts about their ultimate efficacy. Professor Falk counsels domestication of this phenomenon by offering realistic conditions of legitimacy.[241] To some this

---

237 Falk (fn. 217), 423.

238 Res. 2131 (XX), December 21, 1965: "no state shall . . . tolerate subversive, terrorist, or armed activities."

239 See fn. 115.

240 The African states, for instance, regularly condemn foreign intervention in their domestic affairs while openly supporting southern African liberation movements. On the counterrevolutionary side of the political spectrum, one might contrast the various Western Hemisphere codifications of the principle of nonintervention (see von Glahn, fn. 21, 165-66) with the Caracas and Punta del Este Resolution (see fn. 180).

241 Fn. 217, 441-42:

(1) That the burden of persuasion is upon the government that initiates an official use of force across international boundaries;

(2) That the governmental user of force will demonstrate its defensive character convincingly by connecting the use of force to the protection of territorial integrity, national security, or political independence;

(3) That a genuine and substantial link exists between the prior commission or provocative acts and the resultant claim to be acting in retaliation;

(4) That a diligent effort be made to obtain satisfaction by persuasion and pacific means over a reasonable period of time, including recourse to international organizations;

(5) That the use of force is proportional to the provocation and calculated to avoid its repetition in the future, and that every precaution be taken to avoid excessive damage and unnecessary loss of life, especially with respect to innocent civilians;

(6) That the retaliatory force is directed primarily against military and paramilitary targets and against military personnel;

(7) That the user of force make a prompt and serious explanation of its conduct before the relevant organ (s) of community review and seek vindication therefrom of its course of action;

(8) That the use of force amounts to a clear message of communication to the

may appear as the liquidation of a beachhead of nonviolence. But to others it will seem a prudent concession in the name of minimum destruction of values to the reality of a world in which peaceful change may often seem a contradiction in terms.

CONCLUSION

In the era of nuclear weapons, the strong may have more to fear than the weak. Perhaps this is the ultimate explanation for the broadly based consensus which appears to reject overt force as a means of vindicating existing legal rights, other than a modestly defined right of self-defense, or as a means of asserting new ones.[242] Even the superpowers participate to a substantial degree in this consensus.

The United States has been unprepared to employ its own troops in the heart of its sphere of influence for the suppression of a hostile government allied with the other superpower. The Dominican affair can be distinguished because of the absence of an effective government opposed to United States intervention.

In Czechoslovakia, the Soviet Union demonstrated that it will not be a full partner in the consensus. Yet its own efforts to multilateralize the occupation by including other Warsaw Pact troops and its invocation of transnational "socialist" values (the Brezhnev Doctrine) evidence the consensus, though without honoring it. It may be instructive to recall, moreover, that the Soviet Union has not invaded the three remaining fractious Communist states in Eastern Europe despite having every reason to believe that the West would be essentially acquiescent. Nor has it attempted to excise China's nuclear capabilities, though the temptation must be great.

Lesser states test the consensus at their peril, as the British and French discovered at Suez. Property, and probably peripatetic persons as well, must survive without the ministrations of gunboats or marines. Even territorial integrity appears subject to a partial subordination

---

target government so that the contours of what constituted the unacceptable provocation are clearly conveyed;

(9) That the user of force cannot achieve its retaliatory purposes by acting within its own territorial domain and thus cannot avoid interference with the sovereign prerogatives of a foreign state;

(10) That the user of force seek a pacific settlement to the underlying dispute on terms that appear to be just and sensitive to the interests of its adversary;

(11) That the pattern of conduct of which the retaliatory use of force is an instance exhibits deference to considerations (1)-(10), and that a disposition to accord respect to the will of the international community be evident.

(12) That the appraisal of the retaliatory use of force take account of the duration and quality of support, if any, that the target government has given to terroristic enterprises.

242 Cf. Falk (fn. 73), 167.

by the consensus when it restrains effective response to guerrilla intrusion.

While the Vietnamese War drags on, there is a natural tendency to see a world convulsed with violence. But one wonders whether in retrospect the first two and one-half decades under the Charter may not appear as a time of surprisingly widespread peace between states. Despite the ludicrous artificiality of the postcolonial boundaries in Africa, border conflict in that continent has been rare and full-scale war nonexistent. The Western Hemisphere has been free of sustained interstate violence. And Western Europe has experienced years of unrivaled tranquility. The areas devastated by war might without manifest hyperbole be likened to islands in a somewhat roiled and frequently threatening sea of peace.

Most of the violence of our time is internal, subject to the influence but not the control of international law. There is no prospect for its abatement. Since the underlying social and technological forces on which it rides promise undiminished momentum, there is every prospect for its increase. Because of the growing sense of transnational solidarity—ideological, racial, and cultural—internal conflict continuously threatens to burst its geographical shackles. Torn between fear of war and the desire to promote certain deeply preferred values, international society has yet to adopt a coherent approach to the phenomenon of internal strife.

Aid to insurgents is condemned in the abstract, while there is broad and open support for insurgents in southern Africa. In other contexts, community consensus fragments, but nearly every insurgent movement has some foreign friend. Confronting the ubiquity of transnational involvement, authoritative decision-makers prefer castigating the phenomenon in general terms to developing criteria for its regulation. There is, for example, no overt attribution of significance to differing degrees of foreign involvement. Such attribution of significance may be a condition precedent for designing more precise standards to govern the target state's and its allies' response.

We do know that where occupation of the sanctuary has been attempted, it has been condemned. The status of less severe measures does seem to vary in some rough and inarticulate way with the intensity of sanctuary-state involvement. Community reaction to United States bombing of North Vietnam and Israeli counterforce raids since the 1967 war suggest that forceful measures which do not threaten the sanctuary state's independence may enjoy high levels of tolerance once troops of the sanctuary state become directly involved.

The tension between fear of war and sympathy for domestic change probably precludes into the foreseeable future any tidy normative solution to the problem. One can anticipate a continuing series of adjustments which will reflect attempts in constantly changing contexts to maximize the opportunities for free choice, while minimizing the danger of war. If recent precedents are a useful guide, these adjustments will be structured by a few normative parameters including preclusion of attack on civilian targets in the sanctuary state, preclusion of nuclear,[243] chemical, and biological weapons, and preclusion of invasion. If these parameters are respected, we may continue to live dangerously, but, nevertheless, we may entertain quite reasonable hopes of continuing to live.

[243] G. A. Res. 1653 (XVI), "Declaration on the Prohibition of the Use of Nuclear and Thermonuclear Weapons," adopted on November 24, 1961, by a vote of 55-20-26, provides in part that: "Any State using nuclear and thermo-nuclear weapons is to be considered as violating the Charter of the United Nations, as acting contrary to the laws of humanity and as committing a crime against mankind and civilization."

Part II

Central World-Order Concerns

CHAPTER 3

Internal War and International Law

ROSALYN HIGGINS

INTRODUCTION

THIS CHAPTER seeks to examine the role of international law in internal wars and to make suggestions as to the future of the international legal order in this regard. The theme is one which, until fairly recently, was regarded as of limited interest to the international lawyer. International law is largely concerned with international transactions and, to a lesser degree, with the promotion within nations of international standards on certain questions. Events occurring within a state have been regarded as prima facie a matter for the country concerned; but it has long been recognized that the dimensions and duration of a civil conflict may affect the position of outside parties.[1] To the extent that this is so, traditional law has purported to provide certain rules of conduct to be observed by the community of nations in respect to a civil war. And since 1949 international law has also sought to promote a certain minimum standard of conduct by the parties to the hostilities.

Only comparatively recently, however, has there been much critical analysis of the degree to which the stated "rules" in fact conform to experience.[2] Those who believe that law must accurately reflect community expectations, rather than consist of a mere statement of

[1] Hersch Lauterpacht, *Recognition in International Law* (Cambridge 1947), Pt. 3; Georges Berlia, "La guerre civile et la responsabilité internationale de l'état," *Revue Générale de Droit International Public*, XLIV (January-February 1937), 51; Charles G. Fenwick, "Can Civil Wars Be Brought Under the Control of International Law?" *American Journal of International Law*, 32 (1938), 538; James W. Garner, "Recognition of Belligerency," *American Journal of International Law*, same, 106; Leon C. Green, "Le statut des forces rebelles en droit international," *Revue Générale de Droit International Public*, LXVI (January-March 1962), 5; Lothar Kotzsch, *The Concept of War in Contemporary History and International Law* (Geneva 1956), 121; Haig Silvanie, *Responsibility of States for Acts of Unsuccessful Insurgent Governments* (New York 1939); Jean Siotis, *Le droit de la guerre et les conflits armés d'un caractère non-international* (Paris 1958); Wyndam L. Walker, "Recognition of Belligerency and Grant of Belligerent Rights," *Transactions of the Grotius Society*, XXXII (1937), 177; Jean-Pierre Weber, *Problèmes de droit international public posés par les guerres civiles* (Geneva 1940); Hans Wehberg, "La guerre civile et le droit international," *Hague Recueil*, LXIII (Paris 1938), 1; George Grafton Wilson, "Insurgency and International Maritime Law," *American Journal of International Law*, 1 (1907), 46; Erik Castrén, *Civil War* (Helsinki 1966); Roger Pinto, "Les Regles de Droit International Concernant la Guerre Civile," *Hague Recueil*, CXIV (Paris 1965), 451-553.

[2] See for example the comments of Siotis on the practical irrelevance of the notion of recognition of belligerency by the legal government itself: Siotis (fn. 1), 223; cf. Castrén (fn. 1), 138.

often unheeded "rules,"[3] have contended that the traditional rules no longer represent an accurate statement of the law.[4] Further, there has been recently some work of considerable importance on the causes and international implications of civil strife,[5] which has caused the contention to be made that the traditional rules are inimical to the policy interests of the world community.[6]

Major research in this field is now under way,[7] commanding infinitely greater resources than the present writer has at her disposal. The target of this chapter is therefore modest: it seeks to look at current practice, to analyze contentions made by the foremost scholars in the field, and to examine alternative proposals for the future.

I have sought to handle the multitude of relevant factors and variables by presenting "groupings" of claims made by the protagonists. This method has the advantage of highlighting the real issues at stake, and enables one to relate the traditional law to the assertions of legality actually made by the actors.[8] In essence, the claims which are made concern four international aspects of civil strife: (1) claims concerning the existence of a civil war (as opposed to international conflict or mere domestic revolt); (2) claims concerning the conduct of internal war; (3) claims concerning participation in internal wars (the right of third parties to affect the outcome of the war); and (4) claims concerning relations with third states (on the part of the contending factions).

No policy recommendations can be made without distinguishing between various types of civil conflict. To do otherwise would be to paint with too broad a brush, for the interests of the international community are by no means identical in each case. Before proceeding to an analysis of the claims made, therefore, we will briefly refer to the varying motives and situations which lead to internal war.

SITUATIONS

Internal wars may be of a variety of types, occurring for a variety of different reasons. They may be civil conflict *simpliciter*, in which

[3] The present writer would number herself among them. See Myres S. McDougal, "Some Basic Theoretical Concepts About International Law: A Policy-Oriented Framework of Enquiry," *Journal of Conflict Resolution*, IV (1960), 337.

[4] Richard A. Falk, "Janus Tormented: The International Law of Internal War," in *International Aspects of Civil Strife*, James N. Rosenau, ed. (Princeton 1964), 185-92.

[5] See the admirable volume *International Aspects of Civil Strife* (fn. 4), which provides an interdisciplinary analysis of the problems involved.

[6] Falk (fn. 4), 210-48.

[7] By the American Society of International Law, under the direction of Professor Falk.

[8] This is a technique which the present writer has found helpful in other comparatively uncharted areas of international law: see Rosalyn Higgins, *The Development of International Law through the Political Organs of the United Nations* (New York 1963).

two parties are contending for the status of government in all the territory: this was the case in the Spanish Civil War. The incumbent government may be democratically elected, and the insurgents Communists, military junta, Fascists, or other nondemocrats. Alternatively, the incumbent government may be unrepresentative, and the insurgents may be seeking to introduce democracy. Or neither party may command popular or democratic support. The motives of such insurgents vary. They may be seeking to establish certain minimum human rights; they may be acting from ideological motives; they may be seeking to secure a government more acceptable to the majority of the people, or to the neighbors of the territory concerned; or they may be engaged in a simple power struggle.

The civil conflict may also occur not as a dispute over central power, but because one party wishes to secede from the political unit as it is established. The Nigerian civil war was clearly a dispute over secession rather than any attempt by Biafra to seize power in Lagos. The civil war in the Congo was in part—though not solely—caused by the attempted secession of Katanga. The reasons for attempt at secession also vary. Secession may be attempted by a wealthy part of a larger federal unit which does not wish to share its resources with, or pay tax on them to, the central government. It may be encouraged in this attitude by foreign economic interests. Both of these factors are relevant to the Katanga and Biafra secessions. The secession may be felt necessary because tribal groups residing in one area believe that they are not treated as equals and fear for their security: this was clearly the prime motive of Colonel Ojukwu's attempt to establish a separate state of Biafra. And the secession may represent the attempt of a locally charismatic leader to secure a greater measure of power than he has been able to achieve in the federal structure. One can also imagine attempts at secession in order to join with ethnically similar neighbors:[9] although the fighting between the Somalis in Kenya and the Kenya government has never reached the status of civil war, one may note that the rebels' objective has been to unify with the neighboring state of Somalia.

Government persecution, or claimed persecution of minorities, and resistance by those minorities, could lead to civil war. Were the Kurds and the Nagas militarily better organized the internal hostilities could acquire the status of internal warfare. Equally, disputes between ethnic or religious groups as to the constitutional disposition of power and opportunities between them can cause domestic strife on a major scale, as the tragedy of the Cyprus experience shows, as well as current events in Northern Ireland.

[9] In Cyprus the same motive has been evident, though it has not manifested itself in terms of secession. In this case an element in the civil war has been the desire of the majority for *Enosis* with Greece, notwithstanding the fears of the Turkish minority.

A further group of internal wars arise from the process of decolonization. The peoples of colonial territory may take up arms because they have no prospect of obtaining independence from the metropolitan power—such is the case in Angola and Mozambique. In yet other territories, even if independence is promised, the local leaders may insist that the timetable is too slow, or that the people to whom power is to be handed are not representative. These factors were of great significance in the fighting in Aden between British forces and the nationalist groups. Insofar as the administering authority declares that the territory in question is an integral part of the metropolitan territory—as was the claim in respect of Algeria—then, at least from the point of view of the metropolitan power, any conflict is an internal rather than international war. The international community has regarded such claims with some skepticism, and from the point of view of, for example, the United Nations, such a war is not necessarily internal.[10] The evidence points to this imbalance of legal perspective, though certain authors prefer to rest on the formalistic argument that such wars cannot be international "since such areas do not have the status of a subject of international law."[11] A similar problem arises in the case of anticolonial wars in those dependent territories which have a special legal status, such as protectorates or trusteeship areas. In both cases there is some controversy as to the division of sovereignty between the dependent and governing authorities. Some authors view colonial wars in protectorates as internal,[12] and those in trust territories as international.[13] In any event, the international community is taking an increased interest in their outcome, and whatever their precise status they cause important international repercussions.

Rebellions in colonial territories are usually between the colonial authority and those representing the majority of the indigenous population. It can occur, however, that the rebellion against the administering authority is by a minority element in the territory seeking to secure power against the indigenous majority. This has been the case in the seizure of power by Ian Smith's government in Rhodesia.

In all of these cases the policy considerations, from the point of view of the world community, are different. For the moment we merely note the different and the differing motives for which they are fought. In our concluding section on recommendations for the future international legal order, we shall seek to relate these variables to certain proposals.

[10] For a full discussion of the United Nations perspective, see pp. 106-10.
[11] Castrén (fn. 1), 37; cf. Siotis (fn. 1), 47.
[12] Castrén (fn. 1), 37; cf. Frede Castberg, "Borgerkrig og revolusjon," *Studier i folkerett* (Oslo 1952), 83ff.
[13] Castberg, same, 86; Castrén (fn. 1), 38.

Claims Concerning the Existence of a Civil War

1. CLAIM THAT THE WAR IS INTERNAL
   RATHER THAN INTERNATIONAL

The identification of a major conflict as either civil or international war is essential to the correct application of the relevant legal norms. Two main factors operate that make it difficult to appraise a conflict as simply "internal." In the first place, the international community (and the parties themselves) may be divided as to whether the territory concerned is a political unit or state, or two. In the second place, it may be claimed that what appears ostensibly as a civil war is in fact violence fomented from outside. Should this be so, different considerations of both law and policy will ensue.

The appraisal of a conflict as internal war, rather than international conflict, entails legal consequences so far as the status of the warring parties is concerned; so far as the rights of third parties to participate or remain neutral is concerned; and so far as the modalities of the conflict is concerned. All of these aspects are discussed below. For the moment we may note that the war in Vietnam provides a clear example of this problem. Certain observers have regarded Vietnam as legally one state;[14] thus entailing the consequence that the fighting was initially a civil war, and this did not entitle the United States to intervene on one side.[15] Others have contended[16] that, the intentions of the Geneva Accords notwithstanding, North and South Vietnam are now effectively two de facto states; and that, if aggression by one can be shown, there is a right by the other to invite the assistance of another nation in collective self-defense.

Similar arguments, though in more muted terms, were heard in respect of the Korean War. In this case South Korea had been recognized in a resolution of the United Nations General Assembly,[17] and thus the majority of the international community was on record as acknowledging the de facto statehood of the South. The crossing of the

---

[14] It is argued that the Geneva Accords of 1954 established the unity of Vietnam. See, e.g., Lawyers Committee on American Policy toward Vietnam, *American Policy vis-à-vis Vietnam, Memorandum of Law,* in 112 *Congressional Record* 2552; Senator Morse, 112 *Congressional Record* 1975; Henry Steele Commanger, "Our Vietnamese Commitment," in 112 *Congressional Record* 11746; William Standard, "United States Intervention Is Not Legal," *American Bar Association Journal,* 52 (1966), 627; David G. Partan, "Legal Aspects of the Vietnam Conflict," in *The Vietnam War and International Law,* Vol. 1, Richard A. Falk, ed. (Princeton 1969), 216-17; Quincy Wright, "Legal Aspects of the Vietnam Situation," same, 285; Falk, "International Law and the United States Role in the Vietnam War," same, 363-69.

[15] The scope of the right to intervene in a civil war is discussed on pp. 97-106.

[16] E.g., Eliot D. Hawkins, "An Approach to Issues of International Law Raised by United States Actions in Vietnam," in *The Vietnam War and International Law* (fn. 14).

[17] G.A. Res. 195 (III).

parallel by North Korean troops was thus readily deemed an international breach of peace,[18] and not a merely civil conflict.

The sequence of events, as well as the status of the territorial units involved, is also relevant to the determination of a conflict as internal or international. Thus in the case of Vietnam it is argued by some that the conflict was originally between the Diem government and the NLF, but that it was internationalized by the intervention of the United States, leading in turn to a response by regular troops of Hanoi.[19] Others read the evidence differently, asserting that the United States responded only after intervention by the North.[20]

2. CLAIM THAT INTERNATIONAL LAW IS RELEVANT TO THE SITUATION

Clearly, international law is not directly relevant to all domestic conflicts. Traditionally, major domestic violence has been classified as falling within one of three categories: rebellion, insurgency, or belligerency. Rebellion is understood to entail sporadic violence which is capable of containment by the national police or militia. By definition, a government has no need to call for outside help in controlling the situation.[21] International law gives no protection to the rebels, and is relevant only insofar as it entitles the government to promulgate measures which may incidentally inconvenience other nations, and makes help to the rebels an offense.

By contrast, certain traditional norms of international law are—or are said to be—relevant to internal hostilities which are deemed either insurgency or belligerency. Some guidance is given by the records of the Geneva Diplomatic Conference of 1949[22] which lists "convenient criteria"[23] that are useful for "distinguishing a genuine [internal] armed conflict from a mere act of banditry or an unorganized and shortlived insurrection." These criteria are as follows:

(1) That the Party in revolt against the *de jure* government possesses an organized military force, an authority responsible for its acts, acting within a determinate territory and having the means of respecting and ensuring respect for the Convention.

---

18 S.C. Res. S/1501.

19 Falk, "The Legal Status of the United States Involvement in the Vietnam War," in *Legal Order in a Violent World* (Princeton 1968), 276-77, 298.

20 E.g., Memorandum of the Legal Adviser, Dept. of State, "The Legality of United States Participation in the Defense of Viet Nam," reprinted in same, 535-58.

21 Though cf. Falk, same, who states that foreign states, however, are free to help the government against the rebels, 118.

22 The Conference at which the texts of the 1949 Geneva Conventions were adopted.

23 Cited in Marjorie Millace Whiteman, ed., *Digest of International Law*, x (Washington 1963), 41.

(2) That the legal Government is obliged to have recourse to the regular military forces against insurgents—organized as military and in possession of a part of national territory.

(3) (a) That the *de jure* Government has recognized the insurgents as belligerents, or

(b) that it has claimed for itself the rights of a belligerent; or

(c) that it has accorded the insurgents recognition as belligerents for the purposes only of the present Convention; or

(d) that the dispute has been admitted to the agenda of the Security Council or the General Assembly of the United Nations as being a threat to the peace, a breach of the peace, or an act of aggression.

(4) (a) That the insurgents have an organization purporting to have the characteristics of a state;

(b) that the insurgent civil authority exercises *de facto* authority over persons within a determinate territory;

(c) that the armed forces act under the direction of the organized civil authority and are prepared to observe the ordinary laws of war;

(d) that the insurgent civil authority agrees to be bound by the terms of the Convention.[24]

All violent acts against the government, whether rebellion, insurgency, or belligerency, are likely to be punishable under domestic law.[25] However, neither treaty nor customary international law condemns civil war;[26] indeed, many have explicitly asserted that the law of nations permits civil war.[27] There is also a considerable sympathy for the notion that civil war may be the only way by which the peoples of a country can express their will in an authoritarian environment, and that it should thus not be condemned by international law.

While international law neither prohibits nor condemns civil war, it has a relevant role to play where the domestic violence is more than mere rioting or rebellion. This is true even though, as we shall see below, it has become virtually unheard of to grant a formal status of either insurgency or belligerency in recent years. Though the traditional distinctions—and the methods for making them—have become largely irrelevant, it remains correct to observe that minor domestic

[24] Final Record of the Diplomatic Conference of Geneva, 1949, II-B, 121. We shall return on pp. 89-93 to the application of the Geneva Conventions in civil war.

[25] See Grigore Geamanu, *La Résistance à l'oppression et le droit à l'insurrection* (Paris 1934).

[26] Nothing in the United Nations Charter forbids civil war; nor does the Inter-America Havana Convention of 1928.

[27] See Wehberg (fn. 1), 9, 40; Georges Scelle, "La guerre civile espagnole et le droit des gens," in *Extrait de Revue Générale de Droit International Public*, XLV (May-June 1938), 265-66; Lauterpacht (fn. 1), 175; Castrén (fn. 1), 19.

violence entails few international—and thus international legal—repercussions.

3. CLAIM THAT THE STATUS OF THE PROTAGONISTS RENDERS A CONFLICT A CIVIL WAR

Traditional international law recognizes two categories of domestic violence which establish a civil war; and different legal consequences flow from each of these categories.

The lesser, and less well-defined status, is that of insurgency. It is, as Professor Falk has correctly commented, an international acknowledgment of the existence of an internal war, which leaves each state substantially free to control the consequences of this acknowledgment.[28] De Visscher has described the recognition of insurgency as "more elusive in its criteria than recognition of belligerency,"[29] while Lauterpacht has observed that "any attempt to lay down the conditions of recognition of insurgency lends itself to misunderstanding. Recognition of insurgency creates a factual relation in the meaning that legal rights and duties as between insurgents and outside states exist only insofar as they are expressly conceded and agreed upon for reasons of convenience, of humanity, or of economic interest."[30]

The recognition of insurgency—whether implied or expressed, is an indication that the recognizing state regards the insurgents as legal contestants, and not as mere lawbreakers.[31] Such an acknowledgment does not entail the legal burdens of a neutral—possibly the recognizing state is still free to assist the legal government,[32] and would be illegally intervening if it materially assisted the insurgents.[33]

The recognition of belligerency, on the other hand, involves more than the mere acknowledgment of the fact that hostilities are being conducted. Traditionally, four criteria are cited: first, there must exist within the state an armed conflict of a general character; second, the insurgents must occupy and administer a substantial portion of national territory; third, they must conduct the hostilities in accordance with the rules of war and through organized armed forces responsible to an identifiable authority; and fourth, there must exist circumstances that make it necessary for third parties to define their attitude by recognition of belligerency.[34]

---

28 Falk (fn. 19), 119-22.

29 Charles De Visscher, *Theory and Reality in Public International Law*, trans. by P. E. Corbett (Princeton 1957), 238.

30 Lauterpacht (fn. 1), 276-77.

31 Memorandum of Legal Adviser Yingling, cited in Whiteman (fn. 23), II, 487.

32 See the discussion on self-determination, pp. 96-97.

33 Charles Cheney Hyde, *International Law Chiefly as Interpreted and Applied by the United States*, 2nd edn. (Boston 1945), 1, 204.

34 Lauterpacht (fn. 1), 176.

Claims Concerning the Conduct of Internal War

1. CLAIM THAT INTERNATIONAL LAW REGULATING THE METHODS
OF WARFARE IS APPLICABLE IN INTERNAL WAR

Any examination of the purpose of the laws of war—the minimizing of suffering and destruction—reveals that they must in principle be regarded as relevant to internal war. The fact that one party is not, in traditional terminology, a full subject of international law, is not relevant to this proposition. Nor is the characterization of the rebels as criminals under the constitutional law of the country concerned. Lauterpacht's views in 1946 remain appropriate:

A clearly ascertained state of hostilities on a sufficiently large scale, willed as war at least by one of the parties, creates *suo vigore* a condition in which the rules of warfare become operative. . . . Once a situation has been created which, but for the constitutional law of the state concerned, is indistinguishable from war, practice suggests that international law ought to step in in order to fulfill the same function which it performs in wars between sovereign states, namely, to humanize and regularize the conduct of hostilities as between the parties.[35]

To the traditionalist, recognition of belligerency was required before the rights and duties of the laws of war and neutrality were conferred upon the recognized party. Broadly speaking—and certainly in respect to the rights of belligerents as against those of neutrals—this proposition remains true. However, attempts have been made to make operative certain minimum humanitarian standards. These attempts are found in Article 3 of all four Geneva Conventions of 1949,[36] which provide:

In the case of armed conflict not of an international character occurring in the territory of one of the High Contracting Parties, each Party to the conflict shall be bound to apply, as a minimum, the following provisions:
(1) persons taking no active part in the hostilities, including

[35] Same, 246. This is one reason why Lauterpacht contends that the government is under a duty to recognize the insurgents as belligerents. See also Myres S. McDougal and Florentino P. Feliciano, *Toward Minimum World Public Order* (New Haven 1961), 535: "The physical characteristics of exercises of violence and their effects upon people and resources are of course the same, assuming violence of comparable proportions in an internal as in an international conflict. It would thus seem fairly obvious that what has been generalized above as a fundamental policy of minimum unnecessary destruction is equally vital and applicable in one as in the other type of conflict."

[36] On the Wounded and Sick in the Field, On the Wounded, Sick and Shipwrecked at Sea, On Prisoners of War, and on Civilians during War.

members of armed forces who have laid down their arms and those placed *hors de combat* by sickness, wounds, detention, or any other cause, shall in all circumstances be treated humanely, without any adverse distinction founded on race, color, religion or faith, sex, birth or wealth, or any other similar criteria.

To this end, the following acts are and shall remain prohibited at any time and in any place whatsoever with respect to the above-mentioned persons:

(a) violence to life and person, in particular murder of all kinds, mutilation, cruel treatment and torture;

(b) taking of hostages;

(c) outrages upon personal dignity, in particular humiliating and degrading treatment;

(d) the passing of sentences and the carrying out of executions without previous judgment pronounced by a regularly constituted court, affording all the judicial guarantees which are recognized as indispensable by civilized peoples.

(2) The wounded and sick shall be collected and cared for. An impartial humanitarian body, such as the International Committee of the Red Cross, may offer its services to the Parties to the conflict.

The Parties to the conflict should further endeavor to bring into force, by means of special agreements, all or part of the other provisions of the present Convention. The application of the preceding provisions shall not affect the legal status of the Parties to the conflict.[37]

What this provision does is to call for certain humanitarian rules to be applied irrespective of whether the insurgents have been recognized by the legitimate government or by third parties. It also makes clear that interventions by the Red Cross are not to be regarded as unfriendly acts. The provisions of Article 3 have not, unfortunately, been regarded as an integral whole. There have been cases where Red Cross intervention has occurred, but none of the other paragraphs of Article 3 have been employed—and still less have the parties made special agreements to bring the rest of the Convention into effect. Nonetheless, this basis for Red Cross action has still proved useful. The Red Cross was able to act in Guatemala in 1954, and in Costa Rica

---

[37] This Article was a compromise, the Conference being unable to decide whether the Conventions should be automatically applicable to civil wars or not; or whether they should be applicable only in certain major types of civil war. See Castrén (fn. 1), 85; Siotis (fn. 1), 185-206; McDougal and Feliciano (fn. 35), 536-37; and Raymund T. Yingling and Robert W. Ginnane, "The Geneva Conventions of 1949," *American Journal of International Law*, 44 (July 1952), 395-96.

in 1955, though there was no recognition of belligerency.[38] It remains true, however, that the attitude of the constitutional government may still remain hostile to the Red Cross, even while allowing it certain limited rights of action (as in Nigeria).

The Article is binding on both parties, and is not subject to reciprocity. It does not itself define an "armed conflict not of an international character," but—given its humanitarian purposes—it would seem to be applicable to major insurgency and probably also rebellion, as well as to civil war.[39]

While this provision in the Geneva Convention has performed the valuable function of making clear that humanitarian behavior depends neither on recognition nor on the formal status of the parties, actual practice[40] all too often falls lamentably below the standards required by the Geneva Conventions of 1949. This is so whether or not the constitutional government is a party to the Conventions, and whether or not the parties have agreed to heed the humanitarian requirements of the laws of war. The war in Vietnam has been marked by indiscriminate murder, torture, the use of weapons of doubtful legality, and lack of discrimination between civil and military targets. While, so far as one knows, the Nigerian civil war has not occasioned terrorism and torture on any scale, the deliberate bombing of civilian centers has been all too evident.[41]

Behavior is frequently anomalous, and occasionally the humanitarian provisions of Article 3 of the Geneva Conventions are applied in spite of the refusal of the constitutional government to recognize the insurgents as belligerents. France refused to recognize the Algerians as belligerents, but did permit relief activity by the Red Cross. The French government acknowledged that the conflict was not solely a criminal matter but was an armed conflict of the type mentioned in Article 3 of the Geneva Conventions. Nonetheless, she denied the international character of the conflict.[42] Neither side fully adhered to the legal standards of Article 3. Not infrequently, a government permits activity by the Red Cross asserting that it does so as an act of sovereignty, and not because Article 3 is applicable. The United Kingdom

[38] See Castrén (fn. 1), 78; Siotis (fn. 1), 209ff.

[39] To this effect, Siotis, same, 209; Castrén, same, 87.

[40] And note also that Portugal has a reservation in respect of Article 3 to the effect that she reserves the right not to apply the Article if it is considered contradictory to her domestic legislation. Such a reservation would seem to be quite incompatible with the overall intentions of the Convention.

[41] See, for example, the eyewitness accounts of Winston S. Churchill in *The Times* (London) during March 1969.

[42] Castrén (fn. 1), 74. See also Siotis (fn. 1), 211. Mohammed Bedjaoui, *Law and the Algerian Revolution* (Brussels 1961), 159, observes that France engaged in actions that were tantamount to a recognition of belligerency, such as stopping, searching and rerouting foreign ships sending supplies to the Algerian rebels.

never admitted Article 3 applied in respect to the conflicts in Kenya and Cyprus, though it did allow the Red Cross to visit detainees in Cyprus in 1955 and in Kenya in 1957.[43]

In Nigeria the situation seemed confused. The Federal authorities agreed to enter into arrangements with the International Red Cross concerning proposals for airlifting supplies to airports under Federal control but rejected an appeal (on May 23, 1968) for extensive lifting of the blockade on Biafra, the sparing of civilians from bombing attacks, and the exchange of some prisoners of war. The Federal government stated that the I.C.R.C. was "allowing itself, perhaps unwittingly through political naiveté, to be used as a tool of rebel propaganda."[44] The Biafrans agreed to cooperate with the Red Cross, but clearly wanted an airlift operation, rather than a land corridor, for political rather than humanitarian reasons. Although the Federal authorities did not formally deem Article 3 of the Geneva Conventions to be applicable, they invited in international observers to inspect Federal military operations in the field. By and large, their reports were favorable. The Federal government stated that it would voluntarily apply the standards of the Geneva Conventions. At the same time, there were widespread reports about indiscriminate bombing and the holding up of relief supplies.

In Vietnam the United States, viewing the situation as an international rather than a civil war, deems the entirety of the Geneva Conventions applicable, rather than only Article 3. All parties to the conflict—North Vietnam,[45] South Vietnam, and the United States—are bound by the four Geneva Conventions. In reply to a letter from the I.C.R.C., the United States indicated its intention to abide by the provisions of the Geneva Conventions, adding the caveat that given the reliance by the North on disguise and illegal methods of warfare, it is "difficult to develop programs and procedures to resolve fully all the problems arising in the application of the provisions of the Conven-

---

[43] Colonel Gerald Irving A. Dare Draper observed in 1958 ". . . several thousand troops were employed to quell the Mau Mau in Kenya, the terrorists in Malaya, EOKA in Cyprus, and no less than 400,000 are employed in Algeria where the rebels are still active. The refusal of France and the United Kingdom to recognize that these conflicts fall within Article 3 has, it is thought, been determined by political consideration and not by any objective assessment of the facts." *The Red Cross Conventions* (London 1958), 15, n47.

[44] *Keesing's Contemporary Archives*, August 24, 1968, 22877.

[45] The International Committee of the Red Cross classifies the situation as armed conflict between two or more of the Contracting Parties. It also has stated—and has not been contradicted by any of the parties—"The National Liberation Front too is bound by the undertakings signed by Vietnam." See letter from Jacques Freymond to Dean Rusk, June 11, 1965, reproduced in *International Legal Materials* (November 1965), 1171. But cf. contrary reports, e.g., *New York Herald Tribune*, May 7, 1966 which stated that the I.C.R.C. had been informed that the Viet Cong were "freedom fighters," not subject to the responsibility of Hanoi. They were entitled, it was argued, to regard themselves as not bound by the Geneva Conventions.

tions. Continued refinement of these programs and procedures in the light of experience will thus undoubtedly be necessary."[46]

The Republic of Vietnam reported that the Geneva Conventions were applied with respect to Viet Cong prisoners. Visits by the I.C.R.C. would be permitted. The Democratic Republic of Vietnam replied[47] that aerial attacks on the North by the United States, indiscriminate bombing, and the use of napalm were all in breach of the Geneva Agreements of 1949. Consequently, it regarded captured air pilots as "criminals" and liable to judgment under North Vietnamese law.[48] North Vietnam's reply made no mention of the applicability of the Conventions to the situation.[49] North Vietnam has not allowed inspection of camps by the I.C.R.C., nor has it given lists of prisoners. Certain attempts have been made by third parties—such as the U.A.R. —to act as a protecting power for U.S. forces held by Communist forces, but this has been unsuccessful. On occasion, captured military personnel have been paraded in a manner contrary to the Conventions. Undoubtedly, there have also been breaches of the Conventions in the South, though there is evidence that the United States has sought to control these.[50] Given the difficulty of making the Viet Cong fall within the definition of Prisoners of War in Article 4 of the Convention, it could have been argued that they were unprotected by this Convention; yet, because the war was international, the minimum humanitarian provisions of Article 3 did not apply either. Fortunately, this narrow argument has not been advanced, and P.O.W. status has been granted to North Vietnam regulars and to Viet Cong alike. The United States has no doubt been mindful of its own traditions, public opinion, and the hope that it would be able to call for reciprocity.

Claims Concerning Participation in Internal Wars

1. CLAIMS IN FAVOR OF OUTSIDE PARTICIPATION

   A. *Claim by the constitutional government*

   (1) *that it is entitled to ask for help.* Traditional international law is fairly clear in indicating that in relations with third states a lawful government is in a privileged position compared with the insurgents,[51]

---

[46] *International Legal Materials* (November 1965), 1173.

[47] Same, 1174.

[48] At the time of capture of the pilots it was threatened that they would be brought to trial as "war criminals." In fact, this has not occurred.

[49] Reprinted in *International Legal Materials* (January 1966), 124.

[50] Thus in July 1966 the United States decided not to hand over all prisoners directly to the South Vietnamese Army, but to keep them in U.S. hands until transferred to P.O.W. camps. Under Article 12 of the Convention of Prisoners of War, a capturing power is required to turn prisoners over to another country to guarantee their well-being.

[51] This aspect is dealt with under "Claims Concerning Relations with Third Parties."

at least until there has been recognition of belligerency. What is less clear—and it has become still more doubtful in recent years—is the legal authority of the government to ask for military assistance during civil hostilities—either of arms or active participation. While the majority of writers support aid in general terms for the government, they are divided where aid in arms or military forces is concerned. Those supporting[52] the right of the government to call for assistance point to the fact that it is still the recognized government, and that the insurgents have no status under international law. Others suggest that once a government requests foreign military aid it no longer, by definition, represents all the state.[53] What is clear beyond doubt is that governments faced with rebellion do frequently ask for assistance, and other governments see fit to grant it. Given the increasing infrequency of recognition of belligerent status—a legal concept fast becoming irrelevant in the context of internal wars—governments feel more and more free to answer a plea for help from another government, irrespective of whether the rebels are mounting an organized opposition and have control of a substantial portion of the territory.

Calls for assistance in the form of troops usually occur when the government classifies the war as international rather than internal. In Vietnam, the South Vietnamese emphasize that the fight is against North Vietnamese regulars, and that even the Viet Cong are assisted by and directed from Hanoi. Sometimes there is comparatively little evidence that the conflict is anything but internal; thus Chamoun's government in Lebanon sought aid from the U.S.A. in 1958, claiming that the domestic rebellion was being fomented by the U.A.R.; a U.N. observer group found no proof of this.[54] It is comparatively rare for a government faced by a rebellion to call for assistance by foreign troops. East African governments asked with great reluctance for British help in 1964 in putting down mutinies; but this damaged their prestige in the region and would be unlikely to be repeated. Clearly, most governments that have recently secured their independence from their colonial masters are unwilling to invite them to assist in terminating civil conflict. However, requests are made—and met—for arms supplies to the government.[55]

In short, there is a clear community expectation that a government may seek arms supplies from abroad when a civil conflict occurs, and is not prevented from doing so even if the rebels have acquired a posi-

---

[52] Among those supporting the legality of military aid, see Castberg (fn. 12), 104; Ian Brownlie, *International Law and the Use of Force by States* (London 1963), 325-27; Castrén (fn. 1), 110-11.

[53] See Arnold Raestad, "Borgerkrig og Folkeret," in *Nordisk Tidsskrift for International Ret.*, VIII (1938), 5.

[54] For an overall survey of the U.N. role in civil wars, see pp. 106-10.

[55] For a discussion of the right of outside parties to provide arms, see pp. 98-99.

tion that would have been granted the status of belligerency under traditional international law. Most governments are reluctant to ask for foreign military help when the conflict is purely civil, but they and the world community believe that they have the right to do so when the civil war is fomented or supported from outside.

(2) *that it is entitled to belligerent rights.* Although the formal recognition of belligerency is becoming increasingly rare, we may note that under traditional international law the constitutional government is not entitled to claim belligerent rights unless the insurgents have been recognized as belligerent. As we shall observe below, this nominal restriction has little practical effect on the course of the war.

B. *Claims by insurgents*

(1) *that they are entitled to belligerent status.* This claim may be advanced by the insurgents in respect of the constitutional government. There has been academic debate as to whether such recognition is constitutive[56]—bringing into existence certain rights and duties—or whether it is declamatory.[57] Suffice it to say that, since the Spanish war, belligerent recognition of the insurgents by government and by third parties has lost all practical significance,[58] though it can be argued that tacit recognition of this status[59] still brings certain legal consequences into effect. It is arguable that, as a matter of policy, insurgents should be *entitled* to recognition by the government, but there is less case for making such a suggestion in respect of third parties because the recognition of belligerency cannot be gratuitous, but depends upon the necessity of the relations between the insurgents and the third party concerned.[60]

There are arguments for and against the proposition that states are obliged to recognize the belligerent status of insurgents when the appropriate conditions exist. An obligation to recognize belligerency entails subsequent neutrality by the recognizing party (which it may or may not deem to its advantage, depending on the circumstances) and its nonparticipation in the internal conflict.[61] On the other hand, recognition entails highly significant consequences for the recognizing

---

56 Castrén (fn. 1), 138; Castberg (fn. 12), 109.

57 Lauterpacht (fn. 1), 253, who notes that recognition acknowledges that the civil war has fulfilled certain prerequisites for recognition and that the recognition is mandatory. It is recognition of belligerency which brings the laws of war into operation—though Article 3 of the Geneva Conventions applies irrespective of recognition by either the government or third parties.

58 Thus Siotis (fn. 1), 223.

59 Castrén (fn. 1), 136, 147.

60 On which question, see p. 101.

61 This reason—the tendency to limit the scope of civil wars—is emphasized by Lauterpacht when he urges the legal obligation to recognize belligerency (fn. 1), 229ff.

state; and it will be reluctant to acknowledge that insurgents, lacking formal status under traditional international law, can oblige it to embark upon these. We shall suggest later that this is an area in which community procedures could be profitably employed.[62]

(2) *that they are entitled to recognition as either the government of all the territory or of a seceded portion of the territory.* So far as traditional international law is concerned, insurgents may on occasion pursue the claim that they are entitled not merely to recognition as belligerents, but to recognition as a de facto government. Sometimes an insurgent government may be recognized as the de facto government in the area which it controls (though some have said that this is merely tantamount to a recognition of belligerency).[63] However, insurgents may also be recognized as the overall de facto government. Recognition must traditionally be based on factual prerequisites, although the granting of it is discretionary. When the goal of civil war is separation of a portion of the territory, and if the insurgents have already succeeded in establishing their rule, and have been recognized by many states, it is arguable that the internal war has now become an international one.[64]

All this being said, one may note that practice has varied considerably. In the Spanish Civil War, Germany and Italy early recognized Franco as the only lawful government in Spain. Academic arguments as to the propriety of this notwithstanding,[65] these countries opened diplomatic relations and provided Franco with arms and troops. *De jure* recognition was also accorded by Portugal, Albania, El Salvador, Guatemala, and Nicaragua. In addition, other states granted de facto recognition.[66] The Soviet Union and Mexico, on the contrary, recognized the National government as the only lawful government, and Franco as a mere insurgent.

In other cases recognition has taken place in circumstances which the majority of nations regard as premature, because the outcome was uncertain: the recognition by certain nations of the Algerian government was a case in point. Here the traditional criteria were fulfilled and the controversy was about timing. In some recent cases, however, it has become clear that some governments assert a right to recognize

---

[62] Same, 49.

[63] Jean Spiropoulos, *Die de facto Regierung im Völkerrecht* (Kiel 1926), 57.

[64] A point made by Pasquale Fiore, *Il Diritto internazionale codificato e la sua sanzione giuiridica,* 5th edn. (Torino 1915), 556.

[65] The German and Italian action is widely regarded as premature and illegal: Castrén (fn. 1), 58; Frede Castberg, "Folkerettslige Spörsmal Om Kring Den Spanske Borgerkrig," *Nordisk Tidsskrift for International Ret.,* XIII (1937), 164.

[66] Britain sought a middle path by recognizing, in due course, Franco as the local de facto government.

even when the traditional criteria are manifestly not fulfilled. The eloquent statement by President Nyerere of Tanzania on his decision to recognize Biafra[67] reveals a preoccupation with questions of morality and a total indifference to the customary legal factors. International consensus on recognition—both generally and in antiwar situations—has broken down.

C. *Claims by outside states*

1. *Claims in favor of supporting the government*

(1) *that armed assistance, mere rebellion or insurgency is taking place.* It used to be generally accepted that a state may aid a government threatened with riots and insurgency until such time as it has recognized—whether by implication or expressly—the belligerent status of the insurgents. This statement of the traditional rule is now to be qualified by concern for the principle of self-determination: to what extent is such help an intervention preventing the self-determination of the population of the territory concerned, notwithstanding the limited status of the rebels? This aspect is discussed below.[68]

Intervention by invitation is a doctrine to be regarded with suspicion so long as there are no centralized procedures for establishing the support commanded by the rebels, and so long as the openings for abuse are so many.[69] The point was well put as early as 1924:

> [if intervention is] directed against rebels, the fact that it has been necessary to call in foreign help is enough to show that the issue of the conflict would without it be uncertain, and consequently that there is a doubt as to which side would ultimately establish itself as the legal representative of the state. If again, intervention is based upon an opinion as to the merits of the question at issue, the intervening state takes upon itself to pass judgment on a matter which, having nothing to do with the relations of states, must be regarded as being for legal purposes beyond the range of its vision.[70]

A more detailed discussion of the policy considerations at stake in this question will follow in the final section of this chapter. For the moment, we may note that the traditionalist view—allowing a right of intervention where there has been no recognition of belligerency—is losing favor.[71]

---

[67] *Observer*, April 28, 1968.   [68] Pp. 103-05.

[69] On this point generally, see Higgins (fn. 8), 210-13.

[70] William E. Hall, *A Treatise on International Law*, A. Pearce Higgins, ed., 8th edn. (Oxford 1924), 347.

[71] See, e.g., Quincy Wright, "United States Intervention in the Lebanon," *American Journal of International Law*, 53 (January 1959), 121-22.

(2) *that arms may be sold to the lawful government if the belligerency of the rebels has not been recognized.* We have already observed that, given the general desire for international stability, the lawful government starts with a built-in advantage against the rebels. The duty of nonintervention requires states not to furnish arms, munitions, military goods, or financial aid to the rebels, and not to allow their territory to be used as a base for rebel activities against the lawful government.[72] However, it appears in these circumstances to be lawful to continue to provide arms to the lawful government. The U.S. Department of State, in justifying its decision on the 1930 resolution in Brazil to prohibit shipment of all arms to that country except to the government, explained: "Until belligerency is recognized, and the duty of neutrality arises, all the humane predispositions towards stability of government, the preservation of international amity, and the protection of established intercourse between nations are in favor of the Existing Government."[73] Such a view does not appear to be inconsistent with the view that nothing in international law prohibits revolution; and certainly it is consistent with state practice.

(3) *that arms may be sold to the recognized government, irrespective of the status of the rebels.* Given the contemporary infrequency of formal recognition of belligerency, it has become more and more possible for states to deal with the lawful government as if the rebels had not the status of belligerents, even though the facts clearly indicate otherwise. In other words, the legal relevance of the particular rights and duties flowing from the existence of a major civil war is denied. A clear example of this tendency is available in the handling of the Nigeria-Biafra War by the British government. The British government appeared to acknowledge—indeed, it would seem impossible on the facts to do otherwise—that a civil war existed in Nigeria. At the same time, the government regards itself as free to provide the Federal government with arms, merely on the legal ground that it is the recognized government. Speaking in the House of Commons, the Secretary of State for Commonwealth Affairs commented: "Neutrality was not a possible option for Her Majesty's Government at that time. We might have been able to declare ourselves neutral if one independent country was fighting another, but this was not a possible attitude when a Commonwealth country, with which we had long and close ties, was faced with an internal revolt. What would other Commonwealth countries have thought?"[74] Lest it be thought that the Commonwealth

---

[72] Relations between third states and the parties to an internal war are dealt with more fully on p. 101.

[73] Department of State, Latin American Series, No. 4, 1931, cited in Lauterpacht (fn. 1), 231.

[74] *Hansard*, August 27, 1968, col. 1146.

Secretary was implying that this was a mere rebellion, it may be noted that he had earlier classified the situation as "a civil war."[75] The entire speech largely ignores the legal issues, and insofar as they are touched on at all, it is in confusion. Nor was the Secretary endeavoring to draw a distinction, insofar as aid to the government is concerned, between civil war and secession. The Deputy Leader of the Opposition had supported the supply of arms, but added: "However, the position could change if the struggle took on the character of a genuine civil war. . . . Despite the recognition of Biafra by a number of other territories on the African continent, is it not still a fact that this is a matter of secession rather than a civil war?"[76] The suggestion, apparently, was twofold: first, secession was something different from civil war; and that in the case of the former—but not the latter—arms supplies could continue. But the Secretary did not wish to grasp at even this legal straw, for he replied (no doubt correctly):[77] "I do not follow the distinction that the right hon. gentleman was seeking to make between the issue of secession and the fact of a civil war. I would describe this as a civil war over the issue of secession."[78] The historical antecedents of this claim to aid the recognized government, irrespective of the circumstances, lie in the Spanish Civil War. Quincy Wright has pointed out that if an outside state could respond to help from the *de jure* government, then where different states recognize different factions, there is a prescription for the internationalizing of a local dispute. He goes even further, denying the right to help the recognized government even where the insurgents have not attained the status of belligerency. He contends that what is relevant is not recognition of belligerency, but the uncertainty of the outcome.[79]

(4) *that they are under a treaty obligation to sell arms to the lawful government.* Nations which have treaty arrangements for the supply of arms to a particular government are placed in an embarrassing position—and especially if they are the traditional supplier of arms—if a civil war breaks out in the territory. Here the term "nonintervention" is something of a misnomer because the foreign state is already involved; and if it ceases to supply the lawful government, that may be regarded, effectively, as assistance for the rebels. There is considerable evidence that the export of arms *de novo* during a civil war is impermissible. By a Joint Resolution of Congress of January 8, 1937, the

---

[75] Same, col. 1443.

[76] Same, col. 1437.

[77] We approve the definition by McDougal of a civil war, "A genuinely internal conflict within a nation-state in which a counter-elite group seeks forcibly to organize a new political unit separate from the old body politic, or to capture effective control of existing governmental structures." McDougal and Feliciano (fn. 35), 77.

[78] *Hansard*, cols. 1443-44.

[79] Wright (fn. 71), 121-22.

United States prohibited the export of arms and munitions to Spain. Again, during the American Civil War a British proclamation of December 4, 1861 prohibited the export of arms and military stores. The claim of a government engaged in civil war to be able to buy arms in countries to which it has had access hitherto would not seem to be upheld by either principle or practice. But the position where there is a treaty covering the matter is very much more complicated. Policy considerations would seem to indicate the paramountcy of the desirability of nonintervention in a civil war, even over and above treaty commitments. Lauterpacht devised a method of squaring this particular circle by suggesting that "even the provisions of the treaty may have to be read subject to the implied condition of its fulfilment not involving the danger of international complications following upon interference, implied in a unilateral grant of advantages, in a civil war of considerable dimension."[80] *Clausula rebus sic stantibus* might be thought relevant here. But the essential difficulty—that in the case of a long-standing arms supplier, the cessation of supplies is effective intervention on the side of the rebels—remains. Closely related is the argument that the withdrawal of arms by a traditional supplier, far from limiting an internal war, in fact lengthens it because the rebels are also securing arms. This argument has also been advanced in the Nigerian war—Britain has claimed that from a humanitarian point of view it is better that a war which will inevitably be won by the Federals in the long term should be won by them sooner than later.

(5) *that the insurgents are being assisted by one or more other states.* State practice reveals that, even if a civil war is manifestly in progress, governments feel free—regardless of the "rule" of nonintervention—to intervene on the side of the government if the rebels are receiving external assistance. This argument is used with particular vigor where it is believed that the rebellion is not essentially indigenous, but is fomented from outside. Thus the United States in 1958 went to the assistance of President Chamoun of Lebanon, supporting his assertion that rebellion in Lebanon was being fomented by the United Arab Republic.[81] But even where the war is initially a bona fide civil war, the claim of counterintervention is now frequently heard. In 1963 the U.A.R. asserted that it was supporting the Yemen republicans because Saudi Arabia was interfering in the civil war by supporting the Royalists. The mirror claim was made by Saudi Arabia. The United States regards itself as authorized to intervene in war be-

[80] Lauterpacht (fn. 1), 232-33.
[81] But see UNOGIL's (United Nations Observer Group in London) reports denying major intervention by the U.A.R.: S/4040, July 3, 1958; S/4043, July 8, 1958. For a detailed analysis of the U.N. role in the civil strife in Lebanon, see Rosalyn Higgins, *United Nations Peacekeeping 1946-67, Documents and Commentary*, Vol. I, (London, New York, Toronto, 1969), 535-603.

tween the Viet Cong and South Vietnam because North Vietnam has been aiding the Viet Cong. The list could be greatly enlarged. Professor Falk has brilliantly analyzed why this claim is more commonly heard than the traditional emphasis on nonintervention.[82] He notes that in a decentralized system, it is hard to establish authoritatively the sequence of events, and each side is able to claim initial intervention by the other. After describing other reasons for the breakdown of the concept of nonintervention in civil wars, Professor Falk goes on to suggest that "offsetting participation by nations in internal wars may often be more compatible with the notions of nonintervention than is an asymmetrical refusal to participate."[83] These are points of policy to which we shall return below.[84]

(6) *that another state is assisting the lawful government.* This claim is not normally dealt with in the growing literature on internal war, but is very much a reality. If there is a civil war in State A, State B may be inclined to support the government if it sees that State C, its enemy, is supporting the insurgents. However, if it desires the outcome of the civil war to be victory for the government of State A, State B may be distressed to see its rival State C helping the lawful government, and may itself intervene on the side of the lawful government in order to affect the influence of State C in State A. Obviously different policy considerations obtain here. What is disconcerting is the built-in predisposition, in a divided world, to intervention. There is a case for intervention if one's rival enters the field on one's chosen side, *or* against it. This claim was very much at the forefront of the British case for continuing to supply arms to the Nigerian Federal government: "The Russians have already secured a political foothold in Nigeria by supplying military aircraft and bombs, which we refused to supply. If we cut off our arms supplies, Russia would be only too willing to fill the gap and gain the influence which we would lose. Is it seriously argued that this is the best way to help a new Commonwealth to stand up to the pressures of Soviet imperialism?"[85] The depressing logic of this position is that, in an area of any major importance to them, if one superpower intervenes, a competing superpower will also intervene, either on the same side or on the opposing one, according to its preferred outcome to the internal war.

(7) *that the internal war is occurring within a superpower's sphere of interest.* No state, of course, asserts that it is intervening because it has a vital interest in the outcome of an internal conflict within its sphere of influence. Events, however, indicate that this is a common

---

[82] Falk (fn. 4), 206ff., 222-27.

[83] Same, 207. This view is elaborated by Manfred Halpern, "The Morality and Politics of Intervention," same, 249-88.

[84] Same, 50-55. [85] *Hansard*, August 27, 1968, col. 1448.

course of action, and one which given the nuclear confrontation, is increasingly tolerated between the superpowers. The Monroe Doctrine formalizes the interest of the United States in the prevention of successful Communist governments in the Americas. The Bay of Pigs was clearly in breach of traditional norms of nonintervention (though this, of course, occurred some considerable time after the conclusion of the internal hostilities in Cuba). And the United States intervention in the Dominican Republic in 1965 was based on a concern felt by that country that certain persons coming to power were known Communists. The charges, in fact, proved lamentably untenable: but the point at issue was that the United States believed it to be a sufficient legal basis for intervention. In Guatemala, in 1954, the United States intervened for identical reasons in an internal dispute. In eastern Europe the grip of the Soviet Union has been sufficiently strong to prevent situations developing into civil wars. But in a situation that comes very close to it—Hungary in 1956—the Soviet Union showed that it too had a major interest in the outcome of internal conflicts in the Communist world. And it was prepared (and the invasion of Czechoslovakia in 1968 confirms that it is still prepared) to use the most repressive and harsh methods. Though the nations concerned may complain, the interventions by one superpower in its own sphere of influence are in fact tolerated by the other superpowers. They are tolerated for reasons of reciprocity and because other interests—such as the development of a growing détente—are felt to be at stake.

(8) *that humanitarian reasons dictate the necessity of intervention.* Intervention for humanitarian reasons more usually arises in the context of the treatment of minorities. Occasionally, however, this particular problem of intervention occurs in the context of a civil war. The doctrine is obviously open to abuse, and this writer has suggested elsewhere that it is not to be regarded as compatible with contemporary international law.[86] In 1964 the British, American, and Belgian governments, in cooperation with the government of the Congo, intervened in the rebel-held areas of Stanleyville to rescue certain missionaries whose safety was at risk. The operation was a strictly limited one avoiding participation in the outcome of the internal strife. The Department of State emphasized that it was acting with the authorization of the Congo government and "in exercising of our clear responsibility to protect U.S. citizens under the circumstances existing in the Stanleyville area."[87] The State Department communiqué also pointed to the

[86] Higgins (fn. 8), 220.

[87] Department of State statement, November 24, 1964, cited in Whiteman (fn. 23), 476. A good discussion may be found in S. P. Sinha, "Self-Determination in International Law and Its Applicability to the Baltic Peoples," *Res Baltica* (Leyden 1968), 256-58; and Muhammad Aziz Shukri, *The Concept of Self-Determination in the United Nations* (Damascus 1965).

fact that the treatment of the civilian prisoners by the rebels fell lamentably short of the Geneva Conventions. The task force was speedily withdrawn. However, complaints were made both at the United Nations and at the Organization of African Unity, and it is clear that, if even the particular intervention on a specific occasion is reasonable and limited, the international community is reluctant to approve such interventions.

2. Claims in favor of assisting the insurgents

(1) *that a state is at war with the government which is engaged in civil war.* In these circumstances an outside state will feel legally free to help the insurgents rather than to remain neutral.

(2) *that support must be given to the right of self-determination.* The extent to which the self-determination of peoples has become an accepted right under international law is perhaps debatable.[88] This writer has suggested that the right is now established in principle, even if its contents are still somewhat imprecise.[89] The term is now spoken of as a legal right by virtually all the nations of the world, and no state has overtly reserved to itself the right to ignore self-determination. Outside states are under a duty not to hinder the expression of self-determination in a nation torn by civil strife. The promotion of the right of self-determination is counterbalanced by considerations of stability. Thus until the rebels have established themselves with a status tantamount to that traditionally regarded as meriting a recognition of belligerency, normal relations including the supply of arms may continue with the recognized government. However, third states should not, once a civil war occurs, engage in activities preventing the self-determination of peoples. Normally speaking, this is an authorization for nonparticipation. However, where the government is repressive and undemocratic, and where the rebels represent the forces of self-determination, outside countries may seek to support them. It is doubtful, however, whether the right to self-determination can entail more than a neutral posture on the part of a third state.

Where the civil war takes the form of secession, the question arises whether self-determination of the region is a determining factor.[90]

[88] See the debates on this point in the *Pleadings of the South West Africa Cases,* 1966.

[89] Higgins (fn. 8), 90-106. See also J.E.S. Fawcett, "Human Rights and Domestic Jurisdiction," in David Evan Trant, ed., *The International Protection of Human Rights* (New York 1967). Cf. earlier views by L. C. Green, International Law Association, *Report of the 47th Conference* (1956), 56-57; Pitman B. Potter, "Legal Aspects of the Beirut Landing," *American Journal of International Law,* 52 (October 1958), 727-28. For another dissenting opinion, see Linda B. Miller, *World Order and Local Disorder* (Princeton 1967), 53-54.

[90] The difficulty of identifying the unit entitled to self-determination is widely acknowledged. For example, Professor John Norton Moore limits himself to the

Those recognizing Biafra (such as Tanzania and Zambia) and those assisting her with arms (such as France) have emphasized the right of self-determination of the Biafran peoples. The United Kingdom, on the other hand, has spoken darkly of the undesirability of Balkanization on the African continent, as it clearly thinks of self-determination as a concept operating within larger units.

There is a considerable practice to be drawn upon concerning self-determination for colonial peoples. The United Nations has actively intervened to lend its moral support to those seeking emancipation from colonial rule by the use of force. It has, in very recent practice, gone even further and authorized members to grant material and physical support.[91] This has occurred notwithstanding the general principle of nonintervention in domestic affairs and Article 2 (7) of the Charter; the rationale being that colonial questions concern human rights and are beyond the scope of the restriction of Article 2 (7).

Community practice has been considerably less clear in respect of other claims for self-determination. Where the claim has been for the exercise of self-determination by merger with another country (as in the Greek-Cypriot desire for Enosis) no clear position has been taken —though the Assembly's approval of the union of Gibraltar with Spain (notwithstanding the dislike of the people of Gibraltar for this solution), and West Irian with Indonesia, presumably means that it is not in principle ruled out. What the present mood of the General Assembly does not seem to approve is self-determination by union with the former colonial parent. However, so long as free choice is genuinely exercised, there is no reason why this type of self-determination should be resisted.

Human dignity requires that the concept of self-determination be made clearly applicable to all peoples, and not only to colonial peoples. Where these noncolonial peoples are already a nation-state (as in Hungary 1956, or Czechoslovakia 1968) there is no difficulty in asserting their right to self-determination. Difficulty has arisen, however, over the concept of a right of self-determination for peoples who do not comprise a recognized nation-state. What of the Nagas, or Biafrans, or Kurds, or Welsh? The free acceptance by the newer nations of the former colonial boundaries, together with the world community's stake in international stability, militates in favor of intervention if self-determination applies to the unit of the nation-state. This is not

---

broad recommendation that, insofar as this problem is concerned, one must ask "which characterization would best maximize the values at stake for everyone affected and then to apply whatever criteria seem to be most relevant to the particular case." "The Control of Foreign Intervention in Internal Conflict," *Virginia Journal of International Law*, 9 (1969), 206-342.

[91] See, for example, Par. 14, G.A. Res. 2383 (XXIII), and Par. 5, G.A. Res. 2395.

an argument in favor of large units rather than small units, or in favor of integration rather than Balkanization.[92] Rather it is an argument in favor of building on the small consensus which already exists. This preference should be subject to a qualification: that it may become essential to speak of the necessity for self-determination of units within the nation-state where there is clear evidence of great repression of an ethnic, racial, or religious minority, and where this minority is not allowed to play a proper part in the life of the nation.

(3) *that the insurgents are waging a war of liberation.* The traditional doctrine of noninterference has little appeal, either for the revolutionary Marxist or for the newer nations that see no pacific method for altering the status quo in certain areas. The Communist nations have made it clear, both in word and practice, that they regard themselves as free to assist in what they term wars of liberation. To a considerable extent, these are wars in which the indigenous population is fighting against the colonial authority—although the claim could also apply to a revolutionary group engaged in seizing power from a conservative, nonrepresentative government. The justification is advanced that the principle of nonintervention in civil wars cannot be relied on by "reactionary" regimes, and that the principle of self-determination is paramount. Accordingly "It was essential that the principle of nonintervention should be applied in international law in such a way . . . [as not to weaken] the provisions of international law designed to help those countries still under colonial rule."[93] Again, the Soviet Union has made it clear that if African nationalists found themselves in a position to wage a war of liberation against the white minority governments of South Africa, assistance would be forthcoming.

The newer nations find themselves in a similar position, though their motives are not ideological. Given the everyday assistance afforded to the white minority governments of Southern Africa, and given the United Nations' apparent inability to bring about peaceful change in the areas concerned, they believe that they are under no moral obligation to abstain from any civil conflict that may occur. The departure from the traditional rules of law is in the broad area of intervention: members of the OAU are overtly committed to providing military assistance for guerrillas operating in Portuguese, Rhodesian, and South African territory. In Rhodesia and South Africa there is sporadic guerrilla action, but no international war; in Mozambique there is. Non-

[92] Though such an argument can certainly be made. For an interesting contention to the contrary see Leopold Kohr, *The Breakdown of Nations* (London 1957). Kohr contends that social, cultural, administrative, and economic reasons show the superiority of the smaller unit. It is with regard to this last—economic factors—that Kohr would be most widely challenged today.

[93] Czechoslovakian delegate, GAOR 18th Sess., 6th Com., 802nd Mtg.

intervention is regarded as an irrelevant norm in both of these situations. In recent United Nations resolutions there has been a tendency to introduce clauses which whittle away the traditional rule of nonintervention, and instead reflect practice so far as liberation movements are concerned. Thus, in the latest resolution on Rhodesia, the resolution calls upon U.N. members to give moral and material assistance to those in Rhodesia opposing the Smith regime.[94]

(4) *that the insurgents are to be supported for humanitarian or ethnic reasons.* If the internal conflict is due to ethnic or religious controversy, it may be that third states having ties with the rebels will feel constrained to intervene on their behalf. Turkey has on several occasions threatened to intervene in Cyprus on the side of the Turkish Cypriots, who have been—until the U.N. Force established itself[95]— engaged in major hostilities with the Greek-Cypriot authorities.

(5) *that major interests of state require the support of the rebels.* While this claim is not overtly advanced, it is clearly of relevance so far as policy is concerned. There is ample evidence that the Belgian government, heavily committed to the Union Minière, in fact tacitly supported the attempts at secession by Katanga.[96]

3. Claims in favor of participation by international organizations

(1) *The United Nations.* Article 2 (7) of the United Nations Charter provides that "Nothing contained in the present Charter shall authorize the United Nations to intervene in matters which are essentially within the domestic jurisdiction of any state . . . but this principle shall not prejudice the application of enforcement measures under Chapter VII." At the same time, Article 1 of the Charter stipulates that the purposes of the United Nations include the maintenance of international peace and security, and the development of friendly relations based on self-determination of peoples.

To relate these broad propositions to the problem of internal war, we may note that the United Nations has been faced with three main categories of civil war: colonial wars, a major breakdown in internal law and order, and internal conflicts allegedly fomented from outside.[97]

There has been widespread discussion elsewhere as to the meaning

[94] S.C. Res. S/253, May 29, 1968.
[95] See James Stegaga, *The UN Force in Cyprus* (Ohio 1968); Rosalyn Higgins, "The UN Force in Cyprus: Basic Facts," *The World Today* (August 1964).
[96] Catherine Hoskyns, *The Congo Since Independence* (London 1965).
[97] These three classifications are used by Linda Miller in her interesting study (fn. 89).

of "intervention" by the United Nations.[98] In the context of internal wars caused by colonial conflicts, the United Nations has shown itself willing to intervene in the sense of passing resolutions to bring pressure to bear on the colonial authority. Far from remaining "neutral" in such conflicts, the United Nations has indicated that its sympathies lie with the indigenous population; and, in the case of war in Angola and Mozambique, the Security Council has even called for an arms embargo against Portugal.[99] The clearly emerging tendency in U.N. practice points to the acceptance of community pressures against the government when its "internal" conflict occurs in an overseas territory seeking independence. Even Portugal's NATO allies have indicated— by their abstention in the voting—that they do not regard the matter as an essentially internal one, falling within the scope of Article 2(7). In this category of cases the U.N. has also been willing to suggest quite specific measures: thus in Angola it has called for an amnesty[100]—and in the Indonesian-Dutch dispute, ultimately alienated by the second Dutch "police-action," the Security Council spelled out a detailed program for a political settlement. African members of the United Nations have overtly supported the Angolan and Mozambique rebel groups (indeed, some have recognized them *de jure*); and the United Nations itself has shown no inclination to condemn such practice as contrary to the international law requirements of nonparticipation in a civil war. The United Nations has legitimized its intervention in colonial civil wars by reference to human rights and self-determination.[101]

Rhodesia has presented a particularly complex problem in this category. It is not internal war in the full sense, due to the British decision not to use arms; yet it is undoubtedly a rebellion against the lawful government, in which all the normal pressures ancillary to the use of force are being used. In this case a British internally self-governing[102] territory unilaterally declared its independence under a minority government headed by Ian Smith. The issues were extraordinarily complex. If international law concedes the right to revolution, does it recognize a right to revolution by an elite representing minority interests? The international community is being asked, through the United Na-

[98] E.g., Higgins (fn. 8), 64-130; M. S. Rajan, *The United Nations and Domestic Jurisdiction*, 2nd edn. (New York 1961).

[99] S/5380, July 31, 1963.   [100] S/5480, December 11, 1963.

[101] In the context of the Portuguese territories, as Linda Miller correctly points out, there was disagreement on the meaning of the term "self-determination" because Portugal promised new laws designed to ensure local participation in administrative and political life, whereas the Angolans wanted to be free to opt out of Portuguese control altogether (fn. 89), 59.

[102] Although the General Assembly insisted that Rhodesia was *non*self-governing within the meaning of Article 73. See "Britain at the United Nations," *The Round Table*, LVI (March 1966), 132.

tions, not to stay impartial in a conflict between a metropolitan and dependent territory, but on this occasion to help the metropolitan power in suppressing the rebellion. The grounds are similar to those in the case of Angola—discrimination on grounds of color, amounting to a denial of human rights, and the right of all the Rhodesian peoples to self-determination. Throughout, the United Kingdom, recognizing that the question is one of international concern, has used the U.N. to assist it in its attempt to end a rebellion. The United Nations has been offended not so much by UDI as by a long-standing denial of human rights in Rhodesia, and its objectives are not so much the ending of UDI as the achieving of majority rule in that country. In other words, whereas Britain might be satisfied with a return to the situation of 1963, the United Nations would not.[103] The United Nations has in this case gone considerably beyond the traditional norms concerning civil conflict. Not only has the U.K. case been formally supported by the international community, but the United Nations Security Council has formally prohibited states from trading with Southern Rhodesia—not only in war materials, but in all commodities which could assist the survival of Rhodesia as an independent state. Intervention on the side of the lawful government has been for the purpose of sanctioning the rebels. It is because nations are in any event under a general international-law obligation not to support the rebels that the Security Council has legally been able to address its remarks to nonmembers such as West Germany, as well as to U.N. members. The United Nations has also required governments to act more strictly than usual in controlling the activities of individuals in nonmilitary aid and trade.

The Security Council found itself in a predicament in that minority rule and racial discrimination—the questions with which the U.N. has been really concerned—are not themselves grounds for recommendations under Chapter VII. Accordingly, it was necessary to establish a basis for Chapter VII action; this desire to act on the existence of "a threat to international peace"[104]—a course of action strongly resisted by the United Kingdom in the early stages when it feared escalation to Article 42, but agreed to later when it became prepared to use the veto, if necessary, to avoid international military sanctions. The Security Council has thus established the principle that an internal rebellion in which racial questions play a strong part may be a threat to international peace that warrants community sanctions if neighboring states feel compelled to support the majority peoples of the territory.

[103] See Higgins, "International Law, Rhodesia and the United Nations," *The World Today* (March 1967). See also Myres S. McDougal and W. Michael Reisman, "Rhodesia and the UN: The Lawfulness of International Concern," *American Journal of International Law*, 62 (January 1968), 1-19.

[104] For a full discussion, see Higgins (fn. 103), 100-03.

The situation is anomalous enough for the precedents—including authorization to Britain to blockade the port of a third power[105] that was assisting the rebels—to be far from clear. Nonetheless, the U.N. role in Rhodesia does mark a move away from traditional rules of law.

The second major category of internal conflicts which the U.N. has faced are those entailing a breakdown of law and order, which in turn entails international repercussions. The U.N. has shown a preparedness to intervene physically—when invited—in this type of case. In the Congo the United Nations was asked to help at the stage of a mutiny by the *Force Publique*, but before major civil war had developed. Indeed, at this juncture the situation was fairly readily recognizable as a threat to peace, and rather less as a potential civil war, although separatist tendencies had long been evident. After the mutiny of the *Force Publique* against its Belgian officers, Belgian paratroops reentered the Congo, purportedly to protect the life of their nationals. The situation rapidly degenerated. On July 11, 1960, Tshombe announced the secession of Katanga. Having received a cable from Lumumba and Kasavubu,[106] Secretary-General Hammarskjöld used his powers under Article 99 of the Charter to convene a meeting of the Security Council. Hammarskjöld stated that the breakdown in law and order had posed a threat to peace and security. The ensuing resolutions of the Security Council spelled out the U.N. task as securing respect for the territorial integrity and political independence of the Congo. As time went by and various interests began to assert themselves, the U.N. became more and more involved with ending the Katangese secession until, after Hammarskjöld's death, the ONUC was authorized to "use force if necessary in ending the civil war." The U.N. had thus become involved on the side of the central government in ending a secession: though this relied entirely on the fact that foreign elements—Belgian mercenaries—were instigating the secession.

A force with a not dissimilar mandate[107] (though of a very different composition) was established to help restore law and order in Cyprus after civil war between the two communities. Again, international factors were involved—the ethnic ties of Greece and Turkey with the two

[105] The authorization to the Royal Navy to stop the *Joanna V* and any other ships from discharging oil for Rhodesia at Beira, Mozambique. For a full discussion, see same, 95-97.

[106] For a full background, see Colin Legum, *Congo Disaster* (Baltimore 1961); Hoskyns (fn. 96); Alan P. Merriam, *Congo: Background of Conflict* (Evanston 1961); Fernand Van Langenhove, *The Congo and Problems of Decolonization* (Brussels 1960); Miller (fn. 89); Arthur Lee Burns and Nina Heathcote, *Peacekeeping by UN Forces from Suez Through the Congo* (New York 1963); and Ernest Lefevre, *Crisis in the Congo: A United Nations Force in Action* (Washington 1965).

[107] See Miller (fn. 89), 116-48; Stegaga (fn. 95).

communities, and the treaty rights of those two countries and Britain. Again, the consent of the host government was required.

In the third main category of civil wars—internal wars allegedly fomented from without—the United Nations seems to have evolved a particular technique. This is the technique of observation/fact finding. In the cases of Greece (1947), Lebanon (1958), and Yemen,[108] the claim was made that the civil war was externally organized. In each of these cases U.N. observers, with powers limited to observing and reporting facts, went to investigate the charges. A variety of circumstances made it impossible for UNYOM to function efficiently, and it was withdrawn from Yemen. But the experience of UNSCOB and UNOGIL was more favorable. In this area the United Nations has seen fit to participate when invited, but the principle of consent has remained pivotal.[109]

It seems to be the case, therefore, as a rough rule of thumb, that the U.N. is an active participant in several types of civil war. So far as colonial wars are concerned, the U.N. will pass resolutions and engage in certain pressures, but will not itself intervene physically. So far as wars involving the need to restore law and order are concerned, the U.N. has been willing to participate with paramilitary forces, nominally on the basis of neutrality although inevitably with advantage to the incumbent government. And in the case of "proxy wars" the U.N. has found it helpful to offer its services in the field of observation and fact finding.

(2) *Regional organizations.* Regional organizations are usually based on a certain degree of political homogeneity, though the degree required will vary from organization to organization. They have a natural interest in the control of civil wars in their region. The extent to which the regional body will sympathize with the government forces depends upon whether the majority of its members perceive the situation as comparable to one which they might face for themselves; or whether, for other reasons, they identify more readily with the rebels. Either way, there is a predisposition for intervention, in the sense of offering good offices and pressing for humanitarian measures. The civil war in Nigeria afforded an example, with OAU members divided on which side they supported, but united on the relevance of an OAU role in seeking to terminate hostilities. In some circumstances, where nonmember nations within the geographical region are governed by groups regarded as wholly unsympathetic, the regional organization may overtly support the rebels. One OAU position on Rhodesia and South Africa is clearly such a case.

---

[108] For a detailed study of these see Higgins (fn. 81).

[109] Though one may note that in the case of Yemen, the consent of the U.A.R. and Saudi Arabia was regarded as more important than that of Yemen.

The desirability or otherwise of regional intervention in an internal war depends upon a variety of factors.[110] Clearly, there are arguments to be made in favor of the principle that those with the greatest strategic, geographic, and cultural interests should have the greatest participation in the decision. It can also be contended that regional expertise in peacemaking is likely to be more acceptable to the contending parties. At the same time, other factors point strongly to disadvantages in regional intervention.[111] There is a considerable danger of great power domination of regional action,[112] and regional values sometimes run counter to community values. In addition to these questions of substance, there will arise jurisdictional questions related to the allocation of competence between the United Nations and the regional organization concerned.[113] While regional peacemaking techniques may be more effective than universal ones, the international community has reason to be concerned about military regional intervention in internal conflicts, as the Dominican Republic crisis and the invasion of Czechoslovakia show.

Claims Concerning Relations with Third States

Insofar as recognition still remains a relevant factor, the following points may be made. Outside states may not lawfully grant recognition to insurgents unless the traditional criteria are present. Recognition so granted is premature, and a hostile act against the constitutional government. However, it is far less certain that there is a duty to recognize if the conditions are fulfilled[114]—or at least, it is not a verifiable duty, because it is for each state to ascertain whether the criteria for recognition are fulfilled. There are nonetheless strong reasons for a policy which supports the thesis that there is a duty to recognize,[115] and to

---

110 These are analyzed in detail in the admirable chapter by Professor Moore. Whereas his analysis is concerned with regional conflicts in general, and not merely with internal wars, his assessment of the factors for and against intervention are entirely relevant to this section of my chapter, and the reader should consult pp. 132-33 and pp. 150-58.

111 See pp. 162-64.

112 For some Latin American apprehension of the O.A.S. for this reason, see Juan José Arévalo, *The Shark and the Sardines* (New York 1961). An impartial assessment of this fear is to be found in Jerome Slater, "The Limits of Legitimation in International Organization," *International Organization*, XXIII (1969), 48-72.

113 See Ronald Yalem, *Regionalism and World Order* (Washington 1965); Bryce Wood and Minerva Morales, "Latin America and the United Nations," in Norman J. Padelford and Leland M. Goodrich, eds., *The United Nations in the Balance: Accomplishments and Prospects* (New York 1965), 350-63.

114 Though such claims have been made. See, for example, the U.S. claim against Denmark in respect of the failure of the latter to recognize the U.S. as a belligerent in the War of Independence: John Bassett Moore, *A Digest of International Law*, Vol. I, Sec. 60 (Washington 1906), 168.

115 See especially Lauterpacht (fn. 1), 228-30.

this we will return below.[116] If the lawful government itself recognizes the belligerency of the rebels, then third states are bound to grant the insurgents belligerent recognition.[117] But recognition by certain third states places the lawful government under no obligation to accord recognition also.

A government faced with a rebellion can shut off its own ports to all foreign shipping,[118] and outside states must accept this. Some have contended that the government may not blockade the insurgents-held ports unless belligerency is recognized;[119] while others have said that a blockade of the insurgents' ports is permissible so long as no rights on the high seas are infringed.[120] But a blockade, to be legal, must be effective, and this usually involves patrolling on the high seas. Yet others have asserted that, so long as sovereignty over the territory remains with the government, it may at any time blockade insurgent-held ports, and that full effectiveness—a requirement of interstate warfare—is not even essential. A government engaged in civil war would probably be entitled to take action against a foreign merchant vessel seeking to break its blockade on an insurgent port.[121]

The lawful government may also in time of civil war adopt such internal measures as may be necessary, even if they affect aliens. These measures may include limitation on freedom of movement and the requisitioning of property. At the same time, the lawful government is under a duty to protect aliens from dangers arising out of the civil war. But in the absence of fault for negligence there is no liability for injuries to aliens due to civil war, whether caused by the government side or insurgents.[122]

Although an outside state may (subject to a U.N. prohibition, as in the case of Rhodesia) continue normal intercourse with the rebels, it may not engage in any assistance which supports the war effort. The sending of war materials, troops, and financial support is traditionally regarded as prohibited—though claims of counterintervention provide a means for states to ignore this injunction. The action of France and Portugal in aiding Biafra is more easily affirmed as "lawful" since the British and Russians gave aid to Lagos.

---

[116] Same, 49.

[117] For early U.S. and British practice on this point, see same, 188-90.

[118] And can probably also lay mines within its own territorial waters—though not in the high seas—provided that clear warning is given. Wehberg (fn. 1), 51.

[119] E.g., Castrén (fn. 1), 102.

[120] Arnold McNair, "The Law Relating to the Civil War in Spain," *Law Quarterly Review*, CCXII (October 1937), 483.

[121] This situation has some similarities to the question of the Rhodesian rebellion and the *Joanna V*. This case is discussed on pp. 107-09.

[122] Edwin M. Borchard, *The Diplomatic Protection of Citizens Abroad* (New York 1915), 229; Lauterpacht (fn. 1), 248-49; "The Home Missionary Case," *Annual Digest* (1921-22), Case No. 117.

Outside parties—either governments, or private companies—may be placed in an embarrassing position if the rebels demand from them actions which seem *prima facie* to involve active support of the rebellion. This is a predicament which has faced British oil companies in Biafra. The Biafrans decreed that they would deprive the Federal government of all customs' revenue and export duties collected at Port Harcourt, as well as of the erstwhile federal revenue of company taxes and oil rents and revenues. Shell-BP has a £200 million stake in Nigeria, mainly in the East. It normally pays rental and royalties to the Federal government every six months. Suggestions of placing the money into a suspended fund for the duration of hostilities was unacceptable to the Federal government and to Biafra. Biafra then suggested a compromise whereby 57.5 percent of the royalties and rents would be paid to the authorities in Enugu. The position was difficult for the oil companies, and particularly so when the British government was actively pro-Federal. Shell-BP, after prolonged discussions, decided to offer an initial payment of royalties to Biafra. The Federal government now announced a blockade of Port Harcourt and a prohibition on oil exports. The Federal government indicated that if royalty payments were not made, the oil concessions would be lost; and when Shell hesitated to make further payments, their installations were taken over by Biafran forces and their personnel imprisoned. After that, no further payments were made to the Biafran authorities.

RECOMMENDATIONS FOR THE FUTURE INTERNATIONAL LEGAL ORDER

To draw firm conclusions in such an unsatisfactorily charted area of international law is a difficult task. I have sought to show that in a variety of "civil-war" situations international law purports to provide guidance on the identification of a conflict as an internal one; on the methods used to wage internal wars; on the intervention by other states and bodies; and on the relations between the protagonists and third parties.

It is clear beyond doubt that international law operates inadequately in at least the first three of these roles.

So far as the identification of a situation as an internal war is concerned, the horizontal authority whereby it is left to each state to appraise the facts leads inevitably to the pursuit of different practices consequential upon such appraisals. The legal debate on Vietnam has to a large extent been a *"dialogue de sourds"* because certain lawyers have seen the situation as essentially a domestic revolt in which the United States has intervened; while others, with the same information at their disposal, and from within the same cultural background, believe the war to be a truly international one in which the United States is entitled to intervene. The divergence of appraisal is undoubtedly bona fide,[123] and inevitably so in a decentralized system. There would, therefore, seem to be a case for suggesting that efforts be directed toward the process of appraising the domestic or international causes of the conflict.[124] The United Nations has shown a certain ability to fulfil this role successfully, and in a variety of ways. In Laos in 1959, a special representative of the Secretary-General was used, and in Lebanon in 1958 an observer group fulfilled this function. Undoubtedly, in the case of the latter, the clear assertion by UNOGIL of the domestic quality of the fighting made the tenability of the American argument in favor of the intervention very difficult, and this contributed to containment and a speedy solution. National decision-makers should thus support—and informed groups should press for support—of a U.N. fact-finding role in civil wars on a regular basis. Where appropriate, regional organizations should also be encouraged to assert this competence, though it is better to have this task carried out by the United Nations because bodies like the OAS and the OAU obviously have a strong predisposition in favor of the established government. Community procedures for recognition of status could also usefully be employed. The experience of Korea, and the satisfactory way in which the U.N. has handled recognition problems concerning Iraq, Yemen, and the Congo indicates that it could play a helpful role in providing normative judgments on the status of the parties to a civil war. This is true notwithstanding U.N. recognition and the China question, which, while unhappy, is an isolated example.

On the question of conduct, it must be conceded that the provisions of the Geneva Conventions are at once too weak and too open to am-

---

[123] Though this writer has been disturbed by the way in which protagonists on each side seem to have overstated their case. One would have wished to see—and would have felt more intellectual confidence in—a debate in which some contended that the U.S. had indeed behaved badly in supporting Diem and refusing elections, had indeed increased the stakes in the war, had indeed been somewhat indiscriminate in their bombing targets, had indeed used some illegal weapons, but were nonetheless entitled to assist the South Vietnamese; while others contended that the Viet Cong had conducted warfare in a terroristic manner, had at an early stage received support from the North, were seeking to impose their views by force, but were nonetheless entitled to oppose the United States intervention. These two positions seem to this writer far closer to reality than the more extreme cases, unremitting in support for every action of the favored side, that have been advanced. The highly informative and interesting volumes edited by Richard A. Falk, *The Vietnam War and International Law* (2 vols.; Princeton, 1968-69), reveals this deep cleavage, with little give and take on the middle ground.

[124] Though this suggestion does not ignore the view that the categorization of a conflict as "civil" is not a helpful guide to behavior in all circumstances. David Forsythe, "United Nations in Intervention in Conflict Situations Revisited," *International Organization*, XXIII (1969), 129, has argued persuasively that there is much to be gained from seeking to perceive whether a conflict is "local" or "general," rather than "internal" or "international."

biguity. In some cases prisoners are given the status of prisoners of war, in others they are not; in some cases basic humanitarian standards are applied, in others they are not. Clearly, a new international convention to deal specifically with standards of conduct in civil war would be desirable. At the same time, it is clear that there is no practical hope of getting consensus at an international conference on these topics, let alone on such thorny questions as the status to be accorded guerrillas who do not wear uniforms or insignia or bear arms openly, and yet represent a major element in the realities of civil war. The forthcoming study by the U.N. Secretariat on human rights in internal war is clearly going to be of the greatest importance. There is an encouraging trend to invite the International Red Cross or other international observers to witness the fighting, and the international community has a considerable stake in promoting the idea that to refuse international scrutiny is *prima facie* evidence of guilt. The Red Cross has visited South Vietnam camps, and U.N. observers (who have reported in very favorable terms) have visited Nigerian prisoner camps. When the states supporting a party in a civil war have public information media, there is a considerable, and desirable, pressure on them to use their influence to achieve desirable behavior by their "clients." Thus the United States has undoubtedly improved the treatment of the Viet Cong by the South Vietnamese (though undoubtedly much is left to be desired), while Britain perhaps reduced the level of bombing by Nigerians of civilian centers in Biafra. A norm whereby the selling of arms to parties to a civil war would be directly related to their obeying international norms of conduct would obviously be highly desirable, but it is very unlikely to be achieved.

The aspect of civil war which has recently attracted most attention[125] has been that of intervention, or participation by interested third parties. Professor Falk, in a pioneering essay,[126] has analyzed the shortcomings of traditional international law in this regard. This writer agrees with each and every one of his analyses. Professor Falk notes that the tendency to avoid an express bestowal of status on the parties to a civil war makes it hard to establish the precise nature of claims by third states. Further, the decentralized and increasingly arbitrary assertion of claims make it impossible to standardize what is permitted and what is forbidden. He also correctly observes that the traditional rule of noninterference is incompatible with the revolutionary ideology of Communist nations and the anticolonial commitments of the Afro-Asians. With the major powers—and particularly the nuclear powers—wishing to avoid direct confrontation at all costs,

---

[125] See Falk (fn. 4); Wolfgang Friedmann and Tom Farer, "Intervention in Civil Wars: a Modest Proposal," *Columbia Law Review*, 67 (1967), 266.
[126] Falk, same.

ideological wars are increasingly being fought in the guise of civil wars. And this high degree of substantial participation by outside groups makes inadequate the traditional "recognition criteria" of effective government, a willingness to be bound by the laws of war, and the impingement upon the maritime and other interests of third powers. As Falk puts it "The facts of external participation are more important than the extent or character of insurgent aspirations as the basis for invoking transformation rules designed to swing from domestic jurisdiction to international concern." Moreover, the whole problem of civil wars has changed because they are tending to become increasingly prolonged in duration and this makes neutrality increasingly difficult. Three recent events—language riots in Belgium, religious hostilities in India and in Northern Ireland—seem to indicate that purely indigenous causes will also add to the reasons why civil wars may be expected to increase as a phenomenon over the next few decades. In most of these cases, third parties will not wish to intervene, though in others, such as the Irish question, neighboring states feel themselves closely involved.

There are, of course, innumerable competing claims being made—claims employing the normative rhetoric that refers to self-defense, domestic jurisdiction, nonintervention, the maintenance of inter-native claims—and the relevant decision-maker has to choose between them at any given moment of time.[127] Quincy Wright has suggested that, granting that revolution is not prohibited, no state should be allowed to intervene to stop it, although the United Nations could act if the civil war was threatening international peace.[128] Falk goes further, and boldly asserts: "It should be stressed, perhaps, that there is a need to promote certain social changes by organizing and encouraging external participation in anti-governmental insurgencies, but that this participation must itself be legitimized by a central process of decision and implementation."[129] While this writer finds Professor Falk's analysis perceptive and persuasive, she is not convinced as to the practicability of his suggestions. He proposes that a *prima facie* presumption of legitimate status might be given to the incumbent government, but that this would be overcome if the incumbent regime is actually based on colonial subordination or racial superiority—and the regime would be classified as such by the United Nations. But this proposition avoids the realities.

First, so far as the Security Council is concerned, governments will

---

[127] This theme is elaborated by Myres S. McDougal, "The Ethics of Applying Systems of Authority: The Balanced Opposites of a Legal System," in Harold D. Lasswell and Harlan Cleveland, eds., *The Ethics of Power* (New York 1962).

[128] Quincy Wright, "Subversive Intervention," *American Journal of International Law*, 54 (1960), 529.

[129] Same, 235.

only be condemned insofar as no physical intervention is anticipated, and no close parallel is seen to a situation in which one of the veto powers finds itself. Professor Falk's recommendation would, to be sure, avoid the formalistic pretence that sanctions are being mounted against Ian Smith because his regime is a threat to international peace. But this case is a truly unique one. Whereas Britain and America will vote for arms embargoes against South Africa, they would not vote for a resolution classifying it as an "illegitimate" regime if they thought that the consequence was to be international participation on the side of freedom fighters in that unhappy land. (Nor, one imagines, would the United Kingdom have allowed Ian Smith's government so to be designated, if this was the anticipated outcome.) In short, resolutions are passed not simply for what is in them, but for what consequences it is thought they will entail.[130]

So far as the General Assembly is concerned, the same point holds good to a lesser degree. Western and Scandinavian nations would be less prone to add their voice to those condemning particular governments. Further, it is very doubtful if the numerical majority at any particular time is an adequate register of normative legitimacy. Deplorable though recalcitrant colonialism and racial supremacy may be, why should these entail a classification of "illegitimacy," whereas other forms of suppression do not?[131] Are rebels against Duvalier's regime in Haiti really to receive less support from the international community than guerrillas in Rhodesia? Is Western colonialism really more repressive than Communist colonialism? The answer should be in the negative; yet, if the "illegitimating" process is left to the Assembly, one knows that it would be otherwise.[132] Essentially, Professor Falk is arguing that it is premature to find objective criteria for intervention, and that therefore all one can do is to approach the problem *procedurally*, by granting a legitimation function to the United Nations. This writer believes that it is not beyond our capabilities to evolve guides for behavior to be acted on after a contextual appraisal by the appropriate decision-maker. Understandably the present preoccupa-

[130] This factor is relevant to an appraisal of Moore's suggestion (fn. 90) that an intervention be regarded as permissible if specifically authorized by the General Assembly or Security Council.

[131] Moore, same, acknowledges as likely this discrepancy, but regards it as a preferable price to the alternative of continuing unilateral intervention. This writer would dissent from that statement.

[132] Jerome Slater (fn. 112) points to many reservations shared by this author on the scope of the legitimating function of an international organization: "International organization, 'multilateral' and 'collective action' are all honorific words eliciting favorable connotations, especially among the generally liberal and internationalist elite sectors of public opinion. Thus, behind the frequent exhortations to policy makers to allow international organizations to play a greater role in national policies lies the implicit assumption that collective bodies will exert a moderating, liberalizing, or enlightening influence. But this is not invariably so." (48-72)

tion of the U.N. is with black-white relations, but the international lawyer must evolve criteria which are as relevant to a potential civil war in Haiti and in Northern Ireland as in Southern Africa.

If, then, one rejects Falk's attempt to provide centralized procedures on the problem of intervention, where is one left? This writer would reject the notion of regional hegemony. International law should not be molded so that the United States is entitled to dictate the political system of the Dominican Republic; or the Arabs that of Israel; or the Russians that of Czechoslovakia. The importance of self-determination here seems to outweigh in importance the desire for peace at any price. We have already suggested that there is an effective norm which permits intervention by the superpowers in their sphere of influence: but it permits it only in the sense that physical opposition is not usually countenanced. Opposition at every other level—diplomatic and economic—should be encouraged. And the reciprocal powers are in dispute. The risk is here more worth running.[133]

Falk would seem to be correct in suggesting that if centralized procedures break down (or if, as here contended, they are inappropriate), the practice of counterintervention must now be publicly acknowledged as an operational norm.

Professor Farer has suggested that the time is ripe for defining a norm prohibiting overt assistance by armed personnel in a civil war.[134] Certainly all recent practice indicates that states have paid, in either political or military terms, very heavily for direct participation; and that their decisions to send forces would not be lightly repeated.[135] One thinks of the American experience in Vietnam, the British in East Africa, and the Egyptians in Yemen. And direct involvement rarely occurs among nonrevolutionary nations unless a foreign element is perceived participating on the other side. Thus there has been no question of Britain participating on the side of Lagos, even though its political preference has been clearly stated.

One can urge other points as relevant to decision-making. Does the traditional concept of collective defense apply in its full vigor where

[133] Cf. Falk's curious statement—as one who is in principle prepared to have the U.N. physically intervene in specified circumstances—that "It is unfortunate in many respects to compel dissenting national communities to conform to regional political preferences, but it may be indispensable for the maintenance of minimum conditions of international stability." "The Legitimacy of Legislative Intervention by the United Nations," in *Essays in Intervention*, by Roland J. Stanger, ed. (Columbus 1964), 55. Is the concern of the international community with apartheid in South Africa really based on the preference of other states on the continent? Or is not the inherent lack of human dignity—a universal value—the real point on which apartheid is to be judged?

[134] Tom Farer, in his interesting article "Intervention in Civil Wars: A Modest Proposal," *Columbia Law Review*, 67 (1967), 261.

[135] But Professor Moore (fn. 90) sees great practical difficulties in Professor Farer's proposal, 320-27.

the war is primarily international, and where the domestic government is manifestly undemocratic, corrupt, and authoritarian? This has, until comparatively recently, been a major query—though an inadequately debated one—on Vietnam. If the war is a colonial one, and a definite date for independence has been given (as was the case in Aden) should violence to achieve earlier independence be condoned? And by what right does a European power pronounce that Balkanization would be disastrous for another country and that (as in the case of Biafra) this disaster of secession should be prevented by force of arms? And if a civil war is for the control of power throughout the country, does not the international community have a greater stake (though still a limited one) in the outcome than if the war is one of secession?

What I have urged here is not that centralized procedures are wholly irrelevant, but that they should be focused on the question of fact finding and determining the status of the hostilities, rather than on the question of intervention. If the status of the hostilities were internationally determined, this would inevitably have consequences for the participation of other states. And this may be thought a more useful and realistic way of approaching the problem.

Professor John Norton Moore has, however, boldly endeavored to make proposals for norms concerning intervention itself. After providing a detailed classification of internal war situations and claims,[136] he suggests the following:

I. An intervention in internal conflict is permissible if specifically authorized by the General Assembly or Security Council, even though in the absence of such authorization it would be impermissible. Conversely, if the General Assembly or Security Council specifically calls for cessation of a particular intervention, continuation is impermissible.

II. It is impermissible to assist a faction engaged in any type of authority-oriented internal conflict or to use the military instrument in the territory of another state for the purpose of maintaining or altering authority structures. The three qualifications to this basic non-intervention standard are:

(A) Assistance to a widely recognized government is permissible prior to insurgency. After a conflict becomes an insurgency, it is impermissible to increase but permissible to continue the pre-insurgency level of assistance. Criteria for determining insurgency, for this purpose of permitting pre-insurgency assistance, include:

---

[136] "This classification . . . is not intended as a slot machine for mechanical solution of intervention problems. It is offered instead as a useful technique for contextually identifying like cases and for formulating standards for appraisal." Same, 333.

(1) the internal conflict must be an authority-oriented conflict aimed at the overthrow of the recognized government and its replacement by a political organization controlled by the insurgents;

(2) that the recognized government is obliged to make continuing use of most of its regular military forces against the insurgents, or a substantial segment of its regular military forces have ceased to accept orders;

(3) that the insurgents effectively prevent the recognized government from exercising continuing governmental authority over a significant percentage of the population; and

(4) that a significant percentage of the population supports the insurgent movement, as evidenced by military or supply assistance to the insurgents, general strikes, or other actions.

(B) Assistance to a widely recognized government is permissible to offset impermissible assistance to insurgents; if assistance to insurgents or the use of the military instrument against another state constitutes an armed attack within the meaning of Article 51 of the Charter, it is permissible to reply proportionally against the territory of the attacking state.

(C) The use of the military instrument in the territory of another state for the purpose of restoring orderly processes of self-determination in an authority-oriented conflict involving a sudden breakdown of order is permissible if it meets the following conditions:

(1) a genuine invitation by the widely recognized government, or, if there is none, by a major faction;

(2) relative neutrality in military operations;

(3) immediate initiation of and compliance with the decision machinery of appropriate regional organizations;

(4) immediate full reporting to the Security Council and compliance with United Nations determinations;

(5) a prompt disengagement, consistent with the purpose of the action; and

(6) an outcome consistent with self-determination. Such an outcome is one based on internationally observed elections in which all factions are allowed freely to participate on an equal basis, which is freely accepted by all major competing factions, or which is endorsed by the United Nations.

III. Non-authority-oriented intervention for the protection of human rights may sometimes be permissible. Criteria for determining legitimacy include:

(A) An immediate and extensive threat to fundamental human rights, particularly a threat of widespread loss of human life;

(B) a proportional use of force which does not threaten greater destruction of values than the human rights at stake;

(C) a minimal effect on authority structures;

(D) a prompt disengagement, consistent with the purpose of the action; and

(E) immediate full reporting to the Security Council and appropriate regional organizations.

These recommendations are at once thoughtful and bold. I myself have reservations, for reasons already given, as to his paragraph I. I am in sympathy with the rest. But the proposals in paragraphs II(C) and III are particularly open to abuse in a decentralized system. Professor Moore seeks to avoid that abuse by including reference, in each, to reference and compliance with U.N. decisions. But the very reservations of which I have spoken make one a little anxious as to the practical efficacy of this safeguard. Meanwhile, centralized pressures for social change, short of direct intervention, should certainly continue. For, ultimately, the internal war problem will only be resolved by removing the causes for rebellion.[137]

137 James N. Rosenau has helpfully pointed out that civil wars have a twofold characteristic: they are convention-breaking and authority-oriented. "The Concept of Intervention," *Journal of International Affairs*, XXII (1968), 167-70. For other useful contributions to the military, political, and psychological factors operating in the civil war problem, see the essays in the same journal, particularly those by Oran Young, Adam Yarmolinsky, and Andrew Scott.

CHAPTER 4

The Role of Regional Arrangements in the Maintenance of World Order

JOHN NORTON MOORE

I. INTRODUCTION

As THE United Nations ends its first quarter-century, two flaws in its normative structure have become increasingly apparent. The first and perhaps most important of these is the unresponsiveness of the Charter to the problem of control of foreign intervention in internal conflict.[1] The second is the ambiguity surrounding the role of regional arrangements in the maintenance of world order. Unlike the problem of control of unauthorized intervention, the framers of the Charter were largely aware of the problems in the interrelation of regional arrangements and the United Nations. The clash of competing regional and universal interests, however, resulted in an ambiguous resolution of the issues. That ambiguity has been magnified as the original expectations of an effectively functioning Security Council were shattered on the rocks of the cold war. Today there is general agreement that the United Nations has the ultimate responsibility for the maintenance of international peace and security but there are major uncertainties surrounding the initial exercise of regional jurisdiction, the authority of regional arrangements to initiate coercive action, and where necessary, the procedure for United Nations authorization of regional action.

Though the problem of control of unauthorized intervention has received increasing attention in the last few years, the ambiguous interface between the United Nations and regional arrangements has remained largely neglected.[2] Clarification of the role of regional ar-

---

[1] See John Norton Moore, "The Control of Foreign Intervention in Internal Conflict," *Virginia Journal of International Law*, 9, 2 (May 1969), 209-12.

[2] Some of the better recent studies of the role of regional arrangements are Joseph S. Nye, Jr., *International Regionalism* (Boston 1968); Charles G. Fenwick, *The Organization of American States* (Washington, D. C. 1963); The Inter-American Institute of International Legal Studies, *The Inter-American System* (Dobbs Ferry 1966); Ann Van Wynen Thomas and A. J. Thomas, Jr., *The Organization of American States* (Dallas 1963); Robert W. Macdonald, *The League of Arab States* (Princeton 1965); Ellen Frey-Wouters, "The Prospects for Regionalism in World Affairs," in Richard Falk and Cyril Black, eds., *Trends and Patterns*, Vol. I, The Future of the International Legal Order (Princeton 1969), 463; Lynn H. Miller, "The Prospects for Order Through Regional Security," same, 556; Andrew Korbonski, "The Warsaw Pact," *International Conciliation*, 573 (May 1969); Inis L. Claude,

rangements in the maintenance of peace and security is important if the Charter structure is to be made a more viable tool for conflict management. Clarification is also important from a purely national perspective. National actions which seek legitimacy through regional action can succeed only to the extent of underlying regional legitimacy. Moreover, to the extent that such actions are widely regarded as illegitimate they may weaken the authority of the regional system itself. Whatever its other merits, the OAS action initiated by the United States in the 1965 Dominican situation may have resulted in some deflation of OAS authority from such a feedback.[3] It is important, then, that the pursuit of short-run national goals should not be permitted to obscure a perhaps greater national and international interest in the integrity of regional systems.

It has been customary to distinguish three kinds of regional organizations: first, the so-called functional organizations focused on regional economic integration or transnational community-building, such as the British Commonwealth, the European Community, the Council for Mutual Economic Assistance, and the Latin American Free Trade Association; second, the postwar multilateral defense organizations created pursuant to Article 51 of the Charter and focused on extraregional threats such as the North Atlantic Treaty Organization, the South-East Asia Treaty Organization, the Central Treaty Organization, the ANZUS Pact, and the Warsaw Pact; and third, the so-called genuine regional arrangements created pursuant to Chapter VIII of the Charter and focused on intraregional threats, meaning pre-eminently the Organization of American States but also including the

---

Jr., "The OAS, the UN, and the United States," *International Conciliation*, 547 (March 1964); Boutros Boutros-Ghali, "The Addis Ababa Charter," *International Conciliation*, 546 (January 1964); B. Y. Boutros-Ghali, "The Arab League: 1945-1955," *International Conciliation*, 498 (May 1954); Ved P. Nanda, "The United States Action in the 1965 Dominican Crisis: Impact on World Order—Part II," *Denver Law Journal* 44, 2 (Spring 1967), 225; John W. Halderman, "Regional Enforcement Measures and the United Nations," *Georgetown Law Journal* 52, 1 (Fall 1963), 89; Jerome Slater, "The Limits of Legitimization in International Organizations: The Organization of American States and the Dominican Crisis," *International Organization*, XXIII, 1 (Winter 1969), 48; Patricia Berko Wild, "The Organization of African Unity and the Algerian-Moroccan Border Conflict: A Study of New Machinery for Peacekeeping and for the Peaceful Settlement of Disputes Among African States," *International Organization*, XX (1966), 18; Francis O. Wilcox, "Regionalism and the United Nations," *International Organization*, XIX (1965), 789; Norman J. Padelford, "The Organization of African Unity," *International Organization*, XVIII (1964), 521; Leonard C. Meeker, "Defensive Quarantine and the Law," *American Journal of International Law*, 57, 3 (July 1963), 515; Gerhard Bebr, "Regional Organizations: A United Nations Problem," *American Journal of International Law*, 49, 2 (April 1955), 166.

The article by Professor Inis Claude on "The OAS, the UN, and the United States" is probably the best starting point.

[3] Slater (fn. 2), 67.

Organization of African Unity and the Arab League. Although these distinctions have enabled a useful focus, they have also been a potent source of confusion. One reason for the confusion is that all regional organizations are functional in some sense and most are multifunctional. Thus, though NATO and SEATO focus on defense they also perform related economic and political functions. Conversely, though the British Commonwealth focuses on economic and political integration, it also exercises a security function. Moreover, though the Article 51 organizations focus primarily on regional defense against external threats, they may sometimes become involved in intraregional disputes, an example being the NATO involvement in the Cyprus conflict. And conversely, the so-called Chapter VIII organizations, though focusing more heavily than the Article 51 organizations on management of intraregional disputes, may perform the same functions as Article 51 organizations in defense against external threats. The inter-American system is a paradigm example of an organization structured for the handling of both intraregional and extraregional security threats.[4]

An even more potent source of confusion stemming from the usual classification trilogy is the temptation to let legal conclusions concerning relations with the United Nations be dictated by a priori characterization of an organization as either an Article 51 organization or a Chapter VIII organization. Thus, in its most extreme form the argument is that if an organization is an Article 51 organization rather than a Chapter VIII organization, its actions could not be "enforcement action" requiring Security Council approval pursuant to Article 53. Vice versa, if an organization is a Chapter VIII organization its actions must be "enforcement action." Though the claim that particular regional action is "enforcement action" may or may not be sound, such reasoning by a priori organizational characterization is nonsense.

To avoid these confusions, it seems preferable to recognize that regional organizations are located on a series of functional continuums. Thus, though the EEC is intensely concerned with economic integration, and to a lesser extent with the promotion of human rights, the OAS and even SEATO may perform some of the same functions. With respect to the peace and security function, it is useful to construct two continuums, one for focus on intraregional settlement of disputes and one for focus on concern with external threats. Both NATO and the OAS would be high on the external threat continuum, but they would be far apart on the intraregional dispute continuum. Even more important, for purposes of normative clarification we need a more spe-

---

[4] For an analysis of the inter-American system see generally Fenwick (fn. 2); The Inter-American Institute of International Legal Studies (fn. 2); Thomas and Thomas (fn. 2); Claude (fn. 2); and Nanda (fn. 2).

cific functional breakdown by types of issue. Such a breakdown, rather than any classification by types of regional security organization, seems best calculated to assist in clarification.

This chapter will attempt to provide a framework for analysis of the role of regional arrangements in the maintenance of world order. In doing so, an effort will be made first to isolate the initial understandings and misunderstandings behind the Charter framework and the major trends and conditioning factors affecting the development of regional arrangements, then to develop general policy criteria for allocating competence between the United Nations and regional security arrangements, and finally to develop a functional framework for appraising regional security claims.

II. The Development of Regional Arrangements Under the Charter

A. The Initial Understandings and Misunderstandings

Early wartime planning concerning postwar international organization was principally concerned with whether such organization should follow the Churchillian conception of regional councils or place primary emphasis on a universal organization.[5] Secretary of State Cordell Hull's arguments for a strong universal organization eventually won out and were reflected in both the Moscow Declaration and the Dumbarton Oaks Proposals. The Dumbarton Oaks Proposals did not preclude regional organizations but they cautiously stipulated that regional enforcement action should not be undertaken without the approval of the Security Council and that the Council should be kept informed of regional action relating to peace and security.[6] In a more pro-regional vein they also provided for Security Council encouragement and utilization of regional arrangements for the settlement of local disputes.[7] This strong universalist position clashed head on at the San Francisco Conference with the determination of the Latin Americans to ensure a largely autonomous inter-American system. Latin American dissatisfaction, supported by Senator Arthur Vandenberg, focused on two issues. First, the desire to free regional action from the veto implicit in the Dumbarton Oaks Proposals requiring regional enforcement action to be approved by the Security Council, and second,

[5] Claude (fn. 2), 4-5; Cordell Hull, *The Memoirs of Cordell Hull* (New York 1948) II, 1639-48.

[6] See Articles 2 and 3 of Section C, Chapter VIII of the Dumbarton Oaks Proposals for the Establishment of a General International Organization in Ruth B. Russell and Jeannette E. Muther, *A History of the United Nations Charter* (Washington, D. C. 1958), 1026.

[7] See Articles 1 and 2 of Section C, Chapter VIII of the Dumbarton Oaks Proposals. Same, 1026.

the desire to achieve primary jurisdiction for regional agencies with respect to local disputes; that is, to require an exhaustion of regional remedies before Council involvement. The resulting compromise was ambiguous on both issues, allowing spokesmen for both universalist and regionalist viewpoints to claim victory.

The compromise on the first issue resulted in the addition of Article 51 to Chapter VII of the Charter. Article 51 provides that: "Nothing in the present Charter shall impair the inherent right of individual or collective self-defense if an armed attack occurs against a Member of the United Nations, until the Security Council has taken measures necessary to maintain international peace and security." Article 53, embodied in Chapter VIII, however, retained the rhetoric of Dumbarton Oaks that "no enforcement action shall be taken under regional arrangements or by regional agencies without the authorization of the Security Council."

The issue of primary jurisdiction was even more ambiguously resolved by the inclusion of the complementary Articles 52(2) and 52(4). Article 52(2) provides that members of regional arrangements: "shall make every effort to achieve pacific settlement of local disputes through such regional arrangements or by such regional agencies before referring them to the Security Council." But Article 52(4) provides that nothing in Article 52 "impairs the application of Articles 34 and 35," which give authority to the Security Council to "investigate any dispute, or any situation which might lead to international friction," and provide that "any Member of the United Nations may bring . . . [such a dispute or situation] to the attention of the Security Council or . . . General Assembly." Article 52(3) further confuses the compromise on the issue of primary jurisdiction. It provides: "The Security Council shall encourage the development of pacific settlement of local disputes through such regional arrangements or by such regional agencies either on the initiative of the states concerned or by reference from the Security Council."

The Dumbarton Oaks principle that the Security Council should "be kept fully informed of activities undertaken or in contemplation under regional arrangements or by regional agencies for the maintenance of international peace and security,"[8] was embodied in Article 54 of the Charter.

Though the final outcome of the San Francisco Conference clearly recognized a role for regional organizations in the maintenance of international peace and security, the specifics of that role were obscure. As Professor Claude has observed: "The decision of the San Francisco Conference . . . provided no precise indication of the contem-

---

[8] See Article 3 of Section C, Chapter VIII of the Dumbarton Oaks Proposals. Same, 1026.

plated division of competence and responsibility between it [the United Nations] and regional agencies, much less a firm basis for predicting the nature of the relationships that would emerge in the dynamic interplay of the United Nations and regional organizations during the next two decades."[9]

B. Major Trends and Conditioning Factors in the Development of Regional Authority

The ambiguous compromise at San Francisco meant that the authority of regional arrangements would be largely shaped by the forces of the international arena. At least seven conditioning factors seemed to have played a significant role in this development. They were the postwar division between competing public order systems with the consequent breakdown in Chapter VII effectiveness, the increasing influence of the smaller states within the United Nations, major power dominance of key regional organizations, the paramountcy of the OAS in testing regional authority, the increase in revolutionary and interventionary activity within the international system, the trend to regional economic and political integration, and the nuclear arms race. Present trends with respect to each of these factors can be expected to have a continuing impact on the future development of regional authority.

THE POSTWAR DIVISION BETWEEN COMPETING PUBLIC ORDER SYSTEMS AND THE BREAKDOWN IN CHAPTER VII EFFECTIVENESS

Perhaps the principal factor affecting the development of regional arrangements has been the breakdown of the wartime cooperation between the major powers and its replacement by the continuing conflict of the cold war. Within the United Nations this breakdown in the envisaged cooperation of the major powers resulted in inability to conclude an Article 43 agreement which was to have made contingents of national forces available to the Security Council. Moreover, the cold war was reflected in the frequency with which the Soviet Union exercised the veto in the Security Council. The result was substantially reduced Chapter VII effectiveness. In turn, this limited Security Council effectiveness coupled with the high level of East-West conflict provided a major stimulant to the formation of multilateral defense arrangements pursuant to Article 51, since such arrangements would not be subject to Council veto in initial defensive planning or action. This postwar period witnessed the formation of the Rio Treaty (1948), NATO (1949), the Pacific Security Treaty or ANZUS Pact (1952), the Collective Security Pact of the Arab League (1952), SEATO (1955), the Warsaw Pact (1955), and the Baghdad Pact (1955), which became

[9] Claude (fn. 2), 3. The preceding discussion of the initial understandings and misunderstandings draws heavily on Claude's pioneering work.

CENTO in 1959.[10] Although there was some initial questioning whether such organizations were compatible with the Charter,[11] the wide participation in such organizations of states on both sides of the cold war firmly established their legitimacy.

A second major effect of the cold war and the breakdown of Chapter VII effectiveness was to shift the United States position from the largely pro-universalist position of Cordell Hull toward the pro-regionalist position of the Latin American delegates at the San Francisco Conference. The United States, which exercised great influence within the OAS, now saw regional autonomy (meaning largely OAS autonomy) as a way of avoiding the veto in the Security Council. Accordingly, in the 1954 Guatemalan case and the 1960 Cuban case the United States urged that the dispute should first be submitted to the OAS pursuant to Article 52(2).[12] Similarly, the United States began to urge a narrow definition of "enforcement action" in order to increase the regional autonomy of the OAS. The position of the Soviet Union and the Communist states, on the other hand, has generally been in opposition to increased regional autonomy for Chapter VIII arrangements (meaning largely OAS autonomy) in order to maximize the power of the Soviet veto and their own influence within the United Nations.

The trend to greater regional autonomy, supported by the United States, is also reflected in the trend to increased General Assembly authority evidenced in the Uniting for Peace Resolution and the trend to increased Secretary-General authority as evidenced by a host of

[10] See *Keesing's Treaties and Alliances of the World* (New York 1968), 144 (Rio Treaty), 98-99 (NATO), 186 (ANZUS Pact), 170 (Arab League), 187 (SEATO), 120 (Warsaw Pact), 174 (CENTO). See also *Staff of House Committee on Foreign Affairs, Collective Defense Treaties*, 90th Cong., 1st Sess. (Comm. Print 1967).

[11] Differing from Article 53, the so-called inherent right of individual or collective self-defence is what may be termed an emergency right. It is conceived as a spontaneous, temporary reaction to a sudden, illegal armed attack, and it becomes operative only and solely after the event. Hence, differing from Article 53, the proper interpretation of Article 51 precludes regional organs of the States, signatories to the North Atlantic Treaty, to elaborate strategic plans, and to coordinate their military forces under a combined High Command before an armed attack has occurred.

F. B. Schick, "The North Atlantic Treaty and the Problem of Peace," *Juridical Review*, LXII (1950), 26, 49. For a discussion of Soviet objections to NATO see W. W. Kulski, "The Soviet System of Collective Security Compared With the Western System," *American Journal of International Law*, 44, 3 (July 1950), 453. See also Bebr (fn. 2), 173; Hans Kelsen, "Is the North Atlantic Treaty a Regional Arrangement?," *American Journal of International Law*, 45, 1 (January 1951), 162, 164; Richard H. Heindel, Thorsten V. Kalijarvi, and Francis O. Wilcox, "The North Atlantic Treaty in the United States Senate," *American Journal of International Law*, 43, 4 (October 1949), 633; E. N. Van Kleffens, "Regionalism and Political Pacts," *American Journal of International Law*, 43, 4 (October 1949), 666.

[12] See Claude (fn. 2), 21-43.

initiatives, particularly under Secretary-General Dag Hammarskjöld. All three trends are partly attributable to the decreased effectiveness of the Security Council as the result of cold-war tension.

Although in the long run a rapprochement between the Soviet Union and the United States could conceivably reverse the pressures for increased regional autonomy, the possibility of Peking obtaining a seat on the Security Council might provide another strong impetus toward increased regional autonomy.

Though there are too many variables to make a confident prediction, it seems likely that in the immediate future the Security Council will continue to have only limited effectiveness and that those centrifugal forces for increased regional autonomy which result from the breakdown in Security Council effectiveness will continue strong.

THE INCREASING INFLUENCE OF THE SMALLER STATES
WITHIN THE UNITED NATIONS

A second factor affecting the development of regional organizations has been the increasing influence of the smaller states within the United Nations. The great increase in United Nations membership resulting from the large influx of new states since World War II and the resulting increase in 1965 in the size of the Security Council from 11 to 15 members have decreased the power of the major powers within the United Nations. In the case of the United States, the decrease in control has been dramatic. Prior to about 1960, United States influence within the General Assembly was so great that it was appropriate to speak of an automatic majority. Though United States and major power influence still remains high within the United Nations, today no major power exercises influence comparable to that of the earlier influence of the United States. It seems likely that this decline in major power influence within the United Nations will contribute to continued support for regional autonomy by those major powers which are in a position to benefit from increased regional autonomy. Conversely, it can be expected that many smaller states may continue to prefer a United Nations forum.

MAJOR POWER DOMINANCE OF KEY REGIONAL ORGANIZATIONS

A third factor affecting the development of regional organizations has been the continued dominance of many such organizations by a major power. The Warsaw Pact seems to have had as one purpose the continued exercise of Soviet control over Eastern European satellites following de-Stalinization.[13] The South-East Asia Treaty Organization was essentially an instrument of United States foreign policy intended

---

[13] See Korbonski (fn. 2), 11-12.

to assist in the containment of Communism.[14] And even the venerable institutions of the inter-American system were subject to disproportionate United States influence.

This major power dominance of key regional organizations produced a number of effects on the development of regional authority. First, it compounded the effects of the cold war on regional authority by ensuring that regional autonomy would be a cold-war issue. Thus, because it identified increased regional autonomy with a United States cold-war position, the Soviet Union consistently opposed United States efforts to increase regional autonomy, at least with respect to Chapter VIII issues. The United States, on the other hand, had substantial influence over the principal Chapter VIII regional organization, the OAS, and thus sought to increase Chapter VIII autonomy.

A second effect of major power dominance has been to decrease the legitimacy of regional action in the eyes of the smaller states. Since the smaller states were subject to the veto of the major powers in the Security Council, it might have been expected that they would take a pro-regional position similar to that of the Latin American states at the San Francisco Conference. Major power dominance of some regional organizations, however, prompted the smaller states to champion the United Nations forum in preference to regional arrangements dominated by a major power. Thus, within the OAS there has been a substantial shift in the position of many of the Latin American states who now champion tighter United Nations control of regional action. The position of other Latin American states is an ambivalent one which fluctuates between a desire for regional autonomy on local issues and the preservation of a United Nations forum as a counterweight to United States hegemony of the OAS. This desire of the smaller nations to maintain United Nations control over regional action and to maximize what many perceive as an advantageous forum provides a counterweight to centrifugal forces favoring increased regional autonomy.

The withdrawal of France from NATO, the weakness of SEATO in the Vietnam conflict, the disaffection of Albania and to a lesser extent Czechoslovakia and Romania within the Warsaw Pact, and the narrow margin of support within the OAS for United States initiatives in the Dominican conflict suggest a steady lessening of major power influence within regional organizations. In fact, as a result of the authority deflation in the OAS resulting from the 1965 Dominican operation it seems likely that the United States must move toward full cooperative partnership on OAS peace and security decisions if the OAS is to remain effective. The Soviet invasion of Czechoslovakia may have

[14] See generally Russell H. Fifield, *Southeast Asia in United States Policy* (New York 1963), 113-58.

temporarily retarded these forces in both NATO and the Warsaw Pact, but it seems unlikely to alter the long run political trend.[15] Any pronounced trend toward genuine partnership within the OAS and other regional arrangements now dominated by a major power would provide a powerful incentive toward increased regional authority.

THE PARAMOUNTCY OF THE OAS IN TESTING REGIONAL AUTHORITY

A fourth factor significantly affecting the development of regional organizations is the paramountcy of the OAS in testing regional authority. Although most regional organizations focus on intraregional problems to some extent, only three such organizations are sufficiently directed at intraregional disputes to have presented much opportunity for testing the full range of problems in the relationship between regional organizations and the United Nations. They are the OAS, the OAU, and the Arab League. Of these, the OAS has been by far the most important organization in testing regional authority. Unlike the Arab League and the OAU which date from 1945 and 1963 respectively, the OAS is the latest version of a working inter-American system which traces its origins to the International Union of American Republics established in 1889. The OAS also provides more elaborate machinery for settlement of intraregional problems and brings a substantial history of involvement with regional peace and security issues to its task. Moreover, as has been seen, most of the pressure for increased regional autonomy at the San Francisco Conference came from the desire of the Latin Americans to preserve a vigorous inter-American system. Under the circumstances, it is not surprising that the OAS has provided most of the test cases for determining regional authority.

The consequences of this OAS paramountcy have been substantial. Since the major tests of regional authority have involved a regional organization identified with a major cold-war power, tests of regional authority have been perceived by all concerned primarily in cold-war terms. Thus, the United States tends to equate regional autonomy with OAS autonomy and presses for broad regional authority. And the Soviet Union equates regional autonomy with autonomy of a United States dominated OAS and opposes increased regional autonomy. As a result, the general issue of regional versus universal authority tends to be subordinated to more immediate cold-war interests.

In the future, it is possible that African demands for increased autonomy for the OAU or Arab demands for increased autonomy for

---

[15] See generally *Staff of Senate Subcommittee on National Security and International Operations, Czechoslovakia and the Brezhnev Doctrine*, 91st Cong., 1st Sess. (Comm. Print 1969).

the Arab League or even demands for increased autonomy for some new regional organization may introduce new forces into the development of regional autonomy and end the equation that regional autonomy equals OAS autonomy. For the time being, however, the African and Arab states are internally split on objectives and without dominant regional leadership, do not have the power to achieve major objectives regionally, and for the most part receive a sympathetic forum within the United Nations. As long as these factors continue to exert substantial influence, African and Arab pressures for increased regional autonomy will probably develop slowly if at all.

THE INCREASE IN REVOLUTIONARY AND INTERVENTIONARY ACTIVITY WITHIN THE INTERNATIONAL SYSTEM

A fifth factor significantly affecting the development of regional authority has been the increase in revolutionary and interventionary activity within the international system. Former Secretary of Defense Robert McNamara recently reported that while "at the beginning of 1958 there were 23 prolonged insurgencies going on around the world, as of February, 1966, there were 40. Further, the total number of outbreaks of violence has increased each year: in 1958 there were 34; in 1965 there were 58."[16] The trend seems to be more than a passing phenomenon. Professors Leiden and Schmitt, in their summary of revolution in the modern world, assert that "even a cursory view of recent history forces an acknowledgement that we are living in a new era of revolution . . . the last third of the twentieth century promises to be a period of almost constant revolutionary turmoil."[17] As events in Czechoslovakia, the Congo, the Dominican Republic, Laos, Nigeria, Vietnam, and Yemen illustrate, this increase in revolutionary activity has also been accompanied by an increase in interventionary activity. The United Nations Charter, however, was primarily structured in response to the kind of overt aggression which triggered World War II. Although there had been earlier experiences with intervention in internal conflict, notably during the Spanish Civil War, for the most part the lessons learned were not assimilated into the Charter structure. Consequently, as intervention in internal conflict developed into a core public order problem the Charter contributed only an inadequate response. For example, the Article 2(4) proscription of "the threat or use of force against the territorial integrity or political independence of any state," provides little guidance as to permissibility of assistance to either a widely recognized government or insurgents in a situation

[16] Robert McNamara, *The Essence of Security* (New York 1968), 145.

[17] Carl Leiden and Karl M. Schmitt, *The Politics of Violence: Revolution in the Modern World* (Englewood Cliffs 1968), 212.

of internal war. Similarly, when is assistance to one side or another either an armed attack or collective defense within the meaning of Article 51? The principal difficulty in both cases, of course, is in determining which faction represents the state.[18] These Charter ambiguities and gaps also affect the delineation of regional authority, since regional authority is delineated in the Charter by reference to these same provisions. Thus, is regional action which provides assistance to one or another faction on request an "armed attack" or "enforcement action" within the meaning of Articles 51 or 53? Are regional peacekeeping operations such as the Inter-American Peace Force in the Dominican Republic, which are undertaken at the request of a major faction, "enforcement action?" These ambiguities have also contributed to regional support of liberation movements, such as Arab League support of the Palestine Liberation Organization and OAU establishment of a Liberation Committee to support liberation movements directed against the remaining colonial regimes in Africa. These uncertainties and gaps in the Charter concerning the control of intervention in internal conflict coupled with the pressing need to deal with the increased revolutionary and interventionary activity have resulted in increased regional autonomy. Present trends in the frequency of intervention and internal conflict suggest that this factor will continue to exert a significant influence on the development of regional authority.

THE TREND TO REGIONAL ECONOMIC AND POLITICAL INTEGRATION

A sixth factor significantly affecting the development of regional arrangements has been the strong postwar trend to regional economic and political integration. Both the Arab League and the OAU are in part products of this trend. The early enthusiasm for "Arab solidarity," "Pan-Africanism," and regional economic integration has somewhat waned as the difficulties have become more apparent. To the extent that regions are primarily affected by particular decisions or otherwise share common interests, however, regional autonomy seems a likely long-run development. If a significant number of new regional arrangements directed at regional peace and security issues emerge or if existing arrangements become more viable, it will probably strengthen regional autonomy and further generalize the issue of regional versus United Nations authority.

THE NUCLEAR ARMS RACE

In any listing of factors affecting the development of regional arrangements it is prudent to include the nuclear arms race. The enor-

18 See generally Moore (fn. 1), 210-11, 242.

mous economic and technological requirements for maintaining a competitive nuclear position necessarily limit that status to a few superpowers. In matters of nuclear defense, then, this factor could be expected to encourage a proliferation of regional defense arrangements as smaller powers seek to cluster around the competitive nuclear powers. On the other hand, the magnitude of the nuclear threat may itself destroy the credibility of such arrangements and reduce their importance. In any event, it seems probable that within regional arrangements the disparity in nuclear power increases dependence on major power initiatives, particularly when the issue itself involves a nuclear threat, as in the Cuban missile crisis of 1962. The disparity in nuclear power provides a built-in dependence in those regional organizations such as the OAS which include a major power participant.

The Cuban missile crisis illustrates another effect of the nuclear condition. That is, the pressure to enlarge the concept of armed attack when fundamental defense interests are perceived threatened by sudden shifts in nuclear deployment. That nuclear defense matters may be subject to different rules which reflect the immense importance of the stakes is suggested by the virtual absence of Security Council debate challenging OAS action in the missile crisis. In such cases, the interest in avoiding a nuclear war overshadows the problem of allocation of competence between the United Nations and regional organizations.

SUMMARY OF MAJOR TRENDS AND CONDITIONING FACTORS IN THE DEVELOPMENT OF REGIONAL AUTHORITY

A number of long-range trends suggest an increased autonomy and importance for regional arrangements in the maintenance of international peace and security. These include the probable continued limited effectiveness of the Security Council, the decrease in major power influence within both the United Nations and regional arrangements, and the trend to increased identification of regional common interest evident in the movements for regional economic and political integration. In the short run, however, continued cold-war pressures combined with small power preference for a United Nations forum may somewhat restrict regional autonomy. The length of the debate in the Security Council on the 1965 Dominican operation, which was longer than all prior Security Council discussion on the issues of regional autonomy combined,[19] and the resultant Security Council resolution taking action parallel to the OAS action while the OAS was still involved in the situation, suggest that the latter trend may already be under way.

[19] See Nanda (fn. 2), 254-55.

III. Community Policies for Allocating Authority
Between Regional and Universal Security Organizations

There is surprisingly little discussion in the literature of regional arrangements concerning criteria for optimum allocation of authority between regional and universal security organizations.[20] During the wartime planning for postwar international organization there was some debate within the Allied camp as to whether emphasis should be given to regional councils or a universal organization. The Churchill-ian emphasis on regional councils was opposed by Secretary of State Cordell Hull on the ground that emphasis on competing regional councils might create a system conducive to war between regions and that it might encourage great power hegemony within regions.[21] Hull also argued that emphasis on regional councils might create "a haven for the isolationists, who could advocate all-out United States cooperation in a Western Hemisphere council on condition that we did not participate in a European or Pacific council."[22] Within the framework of the United Nations Charter, which adopts a structure of both universal and regional organizations but assigns ultimate responsibility for the maintenance of peace and security to the universal organization, the arguments of Hull do not seem very helpful as criteria for determining the precise role of regional arrangements. In fact, with the partial breakdown in the centralized collective security system envisaged for the United Nations and the consequent proliferation of Article 51 collective defense arrangements, Hull's first and second points have largely been realized despite the initial emphasis on universal rather than regional organizations. And Hull's point concerning a haven for isolationists seems more appropriate to the League era than the present.

Most of the more recent debate following the adoption of the Charter has been heavily influenced by cold-war currents which frequently obscure the criteria for optimum allocation of authority. In the absence of more useful discussion of these issues the following discussion of policies favoring universalism and policies favoring regionalism are necessarily tentative formulations. The background assumption is that both universal and regional organizations may have a role in the main-

[20] What discussion there is focuses on a choice between international organization based on either regional arrangements or a universal organization rather than an optimum allocation of authority between regional and universal organizations in a system made up of both. See Stephen S. Goodspeed, *The Nature and Function of International Organization* (New York 1967), 567-70; Hull (fn. 5), 1639-48. There is some discussion of policy criteria for regional authority under the Charter, however, in Wilcox (fn. 2), 807-811.

[21] Hull (fn. 5), 1644.

[22] Same, 1645.

tenance of peace and security and that the real issue is allocation of authority between them in the most policy-responsive manner.

Policies Favoring Universalism

The principal policies favoring universalism seem to be that states affected by decision should have an opportunity to participate in the decision-making, that effective decision may require that competing major powers be included in security decisions, that wider decision is more likely to reflect community common interest and the corollary of this principle that major power dominance of regional organizations may sometimes result in assertion of special interests.

The first of these, that states affected by decision should have an opportunity to participate in making those decisions, is a widely shared community policy. To the extent that peace and security issues affect the whole community of states, the whole community has an interest in participating in their resolution. And in the kind of interdependent world in which we live today the quality of the international peacekeeping machinery is of concern to every nation. This policy, then, strongly suggests that at least final authority for the maintenance of world order should be vested in a universal organization.

A second policy is the desirability of representation of competing major powers in security decisions. This policy reflects the importance of avoiding conflict between the competitive nuclear powers and of ensuring effective power to implement collective decisions. To the extent that world order decisions are approved by all major powers there is less likelihood of a major power clash. There is also greater likelihood that decisions will be effectively implemented. Moreover, participation in the decision process might moderate positions even if agreement is not possible. As Francis Wilcox puts it: "regional organizations are not capable of bridging the gap between the East and West—or the North and South for that matter—nor are they able to transcend the Cold War in a search for a common ground for the solution of great-power differences."[23] The permanent seats for the major powers in the Security Council reflect these realities.

A third policy is that wider decision is more likely to reflect common community interest. There is, of course, no guarantee that a universal organization will always make just or rational decisions. The United Nations is a political arena with characteristics similar to other such arenas, and it is a mistake to idealize its decisions just because they are collective. Nevertheless, on a continuum from unilateral to universal decision there is greater likelihood that the wider the participation in decision the more the decision will reflect common community inter-

[23] Wilcox (fn. 2), 811.

est. As a corollary to this principle, since major powers exert disproportionate influence in a number of regional organizations, United Nations authority should be preferred as a check on assertion of special
interests.

Policies Favoring Regionalism

Policies favoring regional authority include the principle that those
with greater values at stake in decision ought to have greater participation in decision, the advantages of utilization of local expertise
and interest, the principle of effectiveness, and deference to consensual
arrangements submitting local disputes to regional authority.

The first of these, the principle that those with greater values at
stake in decision ought to have greater participation in decision, reflects the differential impact of decisions. If a decision affects only a
particular region, then that region ought to participate in decision to
the exclusion of nonregional participants. It is self-evident that in matters other than peace and security there are large areas of exclusive
interests in which decision is and should be made unilaterally or regionally. Although few interests are that clearly exclusive if the issue
is one affecting peace and security, nevertheless, even peace and security issues may have differential impact. Thus, the recent El Salvador-Honduras conflict presented a greater threat to the security of
other Central American states than to the security of European or
Asian states.[24] Similarly, it may have posed a greater threat to the integrity of regional peacekeeping machinery than to the structure of the
United Nations. Accordingly, it seems reasonable to accord the regional machinery of the OAS the initial competence to deal with the
situation.

A second policy favoring regional authority is the desirability of taking advantage of local expertise, interest, and capabilities. The inter-
American system, the OAU, and to a lesser extent the Arab League
embody dispute-settlement machinery which may be highly efficient
in settling intraregional conflicts. The relatively quick and efficient
OAS handling of the El Salvador-Honduras conflict is a case in point.
Had the OAS been unsuccessful in obtaining a withdrawal of Salva-
dorian troops, then the greater effective power of the Security Council
might have been required. But in the first instance at least, the OAS
was almost certainly a more efficient forum for dealing with such a
localized intraregional dispute than would have been the United Na-

---

[24] For a history of OAS action in the El Salvador-Honduras conflict see "Docu-
ments Concerning Conflict Between El Salvador and Honduras," *International Legal
Materials*, VIII, 5 (September 1969), 1079-1148; C. G. Fenwick, "Procedure under the
Rio Treaty of Reciprocal Assistance," *American Journal of International Law*, 63,
No. 4 (October 1969), 769.

tions Security Council. Another case which illustrates this regional peacemaking competence is the OAU handling of the Algerian-Moroccan border conflict. It is particularly significant in the Algerian-Moroccan conflict that the major Western powers preferred the OAU forum to the United Nations in order to minimize the chances of cold-war involvement.[25] Francis Wilcox develops several aspects of this second policy for regional authority when he points out:

> Clearly a smaller organization, such as the OAS or the OAU, which is restricted geographically to nations in relatively close proximity to each other, can create the kind of machinery its members need to cope with their common problems more effectively than a world organization. States located several thousand miles away from each other, separated by vast differences in historical background, culture, language, and political and economic interests, may find it difficult to appreciate as fully as they should the mutual problems that afford them a common basis for cooperative action. Even more important, most states have not accepted the idea that world peace is indivisible. Insofar as collective action to repel aggression is concerned, they are inclined to respond with far greater speed and vigor to a security threat in their own area than to a distant danger whose focal point is far from their own frontiers.[26]

A third policy favoring regional authority is the principle of effectiveness. Article 1(1) of the Charter sets forth as a principal purpose of the United Nations the maintenance of "international peace and security, and to that end . . . [the taking of] effective collective measures for the prevention and removal of threats to the peace, and for the suppression of acts of aggression or other breaches of the peace." To the extent that this purpose has been frustrated by the breakdown of the original conception of collective security, particularly the impotence of the Security Council, interpretation may suggest a broader role for regional arrangements. Similar reasoning has been responsible for the growth of General Assembly and Secretary-General authority during the last two decades. This policy supports enlarged regional competence only to the extent that regional arrangements are in fact more effective in achieving the major purposes of the Charter.

A fourth policy favoring a regional role is the desirability of deference to consensual arrangements which submit local disputes to regional authority. The allocation of competence between regional and

---

[25] Wild (fn. 2), 28.

[26] Wilcox (fn. 2), 807. Similarly, Cordell Hull reported that Churchill: "attached great importance to the regional principle, because it was only the countries whose interests were directly affected by a dispute that could be expected to apply themselves with sufficient vigor to secure a settlement. Only vapid and academic discussion would result from calling in countries remote from a dispute." Hull (fn. 5), 1642.

universal organizations ought not place arbitrary limits on the inventiveness of man. Thus, consensual arrangements freely arrived at should not be overturned unless in conflict with clearly articulable community policies. The paradigm case in which this policy would seem applicable is when all parties to a dispute genuinely prefer a regional forum for dispute settlement. Under those circumstances, unless truly compelling community policies suggest otherwise, the universal forum should defer to the regional forum chosen by the parties. Security Council deference to the OAS in the Haitian and Panamanian cases in 1963 and 1964 reflects this policy. In both cases all parties consented to initial reference to OAS machinery, though in both cases the reference seemed to imply residual Security Council authority. The policy favoring consensual arrangements is less clear but may still be applicable under circumstances in which the parties to a dispute have agreed as a condition for joining a regional organization to first submit local disputes to regional dispute-settlement machinery. Article 2 of the Rio Treaty and Article 23 of the Revised Charter of the OAS, both of which purport to create an obligation for members to first submit regional disputes to the machinery of the inter-American system before referring them to the United Nations, present this question squarely. Whatever the resolution in other contexts, in view of the possibility of assertion of special interests inherent in the disproportionate United States influence in the OAS, and the rejection of the purported obligation by many Latin American states, it seems preferable to restrict the principle to situations in which all parties to a dispute genuinely prefer a regional forum. In limiting the effect of these provisions in the inter-American system, reliance can be placed on Article 10 of the Rio Treaty, Article 137 of the Revised OAS Charter, and Article 103 of the United Nations Charter, which make United Nations rights and obligations preeminent when in conflict with the provisions of the inter-American system.

Summary of Criteria for Allocating Authority between Universal and Regional Arrangements

There are strong reasons for urging that a universal organization should have ultimate authority for the maintenance of peace and security. In the interdependent world in which we live, most issues of peace and security affect all of the members of the world community. Moreover, a universal forum is a more broadly based forum for the resolution of security issues, both in the sense of greater assurance that decision will reflect common community interest, and in the sense of greater effectiveness by inclusion of the major powers in the decision process. A universal security organization should encourage regional settlement of disputes, however, in situations in which the interests at stake are primarily regional, in which regional machinery offers more effective conflict management, or in which the parties to a dispute genuinely prefer a regional forum.

IV. Claims Concerning the Authority of Regional Arrangements in the Maintenance of World Order

Study of the present and potential role of regional arrangements in the maintenance of world order can most usefully proceed by reference to the full range of specific issues presented for decision. In the absence of a comprehensive scheme for classification of these specific issues the study of regional authority necessarily remains episodic and pre-theoretical. Unfortunately, however, although a number of studies have perceptively focused on some of the major issues there is still no adequate conceptual framework for inquiry into the full range of claims concerning regional authority. The following enumeration of claims is offered as a tentative foundation for such a framework.

A. *Claims Concerning Participation in Regional Organizations.*
　1. Claims that organization for collective defense is impermissible.
　2. Claims that participants must have a common geographic, ethnic, or religious base.
B. *Claims Concerning Regional Jurisdiction of a Dispute or Situation.*
　1. Claims that the regional organization has primary jurisdiction.
　　a. Claims that members of regional organizations must first exhaust regional remedies.
　　b. Claims that the United Nations may not interfere with the initial exercise of regional jurisdiction.
　2. Claims that the regional organization has exclusive jurisdiction.
　3. Claims that the regional organization has concurrent jurisdiction.
　4. Claims that the United Nations should defer to regional machinery even though the United Nations has jurisdiction.
　5. Claims that the United Nations may terminate regional jurisdiction.
C. *Claims Concerning Regional Authority to Initiate Non-coercive Action.*
D. *Claims Concerning Regional Authority to Initiate Coercive Action.*
　1. Claims to use the military instrument in response to an armed attack.
　2. Claims to use the military instrument in situations not amounting to an armed attack.

    a. Claims that regional action which authorizes but does not require coercive action by member states is not "enforcement action" requiring Security Council authorization.

    b. Claims that regional action not directed against a state is not "enforcement action" requiring Security Council authorization.

    c. Claims that regional assistance to insurgent groups for the purpose of restoring self-determination is not "enforcement action" requiring Security Council authorization.

  3. Claims to use economic or diplomatic sanctions.

E. *Claims Concerning Procedures by Which the United Nations May Authorize or Terminate Regional Action.*

  1. Claims that Security Council authorization of "enforcement action" need not be prior authorization.

  2. Claims that Security Council authorization of "enforcement action" need not be express authorization.

  3. Claims that regional jurisdiction has been revoked by United Nations action.

F. *Claims Concerning the Obligation of Regional Arrangements to Report Activities to the Security Council.*

The following brief exploration of each of these claims is offered more by way of illustration than as a thumbprint of all prior instances of each claim. On each I will attempt to illustrate the problem and to suggest appropriate policy-responsive conclusions.

A. *Claims Concerning Participation in Regional Organizations.*

Claims in this category concern the lawfulness of the existence of a particular regional organization or the lawfulness of a particular state's participation in a regional organization. Two specific claims have been made concerning participation, neither of which has been generally accepted. They are claims that organization for collective defense is impermissible and claims that participants must have a common geographic or ethnic base.

  1. Claims that organization for collective defense is impermissible.

During the period of greatest activity in the formation of regional organizations oriented toward Article 51 collective defense, there was some opposition to such organizations on the ground that they were unconstitutional under the Charter.[27] NATO in particular was subject

[27] Gerhard Bebr (fn. 2), 173, writes:

    Statements have been made denying the right of the United Nations Members to form any regional organization in advance of armed attack and make appropriate military preparations on the basis of the right of collective self-defense. The Soviet note protesting the conclusion of the North Atlantic Treaty argued along

to attack on this ground. The principal criticism was summarized by Grayson Kirk during an address delivered at the 1950 Annual Meeting of the American Society of International Law:

> . . . there is potentially, and perhaps actively, a considerable amount of conflict between the principle of regional arrangements for security purposes and the general principle of collective security as it has usually been thought of in the past. Certainly I do not need to remind the people in this room that one of the driving forces for the principle of collective security as it was developed in the League of Nations and in connection with the creation of the United Nations was the conviction that limited groups, historically called alliances, would inevitably tend to breed counter-alliances and that a world in which alliances bred counter-alliances was an unstable world in terms of political and military security and a world in which, in all probability, controversy would end in conflict.[28]

The breakdown in effectiveness of the Security Council and the participation by all major powers in multilateral treaty arrangements for collective defense, however, resulted in general acceptance of collective defense arrangements. In view of the probable continued limited effectiveness of the Security Council, renewed challenge to multilateral collective defense arrangements such as NATO, SEATO, CENTO, and the Warsaw Pact seems unlikely.

> 2. Claims that participants must have a common geographic, ideological, ethnic, or religious base.

Egypt proposed at the San Francisco Conference that regional arrangements should be defined as:

> organizations of a permanent nature grouping in a given geographical area several countries which, by reason of their proximity, community of interests or cultural, linguistic, historical or spiritual affinities, make themselves jointly responsible for the peaceful settlement of any disputes which may arise . . . as well as for the safeguarding of their interests and the development of their economic and cultural relations.[29]

The proposal was rejected by a Subcommittee of Committee III/4 that seems to have been motivated in part by feelings that the listing of

---

those lines in its attempt to show the incompatibility of the NATO with the United Nations Charter. Such "reasoning" is clearly untenable, given the present development of the technology of war. There is no indication, either in the Charter or the discussions, which would even remotely support such a view.

[28] Grayson Kirk, "Comment," *Proceedings of the American Society of International Law*, 44th Meeting (April 1950), 22-23.

[29] Russell and Muther (fn. 6), 705.

factors was too narrow and in part by fear of reopening the difficult negotiations which had led to agreement on the regional provisions.[30] From time to time since then, there have been similar claims raised that participation by a particular state in a regional organization is impermissible without common geographic, ideological, ethnic, or religious ties. Thus, the claim was raised by "The Lawyers Committee on American Policy Toward Vietnam" in criticizing American sponsorship and participation in SEATO.[31] Although it might be expected that heterogeneous organizations without common geographic, ideological, ethnic, or religious ties might be poor performers in dealing with local disputes, there seems to be nothing in the Charter that limits "regional" organizations (much less Article 51 organizations) to states with a common geographic, ideological, ethnic, or religious base. The United States participation in SEATO is perhaps the clearest example of this practice, but British participation in CENTO and Turkish participation in NATO are additional examples. The extent to which members of a particular grouping share a genuine common interest, of course, may be decisive in the efficient functioning of the organization. The collapse of SEATO demonstrates that such interests cannot be pressure cooked simply by promoting a multilateral arrangement. But there is no reason to believe that genuine common interests cannot be shared across geographic, ideological, ethnic, or religious boundaries.

B. *Claims Concerning Regional Jurisdiction of a Dispute or Situation.*

The issue of regional jurisdiction was one of the two major issues of regional authority argued at the San Francisco Conference. During the Conference the Latin American states vigorously championed broad jurisdiction for the inter-American system. Although the United States position was not completely clear, in theory at least the United States supported strong United Nations control of regional activities. The outcome at San Francisco was a perhaps deliberately ambiguous compromise reflected in Articles 52(2) and 52(4) which could be variously interpreted to fit the position of the interpreter. Thus Professor Inis Claude reports:

[30] Same, 706.

[31] Lawyers Committee on American Policy Toward Vietnam, "Memorandum of Law," *Congressional Record*, 112, Pt. 2 (February 9, 1966), 2665, 2668. The claim that regional organizations may only include states with common ideological or geographic ties has been explicitly rejected by a number of commentators. See Van Kleffens (fn. 11), 670-71; Kulski (fn. 11), 466-67.

Robert Strausz-Hupé points out the fallacy of overemphasizing geographic ties when he says: "Were the idea of Pan Americanism based exclusively upon the facts of geography—the continental relationships of North, Central, and South America—it would hardly be an important factor in world politics. The Americas are not a region." "Regionalism in World Politics," in "The Americas and World Order," *International Conciliation*, 419 (March 1946), 117, 118.

At the meeting of Committee III(4), which approved the package of proposals designed to meet the pro-regionalist demands of the Latin Americans, a Peruvian spokesman articulated his concern that the changes did not clearly preclude the Security Council from asserting jurisdiction over intra-regional disputes at any stage; he was disappointed that the exclusiveness of regional responsibility for dealing initially with local disputes had not been recognized and safeguarded. The president of the Committee, speaking for Colombia, offered reassurance. He saw no problem of double jurisdiction, but believed that the newly adopted provisions established the rule that the Security Council must leave initial efforts at peaceful settlement of local disputes to regional agencies; the Council might investigate to determine whether such disputes threatened international peace, but it could not intrude upon the regional settlement process unless and until the latter had failed.[32]

In the twenty-five years since the San Francisco Conference, the breakdown of Security Council effectiveness contributed to a United States shift to advocacy of broader primary jurisdiction for regional organizations. At the same time, what many Latin American states viewed as United States dominance of the OAS and consequent assertion of special interests, caused many of them to champion United Nations jurisdiction as a check on United States hegemony within the OAS. Today, although there are still occasional statements to the contrary by some United States officials and Latin American spokesmen, there is overwhelming support for a Charter interpretation that the United Nations has jurisdiction over all matters affecting international peace and security and that deference to regional jurisdiction is a matter of pragmatic judgment rather than Charter requirement. The issues have been settled almost exclusively in a context of OAS action, though, and it is possible that as the equation regional autonomy means OAS autonomy breaks down the issues may again be raised and the lines in the debate redrawn. But in view of the present strong consensus for United Nations control it seems likely that the present resolution of the issues will stick.

1. Claims that the regional organization has primary jurisdiction.

The heart of the jurisdictional dispute is the issue of primary jurisdiction. Primary jurisdiction involves two related claims: claims that members of regional organizations must first exhaust regional remedies and claims that the United Nations may not interfere with the initial exercise of regional jurisdiction. Frequently the two are inextricably mixed together.

[32] Claude (fn. 2), 11.

a. Claims that members of regional organizations
   must first exhaust regional remedies.

Although it is frequently not clear whether this claim is one of prior submission or exhaustion of remedies, the usual implication is that members of regional organizations must exhaust the remedies of the regional system prior to referral to the United Nations. Support for this view may be found in Article 52(2) which provides: "The Members of the United Nations entering into such arrangements or constituting such agencies shall make every effort to achieve pacific settlement of local disputes through such regional arrangements or by such regional agencies before referring them to the Security Council." In addition, the inter-American system contains provisions in Article 2 of the Rio Treaty and Article 23 of the Revised Charter of the OAS which purport to create an obligation for members to first submit obligations to the inter-American system before resorting to the United Nations. These provisions were inserted in the inter-American treaties in order to strengthen Charter interpretations taking a broad view of regional jurisdiction. The overriding question, of course, is the interpretation to be given Article 52(2) in the light of Article 52(4), for if the Charter recognizes the right of member states to bring a dispute before the Security Council regardless of regional machinery, then Article 103 of the Charter, Article 10 of the Rio Treaty, and Article 137 of the Revised OAS Charter require that the Charter right prevail.

Though the issue was initially hotly disputed, present United Nations practice strongly supports the right of member states to appeal to the United Nations at any time.[33] Thus, the United States and Colombia argued in the 1954 Guatemalan case that Guatemala had a duty to first submit the dispute to the OAS. Similarly, in the 1960 Cuban case Britain, France, and the United States made a similar contention with respect to Cuba. The argument, however, seems never to have been generally accepted in United Nations discussion of the Guatemalan and Cuban complaints. And in his Annual Report for 1953-54 the Secretary-General seems to have adopted a position in favor of the right of member states to appeal to the United Nations at any time, although his language was somewhat ambiguous: "a policy giving full scope to the proper role of regional agencies can and should at the same time fully preserve the right of a Member nation to a hearing under the Charter."[34] During the ninth General Assembly a number of Latin American states explicitly expressed their understanding that nothing in the inter-American system could restrict their right to have

---

[33] Claude (fn. 2), 21-46.

[34] Introduction to the Annual Report of the Secretary-General on the Work of the Organization, 1 July 1953—30 June 1954, *U.N. Gen. Ass. Off. Rec.*, 9th Sess., Supp. No. 1 (A/2663) (1954), xi.

recourse at any time to the United Nations.[35] This interpretation seems to have been generally accepted within the United Nations during the Haitian case of 1963, the Panamanian case of 1964, and the Dominican case of 1965 despite the fact that the OAS exercised the principal initiative in all three cases. Even if there were an exhaustion of remedies requirement, the requirement should not be interpreted to require a futile appeal to a hostile regional organization. It would seem that the Guatemalan and Cuban appeals could have been decided on this ground alone, since in both cases the regional organization was clearly hostile to the position of the complaining state and in the Cuban case it was the hostile action of the regional organization itself which Cuba sought to raise.

Though the OAS has been the principal crucible for testing the right of regional member states to appeal at any time to the United Nations, one somewhat inconclusive case arose in an OAU context. During the Algerian-Moroccan border conflict of 1963 Morocco sought a hearing within the United Nations rather than the OAU. Eventually she agreed to the OAU forum but the reason was largely lack of political support for a United Nations hearing rather than any victory for a "try OAU first" principle.[36] Although as these cases illustrate, it may frequently be desirable for the United Nations to in fact adopt an exhaustion of regional remedies rule, it seems unwise to constitutionally require such a rule. And certainly any such rule should not require an exhaustion of regional remedies which would obviously be futile.

   b. Claims that the United Nations may not interfere with the
      initial exercise of regional jurisdiction.

This claim is slightly different from the claim that members of regional organizations must first submit disputes to regional machinery. For under Article 35 any member of the United Nations, whether a member of the regional arrangement or not, can bring a dispute or situation to the attention of the Security Council. Thus, it is possible for regional members to resort only to regional machinery and still have the issue raised in the Security Council. Similarly, any state might raise the issue in the General Assembly. The prior submission and interference with initial jurisdiction claims are usually not differentiated, how-

---

[35] Claude (fn. 2), 33-34. The United States continues to support an exhaustion of remedies rule though conceding United Nations "competence to deal with any situation which might threaten international peace and security." See Adlai E. Stevenson, "Principles of U.N.-OAS Relationship in Dominican Republic," *Department of State Bulletin*, LII, 1355 (June 14, 1965), 975, 976. Stevenson took the position that: "the members of the United Nations pursuant to articles 33 and 52 of the charter should seek to deal with threats to the peace within a geographical region through regional arrangements before coming to the United Nations." Same, 976.

[36] Wild (fn. 2), 28.

ever, and as a result their development has been similar. Arguments were made in both the Guatemalan and Cuban cases that the Security Council could not exercise jurisdiction while the OAS was involved in the dispute, and in the Cuban case this argument was made despite Cuba not having filed a complaint with the OAS. The arguments were closely linked to arguments concerning the duty of OAS member states to first resort to regional machinery, and like that claim did not seem to be accepted by the Council. Thus, in the same Annual Report in which he referred to "the right of a Member nation to a hearing under the Charter" the Secretary-General also said: "in those cases where resort to . . . [regional] arrangements is chosen in the first instance, that choice should not be permitted to cast any doubt on the ultimate responsibility of the United Nations."[37] The jurisdiction of the Security Council to consider a dispute or situation concerning international peace and security despite regional exercise of jurisdiction seems to have been largely unchallenged since the Guatemalan and Cuban cases. Security Council competence was implicit in both the 1963 Haitian case and the 1964 Panamanian case. And it was explicit in the 1965 Dominican case in which the Security Council took parallel action by creating a United Nations Mission in the Dominican Republic while the OAS was still actively involved in dispute-settlement efforts.[38] Moreover, in arguing that the United Nations should not interfere with the actions of the OAS in the Dominican Republic, Ambassador Stevenson conceded for the United States that the question of United Nations competence to deal with the situation was not even an issue.[39] That lingering, though seemingly unfounded, doubts remain, however, is illustrated by the declaration of the Inter-American Bar Association at its Fourteenth Conference in May, 1965: ". . . the Organization of American States has original jurisdiction over the situation in the Dominican Republic and no other international organization has competence to interfere in the case until the O.A.S. submits it to the U.N. Security Council."[40]

2. Claims that the regional organization has exclusive jurisdiction.

Claims that the regional organization has primary jurisdiction only assert regional priority. That is, regional disputes must first be submitted to regional agencies and the United Nations must refrain from taking jurisdiction until regional efforts have failed. Sometimes, though, there has been a hint in the debates on primary jurisdiction

---

[37] Introduction to the Annual Report of the Secretary-General on the Work of the Organization, 1 July 1953—30 June 1954 (fn. 34), xi.

[38] See Nanda (fn. 2), 257.

[39] Stevenson (fn. 35), 976.

[40] As reported by Eleanor Finch. See "Inter-American Bar Association," *American Journal of International Law*, 60, 1 (January 1966), 80, 81.

that what is really being asserted is that the United Nations has no jurisdiction at all to deal with disputes within the territory of a regional organization. That is, that the regional agency has exclusive jurisdiction. The United States position in the 1960 Cuban case, in which Cuba had not even referred the dispute to the OAS, is a case in point. The overtones of the debate might be interpreted to indicate a total denial of United Nations jurisdiction over events within the OAS region.[41] If that was the United States position, Ambassador Stevenson's remarks in the 1965 Dominican case indicate that it no longer is.

A second case in which there has been a hint of a claim that regional jurisdiction is exclusive was the 1963 Algerian-Moroccan case. In that case the OAU Council of Ministers adopted a resolution which hinted at OAU supremacy in cases of breach of the peace in Africa. The pertinent language was:

> Considering the imperative necessity to settle differences by peaceful means and in a *strictly African framework.* . . .
>
> Reaffirms the . . . determination of African States to seek constantly, through negotiations and *within the framework of principles and institutions established by the O.A.U. Charter,* a peaceful and fraternal solution to all differences which may arise among them. . . .[42]

In any event, the claim of exclusive regional jurisdiction seems never to have been accepted, if in fact it has ever been made. To accept such a claim would be a giant step toward complete reversal of the decision to give overriding responsibility for resolution of peace and security issues to the United Nations.

3. Claims that the regional organization has concurrent jurisdiction.

Although claims that regional organizations have primary or exclusive jurisdiction have been largely rejected, there seems to be a general understanding that regional organizations may exercise concurrent jurisdiction, at least in the absence of United Nations action terminating regional jurisdiction. The 1965 Dominican case, in which both the United Nations and the OAS were simultaneously engaged in field operations, is an example. Coercive action by regional agencies, of course, may raise claims that the action is "enforcement action" requiring prior Security Council approval.

[41] This seems to have been the Soviet interpretation of the United States position. The interpretation, however, requires a not inconsiderable stretching. See Claude (fn. 2), 34-43.

[42] Wild (fn. 2), 30. Patricia Wild says of this resolution: "The wording . . . appeared to establish the primacy of OAU institutions over the United Nations in case of a breach of the peace in Africa." Same, 30. It is not at all clear, however, that the resolution was intended to announce anything stronger than an exhaustion of remedies rule.

4. **Claims** that the United Nations should defer to regional machinery even though the United Nations has jurisdiction.

Claims in this category are easily and frequently confused with primary jurisdiction claims. Unlike primary jurisdiction claims, however, these claims are based on pragmatic rather than formal jurisdictional grounds for deferring to regional machinery. That is, the primary jurisdiction claims are claims that the United Nations *must* constitutionally defer to regional authority. The pragmatic claims, on the other hand, are based on the premise that such deference is permissive rather than required. And unlike the general rejection of the primary jurisdiction claims, these claims for deference on pragmatic grounds have been highly persuasive. Thus, the United Nations in effect deferred to regional action in the 1954 Guatemalan case, the 1960 Dominican case, the 1960 Cuban case, the 1963 Algerian-Moroccan case, the 1963 Haitian case, and the 1964 Panamanian case. In the 1954 Guatemalan case the Security Council did pass a resolution calling on all states to refrain from giving assistance to the attackers, but subsequent Security Council inaction in fact left the issue to the OAS. Even the Cuban complaint in the Bay-of-Pigs invasion resulted in an equivocal United Nations response.[43] The 1965 Dominican case is apparently the only case in which the United Nations has actually taken parallel action in the face of a claim that a regional dispute should be left to a regional agency. In the Dominican case, however, the parallel action did not go significantly beyond a call for a strict cease-fire and the establishment of a United Nations Mission to the Dominican Republic for the purpose of keeping the Security Council informed of the situation. Even this minimal exercise of concurrent jurisdiction stirred up a hornet's nest of opposition within the OAS. Garcia Amador, the Director of Legal Affairs of the Pan American Union, labeled the Security Council action an "abuse of power," and both the OAS Special Committee and the Inter-American Bar Association issued strong condemnations of the United Nations action.[44]

In evaluating claims for United Nations deference to regional machinery, it is useful to distinguish those cases in which the regional forum was chosen because all parties genuinely preferred regional action, because of genuine regional expertise, or because the interests at stake were primarily regional, from those which were simply cold-war efforts to avoid United Nations consideration of questionable conduct. Those in the first category, such as the consensual deferrals to the OAS in the 1963 Haitian and 1964 Panamanian cases, were largely non-controversial. Cold-war efforts to avoid UN consideration, though, primarily the 1954 Guatemalan and the 1960 Bay-of-Pigs instances, faced

---

[43] See Claude (fn. 2), 21-34 (Guatemala), 40-43 (Cuba).
[44] See Nanda (fn. 2), 259-261.

rougher going. The 1965 Dominican case seems to have some elements of both categories and may foreshadow a tougher United Nations attitude toward deference to regional action. It would seem that claims in this category ought to be decided by reference to the policy criteria whether the interests at stake are primarily regional, whether regional machinery offers more effective conflict management, or whether the parties to the dispute genuinely prefer a regional forum.

5. Claims that the United Nations may terminate regional jurisdiction.

The Security Council would seem to have authority under Articles 24, 25, 39, 51, 52, and 53 taken together, to revoke regional jurisdiction in the handling of any issue affecting international peace and security. Of particular significance, Article 24 confers "on the Security Council primary responsibility for the maintenance of international peace and security." Although claims that the United Nations may terminate regional jurisdiction seemed implicit in the Soviet position in the 1954 Guatemalan and 1960 Cuban cases, the United Nations seems never to have terminated regional jurisdiction over a dispute or situation. That it has not done so even though general authority may be assumed is not surprising in view of the difficulties in obtaining Security Council approval of such a course of action which can frequently be expected to be in opposition to the position of a major power.

C. *Claims Concerning Regional Authority to Initiate Noncoercive Action.*

The principle Charter provision concerning noncoercive regional action is Article 52(1) which requires regional activities to be "consistent with the Purposes and Principles of the United Nations." To date there seem to have been no major claims concerning regional authority to initiate noncoercive action. Since it is clear that noncoercive action is not "enforcement action" within the meaning of Article 53, such authority seems to be assumed in the absence of an allegation of a purpose inconsistent with that of the Charter. In fact, this category probably includes the most likely situations for Security Council referral to regional agencies, as is suggested by Article 52(3) of the Charter.

D. *Claims Concerning Regional Authority to Initiate Coercive Action.*

Regional authority to initiate coercive action without prior Security Council approval, and thus without initial exposure to the possibility of a veto, was the second major issue in regional authority at the San Francisco Conference. The result of the compromise reached at San Francisco was the addition of Article 51. Article 51 provides: "Nothing in the present Charter shall impair the inherent right of individual or collective self-defense if an armed attack occurs against a member of the United Nations, until the Security Council has taken the measures necessary to maintain international peace and security." Article 53, however, embodies a requirement that "no enforcement action shall be taken under regional arrangements or by regional agencies without the authorization of the Security Council." Regional action in response to an armed attack need not have Security Council authorization but "enforcement action" must. Major doctrinal issues in clarifying regional authority with respect to coercive action, then, are the identification of the breadth of the defensive right and the identification of "enforcement action." In addition, pursuant to Article 52(1), coercive action, like noncoercive action, must be consistent with the purposes and principles of the Charter. If, of course, the Security Council authorizes a regional agency to take coercive action for the maintenance of international peace and security, then under Articles 39-42, 48, and 53 such action is clearly valid. Without prior Security Council authorization, however, the parameters of regional authority to take coercive action are less clear.[45]

1. Claims to use the military instrument in response to an armed attack.

Since the essence of the compromise at San Francisco provided for collective defense against armed attack without the need for prior Security Council authorization, it is clear that regional action in defense against an armed attack is permissible. As such, the major controversies concerning defensive action by regional arrangements center on the meaning of armed attack, particularly in relation to external involvement in internal conflict, and whether valid defensive action is limited to situations in which there is a prior armed attack.

The Charter is in large measure unresponsive to the problems of control of unauthorized intervention in internal conflict. On a major purposes rationale, however, it would seem that the defensive exception of Article 51 should be interpreted to permit proportional counterintervention on behalf of a widely recognized government to offset impermissible external assistance to insurgents. Not to permit such counterintervention on behalf of a widely recognized government would be to insulate covert aggression from defensive response.[46] This interpretation should be applicable to regional as well as unilateral action.

Perhaps the potentially most divisive issue in delineating valid defensive regional action is the question of whether such action is limited

45 See generally Claude (fn. 2), 47-60; Halderman (fn. 2); Meeker (fn. 2), 520-22; Nanda (fn. 2), 251-54.
46 See Moore (fn. 1), 279-80, 328-29, 337.

to situations in which there is a prior armed attack. The Cuban missile crisis of 1962 presented this issue since the secret emplacement of Soviet missiles in Cuba could not be classified as a prior armed attack and there was no prior Security Council authorization for the quarantine. A number of scholars have urged in this context that the "defensive quarantine" authorized by the OAS was permissible defensive action under the Charter and that if such action otherwise meets the requirements of the "inherent" right of defense it is not limited by the armed attack requirement of Article 51.[47] Their interpretation, however, which parallels a long-standing dispute about the scope of the defensive right under the Charter, remains controversial.

    2. Claims to use the military instrument in situations not amounting to an armed attack.

Claims to use the military instrument other than in response to an "armed attack," or arguably other than in response to a broader inherent defensive right, raise questions both of whether such action is "enforcement action" requiring Security Council approval and whether such action is otherwise consistent with the Charter.

The meaning of "enforcement action" is disputed. One interpretation is that it refers to all coercive action by any modality (other than defensive action) and does not include noncoercive action.[48] Another interpretation is that it refers only to action which is obligatory on member states as opposed to action which is merely recommended.[49] One scholar indicates that because of the breakdown in Security Council effectiveness some states seem to be tacitly assuming a Charter amendment doing away with the requirement of Security Council approval for enforcement action.[50] Any such assumption, however, would certainly meet widespread opposition within the United Nations.

    a. Claims that regional action which authorizes but does not require coercive action by member states is not "enforcement action" requiring Security Council authorization.

Leonard Meeker, Deputy Legal Adviser of the Department of State at the time, argued with respect to the lawfulness of the OAS action in

[47] See Halderman (fn. 2), 111-16; W. T. Mallison, Jr., "Limited Naval Blockade or Quarantine-Interdiction: National and Collective Defense Claims Valid Under International Law," *George Washington Law Review*, 31, 2 (December 1962), 335, 360-64.

For a restrictive interpretation of the defensive right, limiting it to response against an "armed attack," see, e.g., Philip C. Jessup, *A Modern Law of Nations* (New York 1948), 165-67.

[48] See Claude (fn. 2), 48-53; Halderman (fn. 2), 96.

[49] Meeker (fn. 2), 520-22. Professor Abram Chayes suggests that he shares this view when he indicates that "enforcement action" has been treated "as a rigorously narrow category." See Abram Chayes, "Law and the Quarantine of Cuba," *Foreign Affairs* XLI, 3 (April 1963), 550, 556.

[50] Halderman (fn. 2), 91-92, 105-11.

the Cuban quarantine that " 'enforcement action' does not include action . . . which is not obligatory on all the members."[51] Thus, since Article 20 of the Rio Treaty provides that "no State shall be required to
use armed force without its consent," the military measures authorized
by the OAS could not amount to "enforcement action." The argument
is based principally on a distinction between "a Security Council measure which is obligatory and constitutes 'action,' on the one hand, and
a measure which is recommended either by the Council or by the General Assembly, on the other."[52] Although at least one scholar disputes
this distinction as a delimitation of enforcement action even as applied
to allocation of authority between the General Assembly and the Security Council,[53] the real issue seems to be whether such a definition
of "enforcement action" for the purpose of allocating responsibility
between the General Assembly and the Security Council should be
applied for the purpose of allocating responsibility between the United
Nations and regional agencies. It seems doubtful whether the restriction argued in the one context should be applied literally to the other.
The consequence of such an interpretation would be that Security
Council authorization of regional action would not be required, even
for coercive use of the military instrument, as long as the regional
body merely recommended and did not require that its members take
action. Such action, of course, would still have to be consistent with the
purposes and principles of the Charter, but for all practical purposes
this restrictive interpretation would virtually eliminate the "enforcement action" requirement of Article 53. As long as the OAS remains
the only regional organization seriously asserting regional autonomy,
the United States may have a continued incentive to assert this narrow
construction of "enforcement action." The possibility of the narrower
interpretation being invoked by the Warsaw Pact in taking military
action in Eastern Europe or by the Arab League in taking such action
against Israel, however, suggests some of the dangers in adopting this
interpretation.

    b. Claims that regional action not directed against a state is
       not "enforcement action" requiring Security Council
       authorization.

During the course of the Security Council debates on the 1965
Dominican action the United States took the position that the action
was peacekeeping action not directed against a state and as such was
not "enforcement action." The Cuban representative disputed this contention and argued that the "very presence of foreign military forces
in a sovereign state constituted an act of a coercive nature and made

[51] Meeker (fn. 2), 521.   [52] Meeker (fn. 2), 521.
[53] John W. Halderman, "Regional Enforcement Measures and the United Nations,"
Georgetown Law Journal, 52, 1 (Fall 1963), 89, 97-105.

the measure 'an enforcement action.' "[54] In its broadest formulation "enforcement action" refers to all coercive action other than valid defensive action. The Cuban argument implicitly seems to adopt this view. In its broadest formulation, then, the issue is whether a peacekeeping force (or if the first stage of the Dominican operation is in question, a force for the protection of nationals) undertaken with the permission of the government amounts to coercive action. If the purpose of the force is to restore orderly processes of self-determination and is not simply to render assistance to one side or another in an internal conflict, then there would seem to be a good case for saying that such action is not directed against a state and is thus not "enforcement action." In view of the United Nations financial crisis stemming from and further inhibiting United Nations peacekeeping operations, it seems desirable to permit regional peacekeeping operations without prior Security Council approval. Such operations, of course, should be neutral operations conducted within safeguards designed to ensure genuine self-determination and should be subject to subsequent United Nations review. An interpretation of "enforcement action" which permits regional peacekeeping actions or humanitarian intervention undertaken at the request of a widely recognized government is also supported by the 1962 Advisory Opinion of the International Court of Justice in the *Certain Expenses of the United Nations* case.[55] The Court held that peacekeeping measures that were authorized by the General Assembly in both the Congo and the Middle East were not "enforcement action," in part because they were not directed against the sovereignty of any state and were undertaken with the permission of the Congo and Egyptian governments.[56] Although the issue in the *Certain Expenses* case was the authority of the General Assembly rather than the authority of regional arrangements, many of the same considerations seem applicable on the issue of regional authority.

    c. Claims that regional assistance to insurgent groups for the purpose of restoring self-determination is not "enforcement action" requiring Security Council authorization.

The ambiguity surrounding intervention in internal conflict and the critical political interests at stake have prompted both the OAU and the Arab League to give collective assistance to national liberation movements without Security Council authorization. One of the purposes of the Charter of the OAU is "to eradicate all forms of colonial-

---

54 As reported by Professor Ved P. Nanda. See "The United States Action in the 1965 Dominican Crisis: Impact on World Order—Part II," *Denver Law Journal*, 44, 2 (Spring 1967), 225, 265.

55 *I.C.J.* [1962], 151.

56 *I.C.J.* [1962], 151, 165-66, 170, 177.

ism from Africa."[57] To that end the OAU established a Commission on Liberation Movements which has been active in assisting insurgents in Angola, Mozambique, and South Africa.[58] And the Arab League has supported the Palestine Liberation Organization in its struggle with Israel.[59] Such assistance raises both the issue of lawfulness of assistance to insurgent groups, whether unilateral or regional action, and whether such action, if collective regional action, amounts to "enforcement action" requiring Security Council authorization. On the first issue, the prevailing view seems to be that without United Nations authorization, assistance to insurgent groups is unlawful.[60] The Arab League action against Israel seems unlawful even on this first ground. But in the last few years the General Assembly has passed a series of resolutions authorizing assistance to insurgent movements directed against the colonial and racially discriminatory regimes of Southern Africa and arguably such resolutions would support OAU intervention in Southern Africa.[61] Since regional "enforcement action" requires Security Council approval, however, there is still some question whether such General Assembly authorization would be sufficient authorization for collective regional intervention. Although it seems anomalous that General Assembly action might suffice to authorize unilateral but not regional intervention, it would also seem anomalous to characterize assistance to insurgents as something other than "enforcement action." The issue seems never to have been raised and remains one of many submerged icebergs on the vast and only slightly charted sea of intervention.

3. Claims to use economic or diplomatic sanctions.

There can be little doubt that claims to employ economic or diplomatic sanctions in response to an armed attack (or possibly any other situation triggering an inherent defensive right) are as lawful as claims to respond with the military instrument. The recent OAS action in the Honduras-El Salvador conflict indicates that the threat of economic

[57] Article II (1d) of the Charter of the Organization of African Unity, reprinted in Boutros Boutros-Ghali, "The Addis Ababa Charter," *International Conciliation*, 546 (January 1964), 53, 54.

[58] See same, 31-33; Norman J. Padelford, "The Organization of African Unity," *International Organization*, xviii (1964), 521, 536-37; Francis O. Wilcox, "Regionalism and the United Nations," *International Organization*, xix (1965), 789, 802-803.

[59] See *Keesing's Treaties and Alliances of the World* (fn. 10), 172.

[60] See authorities collected in John Norton Moore, "The Control of Foreign Intervention in Internal Conflict," *Virginia Journal of International Law*, 9, 2 (May 1969), 209, 276-77, 315-332.

[61] See *G.A. Res.* 2262; 22 *U.N. GAOR*, Supp. 16, 45-46; *U.N. Doc.* A/6716 (1967) (Southern Rhodesia); *G.A. Res.* 2307; 22 *U.N. GAOR*, Supp. 16, 19-20; *U.N. Doc.* A/6716 (1967) (South Africa); *G.A. Res.* 2372; 22 *U.N. GAOR*, Supp. 16A, 1-2; *U.N. Doc.* A/6716/Add. 1 (1968) (South-West Africa); *G.A. Res.* 2270; 22 *U.N. GAOR*, Supp. 16, 47-48; *U.N. Doc.* A/6716 (1967) (Portuguese colonies).

and diplomatic sanctions may be all that is necessary to ensure compliance with regional peacemaking efforts. Certainly such sanctions should be as lawful as the more coercive use of the military instrument.

If economic and diplomatic sanctions are employed in the absence of an armed attack, however, then regional authority is less certain. The difficulty, of course, is whether such action amounts to "enforcement action" requiring Security Council approval. One interpretation of "enforcement action" is that such action is restricted to military measures and does not include economic or diplomatic sanctions.[62] In support of this interpretation it is argued that since individual states are not restricted from breaking diplomatic relations or imposing trade or other economic restrictions that states acting collectively within a regional organization may also take such action without Security Council approval. On the other hand, at least one scholar urges that the proper distinction is not between military and nonmilitary measures but is between coercive and noncoercive measures, whatever the modality of coercion.[63] In support of this position, Articles 41 and 42 of the Charter refer alike to both nonmilitary and military actions as "measures" which the Security Council may take "to maintain or restore international peace and security" under Article 39. And Professor Inis Claude refers to some evidence from both the San Francisco Conference and the formation of the Rio Treaty that "enforcement action" was thought to cover collective imposition of nonmilitary as well as military sanctions.[64] Although none of these arguments on either side of the debate appears decisive, there is strong support in United Nations practice for an interpretation which does not consider economic or diplomatic sanctions as "enforcement action."

The first case in which the issue arose seems to have been the 1960 Dominican case in which the OAS condemned the Dominican Republic for "acts of intervention and aggression" against Venezuela and instituted diplomatic and partial economic sanctions against the Dominican Republic. Although the Soviet Union did not oppose the sanctions

---

62 See Halderman (fn. 53), 96.

Francis Wilcox (fn. 58), 800, suggests that this position has merit though "its historical roots" are unimpressive.

The United States' argument that Security Council approval should be limited to enforcement action that involves the use of military power and should not be required for the limited kind of political and economic sanctions the OAS invoked against the Dominican Republic certainly has some merit. Clearly it is within the power of *any* sovereign state—without violating the Charter—to sever diplomatic or economic relations or to interrupt its communications with another state. Why, then, should UN approval be necessary for the same kind of action undertaken by a few states individually or by a *group* of states acting together?

63 Halderman (fn. 53), 96, 116-18.

64 Inis L. Claude, Jr., "The OAS, the UN, and the United States" (fn. 2), 50-51.

against Venezuela it requested a meeting of the Security Council to consider authorizing the OAS sanctions. During the ensuing debate the United States took the position that diplomatic and economic measures of the kind being applied against the Dominican Republic did not constitute "enforcement action." The Soviet Union, on the other hand, argued that all such actions were "enforcement action" within the meaning of Article 53. Despite the adoption of a United States resolution that the Security Council merely acknowledge the OAS report and "take note" of the sanctions, the Dominican case seems merely to have indicated the lack of agreement on whether "enforcement action" includes nonmilitary measures. If the 1960 Dominican case was not decisive, however, Security Council action in the March 1962 phase of the Cuban case seems to have been a clear victory for the view that nonmilitary measures were not to be considered "enforcement action." The March 1962 action in the Cuban case was in response to a complaint by Cuba that the OAS measures taken against Cuba at Punta del Este constituted illegal enforcement action in the absence of Security Council approval. Cuba also sought to refer the issue of whether such sanctions constituted "enforcement action" to the International Court of Justice. During the debate, however, only four members of the Security Council denied or questioned the interpretation advanced by the United States that "enforcement action" did not include nonmilitary measures. Claude says of this case: "Thus the victory that the United States had proclaimed at the close of the Dominican case became belatedly a fact."[65] That the victory was fairly conclusive is suggested by Ved Nanda's observation that: ". . . following the decision of the Ninth Meeting of Consultation to apply even more severe diplomatic and economic measures than had been previously imposed against the Cuban government, the Secretary-General of the OAS, pursuant to article 54, informed the Security Council of this decision, and the Council never even discussed the issue."[66]

The economic boycott of Israel instituted by the Arab League is a non-OAS example of regional nonmilitary sanctions. As is true of OAS nonmilitary sanctions, the Arab League boycott seems to have been generally accepted despite the absence of formal Security Council authorization.[67] Another non-OAS example is the OAU economic and diplomatic sanctions against South Africa and Portugal. Since the OAU nations have also pressed their case within the United Nations, and since the racial and colonial issues at stake largely transcend the cold war, the OAU has not been faced with a major jurisdictional challenge from this action.[68]

[65] Same, 56.　　　　　[66] Nanda (fn. 54), 254.
[67] For a brief discussion of the Arab League boycott see Wilcox (fn. 58), 799.
[68] See same, 802.

Collective nonmilitary sanctions, such as severing diplomatic relations or taking coercive economic measures, do seem to involve more than unilateral state action. As such, the principle that what states are free to do individually they may also do collectively may sometimes prove too much. Realistically, nonmilitary sanctions may sometimes be as coercive as military sanctions, particularly if instituted by a multinational initiative. United Nations practice, however, seems to support a narrow definition of "enforcement action" which does not include nonmilitary measures.

E. Claims Concerning Procedures by Which the United Nations May Authorize or Terminate Regional Action.

The debate in the Security Council on the OAS action in the Cuban missile crisis was drastically curtailed by the overriding concern to avoid a nuclear confrontation between the United States and the Soviet Union. Subsequent discussion of the lawfulness of the "defensive quarantine," however, has raised a number of important issues concerning procedures by which the United Nations may authorize regional "enforcement action." There is no question, of course, that such action may be authorized in advance by an express Security Council resolution. The issues which have been raised concern whether such authorization must be prior authorization and whether it must be express authorization. Although there seem to have been no claims to date concerning the revocation of regional jurisdiction, a separate category is included to consider the related procedural claims.

1. Claims that Security Council authorization of "enforcement action" need not be prior authorization.

Abram Chayes and Leonard Meeker, both former Legal Advisers of the Department of State, have argued in evaluating the OAS actions during the missile crisis that it is reasonable to interpret Article 53 to mean that Security Council authorization of "enforcement action" need not be prior authorization.[69] In support of this interpretation, both scholars rely on the 1960 Dominican case in which the Soviet Union proposed Security Council authorization of OAS sanctions against the Dominican Republic after those sanctions had already been imposed by the OAS. Thus Leonard Meeker says:

On this point it is illuminating to recall a 1960 precedent. In September of that year the Security Council had met, on Soviet request, to consider diplomatic and economic measures voted against the Dominican Republic by the Foreign Ministers of the American Republics meeting at San José the preceding month. The U.S.S.R. asked

[69] Leonard C. Meeker, "Defensive Quarantine and the Law," *American Journal of International Law*, 57, 3 (July 1963), 515, 520; Chayes (fn. 49), 556.

the Council to approve these measures after they had been taken. The Soviet theory quite evidently was that the Council could appropriately give its "authorization" after the fact.[70]

In evaluating this claim it is useful to distinguish the question whether the Security Council may approve regional enforcement action at any time either before or after regional action is taken, from the question whether regional enforcement action is valid until Council authorization is given. On the first question the Soviet position in the Dominican case was clearly that the Security Council could authorize regional enforcement action even after regional action had been taken. On the second question, however, the Soviet Union equally clearly took the position that: "Without authorization from the Security Council, the taking of enforcement action by regional agencies would be contrary to the Charter."[71] There seems to be no policy reason why the Security Council cannot authorize regional enforcement action at any stage, whether before or after such action has been taken. Moreover, if regional action is subsequently authorized it would seem reasonable to grant the Security Council the power to authorize it retroactively to the time when such measures were initiated. In fact, unless the Security Council states otherwise, such retroactive authorization seems implicit in subsequent authorization. That authorization may be subsequent, however, does not mean that regional enforcement action is valid without any authorization at all. Until the Security Council authorizes such action it remains unauthorized enforcement action.

2. Claims that Security Council authorization of "enforcement action" need not be express authorization.

Chayes and Meeker also argue in evaluating the "defensive quarantine" in the missile crisis that in light of the paralysis of the Security Council and the consequent constitutional evolution of the United Nations, it is reasonable to interpret Article 53 to mean that Security Council authorization of regional enforcement action need not be express authorization.[72] During the missile crisis the United States placed the situation before the Security Council and called for an urgent meeting of the Council. The Council met before the "defensive quarantine" was instituted and the Soviet Union introduced a resolution condemning the quarantine. The Soviet resolution, though, was not brought to a vote. In this context Leonard Meeker urges:

The Council let the quarantine continue, rather than supplant it. While the quarantine continued, and with knowledge of it, the Council encouraged the parties to pursue the course of negotiation

---

[70] Meeker (fn. 69), 520.

[71] *U.N. Security Council Off. Rec.* 15th year, 893 Mtg. (S/PV.893) (1960), 4.

[72] Meeker (fn. 69), 522; Chayes (fn. 49), 556-67.

between the United States and the Soviet Union. Thus, if it were thought that authorization was necessary (which was not the view of the United States), such authorization may be said to have been granted by the course which the Council adopted.[73]

It is only a short step to Abram Chayes formulation that:

> . . . surely it is no more surprising to say that failure of the Security Council to disapprove regional action amounts to authorization within the meaning of Article 53 than it was to say that the abstention and even the absence of a permanent member of the Security Council met the requirement of Article 27(3) for "the concurring votes of the permanent members."[74]

But surely it *would* be surprising if failure to disapprove regional enforcement action amounted to authorization. The contention turns the Article 53 authorization requirement into an Article 51 subsequent review requirement. Whereas under the generally accepted interpretation of Article 53 the veto can be used to prevent authorization of regional enforcement action, under the Chayes view the veto could be used to prevent disapproval of regional enforcement action.[75] For all practical purposes, then, the Chayes interpretation amounts to an interpretation that regional action is valid unless disapproved by subsequent Security Council action. If that position is to be taken, it does seem necessary to call it a tacit Charter amendment stemming from changed circumstances rather than a reasonable interpretation of the initial intent of the San Francisco Conference. And as to the Article 27(3) analogy, the interpretation which Chayes refers to seems much stronger on a major purposes rationale than his Article 53 interpretation.[76] In any event, the consequences of accepting this interpretation would seem to be a quite undesirable loosening of Security Council control over regional action. What works for the OAS must also work for the Warsaw Pact, the Arab League, and the OAU.

[73] Meeker (fn. 69), 522.   [74] Chayes (fn. 49), 556.
[75] See Halderman (fn. 53), 105-11.
[76] The interpretation that abstention or absence of a permanent member does not constitute a "veto" within the meaning of Article 27 (3) prevents a permanent member from destroying the Security Council by prolonged absence. Moreover, it does not deprive the permanent members of the "veto" should they choose to exercise it. The Chayes interpretation of Article 53, however, reverses the original understanding regarding Security Council approval of regional "enforcement action" and for all practical purposes deprives the permanent members of the "veto" with respect to regional "enforcement action." For arguments for and against the Article 27 (3) interpretation and a discussion of the policy issues raised see Myres S. McDougal and Richard N. Gardner, "The Veto and the Charter: An Interpretation for Survival," *Yale Law Journal*, 60, 2 (February 1951), 258; Leo Gross, "Voting in the Security Council: Abstention from Voting and Absence from Meetings," *Yale Law Journal*, 60, 2 (February 1951), 209.

It should be kept in mind that the "enforcement action" requirement of Article 53 has both a positive and a negative aspect. Negatively it is a limitation on regional action in addition to the requirement that such action must be consistent with the purposes and principles of the Charter. As such, unauthorized regional action, even if it does not constitute "enforcement action," must still have an independent basis in the Charter. Positively, however, Security Council authorization of regional "enforcement action" is an independent basis for regional action which carries its own authorization. A loosening of the procedures for Security Council authorization of regional action, then, may have far more anarchic consequences than a narrowing of the definition of "enforcement action."

    3. Claims that regional jurisdiction has been revoked by United Nations action.

Apparently no regional action has been revoked by the Security Council pursuant to its authority to do so. Revocation which took the form of an express resolution condemning the regional action would seem fairly clearly to terminate authority. It might also be argued that Security Council action inconsistent with regional action would revoke regional authority. Just as in the case of Security Council authorization of regional authority, though, it seems preferable to require express Council action.

F. *Claims Concerning the Obligation of Regional Arrangements to Report Activities to the Security Council.*

Both Articles 51 and 54 create an obligation for regional arrangements to report certain of their activities to the Security Council. Thus, Article 51 provides: "Measures taken by Members in the exercise of this right of self-defense shall be immediately reported to the Security Council." And Article 54 provides: "The Security Council shall at all times be kept fully informed of activities undertaken or in contemplation under regional arrangements or by regional agencies for the maintenance of international peace and security." Though these two articles create a fairly comprehensive duty to report regional actions concerning international peace and security, in practice that duty does not always seem to have been satisfactorily met.[77] A principal difficulty has been regional involvement in internal conflict. Both the Arab League and the OAU appear to have engaged in assisting favored insurgent groups without reporting such assistance. And SEATO did not meaningfully report its assistance to the South Vietnamese government until several years after such assistance was initiated.[78] If the Security

[77] See Wilcox (fn. 58), 799.   [78] See Moore (fn. 60), 211-12, 300-01.

Council is to assert more meaningful control over regional activities affecting international peace and security it would seem important to make the reporting requirement more responsive to the problem of internal conflict and to more effectively police its effectuation.

V. THE FUTURE ROLE OF REGIONAL ARRANGEMENTS

The wartime debate focusing on a choice between universal and regional security organizations no longer seems relevant. Both universal and regional organizations are here to stay, and rather than an either-or choice the issues for the future are the precise interrelations between regional and universal authority. To date, these judgments concerning specific allocation of competence have tended to be made largely on the basis of the cold-war positions of the protagonists. The result is that discussion of criteria for optimum allocation of authority is long overdue. As a tentative beginning, the pervasiveness of peace and security issues suggests that the United Nations should have ultimate authority with respect to all such issues. It should encourage regional action, however, in situations in which the interests at stake are primarily regional, in which regional machinery offers more effective conflict management (for example, avoidance of cold-war entanglements), or in which the parties to a dispute genuinely prefer a regional forum. These criteria support the general expectation that the United Nations has jurisdiction of any dispute or situation likely to endanger "the maintenance of international peace and security,"[79] but that in particular cases regional jurisdiction may be preferred on pragmatic grounds. It should be emphasized that these pragmatic grounds for deference to regional action may, in a particular case, be quite compelling, and that there are persuasive policy reasons for encouraging strong regional arrangements. If nothing else, the necessity of making security decisions with a high differential impact would strongly support some decentralization of international machinery for dealing with peace and security issues. Greater regional effectiveness in conflict management and deference to genuine preferences for a regional forum for dispute settlement are additional reasons for preferring regional arrangements which have demonstrated real merit. When policies suggest a regional arrangement as the more appropriate forum for dispute settlement, the Security Council should be encouraged to work explicitly through the regional arrangement. There have been too few instances of Security Council authorization or support of regional action when such authorization or support seemed called for. The United Nations should not, however, defer to regional arrangements when deference is sought simply as a technique for insulating

[79] Articles 24 and 34 of the United Nations Charter.

regional action from community appraisal. Both the Guatemalan and Bay-of-Pigs incidents (and the Arab League action against Israel which somehow escaped Security Council scrutiny) suggest an abdication of United Nations responsibility.

In the absence of explicit Security Council authorization, regional action should be tested by conformance with the purposes and principles of the Charter. In addition, coercive regional action may constitute "enforcement action" requiring Security Council authorization. Though some arguments advanced for drastically narrowing the meaning of "enforcement action," such as the argument that regional action which authorizes but does not require coercive action by member states is not "enforcement action," seem to cut too broadly—the real question is why regional action should be more restricted than unilateral action.[80] Theoretically at least, since regional action is less likely to reflect special interests than unilateral action, it would seem that regional action should have broader latitude than unilateral action. Since the "enforcement action" requirement of Article 53 applies only to regional action, however, under the present Charter framework regional action is more restricted than unilateral action. This discrepancy has given rise to a strained narrowing of "enforcement action" to exclude coercive diplomatic or economic action largely on the ground that states are free to take such action unilaterally. It also raises such anomalous possibilities as General Assembly authorization of unilateral intervention while regional intervention, lacking Security Council authorization, would be prohibited "enforcement action," or certain unilateral humanitarian interventions being legal while the same action if regionally initiated would be unauthorized "enforcement action." Though arguably, because of the greater coercive effect

[80] The United Kingdom Representative urged during the Security Council debate on the 1962 Punta del Este resolution that "enforcement action" should be interpreted "as covering only such actions as would not normally be legitimate except on the basis of a Security Council resolution." The argument for this interpretation was:

> There is nothing in international law, in principle, to prevent any State, if it so decides, from breaking off diplomatic relations or instituting a partial interruption of economic relations with any other State. These steps, which are the measures decided upon by the Organization of American States with regard to the Dominican Republic, are acts of policy perfectly within the competence of any sovereign State. It follows, obviously, that they are within the competence of the members of the Organization of American States acting collectively.

U.N. Security Council Off. Rec. 15th year, 893rd Mtg. (S/PV.893) (1960), 16. See also Halderman (fn. 53), 95-96.

This United Kingdom test might be rephrased more explicitly as "collective regional action is lawful (and thus does not constitute "enforcement action") whenever comparable unilateral action would be lawful." Though such a test lacks historical basis, as a policy matter there is a case to be made for it. The test for individual and collective action is the same, of course, under Article 51.

of regional action, coercive regional action should be more restricted than coercive unilateral action, the argument proves too much. In the era of the superpower some unilateral action may be far more coercive than regional action. For the future, there seems to be few policy reasons for appraising regional action by a stricter standard than that applied to comparable unilateral action. It seems likely then, that pressures for a narrow definition of "enforcement action" will continue strong. Perhaps the major policy issue for the future is whether and to what extent regional arrangements should be authorized specific areas of coercive competence which would go beyond unilateral competence, for example authority-oriented humanitarian intervention.[81] The present dominance of key regional organizations by the major powers and their resulting cold-war involvement, as well as the use of the Arab League to wage regional warfare, though, suggest that for the intermediate future such an expanded regional authority not predicated on United Nations authorization in a particular case would be unwise. The challenge for the future is to revitalize the legitimacy of regional arrangements so that regional authority might be expanded to capitalize on their real potential in the maintenance of world order.

[81] For an exploration of the possibility of using regional action as a half-way house between undesirable unilateral and unattainable United Nations intervention see Linda B. Miller, "Regional Organization and the Regulation of Internal Conflict," *World Politics*, xix, No. 4 (July 1967), 582.

CHAPTER 5

Territorial Stability
and Conflict

DANIEL WILKES

THE MAIN DEFECT in most approaches to international law, and especially to territorial problems, is that they concentrate on the *rules for resolution* of conflicts rather than on the *mechanisms or structures* by which conflicts can be *avoided*.[1]

For example, no one seems to worry that, in places where shallow border rivers flow through shifting sands, under existing rules, territorial changes or disputes about them may occur several times a year. "We can always settle this through the World Court or by arbitration" is the international lawyer's classical response. A look at just one such case will illustrate this chapter's assessments as to why—and how—existing rules may prove inadequate as a total system to meet future demands on world public order.

THE BRAVE MEANDERING RIVER AND THE INTERNATIONAL LAWYERS

Part of the boundary between Mexico and the United States follows the Rio Grande, or the Rio Bravo del Norte as it used to be called.[2] Because of its sandy banks, the exact location of the river is constantly changing. Under traditional international law, where a river is the boundary and its banks change, the rule is simple: if the bank is built up slowly by accretion, the border shifts with the river; if the bank results from a sudden shift in course by avulsion, the border stays on the dry land where the old riverbed used to be.[3]

---

[1] The writer spelled this out in two earlier articles, "New Emphases and Techniques for International Law—The Case of the Boundary Dispute," *Western Reserve Law Review*, 15 (September 1964), 623-40, and "Conflict Avoidance in International Law—The Sparsely Peopled Areas and the Sino-Indian Dispute," *William and Mary Law Review*, 9 (Spring 1968), 716-48.

[2] Article 5 of the Treaty of Guadelupe Hidalgo established this border from the Gulf of Mexico up the deepest branch of this river following its deepest navigational channel. See William M. Malloy, *Treaties* (Washington 1910) I, 1110, 1122; *United States Statutes at Large*, IX, 922, and X, 1031 (hereafter cited as *Statutes*). For the history of this settlement, see Robert H. Ferrell, *Foundations of American Diplomacy, 1775-1872* (Columbia 1968), 185 and following. The *thalweg* is also a river boundary in agreements affecting the following borders, among others: Afghanistan-Iran, Algeria-Libya, Argentina-Uruguay, British Honduras-Guatemala, Bulgaria-Greece, Bulgaria-Rumania, Burma-Laos, Cambodia-Laos, China-U.S.S.R., Congo (Leopoldville)-Rwanda, Czechoslovakia-Hungary, Dominican Republic-Haiti, Iran-Turkey, Iran-U.S.S.R., Mexico-United States, Mozambique-Tanzania, Rwanda-Uganda, Tanzania-Uganda, and Zambia-Southern Rhodesia.

[3] See Stephen B. Jones, *Boundary-Making* (Washington 1945), 120-25.

In the *Chamizal Tract Arbitration,* both sides agreed that this was indeed the governing rule on the Rio Grande boundary, but disputed how the particular *bancos* evolved.[4] From 1895 until the arbitral award in 1911, the Mexicans insisted the 630-acre area called El Chamizal resulted from the sudden flood of 1873, thus leaving the tract in Mexico. The Texans, backed by the State Department, cried, "No, it was by accretion!" and, under the international jousting rules, legal combat was joined.

It took until 1910 to get to the arbitral table. The terms of reference were: to decide finally, conclusively, "solely and exclusively" whether title to the tract lay in Mexico or in the United States. The arbitrators found both sides were wrong: an earlier flood in 1864 governed part of the *bancos*—which thus remained Mexican—while gradual erosion and alluvial deposit formed some of the *bancos*—which thus became American.

Then President Theodore Roosevelt's State Department decided to back up the dissenting American arbitrator, who claimed that the terms of reference required nothing less than an all-or-none decision, and yet another legal combat was joined, never to be set before any third party, and only finally ended in 1962 by President Kennedy's agreement to reshift the river's course itself so as to put the entire Chamizal back into Mexico.[5]

Much of the international legal discussion about this case has centered on the United States' refusal to accept the award. The half-century of recurring diplomatic "surfacing" of this dispute is stressed; the fact that it was just as thorny an issue during the 16 years before the award is ignored. It is true that, during the 1930's when the United States was shifting to a Good Neighbor Policy in Latin America, the American Ambassador to Mexico recalls the Chamizal Award dispute as the most recurrent irritant in diplomatic discussions. It is true that, while the March 1938 expropriations by Mexico of American oil concessions had nothing to do with the Chamizal, they did have to be discussed against the background of that issue. However, whether before arbitration or during a refusal to accept an award, the hostile posturing of border states permitted and nourished by traditional rules and procedures about territorial changes has cut down the amount of co-

---

[4] This rule governed via Articles 1 and 2 of the 1884 United States-Mexican boundary treaty. Malloy (fn. 2) 1159; *Statutes,* XXIV, 1011. See generally, "The Chamizal Arbitration between the United States and Mexico," *American Journal of International Law,* 5 (1911), 782ff. (hereafter cited as *Am. J. Int'l L.*).

[5] See *New York Times,* July 3, 1963, p. 1 col. 4, p. 22 col. 1; same, July 19, 1963, p. 1 col. 1, p. 5 col. 1. The text of the resulting 1964 Convention for the Solution of the Problems of the Chamizal is in *Am. J. Int'l. L.,* 58, 241, 336. The relocations of railroad yards, industries, and 655 homes were combined with a $44-million channel project not able to be started until several years after the treaty itself. See *New York Times,* April 17, 1966, p. 29 col. 1.

operation which might have developed along and across the Rio Grande. In this sense, those rules can be said to have failed to foster climates in which the very countries which make the most natural partners for mutual ventures because of their contiguous territory can jointly pursue their developmental goals.

This chapter seeks to demonstrate just how other aspects of existing international rules and procedures on territorial changes have similarly less-than-adequate effects by: (1) analyzing existing rules, then, (2) focusing on the problems of discovering predictors to permit us to see at earlier stages just which territorial disputes are heading for conflicts not likely to be resolved in traditional terms, and finally, (3) exploring the need for "shifters"—devices which can move territorial dispute situations from the noncooperative or explosive arenas of legal dispute to more stable structures in which needed joint help is more likely to occur.

Underlying all is the theme that the future development of international law in this area will lie in a shift away from a rule-centered system aiming as its *summum bonum* at voluntary adherence to agreed rules or to traditional adjudication. This shift will require new mechanisms for minimizing the possibility of disputes arising, and when they do arise, for solution-conscious institutions to handle them.

One warning is in order. This bias of the writer's in favor of moving from resolving conflicts about territorial changes to avoiding them deserves to be looked at critically. It has been suggested by Barkun and Gregg, Coser, Nieburg, and others that "conflict" itself is unnecessarily made a shibboleth; that it is at the very minimum helpful to social change, and possibly even essential for successful conflict management.[6]

An honest appraisal of the history of border conflicts, however, will reveal that, at the very least they must be seen as an exception to the proposed virtue of change-through-struggle; and possibly, too, as some small ground for reexamining it. First, this class of disputes more frequently results in resort to arms than other kinds. Even within the confines of a federal system, Iowan farmers' disputes with Nebraskans over lands on the shifting Missouri River border between these two states "threatened to result in armed conflict" in 1964.[7] How much more so is this the predictable result along disputed international borders.

Second, unlike disputes with distant countries, those with neighbors

---

[6] See, e.g., Robert W. Gregg and Michael Barkun, "Conflict Management" in Gregg and Barkun, *The United Nations System and Its Functions* (Princeton 1968) 243-44; Louis A. Coser, *The Functions of Social Conflict* (Glencoe 1956); see also H. L. Nieburg, "Uses of Violence" in Richard A. Falk and Saul H. Mendlovitz, eds., *The Strategy of World Order* (New York 1966), I, 157-68, at 163-64.

[7] See *New York Times*, July 26, 1964, p. 1 col. 4.

are more likely to spill over into general climates of cooperation or hostility. This is a which-came-first-the-chicken-or-the-egg kind of problem. If there is some other annoyance between bordering states, the disputed boundary itself not only heightens the level of hostility, but once introduced into the verbal fray, prolongs it. On the other hand, if the border dispute came first, a complaint on some other matter which might never have led to diplomatic protests may well be brought up to a more belligerent verbal posture simply because of that dispute.

Third, the ego-identification of self with nation and of nation with territory implicit in every border question makes it more likely to last longer than conflicts of other kinds. In the dispute between the United Kingdom and the United States over the Pacific Northwest in the 1840's for example, despite exclusively British activity north of the 49th parallel, American congressmen crying "54°-40'—or fight!" came to believe their own slogan that the "Oregon country" of America extended that far simply because they had been saying it was so for so long.[8]

I. How Existing International Rules Create Difficulties in Successful Conflict Management

An appraisal of the present state of territorial rules would show that they are inadequate in three ways: first, they do not provide quick, amicable settlements to disputes in the absence of treaty lines; second, often they do not provide an end to disputes after they have been embodied in treaties; and third, they lend themselves to prolonged conflict atmospheres, even during noncombat periods and even after arbitral settlements have been reached.

A brief look at the difficulties with each rule demonstrates just how this occurs.

A. Natural feature boundaries

There are distinct uses of "natural" boundaries in an effort to avoid territorial disputes. First, a natural feature, such as a river, may be taken as the traditional customary line dividing two states. Second, the natural feature, for instance a watershed line, may be taken in a treaty as the embodiment of the agreed line of division—perhaps based upon custom or prior treaty, perhaps not. Third, the feature may be thought to be "the natural place for a boundary," as in the case of the mountain range dividing Timor Island in two.

The key to future growing instabilities of such boundaries, where not supplanted by either agreed closely demarcated lines or agreed

---

[8] Ferrell (fn. 2), 198-203.

large-scale mapped lines, lies in the fact that land use in frontier areas is becoming more and more frequent. This follows from worldwide commercial and international organizational surveying of each nation's hidden wealth resources, coupled with increasing means of access to them. Consequently, if the present rules can be seen to leave room for a squabble over the sovereign rights to exploit—say a tungsten vein, a bauxite deposit, or a diamond bearing river—left alone those rules will ensure that such squabbles will increase.

1. Lakes

a. No treaty or treaty does not cover

In the absence of a treaty, the international law rule would appear to be that a lake along a boundary is divided between the two states at the median points between the opposing shores, or "down the middle," unless some customary right to control up to the far shore exists.[9]

As is frequently the case, the "unless" clause pinpoints one big source of potential dispute. For example, in the past, Tsarist and Soviet leaders have made such customary claims to the whole of the Caspian Sea up to the Iranian shore. Indeed, the Russian navy at times has used the islands off the Astrabad Coast in the extreme southeast corner of the Caspian Sea for naval defenses. Thus, even when these islands were ceded to Iran by the Moscow Treaty of 1921, the underlying "far shore" claim which such defenses had made possible, remained unadjusted.[10]

b. Treaty variations

A study of treaty lines at lake boundaries discloses some of the policy reasons for departing from the traditional rule. For instance, the established median line drawn from circle arcs from points on shore between Switzerland and France in Lake Geneva was deemed inequitable and unworkable. In 1953, these countries solved their problem by arranging a novel polygonal line of six sides out in the middle of the lake which connects with the median lines to Hermance and St. Gingolph on shore and results in an equal division of the surface.[11] Paradoxically, the new treaty for semantic reasons keeps the boundary at the median points "theoretically" while delineating the new polygon "practically."[12] The result is not an unimportant one, for ownership of the subsurface waters and areas may be far more valua-

[9] Sir Hersh Lauterpacht, *Oppenheim's International Law*, 8th edn. (London 1955), I.
[10] See Geographer of the Department of State, *International Boundary Study Series* No. 25 (Washington 1963) 7 (hereafter cited as *Int'l Boundary Study*).
[11] Convention on the Determination of the Frontier in Lake Geneva of February 25, 1953, in force September 10, 1957, Article 1. See *Int'l Boundary Study* No. 11 (1961), 3.
[12] Same.

ble in the future. Cousteau has a sightseeing submarine on another Swiss lake already and there has yet to be any mineral exploitation on Lake Geneva.

Finnish treaties with the Soviet Union provide yet other policies. Where the boundary lakes are also sources for streams or lake chains basically in one country, the border is often rigged to go between lakes. Most of the actual lake crossings are made by straight lines continuing the direction of a border regardless of the division of waters involved. In fact, the one border lake which had been divided at the middle, 1,040-square mile Lake Ladoga, was kept entirely in Soviet hands after World War II.[13]

Finally, it has sometimes made more sense to shift the border to the thalweg of the main navigational channel, especially when going through a strait between islands or promontories, as along the Great Lakes system between the United States and Canada.

c. Stability from existing rules?

It is crucial to note that existing international rules permit at least two borders to be argued for in lake cases not governed by treaty. Further, where differences between these rules and treaty rules exist there is plenty of room for argument about treaty validity. For example, in the Lake Ladoga case just cited, the first treaty shift from the straight midline occurred after the Winter War of 1939-40. This war itself had been labeled by the Assembly and the Council of the League of Nations as one contrary to Article 16 of the League Covenant.[14] If that treaty fell for its invalidity, what greater status has the post World War II Peace Treaty "restoring" to the Soviet Union the rest of the lake? Thus, the stability of the territorial rules can be seen to be inextricably bound up with the stability of boundary agreements under treaty rules.

2. Rivers

a. Location of line when border is a river

The thalweg rule of navigable river borders and the midline rule for nonnavigable ones, already referred to, also has an "unless" clause for historical possession and control up to the far shore.

Two current disputes show how this can lead to increasing clashes over river area development in the future. In the first, Brazilian-Paraguayan plans to build a bridge across the Paraná River once faltered on this very issue. Since Brazil claimed it had customary control on the Paraguayan shore, it would have built the whole bridge with 100 per-

[13] *Int'l Boundary Study* No. 74 (1967). Compare the midline used across Hazapin Gölü on the Soviet-Turkish frontier.

[14] See Marjorie Whiteman, *Digest of International Law* (Washington 1965), v, 962-63.

cent Brazilian funds. Since Paraguay claimed up to the normal median line (near falls making it nonnavigable), it insisted on control over its half while admitting it had no funds for the project.

In the second, the question of repairing the Su P'ung Dam across the Yalu River arose between North Korea and China. The North Korean insistence on repairing the entire dam in 1948 and 1949 keeps alive a vitally significant difference of opinion for the Su P'ung Dam supplies hydroelectric power to large parts of both North Korea and China.[15]

b. Changing rivers and changing uses

International lawyers tend to assume that rivers are quite stable geophysical features. No geologist or Red Cross flood relief specialist would make such a mistake. The result, however, is that established international rules for river boundaries can leave room for disputes as well. Where navigable rivers have changed their course, land that was once geographically considered part of Country *A* with whatever ego-identification its citizens have made with it, becomes arguably shifted to Country *B*. The assumption of the thalweg rule has been that the navigational interest on the boundary river would remain supreme. In point of fact, however, when shipping interests conflict with earlier identifications, dependent populations, or new economic aspirations, the thalweg rule can be expected to lead to clashes in the future.

For instance, under earlier treaty rules, the Argentina-Uruguay border along the Río Uruguay followed the thalweg. When they had to decide in 1961 whether to keep following the deep and wide Filomena Channel, now on the Uruguayan side of large Uruguayan midstream islands, or the narrow El Medio Channel between Argentina's shore and those islands, potential conflict was only barely averted by use of an unusually imaginative device: "The main navigational channel is the 'border' to divide the more significant river waters and permit transport, while the narrow channel near the far shore is a separate 'border' solely for purposes of guaranteeing free access to the separated Uruguayan islands."[16] From the stability point of view, even in case of such a resourceful treaty solution, one has only to ask: which side would an international lawyer prefer to be on if oil were discovered near an Uruguayan island just off the Argentinian shore? The answer is he would be happy with either side, a symptom of a prolonged dispute under traditional role-playing in the juridical-diplomatic arena.

---

15 See *Int'l Boundary Study* No. 17 (1962), 2. Compare Italian willingness to let Switzerland use a source river one mile inside the Italian border for a power plant to bring hydroelectric power to a Swiss canton. Accord between Italy and Switzerland on the subject of cession of water power from the Reno di Lei (Val di Lei) with additional protocol of June 18, 1949. *Int'l Boundary Study* No. 12 (1961), 3.

16 Treaty of Boundaries of 1961, Article I (A) (II). See *Int'l Boundary Study* No. 68 (1968), 3.

c. Future stability from greater precision

As treaties are made in a context of increasingly greater knowledge, such devices as channel demarcation, large-scale mapping of median lines separated by treaty from accretion-avulsion problems, and aerial or satellite photomapping may cut down some of the sources of river border disputes. Such devices might, for instance, have avoided armed conflict at an earlier stage when Damansky Island or Chenpao in the Ussuri River might have been definitively placed in China or in the Soviet Union. As it is, the Soviets were left to rely upon recent occupation while the Chinese were left to rely on a thalweg claim coupled with an *Eastern-Greenland* type of claim that the Soviet Union's negotiators in 1964 border discussions acknowledged this island to be Chinese territory.[17] The huge demonstrations in Peking and in Moscow which followed border clashes over the island in 1969 were examples of the degree to which "citizen-state-land" identification can reduce diplomatic freedom to avoid conflict once the dispute fires are kindled.

There is one area, however, where past conflicts could disappear with future cartographic and surveying technology. Because of the inaccessibility of river borders remote from metropolitan areas, there have been border disputes in the past about which river was the one mentioned in the treaty, as in the St. Croix River Arbitration between the United States and Great Britain over the border between Maine and Canada.[18] In a very few cases, such disputes remain as in the Chinese-North Korean dispute about which river is the "Shi-i-Shui" mentioned in a 1909 Treaty between the Chinese and Japanese imperial governments. Is it the main stem of the Tumen River? Is it the branch Japanese maps called the Shih-i-Shui significantly farther to the north?[19] For such cases, the advantages of sophisticated computer satellite mapping may be more applicable to future treaties relying on those maps than to past ones where the physical location of competing rivers is less relevant than the evidence as to which one was intended long ago. The lesson for the future in sparsely settled areas of Asia, Africa, and Latin America is this: "to seize upon moments of great rapport and mutual interest in cooperation between states with sections of undelineated river borders to agree on *aerial photograph maps*

[17] See *New York Times*, March 12, 1969, p. 1 col. 2. In the Eastern Greenland Case, the World Court held that oral representations about the absence of territorial claims, made by a Minister in negotiations in which the disclaimer was intended to be relied upon for the sake of other agreements, are binding even if never reduced to a ratified treaty in accord with alleged municipal law requirements. Permanent Court of International Justice (1933), Series A/B No. 53. The Chinese also assert that the thalweg rule, according to which the island would be Chinese, governs this obviously navigable river.

[18] John B. Moore, *International Adjudications* (Washington 1929), 367.

[19] *Int'l Boundary Study* No. 17 (1962), 4.

showing the rivers named in past treaties and rementioning them by coordinates in a new one."

3. Mountains

 a. Apart from treaties

In the Sino-Indian border negotiations, the Chinese rejected as not binding upon them treaties made between the Chinese Imperial and British Imperial officials which established the "McMahon Line" through the Himalaya Mountains. Further, they rejected Indian claims to have administered the areas in dispute continuously. Finally, since several of the tribes and the Tibetan form of Buddhism survived on both sides of the McMahon Line, they rejected Indian claims that tradition had clearly placed the peoples in a cultural area distinctly Indian.

The negotiators from India stated that international law upheld succession to pre-independence boundary treaties and then challenged the Chinese maps and evidence with documents of their own.

Both sides were thus left to argue about the mountain boundaries or "natural features" they conceded were a legitimate basis for boundary claims under international law. India was able to point to the water divide of the line surveyed by McMahon. China suggested that the mountains did make a natural boundary between the two countries but that in the northeastern sector this had been the *base* of the Himalayan range on the Indian side. Paradoxically, farther to the west both sides conceded that a watershed line across the Himalayas would do. The Chinese simply pointed to ridges much farther south than those taken by the British in earlier times. Thus, in one sector the dispute was about the historic rule applied to those particular mountains, while in the other place the dispute was over the facts instead.

Conflict was neither avoided nor resolved here by international rules. Instead, after protracted meetings, the Chinese massed a superior invasion force and readjusted the border by partially withdrawing from their most advanced positions. While it is not necessary to view the Chinese resort to force as one solely caused by legal or factual ambiguities, room for dispute was certainly left by every aspect of classic international law rules.[20]

Traditionalists may differ on whether, if there is no governing treaty, the two countries must be divided where possible along the heights which also divide the waters flowing into each country. This was the rule adopted in the *Timor Arbitration*.[21] Or whether they must

---

[20] For a full analysis, see Daniel Wilkes, "Conflict Avoidance in International Law" (fn. 1).

[21] See Island of Timor Arbitration (*Portugal v. Netherlands*) in Scott, ed., *Hague Court Reports* (1916), 355, 383.

be divided at mountains by a line connecting the highest crests or along some central ridge, as was the case in settling the Argentine-Chile dispute.[22]

What is overlooked by those who would rest too much stability on these rules is that, even if you can agree on a single one for specific circumstances, they not too infrequently just are not able to lead to solely one possible line. In the *Temple of Preah Vihear Case*, for instance, the adjudicators had before them no less than four proffered watershed lines to choose from. No small wonder they finally ruled that a choice was "unnecessary" because stability could best be achieved by binding the disputing countries to lines on a map their predecessors had relied upon in earlier negotiations.[23]

b. With treaty definitions

The erroneous presumption of many treaties that a distinct ridge or crest line exists in every mountain range can leave a ratified agreement intended to end dispute actually openended. This is especially true in areas not yet fully explored where some discovery of a valuable mineral resource may make differences in treaty interpretation worth bringing up. Similar false presumptions guided other diplomats' pens in describing water divides by ridge lines.[24]

It is possible to cure some of these problems which enhance the likelihood of conflict by greater clarity in boundary treaties:

> when a watershed is meant, this does not necessarily mean that crests will be joined at all and the treaty should say nothing about them;

[22] The Argentine-Chile Treaty's assumption that the "crest line" would also follow the "ridge" and that these would be the "water divide" proved false, and hostile posturing over much time preceded an arbitrated settlement and demarcation. Note that unqualified references in treaties to ridges or crests or even something like "along the range" are not much less common than watershed clauses; e.g.: Afghanistan-U.S.S.R. (crests dividing drainage), Bolivia-Chile (lines joining high peaks), Bulgaria-Greece (sometimes watershed lines, sometimes ridge lines or summit lines), Bulgaria-Rumania (curves down slopes connecting the crestline forming the southern limit of the basin), Burma-India (watersheds), Cambodia-Thailand (watersheds except where delimitation commission picks other natural lines such as ridges or streams), China-Korea (ridges), China-Nepal (ridge lines or watersheds), China-U.S.S.R. (watersheds or ridge lines forming drainage basin), China-Vietnam (watersheds or crests of ridges), Dominican Republic-Haiti (ridge of hills), France-Italy (ridge line or fair line taking into account the mountains), Guyana-Venezuela (ridge or summit of main ridge or highest point of main range), Iran-Turkey (crests forming watersheds), Iran-U.S.S.R. (crest lines or ridge separating waters), Italy-Switzerland (watersheds), Malaysia-Indonesia (ridge line which constitutes major water divide, watersheds or crest line), Malaysia-Thailand (watersheds), Rwanda-Uganda (crest line), Tanzania-Uganda (watersheds), Turkey-U.S.S.R. (watersheds or divides between a Soviet range and a Turkish mountain).

[23] (*Cambodia v. Thailand*) I.C.J. Reports (1962) 6 (Merits) (hereafter cited as I.C.J. Rep.).

[24] For examples of such presumptions, see fn. 22.

when lines joining peaks along a general direction are meant, this does not necessarily mean that there is a geophysical "ridge line" to follow and the treaty should merely sufficiently identify the location of the summits to be joined by straight lines; or

when a line is intended, it is possible to demarcate it on aerial photos of such scale as to show it unambiguously and to incorporate these photos into a protocol or a new treaty.

Under the rule in the *Temple of Preah Vihear Case*, such maps may ultimately become more important than the geophysical "fact" upon which the border was supposed to be based.

Unfortunately, the ability to have a more sophisticated map does not itself solve all the mountain range or other natural feature problems. The line shown on it must in fact be the one both states still agree to be the only one supportable in the future. The Algerian-Libyan border for example, was mapped "provisionally" in 1956 by aerial photos in which the treaty words "small escarpement," "outcrop," and "track in the desert" were used to find the points to join by straight lines on the photos. When oil exploration and settlements near the boundary in 1961 made the legality of the mapped line a question of no small economic significance, the need for something better arose.[25]

B. Territorial claims based upon "occupation"

Unsophisticated attacks have been made upon many boundary treaties whose age guarantees that one of the parties was an imperial power purporting to agree to boundaries for a now-independent state. The onslaught is quite shortsighted. The probable result in the territorial changes area would be, for example, that many states outside Western Europe would have few agreed boundaries at all. What is far more frightening is that, if the doctrine that colonial treaties are invalid because they were "unequal" were to succeed, the states most affected would be those in which title by occupation would be most difficult to establish.

A look at the traditional rules for evidencing occupation will show just how frequently conflict would be nurtured rather than avoided even by the established rules.

1. The "continuous administrative acts" test

One of the commonest ways to establish occupation is by proof that a given area was administered by the country which claims it.

The first area for future conflict lies in claims based upon some administrational zoning which calls the area one's own, as in municipal departments which ostensibly "administer" Adélie Land in one part of

---

[25] See *Int'l Boundary Studies* No. 1 (1961), 2-3, 5.

Antarctica for France and the Ross Dependency in another part by New Zealand. This stems from the trap some lawyers fall into of confusing the "administration" offered to prove *occupation* with the thing to be proven itself. Acts of administration are but pieces of evidence going to make up the establishing of: "actual continuous and peaceful display of the functions of state within a given region." This was the requirement of international law as noted by Max Huber of Switzerland in his award in *The Island of Las Palmas (Miangas) Arbitration*, still one of the most thorough discussions of traditional territorial rules of international law.[26]

The big question then, is this: "Can acts of continuous functioning of central authority be displayed in the border regions of independent former dependencies?" The extent to which the answer for any given border is "No" is the measure of our instability under existing international occupation doctrines should some governing treaty fall.

The second area for future conflict lies in claims of administration by both states which can be supported by some acts on both sides. This was certainly the case with regard to the Chinese-Indian clash over the Aksai Chin salt flats where the Chinese successfully completed surveying and constructing a road at a time when India was also asserting its traditional authority there in other ways. As access to frontier regions increases, the potential for dual displays of sovereignty can be expected to rise as well.

Even in so densely populated a region as the lowlands of Europe, for example, the Belgians and the Dutch went to the World Court in the *Certain Parcels Case* with proofs on each side of continuous administrative acts which each claimed led to sovereignty.[27] The Belgians, for instance, listed the parcels on their military maps and surveys and delivered the post. The Dutch were able to show that they too put them in their surveys and collected some taxes there; further, they kept registers for land transfers, births, marriages, and deaths for those areas. The 10-4 vote of the World Court in favor of Belgium may reflect as much the judges' acceptance of an 1834 delimitation in Belgium's favor as their talent for weighing acts of administration when both sides have such acts to show.

2. The "effective display of sovereignty" test

Another potential time bomb in the future area of territorial disputes is the doctrine that the amount of display of sovereignty re-

---

[26] See Island of Las Palmas (Miangas) Arbitration (*United States v. Netherlands*), (Permanent Court of Arbitration 1928), *United Nations Reports of International Arbitrations*, II, 829.

[27] See Case concerning Sovereignty over Certain Frontier Parcels (*Belgium v. Netherlands*), *I.C.J. Rep.* 209 (1959).

quired in cases of uninhabited regions is far less than that required in those which are inhabited.[28] The trouble here is that, aside from the Antarctic, all presently uninhabited border stretches are now subject to the beginnings of habitation and commercial exploitation.

It is precisely at this moment that the central government is least likely to be exercising continuous functions of sovereignty. First, post-colonial states are yet coping with the gaps which poor preparations by colonial powers have left behind in the administrative field. Second, central governments may not even be aware that their spasmodic displays of sovereignty which were effective in the past when the region was uninhabited are no longer enough because they have not learned about the habitations involved.

3. The "exercise of jurisdiction" test

Another facet about the sparse border regions of Latin America, Asia, and Africa is that the first need to have some governmental display may be only when criminal activity needs to be dealt with.

For such areas, this is an unfortunate means of attempting to establish sovereignty, for it will normally involve no real continuity and it may frequently involve "police" actions by both sides. For example, the Chinese settlers sent into areas of the Soviet Asiatic hinterland by the Peking government may require a squad of Chinese soldiers to handle some outlawry among them. In another part of the same area, Soviet frontier police may be called upon to handle a criminal problem involving Soviet citizens. As a result, each will end up with some exercise of jurisdiction.

4. The "customary" lands test

Perhaps the greatest invitation to conflict in the territorial rules basket is the notion that what one once possessed may still be claimed because of the continuation of some ethnic group—as in the Sudetenland of Czechoslovakia in 1938—which stayed on there. There is no real support for this in international arbitration cases, nor in the texts. It is a wonder, therefore, how persistently the irredentas of this world are made the bases for claims. They are at their most dangerous when they are taken up during "occupation" disputes and made a way of fallaciously establishing the minimum possible right for conflict as in the Chinese claims to customary ownership of the Brahmaputra Valley because the Tibetan geophysical terms proved it was traditionally part of China.

[28] Compare Island of Las Palmas Arbitration, fn. 26 (uncolonized native inhabitants) with the Clipperton Island Arbitration, *Am. J. Int'l L.*, 26 (1932), 390 (uninhabited guano islands) and the Minquiers and Ecrehos Case (*France v. United Kingdom*) *I.C.J. Rep.* (1953), 47 (mostly uninhabited rocky islets in ocean).

C. Territorial claims based upon agreed boundaries

The weaknesses already outlined in some treaty formulations should not lead the unwary into the trap of thinking successful treaty boundaries are impossible. One might establish a hierarchy of boundary stability, in fact, which is somewhat related to the degree of treaty sophistication, as follows:

Most stable   Denoted in a treaty by verified geographical coordinates connected by straight lines, marked on clear aerial photos and large-scale maps deposited with the Secretary-General of the United Nations annexed to a protocol which states they are agreed upon as the boundaries for all time unless modified by a duly ratified treaty.

Demarcated by permanent pillars at intervisible intervals frequently checked and repaired, with 1:25,000 scale or larger maps deposited with the Secretary-General annexed to a protocol which states they are agreed upon as the boundaries for all time unless modified by a duly ratified treaty.

Set out in a treaty by unambiguous descriptions subsequently reduced to an agreed map series in a large scale and demarcated on the ground by a mixed commission.

Set out in a treaty by general descriptions.

Subject to no treaty but continuous occupation in densely populated administrative units coming up to a road or some other non-shifting feature.

Least stable   Subject to no mutually recognized treaty and sparsely peopled.

This is a list of propensities toward instability, all other things being equal. In the real world, other factors will also operate. For example, it is still conceivable, as happened on the British Guiana-Venezuela Boundary in 1931 and 1932, that several sets of geographic coordinates could come out of equally "official" surveys.[29]

There may also be countries with an area of the border never covered by a treaty both states admit to be still binding, as might be the case along an 80-mile stretch of the Afghanistan-Soviet frontier, for example, in which maps of both countries and official administration still follow identical "borders" quite peaceably. On the other hand, two states depositing a treaty map with a legend of permanence might so

[29] *Int'l Boundary Study* No. 21, (1963), 3.

change their relationship that the tanks of one might drive right over permanent boundary pillars to seize new territory.

What the analysis made above does show, however, is some of the pitfalls of presupposing stability under an unchanged existing system of international rules about territory. Once conflict breaks out, nonetheless, this same legal structure becomes one of the few means for managing it which can be carried out without continuing armed clashes or without relying upon threats of even greater military confrontations, as is explored next below.

D. Is there a role left for the present rules on territory in future conflict management?

Thomas Hobbes looked at society as slipping back into a war of each against all unless controlled by centralized power. If his model of the world were an accurate one, we would have to conclude that, in the absence of such a sufficiently assured centralized world power, border disputes will lead to a chaotic disintegration of efforts to make cohesive attacks on the world's social problems.

The actual world in which men have been socialized by interactions, however, has neither assured central power nor chaos. The reason is sometimes mis-simplified, it is true, into the statement that we have an international system of rules and juridical and diplomatic means of applying them. But it is far more often mis-simplified into the statement that we have an international power system of balancing power blocs against one another. There are, of course, both systems at work.

The truth is, nevertheless, that when the signs of integration are present it is never because of the power system, but always because of the international institutions founded in rules and procedures. Vice versa, when the absence of chaos owes itself to the maintenance of some power balance, we always have some implied kinds of "war"— whether an open one, as in South Vietnam, or subliminal, as between the Soviet Union and the United States in the Middle East after June 1967. Whatever such conflicts involving a "balance of powers" may be, the one thing they are not is "a cohesive attack upon the world's social problems."

In the case of territorial disputes, where "live war" is threatened by the nature of the dispute itself, the existing rules may provide the mechanism for shifting from dispute to greater cooperation in some limited cases. For example, they operate in cases of partners already cooperating so as to permit them to reduce agreed boundaries to settled terms by demarcation on the ground, or even to change them where hardships result. For instance, it was the existing rules on treaty exchanges of territory which provided the framework for the 1949

Italian-Swiss agreement to cede to Switzerland enough land one mile inside Italy to put up a hydroelectric plant on the Reno di Lei which would supply power to Switzerland through a tunnel under Italian territory.

Where parties have already reached a noncooperative state, however, territorial rules manage armed aspects of conflict only. That is to say they have sometimes provided a framework to shift the conflict from the military arena to the diplomatic or judicial one; they have, on the other hand, at best an extremely poor record of shifting from harmful conflict to swift resumption of cooperation.

Perhaps a prime example is the *Temple of Preah Vihear Case* in which the Cambodians took the Thais to the World Court rather than evict the Thai soldiers from a Buddhist temple. The operative rule which took the conflict down from military escalation was the earlier agreement of both countries to the compulsory jurisdiction of the World Court.

The next level at which the Thais and Cambodians were kept from fighting was their expectancy—within the framework of international legal doctrines—that the Court process would result in their vindication.

For example, the Thais expected:

> the Court would hold the treaty between the French and the Siamese to be still binding upon Cambodia after independence under the normal doctrines of succession; and

> the Court would then look at the plain language of the Treaty and where it said "following the watershed" would find the border to be either at the cliff edge or along the watershed line "proven" by Thai survey evidence to put the Temple in Thailand.

The Cambodians expected:

> The Court would hold that the survey party map made by the French officer in pursuance of the survey obligations in the Treaty was the best evidence as to the "fact" that the Temple of Preah Vihear lies on the Cambodian side of the waterdivide, despite the fact that the Mixed Boundary Commission never formally ratified the survey map;

> the Court would also hold that a ceremonial visit from the Siamese at which no protest was made to the flying of the French flag over the Temple stopped the Thais from now claiming the Temple was on their side of the divide; and

> the Court would say further that Thailand could not be allowed to constantly reopen the question of where the boundary lay and had

already in fact accepted the map placing the Temple in French Indochinese territory in earlier negotiations.

The beauty of the practice of international law is that here, as in so many other disputes, one can find precedents and rules for all of these positions and no single one of these expectations can be considered to have been unreasonable. Thus, the traditional system provided an arena of combat, short of a trial-at-arms, to which to shift hostilities.

In that sense, it successfully prevented armed conflict and the consequences of it. This is indeed a legitimate function of the system. It did not, however, foster cooperation because it kept competing spirits high.

This in itself does not diminish the ability of the system to function as a conflict-management device where more cooperative devices cannot—or just will not—be brought into play. On the other hand, it does diminish the ability of the international community during the next 25 years to rely on this traditional system to permit, say, enough cooperation in Southeast Asia for full development of the Mekong River's potential for alleviating poverty in both countries. There is nevertheless, a role to play. In addition to the danger that we do not see beyond that role to measures and methods leading to greater mutual aid, there is a very real danger that even existing rules will not be allowed by parties or organizations on the international scene to play this conflict-managing role.

The Israeli postmandate situation posed just such a danger. One way to assure that the legal system will be unable to shift hostilities to a lower level is to prevent new rules from emerging to deal functionally with new situations. What was needed after the mandate terminated was a clear-cut rule to deal with the General Assembly's authority to handle mandates—when asked by the mandatory power to do what it could not by itself accomplish successfully when that mandatory subsequently refuses to either vote for or against the General Assembly's disposition or to associate itself with it. The members of the General Assembly who asked the Security Council to enforce their Partition Plan and who subsequently voted for Israel's admission acted on the assumption that the existing international law of the Charter did not make the Assembly's acts ineffective merely for a reluctance of the terminating mandatory to associate itself with them, while asserting it "would not impede them." The armed conflicts which ensued indeed were both heightened and prolonged by misperceptions that the world juridical system had failed to make a rule to fill the void, and that the power system was the exclusive arena in which to operate.

It must be remembered that the Arab states did not ignore the legal system. They proposed, and Subcommittee 2 of the Ad Hoc Committee on the Palestine Question asked the full committee to propose, that the General Assembly ask the International Court of Justice for an advisory opinion on eight of the legal questions involved.[30] The 21 years of armed conflict which followed should have demonstrated solidly enough that the ability of Rule of Law to perform its arena-shifting role often depends upon speedy adjudication of the authority to apply those rules whenever this is called into question.

II. THE FUTURE DEVELOPMENT OF "PREDICTORS" FOR TERRITORIAL CONFLICTS

It is necessary to spot areas where disputes over borders are likely to occur before open clashes break out; it is even more vital to spot those aspects within territorial disputes that tend to prevent later shifts to mutual aid. A few examples are suggested below of possible lines for more sophisticated predictive tools which may be expected to come from international lawyers and social scientists during the years ahead.

A. Dispute maintenance by international characterization

The truth is that certain situations can be predicted to lead to conflict because the molds into which the international community has placed them are ones in which nonconflict resolutions are impossible.

As we have seen, Israel's situation in the Middle East is just such an instance. In November 1947, upon a reference to it by the United Kingdom, as the mandate authority, the General Assembly exercised its responsibilities over the mandate of Palestine to provide for that territory after the mandate was to be terminated. In constitutional terms, the decision to divide the area into a Jewish state and an Arab state was one which only the inheritor of the League Council's political authority could make; the obvious heir to that authority under the Charter was the General Assembly,[31] and the International Court of

---

[30] Draft Resolution of November 11, 1947. United Nations document number A/AC. 14/32; see Louis B. Sohn, *The United Nations in Action* (Mineola 1958), 29-30.

[31] The Charter envisaged the General Assembly, rather than the Security Council, as having responsibility over nonstrategic mandates:

Decisions of the General Assembly on important questions shall be made by a two-thirds majority of the members present and voting, including recommendations with respect to . . . the admission of new Members of the United Nations and questions relating to the operation of the trusteeship system. Article 18 (2).

The trusteeship system shall apply if placed under trusteeship agreements, to territories now held under mandate. Article 77 (1).

The trusteeship system shall not apply to territories which have become Members of the United Nations relations among which shall be based on respect for the principle of sovereign equality. Article 78.

Until trusteeship agreements are made with the General Assembly nothing shall be construed . . . to alter . . . existing international instruments, but this shall

Justice has so held in the *International Status of South-West Africa Case*.[32] The Security Council and the General Assembly voted the admission of the Jewish state as a new member of the world community under the name "Israel" and the Economic and Social Council elected that member to its Social Commission.[33]

Despite the acknowledged existence, then, of this United Nations member, the world community has continually characterized disputes about that area as "The Palestine Question." The net result is to re-enforce statements by some officials and radio commentators in the region to the effect that the unaccepted attempt to create a Jewish state and an Arab one, where "only a single Arab state would be a just disposition," must be completely reversed for there to be justice in the area. Since this makes all other concessions merely intermediate rather than stabilizing ones, this very characterization helps to shape an environment in which nonconflict resolutions simply are not possible. This is not to say that there are no other forces involved in that environment; however, a surprising number of them turn on this continued international semanticism.

Similar international characterizations have like re-enforcing effects in other areas, as through such word symbols as "The Vietnam Question" and "The Korean Question."[34]

What must be done, therefore, in the future development of international law is to analyze existing characterizations which produce non-peaceful resolutions; through this analysis, perhaps, a sensitivity to the undesirable long-term effects involved may also lead to prediction of

---

not be interpreted as giving grounds for delay or postponement of . . . the agreements for placing mandated . . . territories under the trusteeship system. Article 80.

The functions of the United Nations with regard to trusteeship agreements for all areas not designated as strategic, including the approval of the terms of the trusteeship agreements and of their alteration or amendment, shall be exercised by the General Assembly. Article 85 (1).

32 "International Status of South-West Africa," *I.C.J. Rep.*, (1950), 128 (advisory opinion). It could be argued that the World Court's opinion requires termination by the mandatory authority and the General Assembly to be in accord with the League Covenant rules, and therefore with its rule of unanimity, thus the General Assembly's recommendation would have no substitute effect. Such a restrictive interpretation would, however, disrobe the General Assembly of the functions envisaged for it, as the Secretary Council implied in its July 15, 1948 Resolution S/902 which kept the Palestine truce in force "subject to further *decision* by the Security Council or the *General Assembly*." (Emphasis added.)

33 See *Report by the President to the Congress for the Year 1951, United States Participation in the United Nations* (Washington 1952), 297.

34 We will never know to what extent the United Nations Command's decision to cross the 38th parallel with such sanguine results is owed to such characterizations, nor to what extent that bloodshed finds its origins in similar characterizations in February 1949 when the North Korean government's telegram to the Security Council requesting admission was not referred to the Security Council's membership committee. See same, 124.

dead-end routes in conflict management before they are chosen—or frozen—by the participants.

B. Dispute maintenance by national characterizations

It is not fair, however, to suggest that only the world community has played this game of fanning the embers by symbolic labeling. The most pressing "territorial" problem of the next 30 years for instance is probably that of defining the territory of the "Republic of China," set forth in Article 23 of the United Nations Charter as one of the five permanent members of the Security Council. Yet this is actually a characterization problem rather than a legal one.

To the extent that the "Republic of China" government on Taiwan claims to govern an area of some 4,300,000 square miles with over 700 million people, it characterizes the irreducible question as: "Which government is the single government of all of pre-1894 China?"

To the extent that the "People's Republic of China" government in Peking claims that the minimum Chinese territory which can be recognized as under its authority includes Taiwan's 13 million people plus the Pescadores, Quemoy, Matsu, and Taiwan islands, it characterizes the irreducible question also as: "Which government is the single government of all of pre-1894 China?"

These identical characterizations have acted as much as any other factor to heighten the barriers to resolution of questions in this area, including membership questions in international organizations, many of which would now contain both governments and their territories if their nationally imposed semantic hurdles were removed.

Other examples, such as the characterizations placed on their national territory by the two states formed from what was once "Germany," show this is not unique to the two states committed to the ideology of one China.

J. David Singer has suggested that there is a general phenomenon in international relations of dealing in fact on the international level while thinking on the national level of analysis.[35] Since international law has traditionally focused on the nation-state as the actor on the international scene, it is not surprising to find some mystical "reality value" is accorded by other states to purely national characterizations. Thus, each disputant tries to get its allies to accept, cling to, and hence re-enforce such characterizations.

For example, from the point of view of conflict management, one of the most important of such sets of national level characterizations is that placed upon Jammu and Kashmir by the Pakistani and Indian governments. Traditional international law re-enforces rather than restrains the symbolic maintenance of conflict here.

[35] J. David Singer, "The Level-of-Analysis Problem in International Relations," in Falk and Mendlovitz (fn. 6), 235-50.

If, as the Pakistani government has maintained, neither the Indian Independence Act nor the United Nations Charter can be so interpreted as to permit the non-Moslem ruler of a largely Moslem state to "opt for India" upon independence, then the existing occupancy by Indian troops and administrators of that part of Kashmir east of the cease-fire line is of land "outside India."

If, as the Indian government has maintained, the same two sources of valid rules authorized the non-Moslem ruler's accession to India, then the territory occupied by Indian authorities is not only properly "India," but so is that west of the cease-fire line now occupied by Pakistani troops.

Once the nation characterizes its area as legitimately part of national territory, interference from outside, such as a recommendation for a plebiscite, becomes unwarranted. The result: nonconflict resolutions become impossible.

What is needed is a greater flexibility in characterization which admits that some parts of a nation's territory may be "sources of dispute," and that special rules are required for such parts. It is not necessary in every case to submit the matter of arbitration, as India and Pakistan successfully did to end hostilities over the Rann of Kutch. It is not necessary to submit to a plebiscite followed by an investigation into its fairness, as was done by Malaysia when it approved a United Nations Mission to look into the Sabah (North Borneo) and Sarawak plebiscites which opted for federation.[36] A simple sensitivity to the greater than average interest a neighboring state has in the treatment accorded inhabitants of the disputed territory—a subject more fully explored below—would often be enough to shift from the purely national characterization level to one where conflicts become resolvable.

Again, the solution for the next few decades is to concentrate, not on resolving territorial disputes at the level in which national characterizations are frozen, but rather on changing the characterizations themselves. Here world stress on transborder river development, transborder power grids from hydroelectric or nuclear sources, or integration into regional economic associations will help to make those changes.

CAVEAT

The shift in level of analysis suggested by Singer is not enough if the national characterization merely receives re-enforcement by corporate adoption at regional or worldwide levels. One can envisage many border or territory conflicts which can be re-enforced by adoption of some

---

[36] Discussed in Thomas M. Franck and Lawrence D. Cherkis, "The Problem of Fact-Finding in International Disputes," *Western Reserve Law Review*, 18 (July 1967) 1483-1524, at 1496-99.

national frames-of-reference at the higher level in NATO, the Warsaw Pact, the Arab League, the OAS, the EEC, or the OAU.

C. Dispute maintenance by characterizations under rules of international law

It is equally unfair to absolve international lawyers of their responsibility for the creation of situations in which nonconflict shifts to cooperation become impossible. A look at only two types of characterization suggested for international law at various times discloses their role in territorial disputes.

1. The "aggressive war" label

Ending an era in which international jurists accepted wars as legitimate tools of diplomacy to enforce international legal rights when pacific means failed, the Covenant of the League of Nations required members to respect and preserve the territorial integrity of all other members against external aggression.[37] The events which followed helped to crystallize a rule which made a war of aggression illegal and made nonrecognition of the fruits of that war at the very least permissible, and for many states required:[38]

> *1923*—League's Draft Treaty of Mutual Assistance declared aggressive war "criminal," unless to enforce an arbitral award, World Court verdict, or unanimous League Council recommendation without intending to violate the territorial integrity of the other state.

> *1924*—League's Draft Protocol for Pacific Settlement of International Disputes asserted a war of aggression violates "the solidarity of the members of the international community" and signatories would have been bound "in no case to resort to war with one another."

> *1925*—League Assembly resolution reiterated that a war of aggression is an international crime.

> *1927*—League Assembly unanimously adopted resolution prohibiting all wars of aggression and enjoining states to employ every pacific means to settle disputes "of every description."

> *1928*—21 American states unanimously resolved that all aggression is prohibited as "illicit" and to employ all pacific means to settle conflicts among them.

[37] Article 10, League of Nations Covenant. Lord Curzon reported this guarantee made "aggressive war, aiming at territorial aggrandisement or political advantage . . . expressly forbidden." See Ian Brownlie, *International Law and the Use of Force by States* (Oxford 1963), 62.

[38] Summarized from Ian Brownlie's study (fn. 37), 66-122, 413-19, and Whiteman (fn. 14), v, 874-965.

—General Treaty for the Renunciation of Wars[39] signed at Paris and ratified by 63 nations condemned resource to war to solve controversies, renounced it as an instrument of national policies, and agreed never to seek to solve disputes or conflicts among them except by pacific means.

1929—United States sought to have parties adhere to Pact of Paris obligations in China-U.S.S.R. border hostilities.

1932—Stimson Doctrine of non-recognition of "any situation, treaty or agreement brought about by means contrary to the pact of Paris" enunciated in notes given China and Japan when a Japanese "Manchukuo" government was set up in Manchuria after armed conquest.

—League Assembly resolution made it "incumbent" upon members not to recognize any situation or agreement brought about by means contrary to the Pact of Paris.

—During the Chaco War, the 19 other American states declared to Bolivia and Paraguay they would not recognize "the validity of territorial acquisitions" obtained by force of arms.

1933—Saavedra Lamas Pact among 21 American nations condemned wars of aggression and agreed not to recognize any territorial arrangement not obtained by pacific means nor the validity of the occupation or acquisition of territories by force of arms.

—Montevideo Convention on Rights and Duties of States established as the rule of conduct for parties "the precise obligation not to recognize territorial acquisition or special advantages" obtained by force, whether of arms, by threats or by "any other effective coercive measure."

1935—Italian invasion of Ethiopia branded as aggression by League Council but Ethiopia fails to get Council vote on non-recognition of Italy's territorial claims. Between 1936 and 1938 some 29 League members did take some action amounting to recognition; the United States and the Soviet Union did not.

1938—German "annexation" of Austria was not followed by League non-recognition, although the United States tried to avoid *de jure* recognition of Nazi sovereignty.

1939—Dr. Benes of Czechoslovakia asked League Council to invoke League powers "convinced" that no member would recognize the German and Hungarian invasions. The Council took no

---

[39] Known in Europe as the Briand-Kellogg Pact, in some English language materials and in the United States as the Kellogg-Briand Pact, and in official instances frequently referred to as the Pact of Paris.

action, although some members establishing consular relations with the new governments did so *de facto* rather than *de jure*; Hungary, Spain, Switzerland, Poland, Japan, the Vatican, and "Manchukuo" alone granted *de jure* recognition.

—King Zog of Albania asked the League members not to recognize Italian take-over. The Council branded it "aggression," by innuendo, and took no action.

—League Assembly and Council condemned Soviet invasion of Finland as aggression; expelled Soviet Union.

From the history of this rule, four things follow: first, insofar as norm-formulation goes, there is a solidly established international legal principle that territorial changes worked by a war of aggression are not to be recognized. Second, insofar, as practice goes, outside the Western Hemisphere there is no uniformity of practice regarding it. Third, even when applied, the rule itself has never resulted in the voluntary relinquishment of seized territory—the 1956 withdrawal of British, French, and Israeli forces from Sinai excepted. Fourth, with the passage of time, application of the rule can in fact imbed conflict into a situation which is crying out for a shift to the cooperative arena.[40]

There is, of course, much room for internationalization of conflicts in the sense that regional or international bodies may work to move them from the military level and, hopefully, to the neighborly one. The consequence of concentrating solely on the first and ignoring the second is to mistake the success of the world community in embodying nonrecognition of wars of aggression into international legislation for success in obtaining ultimate return to nonhostile relations.

The nonrecognition rule has the advantage of its simplicity, as the underlying syllogism shows: (1) "Territorial claims owed to a war of aggression cannot be recognized." (2) "Country A is in possession of Country B's province of Athelia because of a war of aggression." (3) "Therefore, Country A's new province of Athelia cannot be recognized." The trouble with it is that it is a dead-end device least likely to permit normal relations to exist. If this rule were part of a system developed to the point where the world community would displace Country A from Athelia whenever such a situation occurred, the rule would be a good one. Where, as for the foreseeable next few decades, it is part of a world peace system in which displacement of the Korean conflict kind is not likely to be repeated as often as it is passed by, some better rule is needed than this kind of dead-ended one of blanket nonrecognition.

[40] See e.g., Karl Jaspers, "Initial Political Thinking about the New Fact" in Falk and Mendlovitz (fn. 6) 373-82, at 379 ("unjust boundaries must be legally revisable").

Finally, in the future, armistice lines may well become even more common than they are today. The length of time no possible solution can be had to the situation leading to the initial hostilities may—admittedly not "must"—be a product of the nonrecognition doctrine. This is especially true since efforts by United Nations bodies to end the fighting and keep the peace will inevitably move away from the League pattern of labeling one side the aggressor. Thus both sides will have their views as to the other side's "aggression" re-enforced. Both sides will "know" that international law demands nonrecognition of territories seized by the other. And both sides will "know" international organizations and foreign offices which do not accept that characterization are being unreasonable and partial.

2. The "unequal treaty" or "colonial treaty" label

So long as international law assumes that a useful fiction for rules about conduct among nations is that all states are equal in their sovereignty in entering into treaties, boundary treaties of permanence can result.

Thus, before discarding this fiction, the international legal community should look closely at the consequences for boundary stability in regions previously subject to colonial agreements. While the present Sino-Soviet disputes about the effect of Russian-Chinese treaties may be the most dramatic because of the 4,150-mile border between them, it is far from the only border entirely based upon treaties made before the present form of government arose.

The following list shows but a sampling of those countries where 100 percent of the border between them rested solely upon colonial treaties, decrees, or agreements as of 1966.

Algeria-Libya	Mauretania-Senegal
British Honduras-Guatemala	Morocco-Spanish Sahara
China-Hong Kong	Mozambique-Tanzania
China-Korea	Rwanda-Uganda
China-U.S.S.R.	Rwanda-Tanzania
China-North Vietnam	Sudan-Chad
Congo (Leopoldville)-Rwanda	Sudan-Libya
Congo (Leopoldville)-Tanzania	Sudan-United Arab Republic
Guyana-Brazil	Tanzania-Burundi
Guyana-Venezuela	Tanzania-Kenya
Indonesia-Malaysia	Tanzania-Malawi
Laos-Burma	Thailand-Cambodia
Laos-Cambodia	United Arab Republic-Libya
Libya-Chad	Zambia-Southern Rhodesia
Malaysia-Thailand	Zambia-Tanzania

The large number of African states which have a vested interest in conflict-free borders, and to the extent that they are unable to reach current agreement, in the continuation of border treaties, is great. It is an awareness of the powder-keg nature of boundary problems that led the Council of Ministers of the Organization for African Unity to resolve never to fight over boundaries, but to settle all disputes about them either by negotiation or, as a last resort, by arbitration. While there will be a problem for those few African states which announced they would not continue in effect earlier treaties not expressly reconfirmed, it is worth examining whether the others will profit most by stable succession to border treaties, whether among colonial powers or not.

D. Dispute maintenance in sparsely occupied territory

Just as one can pinpoint the borders on which nonresolvable conflicts are most likely by analyzing them in terms of international characterizations, national characterizations, and characterizations under international law, so too can one foresee the special susceptibility to conflict of borders which pass through sparse regions.

If we assume that neighboring governments will not, in any 30-year period, always be at their friendliest, border wars will be the most likely form of that unfriendliness where border expanses are wild or thinly settled.

The special vulnerability of borders along these sparsely settled regions is: (1) it normally takes a relatively small amount of military force to create overwhelming superiority over opposing guard units, and thus the temptation to grab them in an era of hostile feelings is backed up by military assessments of assured victory; and (2) just as often, on the other hand, conflict on them will be by "creeping expansions."

The first type of military adventure leads either to a relatively accepted fait accompli or a prolonged era of nonmilitary hostility. In the event of miscalculation of the local dissatisfaction with the opposing government, as in Finland in 1939 and in Cuba in 1961, the initiator may even be faced with the possibility of prolonged warfare.

The second type, however, is actually the most dangerous. For one thing, it lacks the drama which normally arouses world concern at an early stage. For another, it results in incremental changes very much like the putting together of enough plutonium to exceed the critical mass in an A-bomb. Finally, to the extent that refugees from one decade's regime may become arguable transborder settlers for the next regime, the thinly policed border regions represent major humanitarian problems as well.

E. The dilemma of the self-fulfilling prophecy

In any approach which focuses on the weakness of existing border rules, there is a danger that the statement "Those rules are less stabilizing than you think," will make them even more so. At any given moment, there will even be boundaries with some unresolved past dispute that appears to be no source of conflict. Isn't it rashly fanning the embers, one might say, to stress such possibilities for brushfires before they occur?

There certainly is such a danger. There is a danger, too, that reminding people that the technology to produce nuclear bombs is now a worldwide one will give some government an idea it would not otherwise have had. But neither problem will go away by using the "ostrich scholarship" which has more often proven to be the vice of statesmen and academicians than their virtue.

What is needed to meet both dangers is less preoccupation with rules of international law and more creative development of new devices or institutions. Nowhere is this more true than in territorial cases.

III. Developing "Shifters" as a Conflict Management Device

There are many tools in the international lawyer's kit to shift potential conflicts from dead-ended routes to levels where cooperation is possible. The following list is far from exhaustive; future developments too, can be expected to add to them.

A. Raising the floor of minimal human rights

One of the sources of interest in an old border dispute is a cry of persecution from former citizens across the border. Thus, border stability is inextricably interwoven with the human rights aspects of border region residents. Treatment of Montagnard tribesmen along mountain borders, of Ibo tribes living across national boundaries, of Rwandans in Uganda, or of Mexicans in the United States as anything less than first-class citizens can be expected, ultimately to play some ember-fanning role.

1. Enlarge protection of minority groups

One approach, suggested elsewhere,[41] is to stress the need to increase by large jumps world efforts for protection of minority groups, by, among other devices:

Codes for protection of minority frontier groups, such as the one put forth by the Delhi World Rule of Law conference;

41 See Wilkes, "Conflict Avoidance" (fn. 1), 740-41.

development of the good offices of the High Commissioner for Refugees, and perhaps the increase in effectiveness of that office by creation of Regional High Commissioners at a high prestige level;

institutionalizing the present obligation of the High Commissioner for Refugees to represent the international law rights of stateless persons to be free from denials of justice;

use of more detailed equal protection clauses in treaties to spell out safeguards for minority groups descended from those of foreign origin;

where known border minority problems exist, under the aegis of third-party mediators such as regional social councils to match regional economic ones, work out detailed agreements for minimum rights;[42] and

adoption by states ready to do so of some international minority complaint investigation device, such as that proposed by the Human Rights Committee of the International Law Association at Buenos Aires of 1968.

2. Enlarging devices to obtain redress of grievances in general

Greater abilities of any citizen to challenge failures by officials to abide by the law are needed to shift minority grievances from border conflict-provoking levels, by, among other devices:

creation of more regional courts for civil rights protection, such as the European Human Rights Tribunal, possibly with an "incarcerated prisoner writ" analogous to habeas corpus upon which to obtain summary preliminary relief on prima facie showings of violations of standards administered by the regional courts;[43]

ratification of civil rights conventions with implementing legislation;

extensions of franchise and rights to form political interest groups;

putting into effect procedures for at least one administrative appeal from any adverse administrative decision, with simplified procedures for those in hinterland areas; and

separating military tribunal functions for military men from civilian tribunal functions to be handled by civilian judges, especially in areas where long-term hostilities around borders are foreseeable.

---

[42] Such regional Social Councils would be the logical result of adoption of amendments to the Charter proposed by Grenville Clark and Louis B. Sohn in *World Peace Through World Law* 3rd edn. (Cambridge 1966) to divide in ECOSOC into two separate councils.

[43] As proposed at the Washington World Peace Through Law Conference, September 1965, by Luis Kutner; compare regional United Nations court proposals in Clark and Sohn (fn. 42).

B. Making the boundary make as little difference as possible in daily life

Even among neighborly states, border irritants develop where the border creates difficulties for local inhabitants. A look at some activities which remove potential sources of trouble provides a yardstick against which future progress in this area can be measured.[44]

1. Freedom to cross borders

Inability to visit relatives is a guarantee of border friction whether across armistice lines or Berlin walls or normal boundaries. One device to handle this has been the treaty guarantee of visitation access, as between Rumania and Bulgaria in 1948 for relatives in frontier regions.

Another device, where visits are freely allowed but procedures are irritatingly cumbersome for those close to the border, is unilateral or agreed simplification of regulations for crossing the boundary, as by the increasingly widespread recognition of visa or passport-free travel.

Finally—and probably of even greater importance in the future— devices must be instituted which will avoid humiliations from checkpoint transit. Searches, delays, and border guard attitudes will play a role in direct proportion to the rising traffic to be expected in the future.

2. Freedom of economic movement

The trend toward greater freedom of economic activity across borders, as in the European Community's commitment to permit work anywhere in the EEC, has a two-edged effect on border squabbles. On the "plus" side, it enables a businessman or worker to ignore the border in choosing where to look for a job or a customer. On the "minus" side, it now makes him especially sensitive to: (1) differences in taxes, administrative burdens, or civil rights, and (2) discriminatory practices affecting him.[45]

3. Free use of communicating routes

For water routes, the crystallizing in international law of truly "free navigation" makes it immaterial who has control of part of a border river, as under the cases and customs on which Articles 13 and 14 of the International Law Association's "Helsinki Rules" of 1966 on Waters of International Rivers are based.

[44] An earlier stress on making boundary differences less critical was presented by the late Geographer of the Department of State, S. Wittemore Boggs, in *International Boundaries* (Washington 1940), 201, from which some of the following devices were taken.

[45] For a discussion of this impact from the rise in numbers of "Transnational Man," see Daniel Wilkes, "The World of 1992," *Western Reserve Law Review*, 18 (July 1967), 1449-82, at 1472.

For land routes, then, what is needed are devices to shift disputed regions to cooperating ones by ensuring transit equally free of red tape when they are the natural routes serving border areas. The present habit of treating these links on land so that the border keeps people on one side from using them even when they parallel a long border is going to be increasingly irritating in sparsely occupied regions in dispute. Thus new devices to shift them from the brushfire level will only be those which make the location of the border have no effect on use of uniquely placed communications.

Joint management schemes have tried to do this, at times successfully, but at times unevenly, as in Bolivia's difficulties with Chile over their Joint Arica-La Paz Railway. Also tried has been the device of putting a road, which intersects existing borders annoyingly frequently, into one state, while guaranteeing the right of those from across the border to use it as if it were their own, as in postwar border adjustments between Belgium and West Germany.

In the next 30 years, it may also be necessary to work out regional management schemes to internationalize the very links in disputed areas which have become cause for temptation or complaint.

Finally, the constructive employment of the "free-zone" device, currently used between Swiss and French border regions, may be needed to achieve the same shifting effect for land route locales, where border prediction augurs border friction, that is achieved on rivers by "free navigation" rules.

4. Access to resources

Rising geoeconomic sophistications—which international lawyers are so quick to see in law-of-the-sea problems—are normally ignored in assessing future border stability. With the United Nations agencies, however, making nation-by-nation resource surveys routinely, and with satellite surveying for resources on its way, each side to a potential dispute will eventually know full well what resource stakes are involved.

Needed, then, for the future will be a wide span of devices to shift possible disputants to cooperative arenas, as by:

agreeing to joint use of power from a border hydroelectric dam, as on the Yalu River;

agreeing to free navigational use of a hinterland river for transport of resources, whether that river remains a border one or not, as would be increasingly possible under greater use of fixed border rules such as that in the China-Nepal Treaty which keeps the old boundary no matter how the river changes its course;

encouraging transborder development projects with World Bank assistance, as was contemplated in the creation of 180-mile-long Lake Kariba between Zambia and Southern Rhodesia, or by other funds, as in the jointly financed Iranian-Soviet power-irrigation complex which is to quadruple the crop acreage on the Iranian side;

experimenting with the creation of small transborder administrative planning units for development along rational lines, as was begun for a 30-kilometer stretch on the Czech-Hungarian border in 1960 and then expanded in December 1961 to include joint planning for the Ipoly River basin, including reservoir construction for irrigation and flood control;[46] or

creating border zones where development can take place without regard to national ownership because the governmental rewards for that development are shared between potential disputants, as was done in the agreement between Jordan and Saudi Arabia shifting their border some 9 miles farther south along the Gulf of Aqaba but sharing profits should oil be discovered in a defined zone.[47]

5. Greater degrees of regional integration

A final development that tends to make the boundaries between states less explosive is the growth of regional integration. The dispute about a border may still exist within a regional economic or political organization; a host of institutional exceptions and on-going independent activities, however, make that dispute one less likely both to lead to armed conflict or to impede multinational development.

C. Providing a World Boundary Commission to fix boundaries once and for all

It is easy to say we have survived border conflicts and boundary powderkegs for so long, we can survive them yet a while longer. The truth is that we have not survived them, and the armaments and stakes involved are constantly rising.

It is easy, dangerously easy, to fall back into 19th-century patterns of thinking about boundaries. There is something as intriguing about a border dispute as there is about an act of piracy or the assassination of a president. It provides international lawyers with a clear field in which to operate, and—as we have seen—a wide variety of scalpels with which to go to work on the arguments of the other side.

But there is something entirely anachronistic about a boundary dispute. The transitional international law following the Charter is one

46 *Int'l Boundary Study* No. 66 (1966), 7-8.
47 *Int'l Boundary Study* No. 60 (1965), 4.

looking to a fulfillment of *human* needs for betterment and survival through the international system, not state betterment and survival through human lives.

Further, to meet legitimate aspirations of the real participants—as contrasted with the useful fictitional ones of state or organization—there must be gains in use of resources and growth of wealth to distribute of a magnitude that is just not possible for each state acting by itself. This need for cooperative efforts is highest among bordering states. Ergo, it is precisely among bordering states that world public order must structure the preconditions for those efforts. The following proposals aim to start thinking about the type of institutional changes required.

1. A World Boundary Commission

Provisions for a World Boundary Commission, drawing on an expanded United Nations Cartographic Office, to meet the definite need for impartial demarcation and arbitration skills in newly emerging states, have been set forth elsewhere.[48]

It is important here to stress that a new type of organization is needed: one that can do more than bring its good offices to the disputants, and one that also has the resources to bring joint aid into the pattern of settlement.

2. The Fixed-Border Depository

Nations are currently depositing maps showing their borders. This is done as part of the worldwide project for the International Map of the World to the Millionth Scale. In some cases, they are even encouraged to deposit a map which is jointly agreed upon. Nevertheless, the rules for the "Map" require the legend to then be superimposed on each that it has no political significance.

There is no reason why these rules cannot be changed to allow those states whose rapport at a given time is such that they are willing to agree to deposit a single set of border maps to do so.[49] These maps should be both to the millionth scale and to the largest scales available, with the legend on them that both parties have agreed that this is their border permanently, never to be changed except by (1) an agreement between them certified to be authentic and binding by the executive branch of a World Boundary Commission or some other impartial agency, or (2) a binding decision of the Security Council, the General Assembly, or a competent regional agency.

[48] See Wilkes, "Conflict Avoidance" (fn. 1), 745-47.
[49] Compare the Algerian-Tunisian announcement that they would continue to hold meetings to establish a "temporary frontier line" between them because of oil exploitation in the border zone. Radio Rabat, January 19, 1967, cited in *Africa Research Bulletin*, IV (1967), 696.

3. Moratoria on Boundary Disputes

Finally, in cases where disputes are not resolved, the World Boundary Commission or an appropriate international agency can solicit Agreements to Disagree, or "moratoria" analogous to those in the Antarctic which Chile, Argentina, New Zealand, Australia, France, and Norway have agreed to as to their claims in that region. There the period chosen was 30 years: a similar period would seem appropriate here. Possible optional clauses in connection with such moratoria are suggested by the discussions above: i.e., sharing of resource profits with a third party to supervise the accounting, joint ventures, joint management, minority guarantees, and reduction of administrative barriers at the borders.

4. Is there a role in a fixed-border system for plebiscites?

The history of elective choice by border peoples of the side of the border which they prefer to live on is largely one of postwar and pre-independence elections.[50] The key to the success of the best of these has lain in the presence of relatively disinterested soldiers in control.

Where, on the other hand, one side has kept its soldiers present—as in the Saar under German influence or in Arica during the abortive plebiscite scheduled for a choice between Chile and Peru—the plebiscite record is mostly an unhappy one. For instance, in the Tacna and Arica situation, outside expectancies that a "free choice" would end the dispute over these Chilean-held territories proved to be naive. In fact, when the Committee on Prerequisites set as its first goal the reduction of Chilean army and constabulary units *inside* the area to a point equal to Peruvian forces just *outside* that area, it recognized the nullifying effect of "elections" under any but the most disinterested army's control.[51]

The trouble is that, especially when already independent states are involved, practically every plebiscite situation is never one of disinterest to the army of one of the potential "winners." In the Tacna and Arica case, the regulations provided for fines or imprisonment, in theory, if intimidation, election frauds, or violence occurred.[52] Would

[50] See especially the comprehensive work of Sarah Wambaugh, *Plebiscites Since the World War* (Washington 1933), I and II (postwar), and Marcel Merle, "Les plébiscites organisés par les Nations Unies," *Annuaire français de droit international,* 1961, 425 (pre-independence); see also, Franck and Cherkis (fn. 36) (after independence). On 18th and 19th century plebiscites for Belgian towns, Mayence, Naples, Natal, Nice, Northern Slesvig, Norway-Sweden, Piacenza, Rome, Saint-Barthelemy Island, Savoy, Sicily, and Venice, see discussions in British Foreign Office, *Plebiscites* (Confidential Handbook n.p. 1919), and British Foreign Office, *Peace Handbooks* (London 1920), xxv.

[51] Plebiscitary Commission, Tacna-Arica Arbitration *El Arbitraje de Tacna y Arica—Actas de la Comisión Plebiscitaria* (Lima 1928), I, 866-87.

[52] Plebiscitary Commission, Tacna-Arica Arbitration, *The Registration and Election Regulations of the Tacna-Arica Plebiscite* (La Paz n.d. [1926)], Articles 114-17.

it not be a foregone conclusion, nevertheless, that (1) the Peruvians would protest to the Plebiscitary Commission that a mere reduction was a pitiful way to establish conditions for a "free" election?[53] and (2) the Chilean troops would not of their own initiative suppress coercive groups or the violent pre-election campaigns of local pro-Chilean newspapers?[54]

Yet this major precondition for successful peaceful shifts of territory from one state to another by plebiscite—the presence of enough outside "policers" to ensure the absence of duress—will become less likely, rather than more likely, in future situations. This is so because the disinterest of the colonial power, as in the Togoland plebiscite, will have become a thing of the past, and occupation by an allied force after a world war will have become an interesting, but irrelevant historical experience.

This is not to say that there will be no role for plebiscites. There may yet be cases in which the Security Council, General Assembly, or regional body has accepted the responsibility for supplying such outside troops (and obtaining the withdrawal of the local ones). There may also be cases in which the domestic pressures which nourished the disputed claim have been radically reversed; here, even a locally supervised plebiscite may be the right face-saving device to permit an end to the dispute itself.

The foregoing analysis suggests, however, that consistent steps aiming at more stable world orders may very well have to be taken with a cautious approach to plebiscite proposals during the next 25 years. First, the use of a plebiscite in which a regional organization can supply the disinterested soldiers *or policemen* required already presumes greater advances in replacing purely national concepts with regional ones than have already been made. Thus, use of the plebiscite device before confidence in a sufficiently neutral regional force emerges can be predicted to lead to an unstable resolution more often than not.

Second, if proposals for plebiscites are not intended to be supported by use of such disinterested policing forces, there is a serious risk that the proposals themselves will not be treated as serious, and will thus weaken the step-by-step process of building habits of responsible (and responsive) diplomacy.

[53] Fn. 51, 903.

[54] The local press campaigns of journals like *El Morro* (e.g., "General Pershing is used to ordering negro slaves about," October 28, 1925, 1), and *El Plebiscito* ("The Peruvian plebiscite officials have kidnapped a young native," March 14, 1926, 1) did much to create the chaos in which the plebiscite was aborted. See generally, P. V. Shaw, "The Breakdown of the Tacna-Arica Plebiscite," in *Current History*, 1926, 693. This was despite the fact that actions of the army of Chile and police against Peruvians, as in analogous disputes, were principal grievances leading up to the arbitration and the call for a plebiscite itself. See, e.g., Pio Max Medina, *La Controversia Peruano-Chilena* (Lima 1925) 271 (closing of Peruvian schools, expulsion, suppression of Peruvian periodicals, unjust conscription alleged).

To those who would reply: "At least you can try!" it should be an-swer enough to rejoin that an international lawyer has not fulfilled his task as a social scientist unless he has demanded of himself in this area the same predictive responsibilities he routinely demands of himself in commercial cases.[55] When the Austro-Prussian War ended in 1866 in a treaty promising a plebiscite in Northern Slesvig (subsequently to become Schleswig-Holstein), it is more consistent with the method of analysis suggested in this series of volumes to ask not only whether it was predictable that Bismarck would refuse to hold the plebiscite on the ground that Prussia could not "compromise its strategic security," but also whether the plebiscite proposal tended to produce greater or lesser unity within Europe when that refusal occurred?[56] Today it is no less fitting to ask: is the persistent appeal for the plebiscite in Kash-mir "recommended" by the Security Council any the less destructive of chances for cooperation on the Indian subcontinent simply because it would be the resolution most consistent with the Charter's self-determination values?

Third, plebiscites are most likely to be proposed by one side or an-other, despite strong probabilities of rejection, when a transborder minority is being persecuted or it is under disabilities caused by bor-der regulations. The corollary is equally clear: namely, that (1) the raising of the level of civil rights in general, (2) the heightening of pro-tection for minority groups, and (3) the reduction of the meaning of a boundary in people's daily lives may forestall the doomed call for a plebiscite which portends a "dead-end" conflict situation.

IV. Some Special Sources of Future Rules or Instabilities

A. The armistice or cease-fire line as a boundary

It is apparent that a stable system will need a device for giving the armistice or cease-fire line some status which has the attributes of permanence.

Present international rules build into such lines an inherent instabil-ity, as on each of Israel's frontiers, or on the dividing lines between North and South Korea, and North and South Vietnam. Furthermore, the nature of that instability is bound up with incompletely resolved recognition and succession problems which currently contribute to threats of breakdowns in at best delicate systems of regional public order.

For example, traditional international law makes it possible to agree

[55] Compare the general criticism of social scientists who have traditionally es-chewed these broader policy aspects of the predictive function in Cyril E. Black, "Challenges to an Evolving Legal Order" in *Trends and Patterns*, Vol. 1 of this series, 3-31, at 11-23.

[56] See *Plebiscites* (fn. 50), 18.

to an armistice or cease-fire without recognizing either (1) the legitimacy of the government or state whose army has been opposed, or (2) the line itself as one defining national territory. To the extent that this rule makes it possible to end hostilities not otherwise concludable, it is an essential part of any future system as well.[57] To the extent that attempts to move forward from those cease-fires are more often doomed than not, it is because the current system provides no incentive to resolve the border problem and, indeed, provides potential penalties for attempting to do so. This is amply, but tragically, demonstrated today by the 17 states at cease-fire lines with little, and often no, contact across their borders. The penalty they perceive in negotiating further lies in the concomitant rule that: "Bilateral non-military agreements generally evidence an intent to recognize the other party as legally authorized to speak for the state whose territory it claims to govern."[58]

Here the problem lies not in identifying what is wrong with traditional international law so much as it does in finding the next step to deal with it. R. Y. Jennings rightly suggests that there is a process by which states find their way to recognition of legitimacy under current law which he describes as follows: "We have seen that Sir Hersch Lauterpacht used the evidence of the practice of non-recognition of titles acquired by force as a reinforcement of the argument that such titles are vitiated in the modern law. It seems a reasonable corollary to hold that the international community may, in the alternative, eventually signify assent to the new position and thus by recognition create a title."[59] Under Professor Jennings' analysis, the individual segments of the international community as well as its collective arms can grant —or withhold—recognition of the armistice line's gains and losses of territory. While this provides some clarifying mechanism, it is one by which a long period of uncertainty is assured, even though—as in Kashmir—no ultimate certainty can be likewise assured.

One final complicating factor in border disputes which begin or end with armistice lines is that the very applications of force which precede them almost guarantee that the principle of self-determination has been violated in some way.[60]

The need for a change in the rules of the game in this area is clear. Without attempting to explore every possibility, two devices to make the transition from cease-fire barriers to traversable borders without

[57] See American Law Institute, *Foreign Relations Law of the United States* (restatement of the Law, Second, St. Paul 1965), 330.

[58] Paraphrasing the rule in same, § 104 (2); cf. recent German rapprochement.

[59] R. Y. Jennings, *The Acquisition of Territory in International Law* (Manchester 1963), 62.

[60] For a position stressing the need for greater weight to be given to self-determination when civil strife is involved, see Chap. 3, Rosalyn Higgins, "Internal War and International Law."

completely side-stepping crucial self-determination problems can represent the types of new approaches worth trying.

THE ADJUDICATION-OR-CONFIRMATION DEVICE

The first is to provide an incentive to submit the underlying claims, including those of group preferences, to an impartial body. This could be provided in an individual case, for example, were the Security Council or an appropriate regional body to signify in its resolution that it would recognize the armistice line as final at the end of a period of time if the parties have not submitted their dispute to a binding proceeding. This need not necessarily be before a court or arbitrator; indeed, the power to seek a *solution*, rather than merely a resolution, may lie elsewhere.

It would be naive, however, to suppose that the Security Council would often wish to confirm a victor in its territorial position. Nevertheless, especially where hostilities were not of its own making, this might indeed be the internationally desired result.

THE MORATORIUM-WITH-CEASE-FIRE DEVICE

In cases where the Security Council cannot make such a determination, however, a second device is needed. This is to lend various attributes of permanence to the cease-fire or armistice boundary without conceding the underlying claims of either party to more or less territory. The device itself is the moratorium on claims discussed above.

The value of such a moratorium in this context could lie in the new operational rules to be followed during it. For example, new rules could advance the world system three giant steps forward if they (1) permitted agreements without recognition, (2) provided rules of behavior toward local inhabitants, and (3) provided for transborder activities with minimal formalities.

The incentive for agreeing to a moratorium of this type—or in acquiescing in one declared by the competent international body—would be that, unlike the present-day situation, activities in the disrupted area by the government in possession would not confirm a title by subsequent occupation. For example, the setting up of a civilian magistrate's court to apply Israeli law in the Golan heights, no matter how administratively necessary such a step may seem to its promulgators, could not be used in subsequent years as evidence of Israeli "ownership" of this territory now within its cease-fire line with Syria.

B. Regional differences in approaching potential border instabilities

There is critical interplay between conscious fostering of regional cohesion and the avoidance of boundary wars.

In the *Inter-American region*, for example, all recent outbreaks of armed warfare over borders have been ended by community pressures to go to arbitration, or—as in the case of the Río Coco dispute between Honduras and Nicaragua—to the World Court. Such a pattern is reciprocal: each dispute resolved in this way reinforces perceptions of the need for an effective regional organization just as it strengthens confidence in the regional system itself.

Likewise, the *European approach*, at least in the West, has been characterized by a high degree of readiness to submit border problems to international adjudication, as in disputes between France and the United Kingdom, Belgium and the Netherlands, Denmark and West Germany, and the Netherlands and West Germany. Minor adjustments have repeatedly been worked out by treaty, as in the adjustments permitted 500 metres on either side of the line to be demarcated under the Italian Peace Treaty, or in a host of specific agreements. The consequence of preferring bilateral recourse to courts or negotiating tables is to pass up the chance to raise the effectiveness of regional bodies, such as the Council of Europe, as much as it is a reflection of a belief that such greater cohesiveness is not needed there.

In *Africa*, on the other hand, the Organization for African Unity has shown the cohesion side of its ambivalent approach. It tackled the prospective chaos for postcolonial borders spelled out above, for example, by passing a resolution to collectively minimize threats of conflict: "Considering . . . that the borders of African States, on the day of their independence, constitute a tangible reality. . . . Declare that all the Member States pledge themselves to respect the borders existing on their achievement of national independence."[61] Indeed, the high value which the leaders of African states have placed on the concept of Africa as a family of nations, and on resolving difficulties by successive meetings of ministers or heads of state under regional persuasion, shows perhaps the most highly sophisticated awareness of regional society's usefulness as a provider of third-party presences to increase the odds that border disputes will be settled without force.

Asia is the least cohesive in regional terms; it is thus not entirely unexpected to find that no regional pattern of peaceful settlement has emerged there. The one case which went to the World Court, involving a temple disputed by both Cambodia and Thailand, led to the withdrawal by Thailand from the compulsory jurisdiction of that court, and was followed by aggravation of the strains between these two states when Thailand lost. Yet Asia is also the testing ground for another possible interrelation between border conflicts and transitions to regional systems of public order. We have seen that a cohesive regional approach can provide habits of "palaver" or adjudication which put out flaring border fires. It remains to be seen whether the border conflict can itself become a means to cooperation, as between China

[61] *Africa Research Bulletin*, III (1967), 633.

and the Soviet Union where preliminary contacts were renewed in 1969 in just that context.

C. Antarctica—new rules for polar lands and new laws of the sea?

This continent provides a laboratory for new rules about territory for several reasons. First, it is the last place for large areas of *terra nullius,* land belonging to no state, just when the 70.8 percent of the planet under oceans is unfolding before virginal explorations. Second, it is the first place where the problem of permanent ice spreading beyond any land base has been dealt with by any large group of nations. Third, it is the major example of framing novel devices to hold in arrest threatened conflicts over territory. Fourth, it is the most likely place for modelling new departures from purely state-centered systems of government.

1. The changing rules for unpossessed lands

Classical international law had a few doctrines applicable to the Antarctic which, taken together, created the following rules for converting parts of it to nationally owned lands:

Terra-nullius areas belong to no state so long as they remain unoccupied and undiscovered.

Discovery of an area by a state is not by itself occupancy.[62]

Discovery, where accompanied or followed immediately by acts symbolizing an intent to occupy nationally, initiates a chain of events which accumulate as evidence of (1) an intent to occupy as national territory, and (2) sufficient occupation for the kind of territory it is, as in the case of guano islands requiring no permanent base on them,[63] or of an area partially covered by glaciers.[64]

When two or more states claim the same territory, they may agree upon a division of it between them.

If these rules had been applied to the Antarctic during the last decade, numerous conflicts would have arisen. For example, the first rule was fashioned for pre-1960 technology when expeditions played "discovery roulette" with unseen lands off established sealanes. With today's aerial mapping and satellite photography, such lands do not in fact exist, although there may be individual mountain peaks left to be surveyed from the ground. For instance, since December 1967, British and American planes have been surveying the entire area through aerial photography and radio echo exploration.[65] Do these acts provide

[62] Island of Las Palmas Arbitration (fn. 26).
[63] See Clipperton Island Arbitration (fn. 28).
[64] See Eastern Greenland Case (fn. 17). [65] Note, *Polar Record,* XIV (1966), 211.

the basis for adequate administration by either state on the analogy to Greenland's glacier?

Again, the third rule would distinguish between acts of French expeditions in French-claimed Adélie Land (now flown over annually from a central base on land), and identical activities there by Americans whose government renounces territorial claims from American discoveries. Would this remain the same if France had promulgated regulations there, however, which American explorers refused to follow?

None of the otherwise predictable conflicts is expected for the new Antarctic rules for unpossessed lands set forth below show how successful conflict avoidance can be managed. More important they have implications for other areas, as in the Law of the Sea problems used for illustrative purposes below.

NEW RULE NO. 1: *If conflict is inevitable as the result of old customs, new rules must be promulgated to replace them.*

While this states a common-sense proposition, it does not state one yet extended fully to other territorial problems. This new rule was in fact urged upon the World Court on behalf of both Denmark and the Netherlands in their dispute with West Germany over the end of their respective continental shelves. Admitting (unnecessarily?) that the median line had not been adopted often enough to be a customary rule, counsel argued that new abilities to exploit the shelf demanded a single rule be forged for cases where adjacent nations could not agree. Specifically, in the North Sea Continental Shelf Cases, Denmark and the Netherlands were asking the Court to adopt as that rule the median-line provision of the Convention on the Continental Shelf, signed in Geneva in 1958 by over two-thirds of the states attending and since ratified by more than the 22 states needed to bring it into force—but not by West Germany. The thrust of the majority decision was to reject the claim that any specific new rule was required by international law and to ask the parties to try once more to reach agreement.

NEW RULE NO. 2: *Nations asserting claims to unoccupied territory disputed by other states must, if they desire to act there, hold their claims in abeyance instead of enforcing them by arms.*

This could become one of the most useful devices for the transitional period ahead in which territorial disputes will provide antipodal forces against regional cohesion if old rules are always to prevail. Further, this alternative must now be weighed against the sobering implications of the sales of arms and widespread access to nuclear technology stressed elsewhere in this volume.

For example, the same discoveries of oil, gas, or minerals offshore which beg for a set rule as to continental shelves, also create new motives for conflicts over the final stretch of the border on land. Even if the median rule is binding upon two states because they have ratified the Continental Shelf Convention, nevertheless, they do not always have a settled seabottom frontier. First, the median rule applies only if they have not already agreed otherwise, e.g., as is alleged to be the case with the Treaty of Guadelupe Hidalgo between the United States and Mexico in its straight-line boundary terms. Second, the median rule applies without dispute only if the starting point on shore or on some other baseline is not in dispute. Thus, a possible claim to an alternative land boundary over terrain of hitherto slight importance can indeed be raised to the fighting level if even a small difference in angle out onto a large continental shelf will result.

The use of some sharing device, such as the Jordanian-Saudi Arabian agreement on royalties in the Gulf of Aqaba, referred to above,[66] can then provide a mutually rewarding alternative to the old all-or-none territorial rules.[67]

NEW RULE NO. 3: *The condition for arresting those claims is that neither state's subsequent action there can be used to perfect a claim.*

This device reflects an imaginative shift away from the rule-conscious adversarial world public order implicit in traditional international law. The shift to solution-conscious approaches demands more techniques aimed to permit forward-looking cooperation.

For example, the lack of intense disputes over ocean bottom areas currently matches the lack of ability in neighboring states to work in their underwater environments. As more activities are conducted routinely in these areas, however, fears that they will somehow ripen into "occupation" will be no weaker on the seabed than they were in the Antarctic.

NEW RULE NO. 4: *When all those using an area can agree on conditions for its use, then subsequent entrants can be required to abide by all previously established rules on which use has collectively been conditioned.*

The acceptance of this device for the Antarctic reflects awareness of a critical threat to any new legal system. If a state can claim not to be bound by prior rules of the game forged by others, the system never

---

[66] See fn. 47.

[67] The need in many situations to search for solutions which can be justified in terms of each disputant government's own perceptions of justice has been admirably set forth in Roger Fisher, *International Conflict for Beginners* (New York 1969), esp. in his Jordan-Israel example on 137-38, 205-07.

achieves an assured level of stability. Perhaps it is in part because the People's Republic of China has argued that it cannot accept the United Nations framework, as it has been erected without its representation, that those who see positive advantages to its presence are not always able to set aside fears for Charter benefits already agreed upon.

This binding device for third parties has already been adopted in the Convention on Conservation of the Living Resources of the High Seas. There, states using a fishery can agree on conservation rules which will be binding upon new entrants. The dilemma raised by any such rule is that it may be in one state's interest not to have new rules promulgated before its claim to use of the fishery can be perfected; yet once it is a member of the group exploiting a diminishing stock, it then becomes in that same state's interest to keep all newcomers out.

This dilemma does not, however, destroy the usefulness of NEW RULE NO. 4. There is absolutely nothing in that rule which forbids the states using some underwater *terra nullius* from limiting access to a fair exploiting group when it is functionally necessary to do so. If, for example, any area is to be kept free enough from external influences to provide a place to study seabed ecology *in nature*, protective rules must be made and enforced, even against newcomers.

NEW RULE NO. 5: *Common use of territory, if national claims are held in abeyance, must be nonmilitary use, although "military" units may be used for peaceful tasks.*

This reflects a growth in perception of how conflicts can be avoided if a disputed region can be kept free from displays of arms or threatening emplacements which award some strategic advantages to its holder. If seabed disarmament can provide like security against fortified frontiers, this aspect of the basic Antarctic regime will have been expanded to cover much of the planet.

An analogous device has also been pointed to in order to do this: namely, that of The Undefended Border. There has been one outstanding success here in the more than 3,000 miles of borders between the United States and Canada on which no fence stands and no army unit stands watch. It is notable that, from 1783 these same two states have had more than 125 disputes over the precise line of the longest border; each of them was resolved by arbitration or demarcation, except the presently outstanding continental shelf boundary in the Gulf of Maine.

There is at least one area where this device can be predicted to have a good chance of similar conflict-avoiding results, namely, for territorial water and shelf borders. Agreements to restrict military emplacements and patrols need not necessarily be drawn to preclude all possible naval activities. Canada and the United States, for example, have been able to make and modify agreements for the use of the Great Lakes by specified naval vessels and training facilities which pose no border threat while agreeing to have an undefended border between them.

One caveat remains: there is a distinct relationship between (1) the successful demarcation of the frontier by monuments on the ground, and (2) the effectiveness of compulsory expert resolution of water-use disputes by the International Joint Commission, and the success of the undefended United States-Canadian border. In the long run, therefore, similar devices will be just as essential for undefended sea-bottom lines to have as strong a likelihood of success.

NEW RULE NO. 6: *Even barren territory, when open to common use, should not be used for pollution, at least of the nuclear waste kind, nor should its wildlife be wantonly destroyed.*

The banning of nuclear pollution from the Antarctic Treaty area below 60° South latitude reflected a new world order system. For one thing, it recognized that the potential harms of new technology must be deemed the concern of the relevant community of states as a whole. For another, it "impliedly" recognized that to leave an area without a sovereign state as master would not do if this meant it had to be left free from any protective regulation by the community at large.

The applicability of this new rule to areas of joint ownership or moratoria is no less valid for land and seabed territory than it is for expanded activities in Antarctica. Two types of opportunity are thus opened up from this south polar experience.

The first is the chance to develop alternative models to contrast with the exclusively nation-state systems of the past. This can be done for the Antarctic by expanding the present annual meetings of the 14 nations there which have already provided regulations to conserve wildlife.

In non-Antarctic situations, moratoria also can provide the chance to experiment with new models of collective machinery. In the past, there have been both workable and nonworkable systems for joint operation of territory. On the success side, for instance, there have been: the primary state method for Norwegian administration of Spitsbergen, the international court system for Tangier, the United Nations transitional constitution-forming system for Libya, and the joint communications uses of Christmas Island, to cite but a few.

On the less successful side has been the notable inability of the United Nations to provide both administrative and policing functionaries for West New Guinea, or "West Irian," during the period of almost a year in which the Netherlands had nominally turned that administrative responsibility over to the UN. Whatever circumstances led to the swift turnover of policing to Indonesian authorities but a few weeks after Dutch forces had left, it would provide needed experience with direct United Nations administration if at least one of the disputed territory situations can be used for a renewed experiment of this kind. Others could employ such alternatives as regional operation, or diverse types of multinational councils.

The second opportunity lies in the chance to work toward a system to replace the Antarctic Treaty itself in the 1991-93 period, when new amendments can be proposed, and when failure to adopt any nation's offered amendment can permit it to withdraw from the Treaty regime. If some segment of the international legal research community is not working with alternative models for Antarctica itself during the next 20 years, therefore, this chance also will have been missed.

2. Permanent ice, ice islands, and seamounts

Is there, however, a corollary that, if an area cannot be successfully regulated by an international community and yet must be protected in some way, territorial sovereignty must be extended to it? By treating the permanent coastal ice in Antarctica as part of the land for purposes of applying the Treaty's regulations, did the states involved, while acting collectively, imply unilateral sanction acts in analogous situations?

There is nothing new about framing rules for a body of land together with its permanent coastal ice. Several Tsarist decrees did so for the Russian north, and some Soviet writers have adopted the identical approach.[68] What is new in the Antarctic is the acceptance by all states working there that no meaningful proscriptions can be framed for ice-covered lands without extending them also to the permanent ice connected to them.

Again, the main importance of this new jurisdictional rule may lie in its extension to other areas. The first such extension would be to *ice islands*, such as the huge floating research facility proposed for the Arctic Research Lab—to hold two stations, two planes, and two helicopters.[69]

Another could be *seamounts*, which would seem to raise the same social questions; man can live, work, and explore there, yet a failure to limit his activities there, and the territorial claims he might make as a result of them, raises the specter of conflict just as vividly as with the Antarctic ice shelves.

[68] E.g., Nikolaev, writing in 1954, named the outer edge of the stationary ice as the baseline from which to measure Soviet territorial waters. See William E. Butler, *The Laws of Soviet Territorial Waters* (New York 1967), 32.

[69] See Note, *Polar Record*, XIV (1968), 219, 226.

Conclusion

The stickiest problems in international law today are boundary ones: the two Chinas, two Koreas, two Germanys, Berlin, the two Vietnams, Israel, and its Middle Eastern neighbors. It is obvious that existing techniques have prevented neither (1) actual conflict (2) the threat of conflict, nor (3) the cooperation gap in these areas.

Yet it is equally obvious that, without any changes in the existing system, the future development of the world community can be foreseen to include: a rise in armed border conflicts, a rise in divided state situations, a rise in the recognition and membership dilemmas which previous rules helped to form, and a breakdown of cooperation in those very regions where it is most vital.

There is a school of survival which analyzes the present nation-state system as a temporary one whose eventual demise makes it sound policy to simply survive the altercations it permits, one by one, until an ethos of greater cooperation arrives. The trouble with this approach is that what we do not do today is shaping tomorrow as much as what we do attempt. If there is no greater development of predictive skills to head off border conflicts, there will be increased occasions for that brinkmanship which risks what Herman Kahn so pointedly calculates as a certain percentage of DOE.[70]

Likewise, if we do not move to develop more effective "shifters" to change problem regions into project regions, we will not be enhancing the development of the greater regional cohesiveness which the "ostrich scholar" hopes will come "just in time."

[70] Death of Earth: the amount of probable life surface on the planet destroyed if a given quantity of atomic missiles is unleashed.

CHAPTER 6

The Proliferation of
Conventional Weapons

WILLIAM B. BADER

IN THE YEARS since Hiroshima the nations of the world have been pre-occupied with the potential horrors of nuclear war and with the seemingly inexorable spread of nuclear arms skills. All but ignored in the search for international means of subduing the nuclear arms genie has been the growing challenge to international order offered by the spread of what is now glibly called "conventional" weapons—the traditional weapons of war. While dramatic in character and of major importance for the future of international stability, the significance of this challenge of conventional arms proliferation has been only dimly appreciated by the world community; and painfully little has been done to erect international barriers to the spread of these weapons.

Since 1945 there have been on the order of 56 armed conflicts of such intensity and destruction as to earn the classification of a "war."[1] Although the developed countries of the world are occasionally shocked by the brutalities of these "small" wars, the developed countries, particularly the major powers, seem strangely unconcerned that all but a few of these small wars have been fought in the less-developed areas of the world by countries which do not have the capacity to produce their own weapons. The hard but all-too-often ignored fact is that a few industrialized nations have provided almost all of the weapons used in these conflicts. Although solid estimates are difficult to obtain, one informed estimate is that some $66 billion worth of conventional arms have flowed into the world's markets since 1945—including a contribution of nearly $50 billion from the United States.[2] The worldwide volume of military export sales (excluding military assistance in grants) is now around $5 billion a year—a rate of military sales in current dollars that has at least doubled since 1950 (the im-

---

[1] "The Arms Trade—Part I," remarks of R. Lawrence Coughlin of Pennsylvania in the House of Representatives, July 31, 1969, *Congressional Record*, July 31, 1969, E6503. Representative Coughlin's efforts to educate the Congress and the public on the dimensions and implications of the burgeoning international arms trade have been thoughtful and thorough; for a detailed list of these "wars" and sophisticated analysis of the implications see Lincoln P. Bloomfield and Amelia C. Leiss, *Controlling Small Wars: A Strategy for the 1970's* (New York 1969) 24; see also Appendix C for listing.

[2] Coughlin (fn. 1).

posing U.S. role in the military export sales market is illustrated by the fact that in fiscal year 1969 U.S. sales amounted to $1.745 billion).[3]

What seems to escape most nuclear weapons strategists is the "linkage" of the problems of escalating conventional arms races to the need many nations are beginning to feel to develop nuclear arms (if Israel loses confidence in its qualitative advantage in conventional arms, or the sheer cost of maintaining a conventional arms parity with the Arab countries becomes economically unmanageable, Tel Aviv will almost certainly move to develop nuclear weapons); and to the "linkage" of hostilities among client states with tensions among nuclear powers.

Even if we assume that the major powers will somehow be able to control the level of violence among client states, the same powers should begin to consider carefully the long-term international consequences of underdeveloped nations diverting an important share of scarce human and material resources to defense. In his remarks to the Eighteen Nation Disarmament Conference in January of 1966, President Johnson made a start in defining the problem of diversion of economic resources to the purchase of arms when he reminded the delegates: "As we focus on nuclear arms, let us not forget that resources are being devoted to nonnuclear arms races all around the world. These resources might be better spent on feeding the hungry, healing the sick and teaching the uneducated. The cost of acquiring and maintaining one squadron of supersonic aircraft diverts resources that would build and maintain a university. We suggest therefore that countries, on a regional basis, explore ways to limit competition among themselves for costly weapons often sought for reasons of illusory prestige."[4]

Despite Mr. Johnson's concern, the pursuit of "illusory prestige" has in recent years quickened throughout the world. Consider part of the record:

> In 1967 worldwide military spending reached an all-time high figure of $182 billion. The increase from 1966 to 1967 was over $20 billion—that is, more than twice the current annual total of foreign economic assistance offered by all countries in the world to the less-developed areas.
>
> The number of independent states has risen from 50 in 1945 to over 120. Most of these new nations seek arms for everything from an independence day parade to combating internal subversion, to pursuing a territorial dispute with a neighbor.

[3] "Military Export Sales, Fiscal Years, 1962-69; Foreign Military Sales Orders—Worldwide Summary by Type of Order and Region," Department of Defense. *Congressional Record*, October 15, 1969, E8503.

[4] *Arms Sales and Foreign Policy*; staff study prepared for the use of the Committee on Foreign Relations, January 25, 1967, 90th Cong., 1st Sess., 1.

According to a survey of 93 less-developed nations taken by the U.S. Arms Control and Disarmament Agency, these governments as a group in 1966 spent more on their military budgets than on education and public health combined—$17 billion compared to $16 billion for education and public health. How ill these less-developed countries can afford a $17 billion expenditure for arms is brought home by the fact that these countries now have 72 percent of the world population and the $16 billion they spend for education and public health represents only 10 percent of the total world investment in these two categories.[5]

Putting aside for the moment the problems of the transshipment from the developed countries of surplus military equipment to the underdeveloped world, there is no doubt that, in spite of the enormous drain on the available resources of the have-not nations military purchases represent, the major industrial powers are now in heavy—if often reluctant—competition to sell conventional military equipment to the developing nations. The international record of such sales is long: Soviet aircraft to Iraq, Egypt, and Syria; French aircraft to Peru; American aircraft and missiles to Israel; British jet fighters to Chile— to cite some examples.

The increase in arms expenditures in the developing nations of the world and the consequent diversion of scarce resources comes at a time when the industrial nations are making strenuous efforts to improve their respective balance of payments position by shifting from programs of military grant assistance to active programs of military sales. In the fiscal-year period 1952 to 1961 the total U.S. military grant aid programs and military sales amounted to a total value of $22 billion—$17 billion in grant aid and $5 billion in sales. According to recent Defense Department estimates, the comparative amounts will be dramatically altered in the 1962 to 1971 period—that is $15 billion in military sales and $7 billion in grant aid. For example, in the 1952-61 period, U.S. military sales averaged approximately $300 million annually; by 1967 the annual figure of sales had risen to around $2 billion a year.[6]

It has been a longstanding position of the Defense Department that a proper and fair-minded assessment of the conventional arms transfer problem should begin with a rigid separation of the sales and grants programs to developed countries from those programs to underdeveloped countries. According to this view, if such a separation is made it becomes clear that there are no international problems resulting from American sales programs to developed countries. As for the sales and

[5] Archibald S. Alexander, "The Cost of World Armaments," *Scientific American*, ccxxi, No. 4 (October 1969).

[6] See fn. 4, 2.

grants to underdeveloped countries, it is admitted that there is a potential problem here but the percentage of total grants and sales that go to underdeveloped countries is so low that the problem of stimulating arms races, diverting economic resources, and fueling local conflicts is minimal. The national defense agencies of other countries (i.e., our competitors in the arms sales business) have made similar statements.

Two points are appropriate here. First, using the U.S. sales program as an example, it is certainly true that if we accept the intricate and somewhat misleading definition of "underdeveloped" used by the Pentagon (Iran, Iraq, Libya, and Saudi Arabia are considered as "developed"), only a small percentage of the U.S. total sales goes to the underdeveloped world. During the period 1962-66, for example, $9.85 billion of the total of $11.1 billion in U.S. arms sales went to "developed" countries in Europe and Asia—that is, 89 percent of the total program.[7]

But what does the remaining 11 percent of $11.1 billion—that is, $1.22 billion—represent in terms of diverted resources and problems for regions with sensitive security problems? We have only to consider that $998 million of this "small percentage" of total U.S. sales went into the Middle East and South Asia in order to appreciate that a $10 million sale in a particularly sensitive area of the world—be it Biafra or Jordan—may in its potential for international trouble-making far exceed the monetary worth of the particular arms transfer.

Then there is the surplus arms sales problem that tends to break down the assumption that there is an important policy difference between sales to developed countries as opposed to sales to the underdeveloped world.

The quantities and varieties of military equipment which have been poured into the world markets are impressive. For purposes of illustration, let us consider only the record of the U.S. and the Soviet Union during a period when the Pentagon has provided solid figures. According to the Defense Department, U.S. military exports in the period 1955-67, including grants as well as commercial and governmental sales, totaled $28,111,000,000. This figure does not include the vast outpouring of U.S. military equipment to West Europe during the period of the Korean War when we stimulated a massive conventional buildup in Europe. On the Soviet side, the estimate for the same 1955-67 period is, according to the Department of Defense, $14,320,000,000 worth of equipment—about half the U.S. contribution.[8]

[7] Same, 4-5.

[8] Testimony before the Senate Foreign Relations Committee on the Foreign Military Sales Act, June 20, 1968. See also Senator Claiborne Pell's analysis and elaboration of these figures, *Congressional Record*, June 12, 1969, S6419-S6421.

Where is this $42 billions of equipment today—equipment that from the U.S. side includes some 16,630 aircraft, 8,300 jet fighter-bombers, 258 destroyer escorts, 3 aircraft carriers, 19,827 tanks, 2.1 million rifles, 71,174 machine guns, 26,845 artillery pieces, and 45,360 missiles. Some of this equipment is still in use, some of it has been scrapped, some of it has been resold—but a large amount is still in the hands of developed countries who would like to dispose of it by selling it to their less fortunate and less particular brethren in the underdeveloped world.

Congressional hearings over recent years have shown that there is an enormous amount of surplus military equipment of American origin either in or soon to arrive on the international arms market. There are already over 7,000 tanks of American origin in Europe, most of them ready for distribution to the underdeveloped countries.[9] Some of this equipment has been given to European countries under the military assistance program and some we have sold. The desire of the industrial countries in Europe to resell this military equipment of American origin is rising. In part, the reason for this anxiousness to resell the equipment is that the United States has shifted from a program of military assistance to one of sales. When a European pays for his military equipment he is interested in reclaiming as much of the cost as he can by reselling the now obsolete military equipment into the international market rather than simply scrapping the arms.

Both the Department of State and the Department of Defense are well aware of this growing problem of the sale of surplus military equipment by the industrial countries to underdeveloped countries. Unfortunately, it is difficult to control the distribution of this equipment because surplus military equipment brings a higher return when sold to underdeveloped countries than when it is scrapped locally. According to Samuel Cummings of Interarm (formerly Interarmco), the West Germans are now asking roughly $20,000 for a surplus M-47 tank, while the same tank brings $2,000 as scrap.[10]

If the surplus material now on hand in Europe represents an important market for underdeveloped countries to buy military equipment they do not need, we can only look forward to an increasing amount of such equipment coming onto the international market. The United States has been heavily involved in the Vietnam War for over five years now. Billions of dollars worth of military equipment have gone into that war. Once the war is over much of this equipment will be coming onto the international market.

[9] Hearings before the Subcommittee on Near Eastern and South Asian Affairs of the Committee on Foreign Relations, U.S. Sen., 90th Cong., 1st Sess., March 14, April 13, 20, 25, June 22, 1967.

[10] Same.

THE FUTURE

Quite apart from the probable impact on regional stability of surplus military equipment left over from the Vietnam War, the trend in the conventional arms trade is not encouraging, if the retardation and possible control of the flow of these weapons into the world market are considered to be worthy international goals. The following excerpts are from a speech given by Air Force Lt. Gen. Robert H. Warren, Deputy Assistant Secretary of Defense for Military Assistance, before the Aerospace Industries Association. General Warren, who has taken over the export-sales function of the former Office of International Logistics Negotiations (ILN), headed by Henry Kuss, began his speech by stating that the U.S. sales programs are now running a bit over the $1.5 billion level. General Warren then went on to give his appraisal of the future of U.S. military sales:

> As to future trends, I believe:
> Grant aid will probably remain at its present level in fiscal year 1970, but will gradually decline thereafter.
> Sales to highly developed countries will probably decline as those countries strive to produce their own military equipments. They have already dropped from 97 percent of the total in fiscal year 1962 to 68 percent last year.
> Sales to "oil rich" and less-developed countries will probably increase.
> Technical components and "know-how" are likely to represent a major portion of sales to highly developed countries.
> Complete end items and systems will probably make up sales to "oil rich" and less-developed countries—with increased emphasis on co-production.[11]

In other words, pressure from our competitors in the arms field will increasingly force the U.S. into the arms market in the underdeveloped world, if we are to maintain a high level of arms sales. For their part, competitors of the United States will presumably be equally active in seeking new arms markets in the underdeveloped areas of the world.

How important these sales have become to the industrial interests of the United States—and presumably to America's industrial counterparts in France and Great Britain—is illustrated by the recent cry of alarm by the National Security Industrial Association (NSIA) over sagging military sales. In a letter to Defense Secretary Melvin Laird asking for a Presidential Commission to study the "total export program," the President of the NSIA, J. M. Lyle, complained that: "Our

11 Remarks of Lt. Gen. Robert H. Warren, USAF, Deputy Assistant Secretary of Defense (ISA) before the Aerospace Industries Association of America, March 26, 1969.

military export trade posture has declined from a high of $1.93 billion in 1967 to $1.81 billion in 1968. This is coupled with a decline in our merchandise export surplus of $3.3 billion to a nine-year low of $845 million in 1968."[12]

Mr. Lyle is hardly the Sir Basil Zaharoff or Francis Bannerman of 20th century American business. Mr. Lyle is, in all probability, a good, grey businessman who conscientiously follows the arms export procedures established by the U.S. government; indeed, he is probably very much like the good, grey government officials around the world who ultimately make the arms export decisions. Challenged by the glint of a balance of payments success, these officials are all too often untroubled by, or unknowing of, the cumulative effect of the ever-increasing flow of conventional military supplies into underdeveloped countries.

Concluding Comment and Recommendations

Given the legitimate desire of nation-states to provide military support to friendly countries in the form of conventional arms, it would be impractical, if not unwise, to oppose all forms of conventional arms transfers. The question that should be addressed with regard to the current proliferation of conventional arms is not how to stop the spread of conventional weapons but how to identify and to control the flow, and hopefully to retard the phenomenal growth of these transfers.

In the area of nuclear arms development and spread there have been important and successful international efforts to identify and quantify the flow of atomic materials (The International Atomic Energy Agency and the buy-back programs for plutonium); to control the spread (the Nonproliferation Treaty); and to seal off areas from nuclear competition (the Antarctic Treaty, the Outer Space Treaty, and the recent Seabed Treaty). Despite the fact that the problem of the proliferation of conventional arms is so acute and destined to worsen, there are no comparable steps taken, or even seriously contemplated, in the field of identification, control, or "buy-back" of conventional weapons. Moreover, no comparable effort has been made in the field of conventional weapons control to the Antarctic Treaty or the Outer Space Treaty—that is, the creation of zones where particular varieties of conventional weapons would be excluded.

If a start is to be made to bring some measure of international restraint and regulation to this well-entrenched system of massive exploitation of the weapons of war, the international community must

---

[12] *Government Executive*, I, No. 5 (July 1969), 13

know more than it does now as to why the industrialized nations export weapons—and why the appetite for conventional arms by the developing nations seems insatiable.

As for the responsibility of the exporters of conventional arms, the situation seems to be that no major national exporter of arms is thus far prepared to give up one iota of national control over the ways and means of exporting its conventional weapons. The national export policies of the 15 countries which dominate the military export market are well-rooted in an array of justifications for exporting arms that go well beyond issues of national security. The pattern of justification includes the desire to strengthen the ability of allies to meet alliance obligations, to provide assistance to friendly governments to resist internal or external aggression, and to win the support and loyalties of the national elites of underdeveloped countries, particularly military officers. Moreover, the producers of conventional arms see that trade as one part of a national effort to improve their respective positions on international accounting sheets.

One of the untested propositions which underlie many of the major arms sales decisions is that a major arms sale not only has positive economic benefits, but wins for the supplier influence in the policy process of the purchaser. A most candid exposition of this thesis was offered by Henry J. Kuss, formerly a Deputy Assistant Secretary of Defense charged with handling the military sales program of the United States. In a speech before the American Ordnance Association in October 1966, Mr. Kuss argued against the "tendency of American companies to refrain from entering into the international arms market." Mr. Kuss said in pressing for increased sales: "From the military point of view we stand to lose all of the major international relationships paid for with grant aid money unless we can establish professional military relationships through the sales media."[13]

All of the major powers have in recent years been tempted by the proposition that selling arms buys influence and thereby insures at least some measure of control over the actions of the so-called client states. This proposition should certainly be challenged on a case-by-case basis. Does the fact that the United States is *the* major supplier of arms to Israel actually help when Secretary Rogers puts forward a U.S. position on peace in the Middle East which we hope the Israeli will endorse—a very unpredictable proposition. Can the Russians control the actions of the Arab states with billions of dollars worth of arms? Again, such a proposition should be tested rather than assumed to be correct. One of the most telling and caustic criticisms of the arms-equals-influence theory was offered by Professor John Kenneth

[13] See fn. 4, 4.

Galbraith in his testimony before the Foreign Relations Committee in 1966:

> Let me take note in passing of the recurring argument that if we do not provide arms to a country it will get them from the Soviets or possibly China. This is another example of that curious obtuseness which excessive preoccupation with cold-war strategy produces in otherwise excellent minds. It was Soviet tanks that surrounded Ben Bella's palace in Algiers when that Soviet-supported leader was thrown out. It was a Soviet and Chinese equipped army which deposed the Indonesian Communists, destroyed the Communist Party in that ruthlessness on which one hesitates to dwell and which left Sukarno's vision of an Asian socialism in shambles. It was a Soviet-trained praetorian guard which was expected to supply the ultimate protection to the government of President Nkrumah and which did not. One can only conclude that those who worry about Soviet arms wish to keep the Russians out of trouble. This could be carrying friendship too far.[14]

Interestingly enough, an analysis prepared by the State Department's Bureau of Intelligence and Research in late 1969 of the use of military export cutoffs by all of the major powers since World War II concluded that these cutoffs have uniformly failed to bring about the desired policy changes in the client state. In citing the conclusions of the classified study, Secretary Rogers stated: "It is interesting to me that we have had a study made of how many times we have been able to influence the policy of another government by withholding military aid, and *we find that it has not been successful in any instance.*"[15]

The study referred to by Secretary Rogers also found that the American experience of failure in bringing about policy changes by embargoing military aid was shared by other major exporters. Examples given were the Soviet cutoff of aid to China, the United Nations embargo of arms to South Africa, and France's current embargo on military sales to Israel.

The logical question which flows from reports of the State Department secret analysis is whether this study asked an equally important question: does the actual sale of arms (as opposed to the cutoff of military sales) bring about desired policy changes in the purchasing country? If the classified study in question ultimately provides a rationale for lifting the U.S. arms embargo on major military aid to Greece and Pakistan, should not a case-by-case study be undertaken to determine whether the granting of arms influences the policy decisions of recipient countries? If the selling of arms does not influence the behavior

---

[14] Testimony before the Senate Foreign Relations Committee on the 1966 Foreign Assistance Act, April 25, 1966.

[15] *Washington Post*, December 24, 1969; *New York Times*, December 25, 1969.

of states, and the impact on balance-of-payments accounts of arms sales to underdeveloped countries is as small as the Defense Department contends it is, where, then, is the essential rationale for selling arms?

What is particularly puzzling—and profoundly disturbing—about any effort to review and to quantify this traffic in arms is the paucity of reliable information and the near absence of thoughtful attention to the issues by the United Nations, the major powers, and even the international relations research centers around the world. With the exception of the very excellent work done on the problems of international conventional arms transfers by the Stockholm International Peace Research Institute, the research efforts of the Institute for Strategic Studies, and the promising work done by Lincoln Bloomfield and his associates at the Massachusetts Institute of Technology, the tangled web of international traffic in conventional arms has received scant attention. This is an unfortunate trend. While the United Nations has done thoughtful and important research on the problem of the proliferation of nuclear weapons and the damages of biological and chemical warfare, and the Soviet Union and the United States continue to discuss strategic arms limitations in Vienna, there is as yet no meaningful and sustained international attention given to conventional violence in the international arena—violence that has increasingly developed the potential to escalate into nuclear weapons exchange.

It is most unfortunate that the record of the United Nations on this issue has been so barren of corrective proposals, or even persistent concern. The potential customers worry about their source of supply; the suppliers worry about restrictions on a sensitive foreign policy instrument. Seemingly lost in this wealth of common interest is the hard fact that the nuclear war we all dread will, in all probability, not begin with a calculated "first" strike by one of the nuclear powers but will be the unwanted result of a "small conventional" war. The devising and implementation of international measures to identify and control the flow of conventional arms seems mandatory if the international environment is to have a better chance of orderly development—if not survival—in the decades to come.

The specific recommendations of this study are offered not as an answer to the conventional arms transfer problem, but only in the hope of contributing to the needed international discussion of ways of imposing a minimum of restraint, and possibly control, in the field of conventional arms transfers.

Identification and Quantification

One or more of the major arms suppliers should take the initiative in the United Nations to bring about an international reporting arrangement of all sales and grants of military equipment.

A similar proposal for arms registration was introduced in the UN General Assembly in the form of a draft resolution by the Maltese delegate, Mr. Pardo, in November of 1965. In scope this draft resolution recalled the League of Nations effort to register trade in arms and ammunition. Mr. Pardo called for the "establishment of a system of publicity through the United Nations" for the transfer of the implements of war. The Pardo resolution was defeated 19 to 18, with 39 abstentions (many of the delegations were either without instructions or felt the issue of arms registration was too difficult and too sensitive to confront on such short notice). Unfortunately, the Maltese have not had the same success with the conventional arms transfer issue as another small country, Ireland, had with the question of the proliferation of nuclear weapons. Over a period of years the Irish delegation to the United Nations acted as the conscience of the institution on the nonproliferation issue by offering one resolution after another until the major powers finally saw the spread of nuclear weapons as a powerful threat.

A regional variation of the concept of publicity for arms transfers was advanced by President Johnson in his June 1967 speech on the Middle East. Mr. Johnson proposed for the Middle East area only that "the UN immediately call upon all of its members to report all shipments of all military arms into this area and to keep those shipments on file for all peoples of the world to see." Nothing has been heard since about this proposal, raising some question as to whether this proposal was in the presidential category of "give me an idea, any idea."

What would be the usefulness of an arms publicity program if such a program received the endorsement of the General Assembly?

It will certainly be argued that there would be no incentives for potential arms purchasers to adhere to such an agreement since it would have all of the overtones of a plan on the part of the suppliers of arms to freeze both clients and small power antagonists in an inferior military position—a conventional weapons "have" and "have not" situation. Moreover, it will be argued that there would be wholesale resistance to full disclosure because the disclosure would be voluntary and there would be no possibility of effective penalties for violations.

The validity of these arguments depends largely on how the reporting arrangement is presented to the UN. If the reporting proposal is portrayed *not* as an arms control measure (as was the case with League's registration plan), but as a straightforward effort to provide the Secretary-General with statistics on arms transfers as a means of lifting some of the regional distress and anxieties that usually accompany arms transfers, then a climate disposed to first appreciating and then defining the scope of arms transfers can begin to be created at the UN. With an understanding of the dimensions of the conventional arms problem that a program for reporting arms transfers would induce, I believe the possibilities for UN action will greatly improve.

Moreover, once the publicity on the transfer of arms begins, member nations could hardly ignore international opinion that they should disclose their arms transfers to the Secretary-General. I believe that if these arms sales and grants reported to the UN are limited to reports on major pieces of military equipment such as tanks, aircraft, and armed personnel carriers, the possibility of undisclosed or clandestine shipments will be greatly reduced. You simply cannot hide a tank or an aircraft for very long. If a country participating in the UN reporting program on arms shipments ignores disclosing a sale of major military equipment and then that sale is brought to light by the press or a neighbor of the purchaser, the country selling the weapons will be put in a very difficult and awkward international position.

International reporting then, can be a practical way of not only exposing arms sales but developing the international understanding of the problem that will hopefully lead to an international consensus on control of the trade.

Conventional Arms "Free Zones"

A program of reporting major arms transfers to the Secretary-General of the United Nations would lay the groundwork for the establishment of conventional weapon "free zones"; zones where the introduction or possession of regionally defined "sophisticated" weapons—i.e., missiles, supersonic jet aircraft, tanks of a certain weight or armament—would be prohibited.

The establishment and maintenance of such free zones should be devised by regional organizations such as the OAS and the OAU, or by the UN where outside mediation is required. Latin America and perhaps North and Subsaharan Africa, where the arms race is still very much a crawl, offer the best possibilities for free zones. In other areas where the conventional arms race is more advanced, such prohibitions may have to be limited to advanced models of conventional arms weaponry. Conceivably, the OAS or the OAU, to cite some obvious examples, could contribute to the maintenance of such zones by the creation of regional arms inspectorates similar to the Western European Union's Agency for the Control of Armaments.

The Scrapping of Military Equipment or "Buy-Back"

As noted above, there is enormous amount of surplus military equipment of American origin either in or soon to arrive on the international arms market. The desire of industrial countries to resell American military equipment is rising as the U.S. is shifting its program of military assistance from grants to sales. When a European pays for his military equipment, he is interested in reclaiming as much of the cost as he can by reselling the obsolete equipment in the international market rather than simply scrapping the arms.

What is needed then is a way of discouraging purchasers of U.S. military equipment from reselling U.S. arms to underdeveloped countries; or better, to encourage them to scrap the equipment.

Two factors important as background to the proposal are offered below:

(1) The countries who want to resell military equipment of American origin are the major industrial countries, such as West Germany, France, and Belgium. Underdeveloped countries such as Greece and Turkey rarely resell military equipment because of its domestic usefulness either as scrap or as "cannibalized" parts for commercial vehicles. Thus, the problem centers on developed countries.

(2) We have negotiated agreements fixing the scrap value of American arms. Previous negotiations with the West Germans have led to an agreement that 7.5 percent of the original sales price would be a mutually acceptable figure for scrap value.

One way of attempting to deal with the problem of the disposal of obsolete military equipment would be to add as a condition of eligibility for military sales of the United States Government to any foreign country not receiving assistance under the Foreign Assistance Act that the purchaser must agree to scrap major military items (tanks, aircraft, artillery—the items covered under the UN reporting plan) of American origin when they become obsolete, or return the equipment if the U.S. should so decide. If it is mutually agreed to scrap the equipment, the purchaser would then deposit the receipts from the sale of the scrap in a special account. In return the United States Government would match this amount in funds (not to exceed 7.5 percent) to be held in a special account in the United States.

As for the obsolete military equipment already in the hands of developed countries, a variation of the above proposal could be worked out. For example, the United States could offer to countries now possessing full rights to equipment of American origin that these countries agree to scrap the major military items in return for a credit of 7.5 percent of the original value of the equipment toward payment required on future sales of U.S. military equipment.

The funds derived from scrapping and the U.S. matching grants in the case of agreements on the purchase of new equipment would be made available for use in financing educational and cultural exchange programs under the Mutual Educational and Cultural Exchange Act of 1961.

A proposal of the sort described is obviously similar to the amendment to the Surplus Property Act of 1944 which established the Fulbright program. The proposal to use the scrap value of American arms for educational and cultural exchange programs described above could be brought into effect by an amendment to the Foreign Military Sales Act of 1968. Such an amendment would have the happy result of devising a program limited to the industrial countries where there is a shortage of Fulbright funds and where the surplus military equipment problem exists.

WHAT IS CLEAR is that the world community must begin to think hard and creatively about the problem of the flow of conventional arms into all quarters of the world. In the United States, we have a responsibility not only to the citizens of the underdeveloped countries that wish to get on with the job of economic development, but to our own citizens who do not wish to be drawn into conflicts not of the United States' choosing. The conventional arms question is central to both these issues.

CHAPTER 7

The Proliferation of
Nuclear Weapons

ARNOLD KRAMISH

SINCE HIROSHIMA the specter of nuclear holocaust has haunted and shaped the international policies of all nations, but no nonnuclear nation has felt the burden to the same degree as have those few powers who have progressively mastered, developed, and attempted to control the nuclear and associated technologies. Each new generation of leadership in those nations has acquired a nuclear legacy which they have found to be more difficult to control and work with than did their predecessors. They have found that nuclear superiority does not deter aggression by those who do not have nuclear arms; even "conventional" conflict is more difficult to terminate. Nuclear arms have thus far deterred worldwide conflict but in every other respect are a burden, a burden which cannot be lifted until (and if) a new means for securing world order can be found.

In the United States, President Eisenhower inherited the legacy of a nuclear weapon program too weak to be effective in any strategic or tactical situation; he inherited the thermonuclear program initiated by President Truman as a response to the entrance of the second member into the "club" and to remedy the "deficiencies" of a fission-weapon-based defense posture. Under the Eisenhower administration the thermonuclear program, with its associated systems, developed and began to thrive. To counterbalance the Damoclean swords suspended then also by taut Soviet and British strands, the Eisenhower administration placed great faith in "Atoms for Peace" as something which would presumably draw more attention to the peaceful potential of the atom and eventually serve as a means for de-escalating the nuclear threat everywhere, diverting the atom into purely benign paths of endeavor. But "Atoms for Peace" became a legacy of peril and promise for the next administration. While much less is known of the nuclear decision processes within the Soviet Union, there is much to suggest similar problems, similar "solutions." For the United Kingdom, which has enjoyed a special relationship with the United States, the burden of updating and maintaining increasingly modernized nuclear sources has for years tottered on the brink of its moment of truth. In France, where the decision to embark upon a nuclear weapon program was made before the Fifth Republic of General de Gaulle, there is now a decade of accomplishment and agony over the composition and role of the *force de frappe*, General de Gaulle's uncomfortable legacy to the men who succeed him. The Chinese nuclear program exhibits such technical peculiarities that it must be, and will ever increasingly become, a severe economic burden and decision problem for Mao's successors.

Catalyzed in part by the frightening experience of Cuba, agreement on a long-discussed, long-debated partial test ban treaty was the contribution of President Kennedy and Premier Khrushchev to the problem of alleviating the nuclear specter. Also initiated during that same period of leadership were the discussions on how to achieve a nonproliferation treaty which would limit the spread of nuclear weapons. Those discussions have been tortuous and have necessitated paying their political price. Such is the legacy which will be passed on by present leaders who are trying to muster ratifications of the Nonproliferation Treaty (NPT). It is hoped, but by no means assured, that the Treaty will initiate a process of counterbalancing the still escalating arms race. Nevertheless, the Treaty (and its history) must serve as the base line for any further developments as nations proliferate or elect not to do so.

How realistic are the NPT expectations in view of the inexorable advances of technology? Is the Treaty really worth the political price, in terms of alliance strains, that has been paid and will continue to be paid? In this respect, the analysis must be prefaced by a very strong moderating consideration. It is simply the fact that during a period of strained relationships over Southeast Asia the Nonproliferation Treaty negotiations had preserved a major point of contact between the two great nuclear powers. The value of keeping channels of communication open between the two cannot be overstated.

The Nonproliferation Treaty, which was opened for signature on July 1, 1968, six and a half years after it was first proposed, automatically divides the world into two classes of nations. It defines a nuclear weapon state as "one which had manufactured and exploded a nuclear weapon or other explosive device prior to January 1, 1967." All other states are nonnuclear weapon states. This political artifice in itself merits discussion, since a state which manufactured and/or exploded a nuclear explosive device after that date would be considered a nonnuclear weapon nation and would have to abide by the principles governing those nations if it signs the Treaty after the attainment of such a device. Furthermore, the state which obtains a weapon by transfer, but not by manufacture, also remains a nonnuclear weapon state under the terms of reference of the Treaty. Thus in the very beginning, matters of definition which are most germane to political reality are plagued by political, technological, and security aspects of a nation's policy in relationship to the Nonproliferation Treaty. The key to the success of the NPT lies mainly in the hands of the nonnuclear weapon states, in the manner they wish to exercise the "pressure" options which are theirs by virtue of their signing.

Although attempts to limit the spread of nuclear weapons date back to the Baruch Plan of 1946, the Nonproliferation Treaty finally drafted is essentially the outgrowth of the unanimously approved "Irish Resolution" of December 4, 1961, in the U.N. General Assembly, calling upon all states: "to use their best endeavours to secure the conclusion of an international agreement containing provisions under which the nuclear states would undertake to refrain from relinquishing control of nuclear weapons and from transmitting the information necessary for their manufacture to states not possessing such weapons, and provisions under which states not possessing nuclear weapons would undertake not to manufacture or otherwise acquire control of such weapons."[1]

The Treaty, achieved and finally opened for signature on July 1, 1968, was probably, as the United States Senate Committee on Foreign Relations observed, "the best that can be negotiated at this time."[2] It is complex enough; if any more time had been spent on negotiating it, catering to special circumstances of nations or groups of nations, the Treaty might not just have been "the best that can be negotiated" but one which might have allowed any signatory nation to do as it pleased under a facade of peaceful intent. Thus the present Treaty must be recognized as a mixture of weaknesses which in time must be corrected by common consensus on interpretation or by Treaty amendment. Some significant clauses of the NPT, again by common consensus on interpretation, might well become the basis for further progress in arms control.

The Treaty is preceded by a preamble which declares the dangers of nuclear war and the proliferation of nuclear weapons, recognizes the benefits of the peaceful atom, and declares the hope of easing international tensions. Even this bland introductory statement has already proved contentious. The final paragraph recalls "that, in accordance with the Charter of the United Nations, States must refrain in their international relations from the threat or use of force against the territorial integrity or political independence of any State, or in any manner inconsistent with the Purposes of the United Nations, and that the establishment and maintenance of international peace and security are to be promoted with the least diversion for armaments of the world's human and economic resources."

[1] U.S. Arms Control and Disarmament Agency, *International Negotiations on the Treaty on the Nonproliferation of Nuclear Weapons* (Washington, D.C. 1969), 5.

[2] Executive Report No. 9, U.S. Senate Committee on Foreign Relations, *Treaty on the Nonproliferation of Nuclear Weapons*, 90th Cong., 2nd Sess., September 26, 1968, 13.

Seven weeks after the Treaty was opened for signature and signed by the Warsaw Pact nations, the latter moved into Czechoslovakia to strengthen the "socialist commonwealth" under the rules of the so-called Brezhnev Doctrine, which asserted the right to intervene in socialist states when the Party was deemed to be threatened.[3]

To some states this seemed like a clear refutation of the last paragraph of the preamble of the NPT (as well as Article 2 of the UN Charter and Article 1 of the Warsaw Pact). A point of this was made by Italian Foreign Minister Medici in declaring that his government would delay signing the Treaty. But memories are short and politics fluid. Italy signed the Treaty after the United States Senate agreed to its ratification in early spring of the following year.

The incident illustrates the transient force of broad declarative statements. The rest of the Treaty however contains specifics which are quite restrictive but in some cases enigmatic. The first and second Articles of the Treaty are declarations quite similar to and having the same force as the simple "Irish Resolution" of 1961. Article III is exceedingly complex because it obligates nonnuclear weapon signatories to accept the extension of the control of the International Atomic Energy Agency over all of their peaceful nuclear activities. It does not obligate nuclear weapon states in similar manner. Reflected in Article III are the years of negotiation with individual nations in attempting to assuage their fears of industrial espionage and the seeking of a compromise arrangement between IAEA and regional nuclear energy authorities, particularly the atomic energy arm of the European Economic Community.

Article IV promises that the peaceful nuclear activities of the signatory states shall not meet with interference and that all parties to the Treaty will assist one another in peaceful programs and ends "with due consideration for the needs of the developing areas of the world."

Article V was designed to assure nonnuclear weapon states that they would receive the benefits of peaceful nuclear explosive devices which could only come from the nuclear weapon states.

Article VI represents virtually the only important obligation in the Treaty of the nuclear weapon states in that it is a further declaration of intent that negotiations would proceed on the cessation of the arms race.

The seventh Article affirms the right of states to further pursue a type of arms limitation, the regional exclusion of nuclear weapons.

The final four Articles are of a housekeeping type, referring to rights of amendment, voting, signature, ratification, withdrawal, and review processes. They are not however without complicating features.

[3] *Pravda*, "Sovereignty and International Duties of Socialist Countries," September 25, 1968.

The NPT does not obligate signatory nuclear weapon states to cease further production and improvement of their own nuclear weapons but does pledge them, as all parties to the Treaty "to pursue negotiations in good faith on effective measures relating to cessation of the nuclear arms race at an early date and to nuclear disarmament, and on a treaty on general and complete disarmament under strict and effective international control."[4] (Article IV) Further, all states pledge "fullest possible" peaceful nuclear assistance to other states—including the potential benefits of nuclear explosions for peaceful purposes. It is these obligations, vague as they seem to be, which form the basis of opportunities for the nonnuclear weapon states to begin to assert an even more important role in bringing about and securing international order.

The nuclear weapon states have developed their own strategic outlooks and theories which, unremarkably, have much in common. But there is no common calculus for the other class of nations; perhaps there cannot be. Few "critical" nations, i.e., those on the threshold of nuclear weapon capabilities, display the inclination to entrap themselves in the web of escalation of strategic forces through which three nations, now by treaty as in fact, have set themselves apart from others.

Others, of course, know how to build the bomb, or at least a simple type of bomb. Historians would be remiss if they did not take the opportunity to pass judgment at this point, more than a quarter of a century after the first chain reaction was initiated, on the apocalyptic literature which began to circulate even within the highly secret Manhattan Project after the fall of Germany and openly after the end of World War II. It was prognosticated that all the secrets of making the atomic bomb would soon become known and that within a decade or so many nations would proliferate atomic weapons. The outcome is that, even though the basic secrets and much advanced relevant technology have become known, proliferation has proceeded at a pace far slower than the prophets of doom had foreseen. Therein lies another lesson and a curious self-contradictory tactic which has been taken by some of those more fearful and positive of the rapid dissemination of nuclear weapons throughout the world. On the one hand they maintain that the information is already available and that bombs are cheap; i.e., proliferation is inexorable and rapid. If their simple calculations were valid, that consideration alone could not have helped but spur the rate of proliferation, contrary to the intent of the nuclear soothsayers. Yes, nuclear bombs are not now beyond the capacity of several nations presently not members of the "club," and this circle of

[4] Executive Report No. 9 (fn. 2), 10.

"threshold" nations will widen. But, for nations without enormous technical resources—nuclear and nonnuclear—to draw upon, it is vastly more difficult and more expensive to acquire any significant piece of nuclear weaponry than it is for the two nuclear superpowers. Once a nation possesses the bomb, the stark realization of how inadequate it has become as a junior nuclear weapon power leads to unforeseen costs of probably unbearable magnitude. This asymmetric fact of life, which also relates to the recent furor over the technological gap, is a difficult fact of life for other nations to accept, but nevertheless a rather resolute one.

Inasmuch as this technological asymmetric position exists and is bound to persist, it is difficult or simply galling for many nations to take the declarative position that they will not manufacture or otherwise seek to acquire nuclear weapons while at the same time those powers which already possess such weaponry are left free to maintain, elaborate, and expand those systems. Furthermore, the nonnuclear weapon states must accept international inspection of their nuclear activities, while nuclear weapon signatories are not so obliged. This asymmetry was the crux of the difficulty in obtaining the approval of a minimal number (40) of nonnuclear weapon states before the NPT entered into force on March 5, 1970. Particularly reluctant were certain nations of Latin America, which in February 1967 reached an agreement ("the Treaty of Tlatelolco") on a Latin American Nuclear Free Zone. Some of those states wondered why they should be bound by yet another treaty which they feel may be more restrictive in certain actions involving the peaceful uses of atomic energy. A nation like West Germany, which has already bound itself not to produce nuclear weaponry in the Western European Union agreements, had similar reservations. Nevertheless, the pressures are already so great that in refusing to sign the Nonproliferation Treaty a state does face the possibility of deterioration of relations with other states. West Germany's policy of East-West detente would be placed in grave jeopardy should she not meet Nonproliferation Treaty obligations. India (with a China view) had firmly stated that she will not sign the agreement in its present form; Pakistan naturally followed suit. The latter two states recognized that these stances, at the minimum, would hardly enhance already exacerbated relationships. These were calculated positions undertaken after extensive soul-searching, most considerations being overshadowed by a nuclear China. Nations resent the fact that the Treaty is asymmetric, no doubt about that. And, "Unless this asymmetry is corrected the Treaty will not achieve any useful purpose."[5]

[5] George W. Ball, *The Discipline of Power* (Boston 1968), 213.

OBLIGATIONS TO THE NUCLEAR WEAPON POWERS TO
CONTROL ARMAMENT LEVELS

At this stage, members of the nuclear weapon club, in name, are the original, permanent members of the United Nations Security Council, i.e., the major victors of World War II. If permanent membership in the Security Council were to be restructured to include some significant "threshold" but abstentious powers, such a move might catalyze new world political structure of some significance—perhaps more stabilizing, perhaps not. Alternatives such as this require consideration, and even more "unusual" solutions must be sought. Even when the NPT is signed by a majority of the member nations of the United Nations, France—a nuclear weapon power—may continue to show no inclination to sign; and mainland China, a member of the United Nations or not, will not sign. Even if more than 100 of the 124 member nations should adhere, this would not represent a significant stabilizing shift in the world power structure. An obvious conclusion is that further progress toward widespread reduction of nuclear armament, constantly maintaining certain essential elements which contribute to world security, depends upon better mutual understanding between the two major nuclear powers of reasonable levels of force structure. And the nonnuclear weapon states must also have a clear idea of what constitutes meaningful global force structures to ensure their security. Just as escalations are not unilateral neither can force reduction be. For example, an offer by one superpower to place all of its peaceful nuclear uses under international control could not realistically be followed by an even more drastic unilateral arms reduction initiative unless the earlier action had been reciprocated, at least in part.

Yet whether or not the Nonproliferation Treaty succeeds as a stepping stone to significant disarmament measures, world leaders cannot but be motivated by the desire and necessity of taking additional initiatives. What they will do, or are able to do, has already been largely shaped by the actions and philosophies of their predecessors. As the price for affixing their signatures to the NPT, the nonnuclear weapon states have every right to, and will, expect important new initatives from the states which now by international legal dictum have set themselves apart with special privileges.

In negotiating the NPT the great powers recognized that they would suffer costs—"substantial"[6] costs—in obtaining it, the heavier cost being "the erosion of alliances resulting from the high degree of US–Soviet cooperation which will be required if a non-proliferation pro-

---

[6] William C. Foster, "New Directions in Arms Control and Disarmament," *Foreign Affairs* (July 1965), 587-601.

gram is to be successful."[7] The U.S. has seen this effect in NATO; the U.S.S.R. has felt it with China. So the Nonproliferation Treaty has little meaning if substantial cost benefit does not ensue for the entirety of nations, without distinction.

The key to the hoped-for dividends is Article VI, which reads: "Each of the Parties to the Treaty undertakes to pursue negotiations in good faith on effective measures relating to cessation of the nuclear arms race at an early date and to nuclear disarmament, and on a treaty on general and complete disarmament under strict and effective international control."

Thus, the nuclear weapon powers are placed under the obligation to pursue such measures but it also obliges the nonnuclear weapon powers to press for such measures. They should never let the nuclear weapon powers forget their continuing and evolving obligations under Article VI as their price for the signatures of the nonnuclear weapon states.

If, in addition, the nonnuclear weapon powers play a more aggressive role in forging ahead to solve the nonmilitary problems which face the industrialized and nonindustrialized states, they will be able to demonstrate even more forcibly to the nuclear weapon states why and how resources must be diverted from a continuation of the strategic arms race.

The ability to withhold ratification after a nation signs and the right (Article X) of a nation to withdraw on three months' notice after it has signed are powerful political weapons for the nonnuclear weapon states in asking the nuclear weapon powers to satisfy Article VI.

But, if the demands and requests of the nonnuclear weapon powers are to be reasonable, they must understand the strategic positions of the nuclear weapon powers vis-à-vis one another. There would be great difficulty in meeting the varied security requirements of the nonnuclear nations during a prolonged period of planned reduction of nuclear forces. What the NATO nations would not like to see is what the Warsaw Pact nations would like to see. What India wants with respect to China, she is now almost indifferent to as regards the U.S.S.R. and the U.S. And the present concentration of nuclear strength in the Mediterranean is what almost nobody wants to see.

Nations must begin to know what they may demand under Article VI; they must be able to judge what constitutes escalation of the arms race, and what does not. Some wish the continued protection of the "nuclear umbrella"; others despise the term. The pressures available to the nonnuclear weapon states, if misdirected, could well damage their own near or long-term security—or, if unbearable enough, cause withdrawal of one or more of the nuclear weapon states themselves

[7] Same.

from the NPT. Article VI then constitutes the life seed of the NPT, making it essential to consider how present and new developments in weapon technology and deployment will affect the Treaty.

Czechoslovakia aside, and the NPT now being in force, the Treaty now reinforces the guarantees of the Charter of the United Nations against "the threat or use of force against the territorial integrity or political independence of any State." Further, the Security Council action of June 19, 1968, which accompanied consideration of the NPT, declared that the nuclear permanent members of the Security Council would act immediately through the Security Council to safeguard nonnuclear weapon states against nuclear aggression or threats of nuclear aggression. If some nonnuclear states adhering to the Treaty were ever to become convinced that these security guarantees were shallow or if a nuclear weapon state symbolically (and/or actually) protecting other states were ever in an inferior position such that it could not effect guarantees, clearly the Treaty would be eroded.

Consequently, it is important to reemphasize that the conditions of implementation of Article VI must at all times be consistent with international, regional, and bilateral security guarantees of all signatory states.

SAFEGUARDS

When it was of little importance, the wording of the safeguards article, Article III in the U.S. draft as tabled on August 17, 1965, read, "Each of the States Party to this Treaty undertakes to cooperate in facilitating the application of International Atomic Energy Agency or equivalent international safeguards on all peaceful nuclear activities." The text of Article III of the final treaty of July 1, 1968, is far longer and much more complex than its initial version. Further, the final Article III, subsection 3, guarantees that:

> The safeguards required by this article shall be implemented in a manner designed to comply with article IV of this Treaty, and to avoid hampering the economic or technological development of the Parties or international cooperation in the field of peaceful nuclear activities, including the international exchange of nuclear material and equipment for the processing, use or production of nuclear material for peaceful purposes in accordance with the provisions of this article and the principle of safeguarding set forth in the Preamble of the Treaty.

This is the key expression of the belief that the NPT might aggravate the technological imbalance among nations. For many nations it has become more important to consider safeguards in this context, not necessarily because of concern that nuclear materials might be diverted to bombs.[8] Their concern was mainly whether the IAEA inspection procedures would compromise proprietary peaceful applications and whether the costs of inspection would add unreasonably to the cost of nuclear power.

Ever since the International Atomic Energy Agency was established a decade ago, it has been the hope and express policy of the United States that the Agency would eventually be able to take over the provision of safeguards in a world where most nuclear activity would be confined to peaceful purposes. An initial aim was to assure the United States, as provider of most of the world requirements of nuclear fuels, that those materials were not diverted to military use. In the beginning, it was necessary for the United States to secure these guarantees by means of bilateral treaties with provision of U.S. inspection; but, as the initial bilateral treaties began to expire, the United States renegotiated them on the basis that the inspection responsibilities would be borne either by Euratom (the atomic energy organization of the six nations of the European Economic Community) or by the IAEA. The latter's safeguarding activities were now beginning to receive serious support from both the U.S. and the U.S.S.R. Thus far the IAEA has inspected only those particular facilities it has been requested to inspect by mutual agreement of two parties involved in an assistance pact. The Nonproliferation Treaty requires the IAEA to become a significant new type of international peacekeeping organization.

One of the American reasons for wanting this is that the United States is ceasing to be the sole source of nuclear assistance in the world.[9] The British-Dutch-German "agreement to agree" of March 1969[10] to proceed on a course of independent uranium enrichment plants underscores this. Similar announcements from South Africa, Australia, Japan, and India dramatically emphasize this trend. Thus the flow of nuclear material between and within nations is becoming increasingly complex; it is becoming difficult if not impossible to sort out the various types of donated materials from each other and from those which are the products of a nation's own program. There is also a growing concern on the part of the United States that the types of controls which other donor nations may institute bilaterally are far weaker than those which should be required. There are differences between sharing policies, and there is not only the uncertainty as to

[8] Arnold Kramish, "The Watched and the Unwatched: Inspection in the Non-Proliferation Treaty," Adelphi Paper No. 36, Institute for Strategic Studies, London, 1967.

[9] Lawrence Scheinman, "Nuclear Safeguards, the Peaceful Atom, and the IAEA," *International Conciliation* (March 1969), n. 572.

[10] "Uranium: Three European Nations Plan to Build Centrifuge Plants," *Science* (April 4, 1969), 53-55.

whether atomic energy materials are being fully safeguarded, but also a matter of economic and competitive concern. If a nation is offered two atomic power systems, it may well prefer to purchase the system which costs less to be safeguarded because of economic considerations. Even if two different national systems were identical in operating costs, that which required fewer safeguards would be preferred. Inspection costs have to be borne either directly by one of the contracting nations or indirectly through an international organization. The costs of applying comprehensive safeguards could increase the price of power by several percent; this is significant in commercial competition. For so-called real time[11] safeguard systems, the cost of nuclear power could be increased by fully 30 percent.

More important as a competitive factor however is the political attraction of a "no strings attached" contract. This problem is related to the type of fuel which a power reactor requires. United States reactor vendors used to feel that Britain and Canada have had a bargaining advantage in offering reactors fueled with generally available unenriched uranium, but actual sales statistics did not support this contention. Conversely, the temporary United States monopoly of the manufacture of enriched uranium bothered foreign manufacturers hoping to compete in the sale of advanced types of nuclear power reactors. The competitive implications of various degrees of inspection have been reflected in U.S. statements on nonproliferation policy: "Particularly important are international agreements on uniform standards to prevent critical materials and equipment from being offered for sale with inadequate controls, in order to realize economic or political advantage."[12]

Although there are many differences between the International Atomic Energy Agency and regional and national nuclear material management arrangements, it is not surprising that technical differences are not as hard to resolve as the problem of political acceptance of the different systems.

Both IAEA and Euratom safeguard systems provide for an examination of the plans of principal nuclear facilities in order to ensure that proper safeguards can be applied to them. The definition of "principal nuclear facility" in the IAEA is a broad one, ranging from reactors to isotope separation plants, reprocessing plants, or any type of facility which may be designated by the IAEA board from time to time. Thus the IAEA's access to plans of nuclear facilities is potentially broad, depending upon the mandate given it by treaty. Access to plans in the Euratom system, on the other hand, is in theory narrower, in practice just as broad. In the first place, Euratom feels that the critical points for diversion are the fuel reprocessing facilities and therefore reserves

[11] Where the accountability of materials is high and instantaneously known.
[12] Foster (fn. 6)

the right to approve the plans of such facilities, but not the right to scrutinize the plans of, say, a nuclear research experiment. However, if such an experiment utilizes materials which a country has received under international commitment and it is felt that the design of such an experiment might complicate the safeguard problem, Euratom has the right to review the design of such a facility. It should be noted that Euratom has responsibilities other than exercising safeguards, including consultation on significant investments and the implementation of technical and management standards assuring the safety of nuclear facilities and their proper management. But from the more broadly stated prerogative of the IAEA to examine all plans stem some of the fears within Euratom that industrial proprietary projects would be exposed to external examination by possible competitors from a great many nations. These fears do not apply merely to inspectors from the Soviet bloc, but to inspectors from such industrial competitors as Japan and the U.S. They even apply to some extent to other countries within the European Economic Community, bound by a complex of political and economic relationships.

The NPT requires harmonization of IAEA and state or regional controls over a reasonable period of time. Within 180 days after the Treaty entered into force, negotiations should have commenced with the IAEA, controls must enter into force within 18 months after that; essentially this meant a two-year period of grace to reach satisfactory agreement on safeguards. Whether the final form of harmonization should involve a complete takeover of safeguard responsibilities of the IAEA or a formula whereby the regional and international organizations become compatible, with appropriate consultation and interaction, may remain unresolved for a long time. If there is sufficient recognition that there are distinct advantages to all parties (including the Soviet Union) in accommodating Euratom through a reasonable transition period and that the IAEA can gain valuable experience from such accommodation, this problem is not fundamentally unsolvable.

It is not only the Euratom nations which are sensitive to the scope of the IAEA's inspection powers. Much remains to be done toward the development of technical methods and a philosophy of inspection which infringes to the least possible extent on a nation's right of privacy. Most of the technical methods which have thus far been applied in the IAEA system have been aimed toward guaranteeing that a specific quantity of fissionable material furnished by one nation to another under bilateral arrangement was not diverted into other uninspected sectors of the recipient's nuclear program. Paradoxically, when a nation's entire nuclear program becomes subject to inspection, the inspection problem is changed fundamentally in such a manner that there can be less infringement of national sovereignty and less possibility of compromise of proprietary processes than there would be if a nation had agreed only to inspection of a certain number of its nuclear reactors. When the complete program becomes subject to inspection, it should be possible to apply safeguards at a few key points along the flow path of materials and still obtain a greater measure of assurance against diversion. Identification of the key points however will be different in each country and the pattern will change from time to time as nuclear programs develop.

SHARING TECHNOLOGY

A major concern of the nonnuclear weapon states is that not only may their peaceful nuclear activities be subjected to commercial espionage because of inspection requirements but that nuclear weapon states, remaining relatively immune from inspection if they do not desire it, will forge ahead competitively. While the U.S. and the U.K. have sought to calm these fears by offering to have most of their peaceful nuclear activities subject to the same standards of IAEA inspection, the weapon programs will remain uninspected.

Technology has a bootstrap effect which can be most efficiently exploited by nuclear weapon states. For example, microcircuitry was first developed under a priority program for miniaturization of missile warheads. Then microcircuitry became available to a vast and varied number of industrial users and the science of microcircuitry developed with a momentum not solely attributable to weapon requirements. Then those who developed weapons were able to review the progress to microcircuitry elsewhere and to adapt those developments to new weapon applications, then to new civilian applications. As technology inevitably develops in the civilian sector, nuclear weapon designers will be able to borrow and adapt appropriate parts of the technology to the improvement and refabrication of existing weapon stockpiles.

The belief that nuclear weapon states have harvested enormous by-product dividends from their weapon programs is not valid in an economic sense.[13] It is true that it is easier to obtain appropriations for vast defense systems than for civilian product development, but this is a highly inefficient and unpredictable way to obtain civilian benefit. The art of mobilizing technological resources for direct attack on non-military problems is still primitive but deserves highest priority.

Another important point is that the Nonproliferation Treaty does not prohibit nonnuclear weapon states from developing nuclear weaponry if they are not explosive devices. For example, it will allow a

[13] Kramish, "Atlantic Technological Imbalance: An American Perspective," Defence, Technology and The Western Alliance Paper No. 4, Institute for Strategic Studies, London, August 1967.

nation to develop and build nuclear submarines or nuclear military surface ships. The Treaty would appear to allow the operation of nuclear power reactors serving military equipment at a military base. The Treaty allows the use of nonexplosive nuclear components and equipment in military aircraft. There is no obligation that any of these uses be inspected by the International Atomic Energy Agency. Further, the Treaty (not by wording but by omission) would allow signatory states to receive nonexplosive nuclear equipment of a military nature from signatory or nonsignatory states; and such equipment would not have to be subjected to IAEA safeguards, because it is neither a "nuclear explosive device" nor a "peaceful nuclear activity."

This is both a serious loophole and an advantage, although it may be important only for a very few special situations. It means, for example, that a signatory nation having a noninspected, nuclear-powered naval vessel could, if it wished to clandestinely circumvent the Treaty, produce fissionable material for bombs on board the uninspected ship. It also means that, if there are any industrial by-products from such activities, nonnuclear weapon states may seek them via such routes. One of the major U.S. civilian power reactor systems was based upon the submarine propulsion program.

One of the hindrances in arms control treaty negotiations has been the misunderstanding about the possible benefits of peaceful nuclear explosives (under the euphemism of "Plowshare"). Both the U.S. and the U.S.S.R. have been conducting such experiments and appear to be convinced that they hold great future potential in the digging of canals, tapping of natural resources, creation of underground storage chambers, et cetera. It would have been well if most of the U.S. publicity on these possibilities had been muted. But the United States is not solely at fault. Not to be outshone, at the mid-April 1969 discussions in Geneva the Soviet delegate was quick to point out that *their* work had shown that some types of nuclear explosions for peaceful purposes might come sooner than the United States delegate had indicated, others later.

Because a nuclear explosion for peaceful purposes can also be used as a military explosive device, this obviously precludes adherence to the NPT if a nonnuclear weapon state prefers to retain that option. If the nuclear weapon nations also prefer to retain that option it obviously also complicates agreement on a comprehensive test ban treaty, for there would always be the suspicion that new devices were being developed and tested under the guise of conducting peaceful nuclear explosions.

The Treaty of Tlatelolco is a paragon of this dilemma. The Treaty, unlike the NPT, defines a nuclear weapon. It "is any device which is capable of releasing nuclear energy in an uncontrolled manner and which has a group of characteristics that are appropriate for use for warlike purposes." It is interesting that the Treaty of Tlatelolco specifically excludes from this definition transport vehicles. Consequently, aircraft, missiles, et cetera—even those specifically designed to carry nuclear weapons—are permitted on the Latin American continent.

The first Article of the Treaty of Tlatelolco specifically prohibits any nuclear device being received, manufactured, installed, et cetera. The U.S. has interpreted any Plowshare device as coming under this definition. But Article 18 allows parties to the Treaty of Tlatelolco to use Plowshare techniques on their territory, either by themselves or in collaboration with third parties. Clearly, ample groundwork has been laid for continuous and extended disputation on the meaning of these conflicting Articles.

When it came to drafting the NPT, the nonnuclear weapon nations still wished to reserve the right to benefit from the peaceful uses of nuclear explosives, and fortunately the NPT is less ambiguous than the Treaty of Tlatelolco in this respect. In the first place, nuclear weapons are not defined in the NPT and Article V requires that the benefits of the peaceful applications of nuclear explosions will be made available to the nonnuclear weapon states on a nondiscriminatory basis. Furthermore, the nonnuclear weapon states will not have to bear any charges for research and development (this was somewhat annoying to certain members of an economy-minded U.S. Congress). These benefits would be provided through a special international agreement or through an appropriate international body (not necessarily the IAEA), or even through bilateral agreement between a nuclear weapon state and a nonnuclear weapon state.

Article V has certain other interesting implications. For one, it seems that it circumvents the International Atomic Energy Agency as a control body. The bilateral agreement proviso presumably would allow nuclear weapon states to preserve some of their secrets of construction of nuclear explosive devices and, under certain circumstances, might invite criticism that the peaceful applications were masking tests of nuclear devices.

Another implication is that Plowshare benefits presumably have an indefinite long-range utility; and, if through some miracle the world's nuclear weapon stockpiles were to be substantially reduced and nuclear weapon development stopped, Article V would still seem to stipulate that the nuclear weapon powers maintain and perhaps refine their nuclear explosives expertise.

Finally, many applications of nuclear explosive devices would unavoidably vent radioactivity to the air or water. Such applications would require a permissive amendment to the 1963 Partial Test Ban

Treaty and international agreement on permissible levels of contamination for each use of such devices.

It is obviously necessary for all signatories to the NPT to come to a better understanding of the implication of the applications of the peaceful uses of nuclear explosives. To this end, the U.S. and the U.S.S.R. met in Vienna outside of the usual disarmament discussions in mid-April 1969 and after brief deliberation warned nonnuclear weapon nations against premature optimism about such applications. It was a reasonable stance and important that it had been agreed to by the two major potential supplying nations. Nevertheless, even this type of negotiation met with some criticism from the nonnuclear weapon nations that the big two had been negotiating behind their back.[14] In this and other instances, however, bilateralism between the two great powers may continue to be necessary for more substantial progress. But wherever possible the negotiations should be broader to garner the confidence of the nonnuclear weapon states. The latter have a certain bargaining position which the nuclear weapon states do not. They can always withdraw from the Nonproliferation Treaty and produce nuclear weapons.

What to share and how to share peaceful technology is going to continue to be controversial. The Nonproliferation Treaty asks nations to show two kinds of restraint. It asks parties to refrain from manufacturing nuclear weapons if they do not already have them and it asks all parties to refrain from assisting other nations in manufacturing nuclear weapons. In reality, a strict interpretation of paragraph 2 of Article I of the 1963 Partial Test Ban Treaty already had placed the latter restriction upon nations adhering to it. The paragraph reads: "Each of the Parties to this Treaty undertakes furthermore to refrain from causing, encouraging, or in any way participating in, the carrying out of any nuclear weapon test explosion, or any other nuclear explosion, anywhere which would take place in any of the environments described, or have the effect referred to, in paragraph 1 of this Article."[15]

A rigid interpretation of this Article would mean that nations should not supply to any other nation information, materials, or other forms of assistance which would enable that nation to carry out a nuclear weapon test explosion in the environments covered by the 1963 Treaty. Presumably this will still permit such assistance to nations for tests

[14] E.g., statement by the Brazilian Foreign Minister to the U.N. General Assembly, September 19, 1963, "we cannot refrain from regretting that the Moscow meeting was held outside the province of the Eighteen-Nation Disarmament Committee."

[15] U.S. ACDA Publication 24, *Documents on Disarmament 1963* (Washington, 1964), 292.

conducted underground. But, in rendering assistance, it would in most cases be impossible to determine beforehand the environmental intent of a nation. Consequently, the 1963 Test Ban Treaty can be interpreted as an arrangement which already went halfway to meet the intentions of the Nonproliferation Treaty.

At least in one major instance paragraph 2 of Article I has already been interpreted in that strict sense by a nuclear weapon power, the United States. When France, which would not adhere to the Partial Test Ban Treaty, attempted to arrange for a long-term delivery of large amounts of uranium from Canada without restricted covenants on its use, the U.S. blocked that move by invoking the fact that Canada was a signatory to the Treaty and knew that the supply of such materials could contribute to the French nuclear weapon test program.

This action constitutes an important precedent, for some nations are now apprehensive that the Nonproliferation Treaty will be interpreted by other nations in such a manner as to seriously restrict peaceful nuclear programs. The fundamental raison d'être of the Nonproliferation Treaty is the intimate relationships between peaceful and military nuclear programs. Almost any peaceful nuclear program can be interpreted as having military implications. If, for example, the U.A.R. and Israel should both adhere to the NPT and seize the political opportunities of accusing one another about the intent of their peaceful nuclear programs, this could constitute a continuing nuisance in the implementation of the provisions of the NPT and a serious block to further negotiations.

But the essential point is that nothing in the NPT "shall be interpreted as affecting the inalienable right of all the Parties to the Treaty to develop research, production and use of nuclear energy to peaceful purposes without discrimination." This means that signatories to the Treaty, having agreed that their peaceful nuclear programs will be subject to appropriate safeguards, are perfectly free to conduct peaceful nuclear research and developments, even such activities which might be considered "dangerous" as far as their weapon implications are concerned.

The nuclear programs of the Federal Republic of Germany have, naturally, been the target of much suspicion and criticism from nations of the Warsaw Pact. The criticisms run to extremes. For example, the pseudonymous Ernst Henry[16] is convinced that West Germany is allied with China in circumventing the Nonproliferation Treaty. Lately, the understanding reached between West Germany, the Netherlands, and the U.K. on the establishment of enterprises to manufacture enriched uranium by means of the ultracentrifuge has come

16 *Literaturnaya Gazeta* (April 10, 1968), 14; (April 17, 1968), 15.

under special attack.[17] This agreement does indeed have serious implications for nuclear weapon proliferation. The emergence of independent uranium-235 isotope separation facilities in nonnuclear weapon states appears to be an inevitable trend.[18] But these technologies must be strictly controlled; and this is why German participation in such an enterprise is disturbing, particularly to the Eastern bloc.

The traumatic experience in proffering nuclear aid to China has evidently had a braking effect on Soviet peaceful assistance policies. The U.S.S.R. has not been overly generous even within the Warsaw Pact. A power reactor which should have been built within five years after being offered to Czechoslovakia in the mid-1950's is still not projected to be ready until the early 1970's. Some nations promised only small research reactors never received them. Formally, the U.S.S.R. has only committed itself to supply a symbolic 50 kilograms of nuclear fuel through the International Atomic Energy Agency, but the United States has committed itself to donating, leasing, or selling, many hundreds of thousands of kilograms. Nevertheless, as it must be if the commitments of the great powers under Article IV of the NPT are to be meaningful, the U.S.S.R. is beginning to show signs of more generous peaceful assistance policies. Some of these policies will, of course, be manifested only to match Western initiatives. This is one reason that the latter initiatives must continue and be imaginative.

Already, the U.S.S.R. has had to match certain Western initiatives. In the area of fuel supply the U.S. has long offered generous terms to foreign customers in the enrichment of raw uranium to fuel grade. This was in part to forestall the construction of independent enrichment facilities abroad, a policy which appears not to have been entirely successful. Very late in this game the Soviet Union has offered the enrichment service,[19] although it has not seen fit to publicize it widely.

At a certain point in time which may not be too distant, China too will feel compelled to start tapping the political benefits which accrue to the nuclear weapon nations because of their peaceful nuclear activities. Even when Stalin was pushing his scientists toward the earliest possible possession of the atomic and hydrogen bombs, there were other areas of high priority in nuclear research accelerators and nuclear power. It is inconceivable that the Chinese will not eventually

[17] Boris Gurnov, "Uranium Plan Attacked," Commentary from *Pravda*, *London Times*, February 7, 1969, p. 6.

[18] Kramish, "A Reexamination of the Nuclear Proliferation Problems Presented by World-Wide Requirements for Enriched Fuel; Relating the February 1956 Options to Today," P-3923, Rand Corporation, Santa Monica, California, August 1968.

[19] International Atomic Energy Agency, *Provisional Record of the One Hundred and Twenty-First Plenary Meeting*, GC (XII)/OR.121 (September 30, 1969), 9.

advertise their nuclear capability via demonstrating some important peaceful nuclear capabilities.

And, after this is done, China will begin to strengthen her sphere of influence by modest (but highly publicized) offers of nuclear assistance and by limited exchange of scientific personnel.

While the Nonproliferation Treaty promises favored treatment for nonnuclear weapon states party to the Treaty, there is nothing in the Treaty which says that states which do not sign the Treaty cannot receive peaceful nuclear assistance from a signatory state if the recipient state agrees to appropriate safeguards. This could mean that only the peaceful nuclear activities of a nonsignatory state which were the result of bilateral assistance would have to come under international safeguards. Other peaceful nuclear activities could be exempt. On the other hand, a state which adhered to the Treaty would have to place *all* of its peaceful nuclear activities (presumably its only nuclear activities) under safeguards. Clearly, the promise of nuclear assistance or the threat that nuclear assistance would be cut off may not constitute an overriding incentive for some nations to adhere to the Treaty. With some nations the U.S. has very heavy bilateral assistance obligations. And if such nations, which might include India, Israel, and Japan, did not adhere to the Treaty or were unable to come to an agreement on safeguards with the International Atomic Energy Agency, their future bilateral status could become a matter of acute embarrassment to the United States. Continued rendering of such assistance might be essential for the preservation of bilateral political relationships. On the other hand, such a relationship is bound to come under the fire of other NPT signatory states of both categories.

But if states, independently or with assistance, prematurely succumb to the lure of new technologies, they may experience the disappointments (which have been many) of the nuclear weapon powers. For most nonnuclear states this would be far more disastrous, debilitating their natural resources, and economic and manpower wealth.

The Nonproliferation Treaty and the realization of the cost involved in embarking upon nuclear weapon programs will presumably dampen unrealistic aspirations in nonnuclear weapon states. The problem of whether a nuclear weapon state with the greater resources at its command should or should not proceed (or at what rate it should proceed) in its flirtation with a new concept, be it for peaceful or military application, requires an entirely new approach to research and development management. The so-called systems approach is one which has promise but has been much abused. It has been misused because many of those obsessed with the magical detail of the analysis have become enchanted by the order and logic which appeared to emerge from a small domain of the problem—and were blinded to the fact that they had neglected other pertinent parameters. The other pertinent issues nowadays are an appreciation of just what is the real threat to a nation, how much can a nation afford to spend on weapon systems in the light of all the other demands, the real obligations of nations among nations, et cetera. We are entering a significant new period of reassessment of this nature. There is danger that too much restraint in some areas of challenge may prove to be unfortunate. There is danger that each considered premature response to the same challenges will prove to be even more unfortunate. But there is also a growing conviction, which appears to have some basis in fact, that a reasonable compromise course can be followed if, at last, other nations too begin to think in the same vein.

FUTURE STEPS

The achievement of an initial nuclear weapon capability is not a difficult task for a substantial number of reasonably high technology countries. In each of these countries there has been much internal deliberation on whether to possess nuclear weapons. Usually these dialogues are stratified and simple. Arguments are usually violently for or violently against national weapon capability. But the dialogue is beginning to be refined and it is interesting that, particularly in those nations closest to a nuclear weapon capability, more subtle rationalizations are beginning to emerge. For example, because China has been able to manufacture nuclear weapons, it indicates to some that such manufacture is technically and industrially easier than most had thought; consequently nuclear weapons by themselves cease to be attractive goals.[20] Even in the political sense the value of possession of nuclear weapons may have declined as a result of the Chinese capability. This is curious reasoning, but perhaps has some validity in the context of a nation like Japan. What this indicates is that, if some nations wished to manufacture nuclear weapons, the Chinese lesson shows that they could outdo China. The knowledge that this is possible, coupled with the act of restraint, is more important than the possession of nuclear weapons.

The corollary is that nations which have a more remote possibility of possessing nuclear weapons may desire them more than do those nations which could easily manufacture nuclear weapons. There is also some truth in this belief: nations which possess nuclear weapons, and those which have carefully considered the consequences of possessing them, inevitably gain a sober understanding of factors which paralyze their use.

Consequently, some would urge a strong peaceful program which will have an increasing latent capacity of conversion to nuclear weapons if necessary, This in fact was occurring anyway in all ad-

[20] E.g., see Junnosuke Kishida, "Concerning Nuclear Armament of Japan," *Kikubo* (July 1967).

vanced atomic energy programs. "Such latent capacities will result in increasing the bargaining power in the aspect of international politics, which will not be undesirable for Japan at all."[21]

It should be noted that, even if nations in this position (such as Japan and India) adhere to the Nonproliferation Treaty, there is nothing in the Treaty which prohibits the development of an option including the nonnuclear development and testing of bomb components. Possession of nuclear weaponry is prohibited in nonnuclear weapon states, but research and development on such weaponry is not. Even with respect to the use of special nuclear materials for such R and D, the restrictions of the Treaty are vague. The Treaty requires safeguards on all source or special fissionable material in all peaceful nuclear activities within the territory of such states but does not specify the kind of R and D which is peaceful or nonpeaceful.

Thus, whether or not a nation adheres to the NPT, its nuclear activities may be considered a threat by other nations. First, there is always the possibility of a drastic type of unilateral "control" measure. The anticipation that it is possible might tend to minimize its use. Realism demands that all means of stemming proliferation be considered, if not advocated.

In the apocalyptic lexicon "preemptive strike" or "first strike" has an ambiguous meaning. It may refer to the destruction of another nation's nuclear strike capability (first or second strike forces or both), to destruction of other military capabilities or populations, or a mixture of all. To discuss a scenario which appears to be on its way to becoming more plausible, particularly in light of the NPT, let us consider a type of action to excise another nation's nascent nuclear strike capability and term it a "surgical strike."

When the Soviets first tested a nuclear weapon, the possibility of the surgical strike certainly was discussed although it never reached the level of official policy. The same situation obtained when the Chinese detonated their first weapon in 1964. At this time the surgical strike was more seriously discussed, but again did not become a part of, at least, U.S. policy. On the other hand, the Cuban crisis made surgical strike a credible action; for, if the blockade and other firm elements of the U.S. stand had not proved convincing, it was clear that the next step would have been a surgical strike against Soviet rocket facilities in Cuba. Although two members of the nuclear club may have in some measure been tempted to "sanitize" China, there is little basis for assurance that China would not attempt to eliminate other new nuclear threats from Japan or elsewhere. Other nations, even remaining as nonnuclear weapon states, conceivably might resort to surgical strike against new entries into the nuclear weapon club.

21 Same.

If a nation does not sign the Nonproliferation Treaty and forsakes the accompanying security guarantees, weak or strong as the latter may be, a surgical strike against such a nation becomes especially credible because the nation undertaking this operation can claim a certain moral justification before the rest of the world. If a nation has signed the Nonproliferation Treaty and then breaks it surreptitiously or by exercising its rights of withdrawal under Article X, a surgical strike against such a nation becomes even more credible.

Such then is one method of "control," desired by none but certainly possible if further proliferation occurs or "high option" nuclear programs persist without an accompanying realistic detente atmosphere among states.

There are other more "conventional" control concepts which will have to be extended and new modes sought for all categories of nations.

The United Nations General Assembly in the fall of 1968 focused mainly on two obligations of the nuclear weapon powers as first steps in satisfying Article VI of the NPT. These were (a) cutoff in the production of nuclear materials for weapon purposes and (b) prohibition of underground nuclear weapon tests.

On June 25, 1964, the U.S. had submitted to the Eighteen Nation Disarmament Committee a detailed paper on the procedures which might be applied to effect the cutoff of the production of nuclear material for weapon purposes and the inspection procedure which might be applied. At that time it was suggested that the IAEA might assume the inspection obligations, but the critical suggestion was made that "each nuclear power would have the right to question the declaration of any other nuclear power and, if the other party does not justify its declaration to the satisfaction of the questioning party, to withdraw from the agreement."[22] The Soviet reaction[23] was entirely negative, maintaining that the proposal opened up all manner of espionage possibilities.

To proceed further with the concept, and especially for the purpose of beginning to open the nuclear weapon powers as well as the nonnuclear weapon powers to consistent standards of safeguards, the U.S. proposed on April 8, 1969,[24] that the nuclear weapon powers would not have the right to question the declaration of any other nuclear power. The entire inspection process would be under the aegis of the IAEA, for the nuclear weapon powers as well as the nonnuclear powers just as under the NPT. Within a few days this new proposal was again rejected by the Soviets.

The rejections reflect an information and security outlook which is

[22] U.S. ACDA, "US Cutoff Paper," *Documents on Disarmament 1964* (Washington, 1965), 236.

[23] Same, 339-51. [24] *New York Times*, April 9, 1969, p. 1.

at least a decade old and has no relevance today. For sensitive installations such as U-235 separation plants, the 1964 proposal suggested a method of inspection which involves access only at the perimeters of the processing buildings; for plutonium production more intimate access to reactors and chemical separation plants would be required, but the technology of such plants is well understood by many nations now. Nevertheless, the Soviet delegate in 1964 ignored the critical point of perimeter access to U-235 plants and claimed that "the visits by inspectors to the atomic plants subject to control . . . would reveal the whole technology of the production of nuclear material."[25]

There is inherent in this statement and in many other documents of the disarmament dialogue (often also in official U.S. statements laid on the disarmament table), a genuine naiveté or blindness to the vast and comprehensive materials now available on nuclear production processes—materials which surely will be examined and comprehended in the most minute detail by those wishing to build bombs but which are left most inadequately exploited by those working to ban bombs.

The glossary of nuclear strategists defines the spread of nuclear weaponry to more countries as "horizontal proliferation"; the acquisition of more weapons and their improvement by existing nuclear weapon states is termed "vertical proliferation."

The Partial Test Ban Treaty of 1963 was a temporary setback to vertical proliferation for the three nuclear weapon powers which adhered to the Treaty. It left them only the option of testing weapons underground. Some believed that this would seriously hamper future weapon development but this evidently has not been the case. Both the Soviet Union and the U.S. detonate underground at a merry rate, presumably mainly for the development of advanced nuclear offensive and defensive systems. Of course, a proportion of these underground detonations is devoted to research on the peaceful uses of atomic explosives.

As well as for testing one's own weapons and weapon systems, atmospheric testing was important to determine the effects of nuclear bursts by the enemy. It is unfortunate for the cause of stemming vertical proliferation, but fortunate for defense planners who were uneasy about the Partial Test Ban Treaty of 1963, that technological ingenuity is transcending the political restrictions on atmospheric testing. Testing techniques which do not require actual detonation of a nuclear device permit nuclear weapon states which might adhere even to a comprehensive nuclear test ban to continue the process of vertical proliferation to some degree. This the nonnuclear weapon states would

25 U.S. ACDA (fn. 22), 339-51.

undoubtedly deplore, but these are programs which are completely uninspectable, unverifiable.

Looking at the situation in another way, however, it is quite probable in retrospect that the U.S. would have been forced through such pressures to give up atmospheric testing within a year or so after the Partial Test Ban Treaty of 1963 was actually concluded. The outcry against radioactive contamination of the atmosphere could not long have been resisted. A similar situation is developing with respect to underground testing.

It is conceivable that, even without a negotiated underground test ban, the superpowers will gradually be forced to develop more sophisticated nondestructive nuclear test techniques and to abandon at least higher yield underground tests. If this is the case, there would be some political advantage in negotiating an underground test ban for tests up to at least a certain maximum yield. This decision is vastly more difficult for both the U.S. and U.S.S.R. than in the case of the Partial Test Ban Treaty; but the strength of public opinion and the attitude of the nonnuclear weapon powers toward Article VI may force this.

An argument can be made that some sort of agreement on a verifiable system of arms control and reduction logically should precede a comprehensive test ban. It is clear now that the Partial Test Ban Treaty has not significantly inhibited the development of new nuclear weapons and the testing of the integrity of stockpile weapons. This was provided for by the joint chiefs of staff recommendations adopted by the U.S. upon the signing of the Partial Test Ban Treaty. The high rate of underground testing in the U.S.S.R. is proof that that nation adopted similar measures to ensure that it would not remain behind in nuclear weapon development.

Some weapon design improvement can be achieved without testing. Certain weapon effects against other weapons can be investigated by laboratory simulation methods. However, certain other advanced weapon concepts will always require testing. Consequently, inhibiting testing or restricting it altogether does amount to a brake on the development of advanced weapon systems. And, if certain suspicious events of a seismic nature in a nation are not verifiable, this will mean that there would be a continuous strain on any treaty designed to inhibit or eliminate underground testing.

It is evident that, if "national means" are used by one party to check on another party's arms control obligation, a new philosophy of disclosure is required—something quite different from the current situation where these means of gathering intelligence are used for internal estimates of a potential enemy's capabilities and are therefore considered quite sensitive. If the confidence of nonnuclear weapon states is to be gained a system of intelligence reporting through an international agency must be established. This is important, as it is anticipated that nonnuclear weapon nations may have to make claims that must be verified against others. Further, since the two major nuclear weapon states are not only watching each other's activities but also the activities of other nuclear weapon states and nonnuclear weapon states, the establishment of reporting procedures through an international agency is clearly a prerequisite to the worldwide control of nuclear proliferation. In the long term it is possible that certain "national means" of reporting will be replaced by international inspection satellites and other advanced detection capabilities under a U.N. agency, i.e., by "international means."

At the present time, the nuclear weapon states are devoting their Strategic Arms Limitation Talks (SALT) to the problems of delivery vehicles as opposed to nuclear materials. The curious asymmetry of the nuclear safeguard problem is, thus, that the nonnuclear weapon states will have controls over their nuclear materials production while controls would be sought mainly over delivery vehicles for the nuclear weapon states. It seems ultimately that it will be necessary to find ways of subjecting fissionable material facilities and stockpiles to some sort of equitable control or reduction.

Only a few nonnuclear nations will have the facilities to separate plutonium from their power reactors. The plutonium which is separated for them by servicing nations presumably will be returned to the producing nations for stockpiling and future peaceful uses for the producing nations adhering to the provisions of the Nonproliferation Treaty. The stockpiles of plutonium will presumably be safeguarded adequately by the International Atomic Energy Agency. But if a nation withdraws from the NPT under the legal provisions of Article X, abrogates it illegally, or its government is replaced by another government which chooses not to recognize earlier obligations, there is nothing in the Treaty which assures continued safeguarding and peaceful use of accumulated stockpiles of fissionable materials.

Such stockpiles then become threats to world security even though they are safeguarded by the IAEA as they grow. Several suggestions have been made on how to forestall, or at least minimize, this potential threat. One suggestion[26] has been that it be made attractive for nations to trade accumulated plutonium for fabricated fuel materials for their power reactors. The trade could be made bilaterally with supplying nations, but this would not be too satisfactory. Most of the supplying nations will be the nuclear weapon powers. It seems absurd that the same fissionable material should be subject to international safeguards

26 Kramish, *The Peaceful Atom in Foreign Policy* (New York 1963), 76-80, 226-29.

in nonnuclear weapon nations when, by Treaty, it is not subject to safeguards when it is in a nuclear weapon state. One way out of this dilemma would be an arrangement whereby the U-235 producing nations, particularly the nuclear weapon powers, would supply large amounts of fuel (grade U-235) to the IAEA. The IAEA would then sell or trade this material to other nations.

Instead of subsidizing the IAEA, nuclear weapon powers could well supply the IAEA with nuclear fuel at advantageous rates. The IAEA could then sell or trade the materials at prevailing commercial rates, thus helping to pay for its overall operations. A variation of this suggestion has been that the IAEA safeguard and accumulate plutonium stock simply by buying back accumulated plutonium from power reactors.[27] This suggestion, of course, would be predicated on the provision of substantial monetary reserves by the IAEA. The U-235 trade-back arrangement would appear to be more feasible and to offer additional political dividends.

If a prolonged period of detente occurs there is another circumstance, an economic one, which may generate pressures for the reduction of stockpiles of nuclear warheads in all nuclear weapon nations. Conventional power plants are being succeeded by nuclear-fueled power plants. As early as the mid-1970's drastic demands for nuclear fuel will begin to be felt. For example, the output of the three U.S. uranium isotope separation plants has been cut back drastically because of substantial declines in defense requirements and because our civilian power requirements are not yet great. These plants are currently operating at about half of their full capacity but during the 1970's full capacity will eventually be reached again and the construction of new plants will have to be started to meet new requirements of the 1980's and beyond.

If, when the decision has to be made on the size of these new plants, there has been a prolonged period of detente between the U.S. and U.S.S.R., there is likely to be generated within the U.S. at least serious questions, if not formidable pressures, as to whether existing stockpiles of fissionable materials fabricated as weapon warheads should not be diverted to civilian uses. If this situation should arise, particularly in France and the U.K., it is possible that these circumstances could generate forces leading to withdrawal from the nuclear club. Whether this issue could effect armament levels in the Soviet Union is difficult to say, but their internal economic growth requirements coupled with fuel supply obligations assumed under Article IV of the NPT would indicate that fuel supply is not likely to remain a minor consideration in armaments limitations.

[27] Leonard Beaton, "Safeguards on Plutonium," *Nature* (December 31, 1966).

But, even though numerical limitations may be set on nuclear armament production and of fissionable materials diverted to civilian use, one should not be sanguine about the possibility of producing savings to be applied to other programs of national urgency or saving taxes. Keeping up with new technology, something which will be necessary for a prolonged period even in an era of nuclear arms limitation, will keep effective defense costs at a high level. These considerations must be anticipated even in keeping conventional forces modernized. Moreover, the cost of effectively securing arms limitation agreements via high technology inspection systems will be high.

One final mode of armament control—the regional approach—should be considered, because it has experienced a certain measure of success (in the Antarctica and Latin America).

The disarmament method whereby areas of the earth would be gradually denied the presence of nuclear weapons or even demilitarized completely has a certain attraction. New weapons are already barred by the Outer Space Treaty of 1966. Presumably this Treaty prohibits nuclear weapons from residing in a more or less stable orbit in outer space for an unspecified period of time. It is not clear whether the Treaty would prohibit a nuclear weapon from being placed into partial orbit in outer space. If it did, this would exclude testing and use of the Fractional Orbit Bombardment System (FOBS), which is apparently one of the Soviet weapon systems.

The other step to this type of disarmament is the gradual application of the philosophy to the earth surface, to the continents, and to the seas. The Antarctic Treaty of 1959 provides for complete demilitarization of that area and is apparently quite successful. It was easy to apply demilitarization there because no nation had yet attempted to integrate the Antarctica into its defense system. Looking to other continents, this situation becomes more difficult because of preexisting conditions.

Nevertheless, the Latin American nations, meeting in Mexico, were able to reach agreement in early 1967 on a Treaty for the Prohibition of Nuclear Weapons in Latin America (the Treaty of Tlatelolco). In many ways the Treaty of Tlatelolco is more comprehensive and specific than the NPT. It was attainable because no Latin American nation had achieved the status of a nuclear weapon power, although nuclear weapons had been installed and deployed in Latin America, e.g., Cuba. The Tlatelolco Treaty not only denies the nations of that continent the right to test, use, manufacture, or acquire nuclear weapons but also does not allow them to receive, store, install, or deploy nuclear weapons. Cuba has not signed the Treaty.

The Tlatelolco Treaty is consistent with the NPT in that it provides that it be safeguarded by the International Atomic Energy Agency. Precedent has been set by Mexico, which in September 1968 concluded a comprehensive agreement with the IAEA under the provisions of the Tlatelolco Treaty. This Treaty will mesh with the obligations assumed by Mexico in signing the NPT. This entwining of various Treaty structures, when it can be accomplished, will undoubtedly have a stabilizing effect on international order.

Looking to other continents, regional arms control arrangements become more difficult. Africa might be the next logical continent to go along with such an arrangement, but there are certain difficulties. The United Arab Republic is on the continent of Africa and Israel is not. The Union of South Africa, with its large reserves of uranium and not insignificant technical capabilities, maintains policies aloof from the rest of Africa. Nuclear arsenals cruise in the Mediterranean north of Africa, and the question of the extent of the continental shelves of all continents remains controversial.

Europe, Asia, and North America obviously cannot be subjected to an area-by-area disarmament solution in the foreseeable future. Australia, that unique single nation continent, will probably continue indefinitely the option to host friendly nuclear forces.

This leaves the rest of the earth, two-thirds of it, the seas. As one of the initial moves to implement the spirit of Article VI of the NPT, the question of demilitarization of the seabeds was discussed in Geneva in the spring of 1969. The initial position of the Soviet Union, strongly supported by Sweden and most of the other nonaligned nations at Geneva, was that the seabed should be completely demilitarized, excluding anything that could be construed as having a function—such as underwater listening devices. The United States position was that only nuclear weapons should not be placed on the ocean floors. Even though the Soviet Union eventually moved toward the U.S. view, both positions were unrealistic in that both ignored what already existed: nuclear, and other kinds of weapons on the surface of the seas, and in submarines cruising under the seas. Essentially, everyone was willing to agree on banning weapon systems they never wanted in the first place.

But such efforts are perhaps important and what is significant in this instance is not the seabed treaty itself but the fact that two great nations (and it will have to be more in a multipolar world) in the brief period of two years moved toward each other's views to enable the signing of a treaty in February 1971. Did this portend a new era of urgency and compromise? If it did, compromises such as these are the bases of major hope for stemming further nuclear proliferation.

CHAPTER 8

Civil Nuclear Power:
Conflict Potential and Management

MASON WILLRICH

AN ABUNDANT supply of energy is one of the essential bases for economic and social development. Electricity is considered one of the most desirable forms of energy throughout the world. The demand for electricity is doubling about every ten years in industrially advanced nations.[1] The principal peaceful use of nuclear energy in the next decade will be to generate electric power.[2] It is forecast that by 1980 nuclear power plants will represent about 25 percent of the electric generating capacities installed in several industrially advanced nations, and a lesser but significant proportion of the capacities in a few less-developed nations. By 2000 it is expected that nuclear fuel will be used to produce about half the world's electricity.[3]

Ever since President Eisenhower's dramatic "Atoms for Peace" address to the United Nations General Assembly in 1953,[4] the peaceful uses of nuclear energy have been an important focus of international cooperation. The primary objective of the International Atomic Energy Agency (IAEA) with a global membership approaching one hundred member nations is to "accelerate and enlarge" the peaceful uses of nuclear energy "throughout the world."[5] Moreover, the Nonproliferation Treaty, which entered into force in March 1970, would declare the use of nuclear energy for peaceful purposes an "inalienable

---

[1] Federal Power Commission, *National Power Survey—1964*, Pt. II (Washington 1964), 9; Commission of the European Communities, *Survey of the Nuclear Policy of the European Communities*, Supplement to Bulletin 9/10-1968 of the European Communities (Secretariat General of the Commission 1968), 9.

[2] Another use still in the developmental stage is in dual-purpose plants to generate electric power and desalt sea water. Beyond this, a range of possibilities are being explored under the broad concept of a nuclear-powered argo-industrial complex. See Oak Ridge National Laboratory, *Nuclear Energy Centers, Industrial and Agro-Industrial Complexes*, ORNL—4290 (Oak Ridge 1968).
A wide variety of possible applications of thermonuclear explosives for underground resource development and surface excavation are also in the developmental stage. Such "Plowshare" applications are not discussed in this paper because they require a different framework for analysis. Moreover, Plowshare is not likely to be a widespread source of international conflict in the decade ahead.

[3] U.S. Atomic Energy Commission, *Forecast of Growth of Nuclear Power*, WASH—1084 (December 1967, 2nd printing with Corrections, June 1968); European Nuclear Energy Agency, Organisation for Economic Co-operation and Development, *Illustrative Power Reactor Programmes* (Paris May 1968).

[4] U.S. Department of State, *Documents on Disarmament, 1945-1959*, Vol. 1 (Washington 1960), 393.

[5] International Atomic Energy Agency Stat. Art. II, opened for signature October 26, 1956, (1957) 1 U.S.T. 1093, TIAS No. 3873, 276 U.N. Treaty Series 3.

right of all the Parties" and obligate each Party to "the fullest possible exchange" of materials and equipment used in peaceful nuclear activities.[6]

The central thrust of international policy and law with respect to peaceful uses of nuclear energy has been, therefore, in the opposite direction from major efforts with respect to warlike uses of the same source of energy. Important attempts have been made *to control* the build up and spread of nuclear armaments among the nations of the world. Concurrently, major efforts have been made *to promote* the rapid development, diffusion, and widespread application of civil nuclear power. The former have by and large failed, while the latter have been highly successful.

Then, why should a volume dedicated to discussion and analysis of problems of conflict management as they relate to the future of the international legal order contain a chapter on the peaceful uses of nuclear power? Every nuclear reactor which produces electric power also produces plutonium, a fissionable material used in nuclear weapons. A small nuclear power reactor with about 200,000 kilowatts electric generating capacity produces every year more than 100 kilograms of plutonium—enough for 5 to 10 crude fission weapons comparable to the bomb dropped by the United States on Nagasaki during World War II. The aggregate worldwide plutonium production rate in civil nuclear power reactors is forecast to reach 8,000 kilograms annually in 1970, and 50,000 to 70,000 kilograms by 1980. This will result in an estimated accumulation in civil nuclear power programs of 300,000 to 450,000 kilograms by 1980.[7] Yet, less than 10 kilograms of plutonium are needed to destroy a medium-sized city.

The stockpiles of plutonium used in civil nuclear programs will soon exceed the amounts of fissionable materials in the nuclear weapons stockpiles of nuclear weapon nations. Moreover, tens of thousands of kilograms of plutonium will be available in nonnuclear weapon nations. If nuclear weapons are acquired by an additional nation in the future, it may well be as an "add-on" to a civil nuclear power program. Therefore, the widespread and growing use of nuclear energy to generate electric power will surely have a major impact on the potential for international conflict and the possibilities for conflict management in the future.

Furthermore, the process by which nuclear energy is being developed and exploited for a variety of peaceful purposes is one of the principal forces of change in the human environment. Science discovered the energy latent in the nucleus of the atom, and technology

[6] Treaty on the Nonproliferation of Nuclear Weapons, Art. IV. For a full analysis and assessment of the Treaty by the author, see Mason Willrich, *Non-Proliferation Treaty: Framework for Nuclear Arms Control* (Charlottesville 1969).

[7] David W. Wainhouse and others, *Arms Control Agreements: Designs for Verification and Organization* (Baltimore 1968), 13.

harnessed that energy to achieve human purposes. From a global perspective, the dynamic and increasingly integrated processes of scientific research, technological development, and application take place within and among certain nation-states in a predominantly decentralized and competitive international system. Since the results of research and development activities are unpredictable by definition, the magnitude and direction of the forces for change unleashed by these processes within particular nations and throughout the world are inherently unpredictable. Thus, science and technology pose continuing yet always changing challenges to the stability of the international legal order and the political institutions of the world community.

One of the central issues for the foreseeable future is whether we can evolve adequate political and legal mechanisms within the international arena to control the risks as we enjoy the benefits of continuous technological revolution. The outcome of this issue will largely determine whether technology will remain the servant or become the master—if not the destroyer—of mankind.

Clear and urgent proof of the preceding assertions is offered by the implications of the exploitation of nuclear energy to generate electric power for future conflict and security within the international system. In order to grasp these implications we must first take a brief tour through the cycle of operations necessary to obtain usable power from nuclear fuel and observe the pattern of distribution of the required resources throughout the world. Then, we will proceed to assess the conflict potential of civil nuclear power. Finally, we will explore various possibilities for keeping that potential within reasonable bounds.

We will limit our time frame to the 1970's. Thus, we are dealing primarily with the implications of technology that has already been developed and is now available for practical application.[8]

NUCLEAR FUEL CYCLE AND THE GLOBAL CONTEXT

The starting point of any nuclear capability, whether for warlike or peaceful purposes, is fissionable material. The two fissionable materials of primary interest are uranium in the form of the isotope 235 and

---

[8] The major technology development effort is aimed at "breeder" reactors which are intended to produce fissionable material from fertile material at a greater rate than fissionable material is consumed in the generation of power. If successfully developed, the introduction of breeder reactors in the 1980's will substantially magnify and further complicate the problems discussed in this paper.

Thorium-232 is the only other important "fertile" material (i.e., material which can be transformed into fissionable material) that occurs in nature, in addition to uranium-238. Thorium-232 will convert upon neutron capture into uranium-233, a fissionable material. Therefore, the possibility exists of a thorium-232/uranium-233 fuel cycle which parallels the uranium-238/plutonium-239 fuel cycle. In either case, a fissionable material is needed to begin with. Thorium technology is still in the development stage.

plutonium. The former is the only fissionable material known to occur in nature. Natural uranium consists of only 0.7 percent uranium-235 and 99.3 percent nonfissionable uranium-238. Uranium-238, however, is converted into plutonium when it is subjected to a neutron flux in a nuclear reactor.[9]

In order to generate electricity with nuclear energy, the heat derived from fission of uranium or plutonium is converted into steam which is then used to drive turbine generators. A nuclear power plant is in many respects comparable to a conventional power plant which uses coal, oil, or natural gas as fuel. The basic distinction is that in a nuclear-fueled plant heat is derived from physical fission in a reactor, whereas in a fossil-fueled plant heat is derived from chemical combustion in a boiler.

Two basic types of reactor technology have been developed, one using natural uranium as fuel and the other uranium that has been slightly enriched (3 to 5 percent) in the fissionable isotope 235. Depending on which type of reactor fuel is used, the cycle of operations required to generate electricity will include four or six major steps. In the case of natural uranium fuel, these steps will include: mining and milling of uranium ore; fuel element fabrication; fuel irradiation in a reactor; and spent fuel reprocessing to separate residual uranium and produced plutonium from radioactive waste products. Enriched fuel requires two additional steps: conversion of uranium into gaseous form; and increasing the uranium-235 concentration.

Each of the steps of the nuclear-fuel cycle, following mining of uranium, entails distinctive physical or chemical processes and facilities of varying technological complexity and cost in which to carry on these processes. The worldwide pattern of distribution of the raw materials, principally uranium, the sophistication of the scientific and engineering talents, the large size of the facilities required for economic utilization, and the resulting capital-intensive nature of nuclear industry have so far limited self-sufficiency in civil nuclear power to a very few nations.

Information related to all aspects of the nuclear fuel cycle except uranium enrichment is unclassified, well understood, and widely diffused throughout the world, in substantial part as a result of international cooperation through the IAEA and United Nations Conferences on the Peaceful Uses of Atomic Energy which have been held periodi-

---

[9] Plutonium in the isotope 239 and 241 is fissionable, but not all the isotopes of plutonium are. The isotopic composition of the plutonium produced in a nuclear power reactor will vary depending largely on the characteristics of the fuel and on the length of time the nuclear fuel is irradiated in the reactor. The fissionable content of plutonium produced in a natural-uranium fueled reactor will be higher than that produced in an enriched uranium-fueled reactor when both are operated for the most economical production of electric power.

cally since 1955. Information related to the materials and technology for the porous barriers used to enrich uranium by the gaseous diffusion process, as well as information related to the gas centrifuge process, remains highly classified within various national and international programs.[10] However, as the need for additional uranium enrichment plant capacity approaches, pressure is increasing to relax controls on the dissemination of information pertaining to enrichment technology.

Costs of the various facilities in the nuclear-fuel cycle vary widely depending upon a large number of variables. Simply for an impression, a recent estimate for capital costs of nuclear power plants in the United States covered a range from $100 to $280 per installed kilowatt.[11] This would mean that an 800,000 kilowatt plant, a standard large size, could cost from $80 million to $224 million to build. The cost per kilowatt of smaller plants is much higher, so that $50 to $80 million is probably a minimal price range for a nuclear power plant large enough to be economically justifiable. The costs of fuel fabrication and chemical processing plants of an economic size run above $20 million each.

Gaseous diffusion plants are the most expensive facilities in the entire nuclear-fuel cycle. The United States has invested a total of $2,326,000,000 in its three gaseous diffusion plants, the cheapest having cost $755 million. Furthermore, each of these plants requires 1,700,000 to 2,500,000 kilowatts of electric power when operating at full capacity to produce low enrichment fuel for nuclear power reactors.[12] To give meaning to this last figure, at present only Argentina, Brazil, India, and Mexico of all the less-developed nations have total electric power generating capacities which exceed 2 million kilowatts. However, if the gas centrifuge process, an alternate enrichment method, is demonstrated to be economically feasible, it is possible that these cost barriers to enriched uranium will be lowered somewhat in the future.

[10] The United States government announced on March 21, 1967, that "national security interests would best be served if privately sponsored work on the gas centrifuge process for separation of isotopes were discontinued." USAEC Release No. K-70 (March 21, 1967). Certain private firms affected by the U.S. Atomic Energy Commission decision have since contracted with the Commission to continue their research and development work in this field on a classified basis. USAEC Release No. K-163 (June 29, 1967). West Germany, the Netherlands, and the United Kingdom are engaged in a major cooperative international research and development program concerning the gas centrifuge process. This program contemplates the construction of one or two demonstration plants in the near future. Japan also has an established program of gas centrifuge research which, unlike the others, is being carried out on an unclassified basis.

[11] Letter from William Webster, Chairman, Yankee Atomic Electric Company, to Chet Holifield, Chairman, Joint Committee on Atomic Energy, April 8, 1969. Reprinted in *Hearings before the Joint Committee on Atomic Energy*, 91st Cong., 1st Sess., AEC Authorizing Legislation—Fiscal Year 1970, Pt. 2, 902-19.

[12] U.S. Atomic Energy Commission, *A.E.C. Gaseous Diffusion Plant Operations*, ORO-658 (Washington 1968).

Outside the Communist states, roughly 80 percent of the known reserves of uranium are located in three countries: the United States, Canada, and South Africa. Within Western Europe, France has deposits that are sufficient for its own nuclear weapons program, but probably not for its civil nuclear power needs as well. In addition, Sweden, Australia, Argentina, and a few African states have substantial uranium reserves. Significantly, the United Kingdom and West Germany lack their own uranium.[13]

Of the Communist states, both the Soviet Union and China are believed to have adequate uranium reserves. In Eastern Europe the largest uranium deposits are located in East Germany,[14] with smaller deposits in Czechoslovakia. Of course, increased demand for uranium is leading to the discovery of fresh deposits, increasing the reserves of nations already producing uranium and perhaps adding nations to the list of uranium producers.

Over 400 small research, experimental, and test reactors are located throughout the world.[15] Plutonium production is nominal in most research reactors, but it can be significant in certain materials test facilities.[16] Nevertheless, it is important to recognize that research and test reactors are essential facilities for the education and training of the manpower required for a nation to translate nuclear ambitions into capabilities.

Power reactors with an output above 100 megawatts, each producing militarily important quantities of plutonium, are in operation, under construction, or planned in all nuclear weapon nations, except possibly China, and in a growing number of nonnuclear weapon states, including Argentina, Australia, Belgium, Bulgaria, Canada, Czechoslovakia, Nationalist China, Denmark, Finland, West Germany, East Germany, Hungary, India, Israel, Italy, Japan, South Korea, the Neth-

[13] Organisation for Economic Co-operation and Development, ENEA-IAEA Report, *Uranium Resources—Revised Estimates* (Paris 1967), 24-25. Of course, reserves must be placed in various price ranges based on costs of recovery. The estimates quoted are an approximation at the $5 to $10 per pound range. While India lacks large uranium reserves, it has one of the largest known thorium reserves in the world.

[14] The implications for German reunification of West Germany's growing civil nuclear industry and East Germany's uranium reserves are substantial. East Germany was in the forefront of the signers of the Nonproliferation Treaty, although that country is not presently a member of the IAEA. The application of IAEA safeguards to peaceful nuclear activities in East Germany in accordance with Art. III of the Nonproliferation Treaty would raise a number of fascinating problems concerning the future of East Germany's participation in the work of the IAEA and recognition of the government and state of the German Democratic Republic.

[15] International Atomic Energy Agency, *Power and Research Reactors in Member States* (Vienna, May 1969), 10.

[16] An example of a research reactor which is a source of genuine international concern is the 24 megawatt materials test reactor at Dimona, Israel, secretly built with French assistance. This reactor is capable of producing enough plutonium for about one bomb per year.

erlands, Pakistan, Spain, Sweden, Switzerland, and the United Arab Republic. Almost 300 power reactors will be in operation in the world by 1975.[17] It is clear that the spread of nuclear power and plutonium production capacity is not confined to particular geographic regions, or to specific political or ideological persuasions, or to countries advanced in economic development.

Fuel fabrication plants to supply the input and chemical separation plants to process the output of nuclear reactors are not yet as widely dispersed around the world as the reactors themselves. Since nuclear fuels are readily available in international commerce, the lag seems due primarily to the absence of economic justification for a complete uranium-plutonium fuel cycle within one nation unless that nation's civil nuclear power program exceeds a minimum size. All the nuclear weapon nations, of course, already possess their own fuel fabrication and chemical separation plants. Chemical separation plants large enough to process industrial quantities of irradiated nuclear fuels are also located in Belgium (under international ownership and operation) and India, and construction is planned for the near future in West Germany, Japan, and Sweden.

Wherever a chemical separation plant is located, militarily significant quantities of plutonium will be available in a chemically pure form. This is a technological fact of enormous political and military importance. As chemical separation plants are constructed in additional nations, that many more will be only one step away from a nuclear weapons capability.

Facilities for enriching uranium are presently located in each of the five nuclear weapon nations. Such facilities are not known to have been built yet in any nonnuclear weapon nation. The growth in size and number of nuclear power plants under construction and planned for the future, however, foreshadows a corresponding increase in the demand for enriched uranium. This in turn will require expansion of existing plant capacity, or the construction of new plants, and probably both. The necessity for new uranium enrichment facilities has also been under consideration for some time both in the United States and Western Europe.[18] It is quite possible that in the future uranium enrichment plants will be built on the territory of one or more nonnuclear weapon nations.

As indicated previously, a decision to build a nuclear power plant involves a choice between natural uranium and slightly enriched uranium as fuel. Plutonium is produced in either case, but the tech-

[17] International Atomic Energy Agency (fn. 15).

[18] Joint Committee on Atomic Energy, *Selected Materials Concerning Future Ownership of the AEC's Gaseous Diffusion Plants*, 91st Cong., 1st Sess., 1969; Forum Atomique Européen, *Report on European Uranium Enrichment* (January 1969).

nologies and economics are different. On economic grounds alone, enriched reactor technology has the edge in most cases, assuming enrichment services are available at reasonable cost. Further, the resulting degrees of nuclear self-sufficiency may be very different. If a nation uses nuclear power and lacks its own uranium reserves, it must rely on foreign fuel supplies. And even if a nation has its own uranium deposits, it must rely on foreign enrichment services if it uses enriched reactor technology but lacks a uranium isotope separation plant. Therefore, a series of complex technological, economic, political, and security comparisons must be made in evaluating natural uranium and slightly enriched uranium as potential fuels for a planned nuclear power reactor.

Virtually all nuclear power reactors built and planned in the United States and a large majority in the Soviet Union will use enriched uranium fuel. Outside the United States and the Communist bloc, it is estimated that about 70 percent of the total nuclear power capacity will be in enriched uranium reactors by 1980, and about 30 percent will be reactors using natural uranium for fuel.[19]

The United States, with its large stake in a future share of the world's nuclear power industry, has given repeated assurances concerning the future availability of United States enrichment services to foreign countries on a long-term, nondiscriminatory basis at attractive and stable prices. This "toll enrichment" policy is intended not only to aid the export of United States enriched reactor technology, but also to minimize incentives for construction of additional uranium isotope separation plants outside the United States.[20] It is extremely doubtful that this policy will forestall the construction of new enrichment capacity in Western Europe within the latter half of the 1970's. Quite possibly, this capacity will be in plants using gas centrifuge technology.

The present distribution of raw materials and production capabilities for obtaining fissionable materials reveals that the United States and the Soviet Union are the only nuclear weapon nations with large and self-sufficient military and civil nuclear programs. The United Kingdom has no uranium, and France lacks adequate indigenous uranium to supply both its civil and military needs. China, which probably has sufficient uranium to service both a military and civil program, has thus far focused its limited scientific and technical resources on the acquisition of a nuclear weapons capability.

[19] A. D. Little, *The Growth of Foreign Nuclear Power*, U.S. Atomic Energy Commission, Division of Technical Information, TID-22973 (Washington 1966).

[20] For a description of the U.S. Atomic Energy Commission toll enrichment services and its uranium supply policies applicable to sales of either enriched uranium or natural uranium to be toll enriched, see USAEC Release No. L-210 (Sept. 6, 1968).

Canada is the only nonnuclear weapon nation which possesses both large uranium deposits and a strong base in nuclear technology. West Germany and Japan are making bids for leadership in peaceful nuclear technology, in each case backed by a broad industrial capability and a firm commitment of governmental support. India has embarked on a civil nuclear power program of substantial size. And Israel, which has developed a strong scientific and technical base, is now considering a variety of power applications. But aside from Canada, each of these nonnuclear weapon nations lacks a uranium supply of its own. While South Africa's large uranium reserves make that nation a major factor in the nuclear power context, its nuclear power program is not far advanced.

Conflict Potential

Most nations, because of their small size, lack of industrial base, or limited raw materials, will have little to do with nuclear technology in the near future. Many less-developed nations will continue to limit themselves to so-called nuclear research, which will frequently mean merely utilizing a research reactor and foreign fellowships in what is essentially an educational program. However, many industrialized and some less-developed nations with established industrial enclaves will have a much deeper interest in the possible application of nuclear energy to meet their growing requirements for electric power. It is this latter category that warrants major attention, for it is among these nations that significant security questions will arise from the development of civil nuclear power programs. Furthermore, it is the civil nuclear power programs of nations presently without nuclear weapons which will add the new dimensions which concern us here.

Every nation contemplating the opportunities for exploitation of the peaceful uses of nuclear energy will establish its own goals and develop its own program for achieving them. Arising out of circumstances, attitudes, and perceptions relevant to each, these goals will not be identical, will not necessarily be based on the same assumptions, and in some cases will overlap and in other cases conflict. For purposes of analysis, it is helpful to categorize the principal national objectives as: cheap electric power; the creation of a nuclear power option for the future; energy security; and the creation of a nuclear weapons option.[21]

Low-cost electric power is widely assumed to be the objective of most nations with ambitious nuclear power programs. How realistic will such a national policy objective be in the near future?

[21] Prestige may be another important objective in some cases. While prestige as a secondary objective associated with achievement of one or more of the other nuclear power objectives is sensible to a degree, a nuclear power program would seem to be an extremely costly way to enhance prestige alone.

For several reasons nuclear technology will retain much of its new-ness for most nations through the 1970's. One reason is the long lead-time between a decision to build a power plant and commencement of its operation, presently from five to seven years. Another is the continuing process of technological improvement. Operating experi-ence is causing modifications in proven reactors, as well as new de-velopments in the technology. Substantial changes can thus be expected to the economics applicable to all phases of the nuclear fuel cycle.[22]

Much will depend on how large power reactors actually perform in their early years of operation. Predicted economies can be demon-strated and realized only if the reactors can be operated successfully under a variety of conditions. Important external factors will be the comparable trends in the costs of alternative energy sources for elec-tric power, trends in the overall pattern of consumption of all energy sources, and the extent to which control of various forms of environ-mental pollution becomes, by virtue of government regulation, an added cost in the production of electric power.

In the case of industrially advanced nations, organization of the energy economy will have a major influence on whether cheaper elec-tricity is a realistic nuclear power objective in the near future. In order to utilize the cost advantages of nuclear power, the production and distribution of electric power must be organized so as to make possi-ble the addition of large blocs of power-generating capacity.

For less-developed nations, cheap power is a realizable nuclear objective in the near future only where growing demand for electric power is concentrated in urban or industrial enclaves. Even where these conditions exist, much will depend on the future availability and performance of smaller-sized nuclear power reactors as well as the availability of favorable financing arrangements to cover the large capital requirements. Usually a significant proportion of capital, along with technology, will have to come from external sources. Thus, civil nuclear power in less-developed nations will probably not be feasible except on a heavily subsidized basis.

Although lower cost electricity may not be a realistic immediate nuclear power objective for most nations, many will, nevertheless, opt for a program in order to gain experience with this new form of energy and the complicated technology associated with it. These na-tions will have as their objective what may be termed the creation of a nuclear power option. Such an objective may be dominant among nations which do not have a major proprietary interest in all or part of the nuclear fuel cycle, such as many small industrially advanced nations and the less-developed nations, with the exception of India.

Every nation has a vital interest in its energy resources. The achieve-

[22] These changes have been in an upward direction, at least temporarily, as far as the cost of nuclear power in the United States is concerned. See fn. 11.

ment and maintenance of a secure energy supply sufficient for its present and projected future needs is a major national policy objective. A particular nation may be willing to pay a premium in order to increase the security of its energy supply because of the pervasive effects of energy throughout its economy. Thus, energy security may be more important than low-cost electric power and be the factor which will steer decision-making toward or away from nuclear power in some cases. But, whether or not nuclear power will increase a nation's energy security depends on its degree of self-sufficiency in nuclear raw materials and technology.

Creation of a nuclear weapons option may be the conscious, tacit objective of only a few nations establishing nuclear power programs. But, a weapons option will be the inevitable by-product of all large-scale programs. This will be especially the case for those nations which construct all the facilities necessary for a complete fuel cycle within their territories, including chemical separation and fuel fabrication plants in addition to nuclear power reactors.

It may take several years to create a nuclear weapons option. Once such an option exists in the form of a viable civil nuclear power industry, the time from decision to acquisition of nuclear weapons could be shortened to a few months.[23] In conflict situations short of nuclear war, therefore, the distinction between nations with and without an immediate nuclear weapons option may become as important as the present distinction between nations with and without nuclear weapons. Furthermore, there is a substantial risk that one nation's posture regarding civil nuclear power may be perceived by another as a clear threat to its security requiring a response. Thus, in a conflict relationship among two or more nations, the conscious or unconscious achievement of nuclear weapons options could produce a nuclear power race and might even lead a nation to acquire nuclear weapons primarily to offset an inferior position regarding availability of fissionable materials.

CONFLICT MANAGEMENT

It is clear that the availability of fissionable materials resulting from the pursuit of a variety of nuclear power objectives will in the near future create a major and widespread threat to international security and stability, at least in the absence of external controls on national

[23] Once fissionable material is available, manufacture of fission weapons is no longer a particularly demanding or costly task, although weapons design information is still cloaked in secrecy. A weapons fabrication and assembly plant which can manufacture ten fission warheads per year has been estimated to cost only $8 million to construct and $1 million per year to operate. The successful development of a thermonuclear (fusion) device, however, still represents a significant technological achievement.

nuclear power programs. The primary external control mechanisms that have been developed are referred to as "safeguards."[24] Safeguards consist merely of a system of international accountability applied to the nuclear materials used, produced, and processed in a peaceful nuclear activity located in a nation. The system includes reports to an external authority and physical inspection by inspectors representing that authority to verify the accuracy of the reports. The major purpose of safeguards is to ensure that materials and equipment in civil nuclear activities are not diverted to military uses.

Safeguards may be administered by a variety of authorities: bilaterally by a nation which has previously supplied materials or equipment to the particular nuclear activity concerned;[25] by a regional authority such as the European Atomic Energy Community (Euratom) to all peaceful nuclear activities within the region;[26] or by an international organization such as the IAEA with a potentially global reach.[27]

[24] For discussion of the history and operational effects of safeguards, see Paul Szasz, "The Law of International Atomic Energy Safeguards," *Rev. Belge de Droit International*, 3 (1967), 196; Mason Willrich, "Safeguarding Atoms for Peace," *American Journal of International Law*, 60 (1966), 34.

[25] Prior to the development of specific safeguards procedures by the IAEA, the United States entered into a series of bilateral agreements for cooperation in the peaceful uses of nuclear energy with a large number of foreign nations. These agreements contained safeguards provisions which were administered on a bilateral basis by the U.S. Atomic Energy Commission until 1962. At that time the decision was taken to transfer to the IAEA the responsibility for administration of safeguards with respect to these agreements for cooperation as the agreements became subject to renewal. A number of other supplier nations have followed the same practice with some or all of their bilateral agreements. These transfers have been the major cause of growth in the IAEA's safeguards role.

[26] The Euratom system of safeguards does not extend to "materials intended for the purpose of defence, which are in course of being specially prepared for such purposes or which, after being so prepared, are, in accordance with an operational plan, installed or stocked in a military establishment." Treaty Establishing the European Atomic Energy Community, March 25, 1957, Art. 84, Par. 3, 298 U.N. Treaty Series 167. For a comparison of the Euratom and IAEA safeguards systems, see *Hearings on the Treaty on the Non-Proliferation of Nuclear Weapons before the Senate Committee on Foreign Relations*, 90th Cong., 2d Sess., 1968, 266-76.

[27] The reach of IAEA safeguards depends, in the case of transactions where the Agency is not used as a supply channel, on the voluntary consent of the parties to the transaction. As of June 30, 1969, the Agency had approved 40 safeguards agreements involving 30 member states covering 68 reactors. However, only 6 of the reactors subject to IAEA safeguards were power reactors, these being located in the United States, the United Kingdom, Japan, Spain, and Nationalist China. The majority were small research reactors. In addition, the United States has opened a chemical process plant to IAEA inspection while the plant is engaged in reprocessing fuel from the power reactor in the United States which is subject to IAEA safeguards. *Annual Report of the Board of Governors to the General Conference, 1 July, 1968-30 June, 1969*, IAEA Doc. GC (XIII)/404, 32-39. The Board of Governors approved in June 1968, an agreement between Mexico and the IAEA under which the Agency will apply safeguards to all nuclear activities in Mexico. This agreement is in accordance with the terms of the Treaty for the Prohibition of Nuclear Weapons in Latin America (Treaty of Tlatelolco), and is the first such agreement under that Treaty.

The nature and effectiveness of safeguards as an external control will depend on the margins of the uncertainties in the accountability system, the anticipated and forthcoming responses of nations which might suspect diversion in other nations, and the resulting reliance which nations will place on safeguards in relation to their national security. These factors are, of course, interrelated.

No system of safeguards will be able to account for every kilogram of fissionable material used, produced, or processed in a nuclear power program. The accountability system will contain its own internal margins of uncertainty, and the system will be applied to a nuclear fuel cycle in which processing losses are inevitable in every phase.[28] As nuclear power programs are established in more and more nations, and as these programs increase in size, a corresponding growth in the international authority administering safeguards will be required. This will, in turn, require development of more definite accountability standards. In the process of establishing standards, the development of parameters may be a technical task, but the choice of standards within those parameters will be political.[29]

[28] A United States contractor operating a fuel fabrication plant has reported losses, which have not been accounted for, in excess of 100 kilograms of uranium-235. Address by John T. Conway, Executive Director, Joint Committee on Atomic Energy, to 7th Annual Mtg., Institute of Nuclear Materials Management, June 14, 1966. This triggered the convening of an outside review panel and the establishment of a new Office of Safeguards and Materials Management within the U.S. Atomic Energy Commission. USAEC Release No. K-108 (May 3, 1967). Furthermore, a resident AEC inspector is now stationed at four private facilities in the United States which process significant quantities of fissionable material. USAEC Release No. K-121 (May 12, 1967).

[29] This choice of standards for IAEA safeguards is made by the Board of Governors. Complicated provisions in the Statute of the Agency attempt to strike a delicate balance in the composition of the Board between atomic "haves" and "have-nots," and between East and West, with perhaps some bias in favor of the atomic "haves" and the West. Under Art. VI of the Statute, the outgoing Board of Governors, by majority vote, makes the following designations of membership for the succeeding Board: "the five members most advanced in the technology of atomic energy"; the member most advanced in the technology of atomic energy, including the production of source materials, not represented by the original five in each of the following eight geographic regions: (1) North America, (2) Latin America, (3) Western Europe, (4) Eastern Europe, (5) Africa and the Middle East, (6) South Asia, (7) Southeast Asia and the Pacific, (8) Far East; two members from among Belgium, Czechoslovakia, Poland, and Portugal as producers of source material; and one additional member as a supplier of technical assistance. The five members most advanced in the technology of atomic energy are Canada, France, United Kingdom, United States, and U.S.S.R. (from North America, Western Europe, and Eastern Europe). These five are thus assured, in fact, permanent seats on the Board. The members most advanced in the technology of atomic energy in each of the eight regions, not represented by the original five, are Argentina, Australia, Brazil, India, Japan, and South Africa. Argentina and Brazil share the seat going to the most advanced country in Latin America and one of the seats going to Latin America on the basis of equitable representation. Since the negotiation of the Nonproliferation Treaty, several nonnuclear weapon nations with civil nuclear power ambitions have

Disparities among nations in the amounts of fissionable materials accumulated in their peaceful nuclear power programs are likely to increase over time. As the gaps widen, the interests of nations with very large nuclear power programs, such as West Germany and Japan, with respect to international safeguards are likely to diverge increasingly from those of nations with smaller programs. The divergence of interest may well become manifest and concrete in conflicting views of what constitutes an adequate safeguards system.

Nations with large nuclear power programs, perceiving less of a threat in the nuclear power programs of other nations and more burdened by the application of safeguards to their own programs, may be expected to resist measures to reduce uncertainties, especially if such tightening would increase the intensity of the intrusion into their nuclear activities. Nations with small nuclear power programs, on the other hand, especially those without the chemical processing plants necessary to separate produced plutonium, are likely to view a safeguards system that is merely maintained at its initial level of effectiveness as a security assurance that diminishes over time.

Assuming safeguards are generally accepted and applied consistent with the Nonproliferation Treaty,[30] how will nations respond if diversion of fissionable materials from a nuclear power to a nuclear weapons program is suspected? It is highly unlikely that an IAEA inspector will ever be an eyewitness to, or receive direct evidence of, a diversion.[31] The most that can be expected from safeguards is indirect evidence—an ambiguous discrepancy in the suspect nation's nuclear materials balance system, or procedural roadblocks put in the way of IAEA inspection of a particular nuclear facility at a certain time. In either event, the suspect nation could involve the IAEA system and nations most immediately concerned in a lengthy process of clarification and debate. Throughout this process the IAEA, and each nation

---

complained strongly that their interests were underrepresented on the Board of Governors.

[30] The requirement for safeguards is contained in Art. III of the Nonproliferation Treaty. The provisions are very complicated. For an explanation and interpretation, see Willrich (fn. 6), 99-126.

[31] Concerning sanctions, the IAEA Board of Governors has not ventured beyond references to the relevant statutory provisions in its development of a system of Agency safeguards. Art. XII, Par. C, sets forth procedures to be followed in the event of noncompliance. These include: a report by the inspectors to the Director General; the transmittal of the report by the Director General to the Board of Governors; a call upon the state concerned to remedy the situation if noncompliance is found by the Board; a report by the Board to the members of IAEA and to the U.N. Security Council and General Assembly; and the Board's decision to curtail or suspend assistance in event of failure of the state concerned to take "fully corrective action within a reasonable time," or to call for the return of materials and equipment made available. Provision is also made for suspension of the noncomplying state from membership in the IAEA.

for itself, would have to determine whether and how far it wished to press the matter. But, it is doubtful that any nation would embark upon a secret nuclear weapons program unless, upon discovery, it was prepared to continue. Thus, the course of action of a suspect nation would be pre-determined while that required of other nations to stop the weapons acquisition process would be difficult to launch.

Forcible intervention would probably have to occur, if at all, before a nuclear weapons capability became operational. Yet, the safeguards system would give few clues as to exactly how far a clandestine nuclear weapons program had proceeded. The nations which would call the loudest for intervention would be those which believed themselves to be immediately threatened, for example, the Arab nations in the case of Israel, or the East European nations in the case of West Germany (assuming all nations concerned were parties to the Nonproliferation Treaty). But these nations would be unable to execute the sanctions required without starting a dangerous local war which they might lose. The burden of effective action might well fall, therefore, upon one or the other of the two superpowers, the United States and the Soviet Union. However, the use of force by either of these powers to deny a sixth or seventh nation a nuclear weapons capability would seem to place the nuclear superpowers in a morally untenable position in the world community.

Thus far, we have assumed that safeguards are accepted by all non-nuclear weapon nations with significant nuclear power programs. The most probable world in the 1970's, however, will be a context in which Nonproliferation Treaty safeguards are applied to peaceful nuclear activities in some, but not all, nonnuclear weapon nations. It becomes important to determine, therefore, what difference the failure of particular nations to accept Treaty safeguards would make in the preceding analysis. West Germany's ratification of the Nonproliferation Treaty may be delayed for some time, and even if the Germans make an affirmative decision, it could take several years before Treaty safeguards provisions go into effect. Fortunately for the stability of Europe, West German delay in ratifying the Nonproliferation Treaty and accepting the Treaty's safeguards on its nuclear power program need not be fatal. West Germany pledged not to acquire nuclear weapons in 1954, and it has never questioned the validity of this obligation which it undertook as part of the arrangements whereby it joined NATO.[32] Quite the opposite, West Germany has repeatedly reiterated

[32] The West German undertaking not to manufacture nuclear weapons is incorporated into the protocols modifying and extending the Brussels Treaty, which were signed at Paris on October 23, 1954. Four separate protocols comprise this group. These documents are conveniently collected in *Message from the President of the United States to the Senate, Protocol on the Termination of the Occupation Regime in the Federal Republic of Germany and Protocol to the North Atlantic*

this renunciation as proof of its intention and policy to refrain from acquiring nuclear weapons.

Furthermore, West Germany's entire nuclear program is already subject to Euratom safeguards. The longer West Germany refrains from adhering to the Nonproliferation Treaty, the more important the continuing application of Euratom safeguards will become, not only to the members of the European Community, but also to all nations involved in European security. The Soviet Union and East European nations have in the past attacked Euratom as self-inspection and a guise for the nuclear armament of West Germany. If this hostile line of policy toward West Germany is maintained, the nations of East Europe may have no choice but to rely on Euratom safeguards more than if they were to permit a normalization of relations to occur in order to induce West Germany to ratify the Nonproliferation Treaty.

Japan is another nonnuclear weapon nation whose nuclear power program will probably achieve large-scale proportions in the near future. At this writing Japan has not ratified the Nonproliferation Treaty, although it may well do so in the future. Japan's acceptance of IAEA safeguards in connection with nuclear imports, which pre-dated the Nonproliferation Treaty, is extremely important since there are no regional safeguards applicable. Japan's nuclear power program will achieve dimensions in the 1970's such that if safeguards are not applied on a comprehensive basis as required under the Nonproliferation Treaty, production free of safeguards will soon exceed what can later be accounted for within any acceptable limits.

India is in a very different position from Japan strategically, of course, and also with respect to its nuclear power program. India has declared it will not become a party to the Nonproliferation Treaty, although it will accept safeguards which are negotiated bilaterally as a part of nuclear assistance it has received or may receive from other countries in the future. The size of India's nuclear power program will not approach Japan's for the foreseeable future. However, India is clearly striving to achieve maximum self-sufficiency throughout the nuclear fuel cycle as soon as possible. It already has a chemical processing plant in operation and is making a concerted effort to reduce the amount of nuclear imports required in each successive power reactor it is building.

Leverage could be exerted on India if all potential suppliers of nuclear assistance refused to furnish India any materials or equipment unless it accepted safeguards on *all* its peaceful nuclear activities, in-

---

Treaty on the Accession of the Federal Republic of Germany, Executives L and M, 83d Cong., 2d Sess., 1954. See Mason Willrich, "West Germany's Pledge Not to Manufacture Nuclear Weapons," *Virginia Journal of International Law,* 7 (1966), 91.

cluding those using only indigenous resources. Such action would extend beyond the obligations assumed by the supplier nations under the Nonproliferation Treaty, however, and would require a deeper consensus in favor of the Treaty than presently exists.[33] Possibly such a consensus will develop over time, especially if Pakistan becomes a party to the Treaty and later threatens to withdraw unless India's entire nuclear program is subject to inspection.[34]

How much time exists in which to bring about Indian acceptance of safeguards on all its nuclear activities would depend on India's plutonium production free of safeguards. As plutonium production and separation continue free of safeguards, a threshold will eventually be reached beyond which, even if India were then to accept IAEA safeguards, uncertain estimates of past production of unsafeguarded plutonium would create a continuing threat that India possessed a secret stockpile of plutonium or nuclear weapons.

There will be a grace period for obtaining comprehensive acceptance of safeguards by many nations. The length of this period will vary depending on the size of a nuclear power program, the fraction of it that is not tied to nuclear imports, and the presence or absence of a plant for separating plutonium. Ultimately, if international safeguards are to play a significant role in reducing the conflict potential of civil nuclear power, there will be no substitute for a safeguards system that is applied to all major nuclear activities in nonnuclear weapon nations. Because of the additional discrimination this would introduce between nuclear weapon and nonnuclear weapon nations, it is unlikely that nonnuclear nations would accept safeguards on all their nuclear activities unless the nuclear nations, especially those engaged in international commercial competition in the civil nuclear field, accepted safeguards on their civil nuclear programs. The United States and United Kingdom have agreed in principle to do this,[35] but the Soviet Union has not and probably will not.

However, even if widely accepted, safeguards should not be overvalued as a mechanism of international control over civil nuclear power. Safeguards provide *verification* that fissionable materials used in peaceful nuclear power programs are not *being* diverted to nuclear weapons. They do not give *assurance* that fissionable materials *will not be* diverted. Safeguards provide a reasonably accurate measurement

[33] Willrich (fn. 6), 123-26.

[34] Art. X, Par. 1 of the Nonproliferation Treaty would permit a party to withdraw if it decides that "extraordinary events, related to the subject matter of this Treaty, have jeopardized the supreme interests of its country." This provision is derived from the Limited Nuclear Test Ban Treaty.

[35] Address by President Johnson, December 2, 1967, *Department of State Bulletin* 862, 863 (1967); Documents on Disarmament (1967), 613, 615. Statement by United Kingdom Disarmament Minister Mully to the House of Commons, December 4, 1967, ENDC/207 (December 5, 1967); Documents on Disarmament (1967), 616.

of the potential security threat in national nuclear power programs. They do not diminish the size of that potential, but rather chart its growth. Safeguards are thus more analogous to observation satellites which provide information concerning the build up of a potential adversary's strategic nuclear forces than to an international inspection system associated with a disarmament scheme.

Without more, therefore, a system of international accountability and inspection is not an adequate response to the challenge presented by continuing exploitation of nuclear energy for peaceful purposes. Further structural innovation is required in the international political system to meet this challenge.

For example, it may be possible to ascertain an optimum way for the component facilities of the nuclear energy fuel cycle to be distributed throughout the world to increase the efficacy of safeguards and to decrease the burden of administration.[36] Beyond this, international ownership of fissionable materials and international operation of key nuclear facilities such as enrichment, chemical separation, and fuel fabrication plants could provide greater security control over fissionable materials than any system of safeguards.[37]

The concept of interdependence also merits exploration. We have seen previously that very few nations now have nuclear power programs that are self-sufficient and autonomous. Thus, the opportunity exists at present for nations to move toward either autonomy or interdependence in their civil nuclear industries.

The drive for autonomy is derived from the very nature of the existing nation-state system with its emphasis upon sovereignty. With respect to energy, the desires for security of supply have generally prevailed, and the theory of comparative economic advantage has not been applicable. The justification for reversing the course of economic and political nationalism with respect to nuclear power must rest essentially on military security grounds and on the assumption that nonproliferation of nuclear weapons is a worthwhile policy objective in this regard. Of course, this assumption has never been universally accepted, and has been eroded repeatedly.

The objective of a policy of nuclear power interdependence would be to place the nuclear share of each nation's electric power generating capacity under some degree of physical dependence on external support and hence control from the outside. A nation beginning the weapons acquisition process would thus risk impairment, probably with some time lag, of its electric power generating capacity.

36 Theodore Taylor, "The Rapid Growth of Nuclear Technology—Implication for Nuclear Safeguards," *International Research and Technology Journal* (January 1, 1968), 16.

37 Leonard Beaton, "Nuclear Fuel-for-All," *Foreign Affairs*, XLV (1967), 662-67.

A range of options for achieving the objective exist. Fuel fabrication and chemical processing facilities could be jointly constructed and operated along the lines of the Eurochemic plant in Belgium.[38] Nuclear power plants could be sited so as to distribute electric power on both sides of a national boundary. Perhaps, most important, stockpiling of uranium fuel or separated plutonium by nonnuclear weapon nations should not be permitted.[39]

If civil nuclear power programs were made functionally interdependent, safeguards and sanctions would then reinforce each other, and both would be substantially more effective. The function of safeguards would be strengthened because a credible response would be available. The sanction of disruption of a nation's electric power supply would be credible because the safeguards system would supply the factual basis for its invocation, and the use of force or territorial intervention would not be necessary for its application.

AT THIS WRITING, none of the nations at the threshold of a nuclear weapons capability are firmly committed to maintaining a world order that includes room for only five nuclear weapon nations. Most governments are extremely reluctant to accept any form of external control over their nuclear industries. What is most alarming is that governments have not yet acknowledged frankly to each other, or to their peoples, the enormity of the security problem that will be an inevitable result of the general availability of huge amounts of fissionable materials.

Thus, the drift toward nuclear catastrophe continues.

[38] The chemical processing plant in Belgium is owned by Eurochemic, an undertaking of the European Nuclear Energy Agency (ENEA) in the form of a joint stock company. The governments or energy authorities of 12 ENEA members own Eurochemic shares. See Convention on the Constitution of the European Company for the Chemical Processing of Irradiated Fuels (Eurochemic) and Statute of Eurochemic, IAEA Legal Series No. 1, Multilateral Agreements (1959).

[39] Present United States policy would permit, and in some cases encourage, stockpiling uranium that has been "toll enriched" in United States gaseous diffusion plants. See fn. 20.

Part III

The Moderation of Conflict

CHAPTER 9

Sanctions and Enforcement

W. MICHAEL REISMAN

IN LEGAL THEORY and in legal practice, the processes of sanctions and enforcement have fared poorly. For all their ubiquity, they are almost treated as ugly and unpleasant aspects of reality, unfit for polite discourse. When the literature of the law has taken notice, sanctions and enforcement have been accorded an unequal, relatively sporadic and anecdotal treatment. Sanctions, for example, are often approached as a discrete sequence, separate from and following lawful decision: they are treated itemistically;[1] and they are, at times, considered almost theologically. To Austin,[2] sanctions are a disembodied doctrinal notion

---

[1] Examples of such itemism are Jacques Dumas, *Les Sanctions de l'arbitrage international* (Paris 1905); Payson S. Wild Jr., *Sanctions and Treaty Enforcement* (Cambridge 1934). An itemistic approach without a comprehensive frame of reference frequently leads writers to dismiss too hastily certain sanctions as obsolete. Dumas, for example, found little effectiveness in religious sanctions. But shared rectitude demands can be a determinant of transnational behavior in certain circumstances; in particular, they can subtly preclude the *sanctioner* from resorting to certain strategies because of his own ethical biases. Wild believed that the institution of hostages had obsolesced as a sanction. But control over irredentist populations continues to be a form of international blackmail and a means of influencing the conduct of adversaries. The point to be emphasized is that a frame of reference which seeks to identify explicitly the range of factors which can influence others is crucial to a comprehensive and realistic grasp of sanctions and enforcement.

[2] A sanction, according to Austin, is "the evil which will probably be incurred in case a command be disobeyed." John Austin, *The Province of Jurisprudence Determined and the Uses of the Study of Jurisprudence*, H.L.A. Hart, ed. (London 1954), 15. For a general critique of the structural biases of analytical jurisprudence in general and of John Austin in particular, see Myres S. McDougal, Harold D. Lasswell, and W. Michael Reisman, "Theories about International Law: Prologue to a Configurative Jurisprudence," *Virginia Journal of International Law* 8 (1968), 188, 243ff.
One of the recurring difficulties of the Austinian definition of sanction has been its inapplicability to societies which are structured in forms other than those of Western Europe and, for that matter, to subgroups within Western civilization which manifest stable public order over time, but are not structurally comparable to or closely associated with official state institutions. See Leopold J. Pospisil, *Kapauku Papuans and Their Law* (New York 1958), 272. Maine, one of Austin's harshest critics, remarked that "customary law is not enforced by a sanction. In the almost inconceivable case of disobedience to the award of the village council, the sole punishment, or the sole certain punishment, would appear to be universal disapprobation. And hence, under the system of Bentham and Austin, the customary law of India would have to be called morality—an inversion of language which scarcely requires to be formally protested against." Sir Henry Maine, *Village Communities in the East and West* (7th edn., 1907, London 1871), 68. The problem here, of course, is definitional: sanctions have been defined anecdotally and itemistically rather than functionally. This has been a persisting flaw in the literature. See, for example, E. Adamson Hoebel, *The Law of Primitive Man* (New York 1954), 52, and Hoebel and Karl N. Llewellyn, *The Cheyenne Way* (Norman, Okla. 1941). It em-

(as they are to Kelsen),[3] conceded to be a requisite element of a norm, but an element which is exhausted of juridical significance once its existence has been registered. Sanctions, it is posited, follow decision. Austin and Kelsen also converge in their bland acceptance of the automatic mechanical imposition of sanctions for delictual behavior,[4] implying notions of social causality regularly denied by the complex experience of our century.

Considering the almost compulsive detail of legal methodology, this strange treatment of phenomena which are quite inseparable from law is baffling. In some representative writings, one senses a deep cultural postulate, perhaps the product of the early socialization and acculturation of the child.[5] It is revealing that Austin defined sanctions as "evils"[6] and with Austin's gloomy and magnificent monument to jurisprudence in the background, one begins to comprehend the real anguish of that self-perceived abstraction "the respectable citizen": someone has broken the law and yet is getting away with it. It becomes possible to understand how these well-meaning but frightened and perplexed citizens can ignore the voluminous data and impassioned arguments of social scientists, criminologists, and penologists about the root causes of antisocietal nonconforming behavior and can resort to

---

phasizes the need for new functional and socially grounded formulations for these conventional terms.

[3] Hans Kelsen, *General Theory of Law and State*, Wedberg trans. (New York 1961), 21, 50-51.

[4] In his study of international law, Professor Kelsen develops two models of sociolegal organization: the primitive system in which the applicative function is primarily by self help and the advanced system, which is characterized by a "monopoly of force" and the technique of collective security. In the latter, a right continues to relate to the individual community member, but its implementation is reserved to community organs. Throughout Kelsen's discussion, one is struck by the automatic quality of the operation: for each right, regardless of special contextual considerations, there is a single authoritative response. Such a view renders sanctions as the abstract perfection of rights and severs both rights and their supporting sanction expectations from values and order in social process. See Hans Kelsen, *Principles of International Law* (New York 1952), 13-17.

[5] Jean Piaget, *The Morality of the Child*, Babain trans. (New York 1965). A different emphasis is offered in Sigmund Freud, *Civilization and its Discontents*, Riviere trans. (London 1951). A recent experiment has suggested that those who have benefited from a deviation from goal patterns may manifest a higher demand for punishment than those who have suffered from the deviation: Philip W. Blumstein and E. A. Weinstein, "The Redress of Distributive Injustice," *American Journal of Sociology* 74 (1969), 408. The obvious point, of course, is that wrongdoing and punishment should not be viewed as symbiotic parts of a whole, in which neither is complete without the other. The appropriate concern for rational decision is predispositions for and behavioral conformity with group norms; under certain circumstances, punishment may neither create nor reinforce predispositions for conformity or may promise a lower net social gain than would other public order techniques.

[6] See fn. 2 and pp. 303-04.

veneer symbols such as "law and order." These words, like any others, draw their meaning and symbolic import from the context in which they are uttered. In contemporary America, they are becoming a hendiadys, too often meaning the imposition of increasingly severe deprivations upon the symptoms rather than the causes of the violation of group norms.

Sanctions and enforcement, at all levels of organization, are appropriate legal questions because they represent the crucible of law, the test of its reality.[7] Law which is not effective is a semantic exercise of minimum social significance. The problem of sanctions cannot be resolved by ritualistic formulations or by definitions which conveniently remove them from the purview of the legal scholar. Having accepted the crucial relevance of sanctions to almost all legal operations, the complexity of the problem must be faced squarely. There are policy problems regarding sanctions and enforcement which are as thorny as the questions about the optimum content of a prescription; the procedural questions of application require a focus on the entire realm of social process.

In this chapter I intend to develop a general theory of sanctions on the one hand, and a programmatic method for solving enforcement problems on the other. While sanctions and enforcement are closely interrelated, the intellectual tasks facing the scholar and the enforcer can be facilitated by focusing upon each problem *seriatim*. The creation of sanction expectations supporting public order prescriptions and the extent to which this has been accomplished in different sectors of the system of world public order will be examined in Part I; enforcement, the actual mobilization and application of sanctions in support of a particular authoritative decision, will be considered in Part II.

I. Sanctions

Sanctions are techniques and strategies for supporting public order.[8] They cannot be divorced from the sociopolitical context in which they operate because they are integral to it. When we speak of group life,

[7] Oliver W. Holmes, who was intensely concerned with the problem of sanctions in public order (see Miriam T. Rooney, *Lawlessness, Law and Sanction* [Washington, D.C. 1937] 114-36) tersely aphorized the problem when he said that a right without a remedy is no right at all.

[8] The scholastic literature on sanctions is surveyed in detail in Rooney (fn. 7), 20-90. In English jurisprudence, sanctions have excited sharp doctrinal controversy for generations. Blackstone's conception of sanction was punishment: "Of all the parts of a law, the most effectual is the vindicatory; for it is but lost labor to say, 'do this, or avoid that' unless we also declare 'this shall be the consequence of your non-compliance.' We must, therefore, observe, that the main strength and force of a law consists in the penalty annexed to it. Herein is to be found the principal obligation of human laws. . . . Rewards, in their nature, can only persuade and allure;

whether it be the microcosmic level of the smallest group of short temporal duration or the level of the most comprehensive world community, extending to all the geographic limits of man's interaction, we are speaking, in some sense, of a system of sanctions: coordinated expectations of indulgences and deprivations, of rewards and punishments, meted out in authoritatively expected procedures, with either the active support or the passive acquiescence of the rank and file and with the ostensible objective of maintaining public order. Separating sanctions from their plenary social context is comparable to the quixotic attempt to separate law from its context.[9] And the product is the same: a disembodied notion, with scant similarity to actual processes of human interaction, a notion descriptively and manipulatively useless.

---

nothing is compulsory but punishment." William Blackstone, *Works*, ii (London 1765-69), 90. Jeremy Bentham's criticism of Blackstone was begun in his *Comment on the Commentaries* (Oxford 1928) 55ff., where he developed three sanctioning instrumentalities. In his subsequent *Introduction to the Principles of Morals and Legislation* (London 1823), he expanded the instrumentalities to four and integrated them with his postulate of maximization: "There are four distinguishable sources from which pleasure and pain are in use to flow: considered separately, they may be termed the physical, the political, the moral, and the religious; and inasmuch as the pleasures and pains belonging to each of them are capable of giving a binding force to any law or rule of conduct, they may all of them be termed sanctions." Same, 41-42. Contemporary efforts which have been considerably more successful in creating comprehensive attention foci are found in Harold D. Lasswell and Richard Arens, *In Defense of Public Order* (New York 1961), and "Toward a General Theory of Sanctions," *Iowa Law Review*, 49 (1964), 233; same, "The Role of Sanctions in Conflict Resolution," *Conflict Resolution*, xi (1967), 27; Myres S. McDougal, "The Impact of International Law upon National Law: A Policy Oriented Resolution," *South Dakota Law Review* 4 (1959), 25; Myres S. McDougal and Florentino P. Feliciano, *Law and Minimum World Public Order* (New Haven 1961); George Dession, "The Technique of Public Order: Evolving Concepts of Criminal Law," *Buffalo Law Review*, 5 (1955), 22.

[9] The integrality of public order and public sanctioning is a recurrent theme in anthropological literature, although the emphases have varied. Both Durkheim and Maine, for example, tended to posit the nexus, but unconsciously assimilated the structures of their own societies to their initially functional definitions.

An extremely clear expression is found in Bronislaw Malinowski, *Crime and Custom in Savage Society* (New York 1926), 55-59. For a concise recent statement, see A. L. Epstein, "Sanctions," *International Encyclopedia of the Social Sciences*, Vol. 14 (1968), 1 and references there. Professor Gluckman remarks: "Sanctions maintaining Lozi relationships are general and diffuse, and breaches of their rules lead to far more than a lawsuit in court. General economic penalties attach to the erring kinsman: he may lose not only rights to cattle and land, but also the support of his fellows in many of his activities. The ancestral spirits may intervene, or fears of sorcery are likely to arise and accusations of sorcery to be hurled. Sentiments and conscience operate to bring the wrongdoer to conform or make redress. It will emerge in the present book that this complex process of social control can be understood only in an analysis of the social relationships which are controlled." Max Gluckman, *The Judicial Process among the Barotse of Northern Rhodesia* (New York 1955), 25.

Utopian visions are striking for their projection of a society charac-terized by the absence of disputes and hence of dispute-resolving mechanisms. The absence is not inadvertent, but rather implies that an appropriately structured group or polity will no longer require sanc-tioning procedures. A number of sociopolitical theories have given for-mal and systematic expression to this notion[10] and if they beg certain knotty problems, they do nonetheless underline a critical characteristic of group homogeneity: laws or authoritative prescriptions which con-form to the most intense expectations and demands of all the politically relevant strata of a polity will secure more spontaneous compliance and require less enforcement than will prescriptions that diverge sharply from expectations and demands. Popular laws, to put it for the moment simply and inexactly, are more easily enforceable than are unpopular laws.[11] In the highly homogenous society, or in the utopia, sanctioning is present *in posse*, but it is below the threshold of visibil-ity. A different social and political structure may, by dispersing values and minimizing dissatisfactions, lower the needs for broad ranging and coercive enforcement. But there is no indication that it can banish it. For sanctions are synonymous with public order.

Every relatively stable pattern of activity generates coordinate expectations among participants. These expectations include, at the minimal level, implied promises of reciprocity and tacit implications of retaliation. Whether our focus is the family circle,[12] the skill

---

[10] For years, the Soviet Union refused to concede the existence of juvenile or adult delinquency, since these were, according to the dogma, a product of a capitalist society and would disappear with the restructuring of society into a socialist polity. Where criminality was conceded, it was significantly characterized in terms of polit-ical pathology. In a corollary manner, progressive Western criminology and penol-ogy insist upon viewing criminality as a form of illness, where the Marxist would emphasize that it is the structured society as a whole which is sick. On the same order, humorously bizarre comments were heard in Israel immediately after the establishment of the state, expressing satisfaction over the emergence of criminals; this was supposedly an indication of the long-sought "normality" of Jewish society.

[11] The converse may be equally true; the costs of enforcing an unpopular and/or unsupported prescription may be more deleterious to total public order than the gains secured by coerced conformity: "the less threatening the conduct with which it is called upon to deal, the greater the social costs that enforcement incurs. We alienate people from the society in which they live. We drive enforcement authori-ties to more extreme measures of intrusion and coercion. We taint the quality of life for free men." Herbert L. Packer, *The Limits of the Criminal Sanction* (Stan-ford 1968), 365.

[12] Pospisil (fn. 2), 274ff. has detailed the family sanctions within one culture. It is a matter of common experience that the family unit is a primary social and socializing unit and that the general community allocates a broad measure of dis-cretion to parents in choice of purposes and modalities of disciplining, intervening, perhaps too rarely, only when gross deprivations of intensely demanded community standards occur.

group,[13] religious groups,[14] the municipality, the state, the region or the globe, assurances of indulgence and/or deprivation are integral elements of expectations about appropriate and demanded behavior. In this sequence, the crucial aspect of a sanction is not its content—which may include any combination of values cherished by the specific participants and imposed in any number of life situations—but rather the inchoate expectation that sanctions will be imposed upon breach of group norms. In the conventional language of the law, this means that at some level of consciousness individuals can frame their expectations in typical normative formulations: appropriate behavior supported by implications of sanctions upon deviation. The critical point is that the vein structure of any group is comprised of sets of prescriptions, from the most explicit to the most implicit and customary and from the most formally authoritative to those of the most diffuse, situational authority. Each of these prescriptions involves a sanction component, with an equally wide variation in regard to content and to either concentration or diffusion of authority.

Authoritative sanctions are frequently associated with the state, but this is a drastic attenuation of focus. The state, or more appropriately, individuals operating in institutionalized patterns and ascribed with special symbols of one form of group authoritative power, prescribe and sanction a range of activities which by no means exhausts all, or even all the important sectors, of group life. Examined from an anthropological perspective, it will readily be seen that in any society, a variety of other groups, wealth associations, skill groups, affection and kin groups, churches and other groups specializing in rectitude and so on, prescribe and effectively sanction in crucial life areas. In many instances, these sanctions are considered authoritative and the degree of dysphoria which they may create in a norm violator will not fall below that activated by formal state sanctions. In this respect, one can distinguish public sanctioning and civic sanctioning and appreciate, from the configurative perspective, the complex policy problems in-

---

[13] Lasswell and Arens (fn. 8), note the Constitution and Rules of the New York Stock Exchange of 1933 as a clear example of skill group regulation, replete with institutional decision processes and specified sanctions. The legal and medical professions exercise an enormous power over members of their respective skill groups, to the point of exclusion and the denial of practice rights. Guilds and unions have exercised comparable sanctioning systems in their sectors. The point has been generalized by Professor Pospisil: "law is not limited to the society as a whole. Every functioning subgroup of the society has its own legal system which is necessarily different in some respects from those of the other subgroups." Pospisil (fn. 2), 272.

[14] See, for example, John A. Abbo and Jerome D. Hannan, *The Sacred Canons*, 2nd rev. edn., Vol. 2 (St. Louis 1960), 781. Sanctioning need not be part of a hierarchically organized religious group. Wherever participation in group rites is a fundamental sacramental activity, any form of excommunication is an effective sanction.

volved in allocating and supervising different prescribing and sanctioning competences.[15] The actual sanction cohesion of a community can be grasped only by viewing the aggregate social processes of that community. An appreciation of the full range of sanctions cannot be viewed in social cross section but must also be considered through time. A group of individuals, a state or a collectivity of states may be hegemonial, in the sense that it is formed and maintained by a single participant disposing of sufficient effective power to hold others in some form of fealty. Unless and until this grouping stabilizes,[16] the public order and sanctioning system is coercive in the sense that the hegemon maintains the structures and patterns of value allocation preferable to him by threats and applications of naked power.

The more usual phenomenon encountered by the student of public sanctioning is a relatively collaborative group, in which the members share significant perspectives and the group's structure is appropriately characterized, or so it seems, in terms of persuasive public order rather than by coercive sanctioning. But this impression is gained only by a momentary cross section: viewed over time, it becomes evident that complex and interlocking cultural processes operate and are operated to internalize sanctioning, such that an impression of public order rather than public sanctioning is the dominant apparent characteristic. The application of relatively brutal force will be found applied not to full fledged participants, as in the hegemonial model, but rather to pre-participants, children, who are socialized and acculturated to accept the group authority system and to internalize its scale of rewards and punishment. When the lawyer speaks of a society with the "law habit" or the political scientist speaks of a persuasive public order system, they are referring to a stable and relatively homogeneous group in which sanctioning has been internalized. In such a group, violence—direct or oblique—will continue to be used. But the significant point is that the modalities and forms of coercion are themselves authorized in the expectations of community participants. Consider, for example, the toleration of capital punishment in a society which puts high premium on human life and internalizes tremendous restraints against impulses of intense hostility.

Where sanctions are internalized, prescriptions related to those internalized signals will ordinarily achieve a higher degree of positive response from their target. We encounter a group which may be variously described as cohesive, homogeneous or, as lawyers put it, manifesting the "law habit." Deviations or tendencies toward deviations may activate autopunitive sanctions, which are frequently severe

[15] Lasswell and Arens (fn. 8), 161 ff.
[16] Harold D. Lasswell and Abraham Kaplan, *Power and Society* (New Haven 1950), 140-41.

enough to secure the demanded group conformity.[17] There is less need for enforcement and where enforcement is necessary, there is more social approval of it. Whether the prescriptions are viewed as hetero-nomic or autonomic in origin, there is a basic predilection to support them. The norm-sanction components of a prescription seem almost self-enforcing. The sanction component here is not, of course, discrete, but is integral to the content of the prescription and to the degree to which the individual identifies with a coherent sociocultural system.[18] Hence prescriptions deviating from basic cultural postulates will acti-vate considerably lower predilections for compliance and may even arouse hostility and opposition. Such a response does not negate the efficacy of sanctions; rather it reemphasizes the integrality of sanctions and the value content of a public order system. Conversely, sanctions achieve a more "floating" quality in a direct or derived charismatic system of authority where a basic postulate of public order is *quod voluit Caesar habet lex vigorem*.[19] Only a deviation from the leader's command activates autopunitive sanctions: the Nazi who experienced dysphoria because of a discrepancy between the Fuehrer's edict and his preexisting moral code was (to his credit) an imperfect Nazi.

To the extent that we encounter the contours of a system of public order of local, national, regional, or global scope, we will encounter a coordinate system of sanctioning, of varying degrees of visibility. The sanctions need not be deprivatory nor need they be organized in struc-tures approximating those we are conditioned to associate with mod-ern government.[20] In the absence of formal structures and hierarchical institutions of authority, the public order sectors may appear to be the

[17] It is Freudian psychology rather than traditional sociology which has until re-cently emphasized the regulator function of the superego and suggested its role in securing conformity with those groups with which the ego identifies: see, for ex-ample, Erik H. Erikson, *Childhood and Society* (New York 1950). In a comparable manner, Professor Pospisil (fn. 2), 279, an anthropologist, locates the efficacy of cus-tomary law in its internalization in the individual personality and its activation of feelings of conscience or shame upon deviation. Leo Petrazhitski, with a unique psychological system, attempted to develop some of these ideas jurisprudentially: Leo Petrazhitski, *Law and Morality*, Babb trans. (Cambridge 1955).

[18] W. H. Rivers, Edwin S. Hartland, and Emile Durkheim posited the basic ef-ficacy of primitive law upon intensive identification with the group: group con-sciousness. Malinowski (fn. 9), 55-56, criticized this view, arguing that "[t]he savage is neither an extreme 'collectivist' nor an intransigent 'individualist'—he is, like man in general, a mixture of both." Group identifications are a function of the total context; in certain circumstances, conformity to group norms may be activated in high degree by intensive group identifications, while in others, a variety of external constraints—applied or expected—are the crucial factor in securing conformity.

[19] Max Weber, *Theory of Social and Economic Organization* (New York 1947), 357ff.; see also Robert C. Tucker, "The Theory of Charismatic Leadership," *Daed-alus* (1968), 731.

[20] In this respect, the reader will note a divergence from Michael Barkun, *Law Without Sanctions* (New Haven 1968), a work with which I am otherwise quite in agreement. Professor Barkun means, as I understand him, that one may and does encounter systems of law without specialized enforcement institutions. One does not, however, encounter law without sanctions. See also Gluckman, fn. 9, 25.

result of voluntary collaboration rather than constraint, a system which neither needs nor has a sanction buttress.[21] But the impression is misleading, for the implicit promises of reciprocity and the tacit threats of retaliation which accompany every interaction provide the underpinning of a sanction system.[22] Value investments are simply not hazarded without some assurances of techniques for maintaining stable expectations. Inadequate sanction techniques imply either a fragmented or extremely fragile system of public order.

We need not engage in a detailed taxonomy of the minimum components of a community which maintains both effective public order and public sanctioning. The varieties of organization are multiple, from intense elite coercion at one pole, to broad rank and file collaboration at the other—and from externalized enforcement to internalized sanctioning. The critical component of any system is the functional convergence of authority and control: the copresence of widely shared expectations about the appropriate procedures for deciding upon and applying sanctions and sufficient evidence of the potential for effective control to sustain the reality of these expectations.[23] Ideally, authority and control should converge at every point of public order concern. But a lesser convergence does not negate group life. Members of any group develop refined awarenesses of those life sectors in which authoritative prescriptions are effective and those sectors in which they are not; and they regulate their behavior accordingly.

[21] See, for example, Gerhart Niemeyer, *Law without Force; The Function of Politics in International Law* (Princeton 1941). A position given its original authority by Durkheim and Weber and reflected in Austin and in the analytical jurists' work has associated law with certain institutional structures. In this country, sociological jurists such as Hoebel and Llewellyn have promoted this view. In regard to sanctions, for example, Hoebel has written that "A social norm is legal if its neglect or infraction is regularly met, in threat or in fact, by the application of physical force by an individual or group possessing the socially recognized privilege of so acting." Hoebel (fn. 2), 28: "the exercise of physical force to control or prevent action is the absolute form of compulsion . . . the characteristic feature of law, as distinct from mere force, is the recognized privilege of a person or social group to apply the absolute form of coercion to a transgressor when conduct deemed improper may occur." Same, 47. Pospisil remarks, that were this definition accepted, "law would not be a universal phenomenon, for cultures exist where physical sanction is practically lacking." Pospisil (fn. 2), 267. Pospisil correctly asks: "Is not the effect (social control, conformity) of a sanction more important than its form? . . . effective social control is the important qualification of a legal sanction." Same.

[22] The prospective effect of these expectations was well expressed by Raymond Buell, in the course of the long, public debate in the United States, in the interwar period, regarding sanctions as opposed to neutrality. Buell noted that "International sanctions are much more than a repressive measure employed to stop fighting after war has illegally broken out; the mere knowledge that sanctions may be imposed will prove a deterrent to, if not a preventive of aggression." Raymond Buell, "Are Sanctions Necessary to International Organizations?," *Foreign Policy Association*, 82 (1932), 6.

[23] See Myres S. McDougal, Harold D. Lasswell, and W. Michael Reisman, "The World Constitutive Process of Authoritative Decision, *Journal of Legal Education*, 19 (1967), 253, 256-57.

Even in periods of apparent social disruption on a wide scale, many sectors of life continue as usual, with normal civic if not public sanctioning procedures.[24]

International Public Order and Sanctions

The most striking feature of the contemporary global process is not diversity, but the very apparent and vigorous trends toward homogeneity. Technology, communications, awesome weapons, and invincible delivery systems have successively obsolesced the castle, the fortified city, and the impregnable nation-state, and to an extent have even obsolesced the concept of interdependence, supplanting it with a global state of simultaneity. We are rapidly approaching a world on the order of a global village and the consensus on shared features of world public order, despite the disparity of ideological symbols, is increasingly broadening. The growth in world public order is paralleled by a growth in world public sanctioning.

International *enforcement* can be understood as collaborative transnational policing of events which a plurality or a majority of states commonly characterize as delictual. In a predominantly coarchical system, it does not mean the operation of an international sheriff, but rather its functional equivalents such that stable patterns of expectations are sustained, holding that certain types of behavior will be enjoined.[25] International sanctions, in contrast, are shared expectations of inchoate deprivations attendant upon delictual deviation. Whether they relate to transcultural delicts or to formally prescribed international crimes, the deviations involved are accompanied by sanction expectations of varying degrees of intensity. To speak of international crimes attenuates the focus, for we are concerned not only with the conventional targets of the criminal code of a variety of national jurisdictions, but rather with the total category of activities which a sig-

[24] Professor Daniel Reisman of the Department of Semitics of Wayne State University informs me that a study of ancient Near Eastern legal documents is striking for the fact that entire sectors of group life continued with a high degree of organization, despite effective invasions from without. The fact that social substructures which have developed their own dynamism and have achieved a high degree of autonomy should continue to function effectively while the overarching structures are disrupted is not surprising. Yet the diversity may manifest itself in the contrary direction: subgroup order systems may be disrupted while inclusive group structures continue to function and to retain stability. E. E. Evans-Pritchard, "Some Aspects of the Family Among the Nuer," *African Political System*, 1st edn. (London 1940), 83, and D. Forde, "Marriage and the Family Among the Yako," have noted that lineage and territorial groups can remain stable despite high instability in domestic groupings. Commenting on these examples, Gluckman suggests the relevance of time-continuity in different sanction systems within one group. Max Gluckman, *Order and Rebellion in Tribal Africa* (New York 1963), 80.

[25] W. Michael Reisman, "The Enforcement of International Judgments," *American Journal of International Law* 63 (1969), 1, 6-8.

nificant portion of the nations of the world stigmatize as delictual to the point where patterns of active collaboration or passive deference stabilize and, to a degree, institutionalize in expectations of common suppression.

If sanctions and public order are recognized as integral, there can be no surprise in the assertion of a functioning system of international sanctions, fragmentary, but nonetheless highly effective in many sectors of transnational interaction. A picture of wide trends toward public order consensus emerges from an inventory of shared international perspectives. Consider a number of global value processes.

POWER

On the verbal level, the most inclusive international documents emphasize political democracy, equal participation in power processes at different levels of global organization, and responsible participation.[26] The prohibition of the unauthorized use of coercion extends from the United Nations Charter[27] throughout national legislation.[28] Many of these high level policies excite disagreements at lower levels of application, but this is certainly not unique to international law. Even in a relatively homogeneous society, the application of punitive sanctions upon breach of a community norm will arouse opposing advocates, because of disagreements over assessments of context, the full range of policies called into operation in each sanction application, and so on. Given the daily political tensions in the international arena, what is surprising is the extent of de facto agreement. An unlawful coercion such as an airline hijacking, from the U.S. to Cuba,[29] or from

[26] See, for example, Charter Articles 2 (1), 4 (1), 55, 56 and 76d. See also "Conditions of Admission of a State to Membership in the U.N." [1950], *ICJ Reports* 4. Many of these basic goal propositions have been applied, by international prescription, to the internal public order systems within nation-states: see the Universal Declaration of Human Rights, G.A. Res. 217 A (III), December 10, 1948, Article 21; International Covenant on Civil and Political Rights, G.A. Res. 2200 A (XXI), December 16, 1966, Article 25.

[27] Charter Article 2 (4).

[28] In point of fact, there is a grievous disparity between proclaimed goal and actual practice. In varying degree, terror and violence are frequently used political techniques in nation-states; see generally, Eugene V. Walter, *Terror and Resistance: A Study of Political Violence* (New York 1969).

[29] See Article 11, Convention on Offences and Certain Other Acts Committed on Board Aircraft, 3 *International Legal Materials* 1042 (1963). In February 1969, the United States government announced a plan to ask the ICAO to make hijacking an international crime and to require the return of hijackers to the country where the craft was registered. *New York Times*, February 6, 1969, p. 1, col. 7. This plan was generally opposed by delegates to the ICAO Convention, *New York Times*, February 11, 1969, p. 62, cols. 5-6. At the same time, pressure was put on the United States to become a party to the Tokyo Convention requiring safe return of passengers, crew, cargo, and planes to their country of origin. *New York Times*, February 14, 1969, p. 77, col. 5. Shortly after this, the International Federation of Airline Pilots Associations planned a resolution to ban service to any country failing to return hi-

Israel to Algeria,[30] will ultimately be subjected to rather unequivocal international policy and will be sanctioned and generally prevented thereafter.

WEALTH

The basic notion of an individual's right to own property as a protected feature of world public order is recurrent in international arbitral awards and judgments and is reiterated in recent United Nations' prescriptions.[31] Dissensions at lower levels of abstraction relate less to the idea of property than to fair allocations of wealth within and between nation-states.[32] Sabotage and wilful destruction and the coercive transfer of wealth assets are condemned by all and there is a high degree of collaboration in suppression or compensation.[33]

AFFECTION

There is no question of the universality of this phenomenon. The institution of marriage is protected in international prescriptions[34] as well as in national legislation and there is a broad stream of transnational collaboration in realizing the reciprocal rights and obligations

---

jacked craft and passengers within 48 hours. *New York Times*, February 15, 1969, p. 58, col. 6. On March 2, the Council of the ICAO acceded to an American request to treat the problem of hijacking at its coming session. *New York Times*, March 4, 1969, p. 85, col. 1. The ICAO has formed an 11-member committee to deal with hijacking and related problems. *New York Times*, May 25, 1969, p. 82, col. 7. Events thus seem to be pushing aviation interests toward a formal agreement on a system of policing the proliferating crime of plane hijacking. In the summer of 1969, the United States ratified the Tokyo Convention.

30 *New York Times*, July 23, 1968, p. 1, col. 7.

31 The frequently overlooked Article 17 of the Universal Declaration of Human Rights (Resolution 217 A (III), December 10, 1948) provides: "1. Everyone has the right to own property alone as well as in association with others. 2. No one shall be arbitrarily deprived of his property."

32 A transcultural perspective on the notion of property is offered in Kenneth S. Carlston, *Law and Organization in World Society* (Urbana 1962). See also W. Michael Reisman, "The Multifaceted Phenomenon of International Arbitration," *Arbitration Journal* 24 (1969), 69, 84.

33 S/PV. 1462 at 6; *American Journal of International Law* 63 (1969) 681; see also the remarks of Professor R. Y. Jennings in "The Aftermath of Sabbatino," same (1965), 87, 92, 96-97. A number of writers have sought to infer from the practice of lump sum settlement in which the agreed liquidated damages are less than those claimed by the plaintiff state that the international doctrine of plenary compensation has been terminated or severely restricted. This appears to be based upon a misconstruction of the cases, as Professor Lillich demonstrates: Richard B. Lillich, "International Claims: Their Settlement by Lump Sum Agreement," in *International Arbitration, Liber Amicorum for Martin Domke*, P. Sanders, ed. (The Hague 1967), 143.

34 International Covenant on Civil and Political Rights, G.A. Res. 2200 A(XXI), December 16, 1966, Article 23; Convention on Consent to Marriage, Minimum Age for Marriage and Registration of Marriages, G.A. Res. 1763 A (XVII), November 7, 1962.

of spouses across state lines.[35] There are comparable areas of agreement in regard to custody of children.[36] In the future, many of the traditional conceptions of affection units, such as the family, may undergo radical changes and the family, as such, may become a less protected feature of domestic and international public order. Whether or not new structures will better fulfil the individual's affection demands, it is quite clear that changes will be presented as affirmations and extensions of the individual's right to give and receive affection.

RESPECT

One of the most radical developments of contemporary international law is the articulation of doctrines of the inherent dignity of all human beings. This is supported by a flow of detailed international prescriptions,[37] the seminal beginnings of institutional structures of enforcement[38] as well as broad political jurisdiction applied by the United Nations Security Council.[39]

[35] A survey of current practice is available in Albert V. Dicey and John H. Morris, *The Conflict of Laws*, 8th edn. (New York 1967), 232-380; a focus upon some of the conventional problems in this area is offered in Daniel C. O'Connell, *International Law*, Vol. I (Dobbs Ferry 1965), 184-97. See also Otto C. Sommerich, ed., "Recognition of Mexican Divorces in Europe," *International Lawyer*, 1 (1967), 39, 202.

[36] See, for example, Declaration of the Rights of the Child, G.A. Res. 1386 (XIV), November 20, 1959. See also case concerning the Application of the Convention of 1902 Governing the Guardianship of Infants *(Netherlands v. Sweden)* [1958] *ICJ Reports*, 55. For a survey of private international practice, see Dicey and Morris, fn. 35, 381-478. There are a number of contemporary efforts to prescribe on the international level for the maintenance of minimum standards for infants. See also David J. Saario, *Study of Discrimination against Persons Born out of Wedlock*, E/CN.4/Sub.2/265/Rev. 1. This area is, of course, extremely complex, for the subjects of decision are preparticipants, who are generally viewed as unable to exercise the plenum of civil privileges and hence, whose welfare is "adopted" by the courts of the forum, according to their own lights. See, in this regard, K. Lipstein, "The Hague Conventions on Private International Law, Public Law and Public Policy," *International Comparative Law Quarterly*, 8 (1959) 506. For a critique of the ICJ's decision in the *Infants* case, see W. Michael Reisman, "International Non Liquet: Recrudescence and Transformation," *International Lawyer*, 3 (1969), 771, 785-86.

[37] Universal Declaration of Human Rights, G.A. Res. 217 A (III), December 10, 1948, Articles 1, 2, 6; International Convention on the Elimination of All Forms of Racial Discrimination, G.A. Res. 2106 A (XX), December 21, 1965.

[38] See generally, Egon Schwelb, "Some Aspects of the Measures of Implementation of the International Covenant on Economy, Social and Cultural Rights" in *Les Droits de l'homme: Human Rights*, 1, (1968), 363; R. B. Bilder, "Rethinking International Human Rights: Some Basic Questions," *Wisconsin Law Review* (1969) 171, 193ff.

[39] The most current example is, of course, Rhodesia. See G.A. Res. 2022 (XX), November 5, 1965; Res. 2024 (XX), November 11, 1965; S.C. Res. 217 (1965), November 20, 1965; Res. 221 (1966), April 9, 1966; Res. 232 (1966), December 16, 1966. See also Myres S. McDougal and W. Michael Reisman, "Rhodesia, and the United Nations: The Lawfulness of International Concern," *American Journal of International Law* 62 (1968), 1; Rosalyn Higgins, "International Law, Rhodesia and the

These selections from transnational value processes are sufficient to indicate the contours of a world public order which is, in surprisingly large part, effectively supported by sanction expectations. This is not to suggest that global order has reached or is near the effective level which it requires for the plenary realization of the goals of the world community. Let us examine, first, the goals which an observer seeking impartiality might recommend to that community and, then, in the light of those goals consider the degree of approximation of past and future trends with those goals. Insofar as projected trends indicate probable deviance, we may consider strategies to secure better conformity to goals in the future.

Sanction Goals for Constitutive and World Public Order

The integrality of public order and sanctions imports that the optimum system of sanctions must support the optimum public order system, one which my colleagues and I have characterized elsewhere as a public order of human dignity.[40] Order, without reference to the value allocations it maintains, is not a goal in itself; while the importance of social stability cannot be gainsaid, it must be viewed as instrumental to achieving a preferred value allocation. We insist that symbols such as "law and order" be subjected to the same contextual analysis to which all other invocations are subjected: who is claiming it, with what perspectives and with what objectives, where, how, with what outcomes, and with what intended and/or unintended aggregate effects. Order in support of tyranny is not a demanded goal, although order as a sequence from a state of disorder to a preferred public order system may achieve a contextual validity. A crucial dimension of sound political appraisal is, of course, an appropriate temporal span within which a single event or event-cluster can be meaningfully related to the manifold of events spanning the past and future. From a goal-oriented perspective, the critical question is always whether events and their context are vectoring toward or away from a social system of human dignity. The coordinate question of sanctions is what is the content of the prescriptions for which control is sought.

We recommend a comprehensive sanction system, effectively and patently supporting policies and prescriptions for the constitutive process and the most inclusive sectors of world public order. We urge delineated sanctions for each of the component decision functions of

UN," *The World Today*, 23 (1967), 94; Thomas M. Franck and Louis B. Sohn, "Policy Paper on the Legality of Mandatory Sanctions by the United Nations against Rhodesia," Center of International Studies Policy Paper: Studies in the Theory and Structure of Peaceful Change: New York University (1967).

40 For a detailed specification, see Myres S. McDougal, Harold D. Lasswell, and Ivan A. Vlasic, *Law and Public Order in Space* (New Haven 1963), 1025ff.

the constitutive process guaranteeing their continuously effective performance: intelligence, promotion, prescription, invocation, application, termination, and appraisal.[41] Allocations of sanctioning competences within the public order sectors should follow patterns of localization of delict, such that at different levels of social organization one can demark public and civic sanctioning processes.[42]

The integrality of public order and sanctioning must be appreciated in order to maximize and economize the sanctioning process. Public order should be structured to represent a positive realization of widely shared expectations and demands and, from the earliest life stages, sanctions should be internalized by the inculcation of appropriate perspectives. To reduce the need for and intensity of sanctions, an effective intelligence flow should identify probable breach areas and seek to avoid breach by prescriptive accommodation and the structuring of new incentives for compliance. I have referred to this elsewhere as the principle of anterior sanctioning.[43]

The objectives of sanctions should constantly be linked back to the needs of public order. Sanctions are not legitimized patterns of vengeance,[44] but of maintenance and improvement of public order. Hence an element of the legitimacy of any sanction is its contribution to constitutive, regulative, enterprisory, or supervisory operations in support of preferred public order, by means of corrective, deterrent, rehabilitative, and reconstructive strategies.[45]

A corollary of human dignity is the preference for persuasive rather

41 Myres S. McDougal, Harold D. Lasswell, and W. Michael Reisman, "The World Constitutive Process of Authoritative Decision," *Journal of Legal Education*, 19 (1967), 253, 403, 415.

42 Lasswell and Arens (fn. 8); Reisman (fn. 30).

43 W. Michael Reisman, "The Enforcement of International Judgments," *1968 Proceedings of the American Society of International Law* 13, 23, 24.

44 Better stated, perhaps, is that they should not be legitimated patterns of vengeance. There are natural law arguments for vengeance. Thomas Aquinas, for example, in his *Summa contra Gentiles*, wrote that "Man resists harm by defending himself against wrongs, lest they be inflicted on him, or he avenges those which have already been inflicted on him with the intention, not of harmony, but of removing harm done. And this belongs to vengeance . . . a special virtue." II, II, q. 108, a. 2, quoted in Rooney (fn. 7), 45. This is not a logically defensible position, unless the form of vengeance chosen is death and all those who are liable to identify with the executed are also killed, a terrifying and possibly limitless operation. The reduction of Aquinas' doctrine is found in the practice of Shaka, the 19th-century Zulu king, whose mode of attack was to exterminate an entire tribe. A contemporary European observer recounts: "We remonstrated against the barbarity and great impropriety of destroying women and children, who, poor unoffending innocents, were not culpable, and could do no injury. 'Yes they could,' he said; 'they can propagate and bring children, who may become my enemies. It is the custom I pursue not to give quarter to my enemies, therefore I command you to kill all.'" Nathanial Isaacs, *Travels and Adventures in Eastern Africa*, I (Capetown 1836), 130, quoted in Walter (fn. 28), 141. An elegant refutation of the deterrence theory is found in Oliver W. Holmes' "The Path of the Law," *Collected Legal Papers* (New York 1920), 189.

45 McDougal and Feliciano (fn. 8), 288-96.

than coercive strategies in all interpersonal transactions. And this extends to sanctioning. Coercive sanctions should be used only when no lesser sanction will avail or a genuine overriding crisis requires exigent and intensely coercive action in the defense of public order.[46]

Trends in Constitutive Sanctioning

In an earlier study my colleagues and I delineated the phases of the world constitutive process and noted cursory trend indications.[47] It will be useful to survey the global constitutive process briefly, with primary emphasis upon emergent sanctioning expectations.

PARTICIPANTS

The most fundamental goals in regard to participation in the world constitutive process may be summarized as democracy and responsibility: the widest sharing of power, commensurate with the responsibility and capacity of putative participants to comply with basic international norms. The United Nations Charter and the Human Rights Conventions and declarations spell out these policies at a lower level of abstraction[48] and the Charter regime does indicate structures for policing the policies.[49] Even with the correction of an appropriate time span, sanctioning techniques in terms of correction, deterrence, and rehabilitation remain fragmentary. Germany and Japan are the sole examples of massive international effort to reconstruct an entire national public order system such that it could be a responsible participant in the world constitutive process. But the importance of this example as a precedent cannot be overemphasized. On a number of occasions, participants worthy of access to crucial international arenas have been blocked for less than lawful reasons,[50] but these deviations are generally corrected over time.

Contemporary international prescriptions are not restricted to a notion of an abstract equality of states. The principles of democracy and responsibility extend ultimately to the internal features of national public order systems. Both the Charter and the authoritative communications illuminating its human rights provisions indicate the ultimate thrust of its policies,[51] but there are, as yet, only seminal indica-

[46] On the need for the recognition of the lawful use of force in appropriate circumstances, see pp. 332-33.

[47] McDougal, Lasswell, and Reisman (fn. 41), 253.

[48] See fn. 6 for citations.   [49] See Charter Articles 5 and 6.

[50] See "Conditions of Admission of a State to Membership in the U.N." [1947-48], *ICJ Reports* 57; "Competence of the General Assembly for the Admission of a State to the U.N." [1950] *ICJ Reports* 4. See also "Memorandum on the Historical Background of the Question of the Admission of New Members," A/AC. 64/L.I. 22 (1953); Aleksander W. Rudzinski, "Admission of New Members: The U.N. and the League of Nations," *International Conciliation* No. 480 (1952).

[51] See fn. 25.

tions of expectations of sanction-effectiveness. The Rhodesian case[52] may augur some development. More equivocal is the response of the world to the Soviet invasion of Czechoslovakia. Through the cloud of apparent official apathy, one can discern the operation of a variety of deprivatory, sanctioning responses which have been imposed upon the U.S.S.R.[53]

PERSPECTIVES

Appropriate perspectives for the world constitutive process involve widely shared subjectivities in regard to identifications, expectations, and demands. To persisting parochial identification patterns, identifications with symbols of the inclusive world community must be developed and they must be maintained at a minimum intensity such that they facilitate participation in international sanctions and enforcement. A number of international programs aim at this objective,[54] but they may expect to be obstructed by national elite counterobjectives. Nevertheless, a variety of environmental factors, which are widely perceived with increasing clarity, tend to generate inclusive identifications despite elite counterefforts. Interdependence and simultaneity, for example, act to clarify the inclusively indiscriminate threat of crises which can only be neutralized by collaborative transnational behavior. Overpopulation, food scarcity, environmental pollution, and weapons proliferation, to cite only the more prominent and dramatic threats to mankind, are widely perceived as common threats; a by-product of this perception is the gradual consolidation of inclusive identifications. This trend is by no means inexorable. Certain crisis situations may deflect the movement toward inclusive identifications and increase, instead, parochialism. The result will, of course, be a lowered sanction effectiveness in international decision.

The expectation most crucial to a viable system of public order and public sanctions involves expectations of the effectiveness of authority. Such an expectation is either consolidated over time from experiences of controlling international prescriptions or is weakened over time by experiences of purely semantic prescriptions. These expectations need not relate to specific structures or institutionalized processes of decision. One can, for example, expect that the United Nations will be thoroughly ineffective as an enforcer of a variety of prescriptions

[52] See fn. 40.

[53] Foremost among these is the fractionation of whatever solidarity still existed in the Soviet wings of national Communist parties. This represents a serious deprivation for the U.S.S.R. The general loss of reputation suffered by the Soviet Union among nations of the Third World cannot be discounted, transient though it may prove to be.

[54] See Otto Klineberg, *The Human Dimension in International Relations* (New York 1965). Same, *Tensions Affecting International Understanding* (New York 1950).

and yet make matter of fact assumptions of the effectiveness of a variety of other prescriptions which may or may not be associated with the U.N. Sanctions, as we have emphasized, are inchoate expectations accompanying prescriptions and they may be inferred by participants from a multitude of diverse interactive patterns. Hence there is no surprise over the fact that the observer may chart the consolidation of expectations of public order and public sanction effectiveness in certain sectors and the deterioration of such expectations in others. One can, as Carr,[55] Friedmann,[56] and Haas[57] have observed, demark simultaneous patterns of collaboration and conflict between two composite participants. More significant is the fact that in the crisscross pattern of transnational relationships, participants may entertain expectations of high public order and public sanction effectiveness for certain regions or certain bilateral relationships and expectations of low order and sanctions for others. The point to be emphasized is that the observer cannot usefully generalize high or low expectations of effectiveness without specifying value sector, geographical range and conditions.

Demands for radical change may have moved a philosopher such as Sartre to generalize a basic ethological drive for violence and to pontificate that its satisfaction can be essential to individual health.[58] But with the exception of a minuscule fringe of violent people, individuals demanding radical change and contemplating violence as a mode for securing it, claim to seek ultimately a system of minimum order approximating their own optimum value demands; once ascendant, they condemn nonofficial violence. A detailed specification of the value demands of the peoples of the world would indicate an equally high consensus in regard to many features of a preferred optimum order: demands for a share of power, wealth, enlightenment, well-being, respect, and so on. While many of these demands can be formulated as importing by implication an urgent demand for effective prescriptions within an effective public order system, the conceptual clarity with which we associate the term "interest"—demands supported by expectations of their feasibility—is only fragmentary. Until there is wider recognition of the fact that demands for stable value allocations involve effective public order and sanctioning systems, the extension of collaborative transnational interchanges will be impeded.

[55] Edward H. Carr, *The Twenty Years' Crisis 1919-1939*, 2nd edn. (London 1946).
[56] Wolfgang Friedmann, *The Changing Structure of International Law* (New York 1964).
[57] Ernest B. Haas, *Beyond the Nation-State* (Stanford 1964). See also Georg Schwarzenberger, *The Frontiers of International Law* (New York 1962); Raymond Aron, *Peace and War: A Theory of International Relations* (New York 1966).
[58] "Violence, like the Achilles lance, can heal the wounds it has inflicted." Jean-Paul Sartre, Preface to Frantz Fanon, *The Wretched of the Earth* (New York 1968). One notes with concern the recrudescence of an extreme nihilism, preaching even a self-destruction among many militant groups in this country.

In this respect, it is no surprise that the popular demand for punitive response, which attends breach of community norms—a demand characteristic of effective public order—is partial and fragmentary in the international arena.[59] Such demands are not, of course, autocthonous in any public order system; they are affected by a variety of changing contextual factors. In a period of high crisis, for example, widespread privitization and withdrawal of attention from all but the most immediate interactions, may dull the otherwise ordinary demand for effectiveness of community prescriptions. But these demands are, under ordinary circumstances, a facet of the perspectives supporting an effective public order system. When such demands become enfeebled, public order is weakening.

In the international arena, these demands can be considered under three headings. First, the demand for the suppression of transcultural delicts: behavior which is stigmatized as delictual in all sociocultural systems. Murder, terrorism,[60] genocide,[61] crimes against humanity,[62] piracy, and the general category of *delicta juris gentium*. Second, the demand for the suppression of international delicts: behavior which is stigmatized by formal international agreement, but for which the demand for suppression is somewhat lower than for transcultural delicts.[63] Finally, jurisdictional delicts: behavior which other communities recognize as properly within the jurisdiction of the state within which it was executed. The homogenization of a global culture will, presumably, shift many of these delicts to the transcultural category, with an attendant increase in the intensity of demand for their suppression.[64]

Situations

Anthropological data indicates, as we have seen, that societies of minimal geographical scope and limited complexity may consolidate

[59] See, Lasswell and Arens (fn. 8).

[60] Raphael Lemkin, "Le terrorisme," *Rapport à la IVe Conference Internationale pour l'Unification du Droit Penal, 1931, Actes de la Conference* (1933); Donnedieu De Vabres, "La repression internationale du terrorisme," *R.D.I.L.C.* 19 (1938), 37.

[61] G.A. Res. 96 (I); Genocide Convention 78 *U.N.T.S.* 237; for a detailed discussion, see W. Michael Reisman, "Memorandum Upon Humanitarian Intervention to Protect the Ibos" (1968).

[62] Charter of the International Military Tribunal, Article 6 (c). And see "The Charter and Judgment of the Nuremberg Tribunal: History and Analysis," Memorandum Submitted by the Secretary-General (1949) 66ff.

[63] Drugs are an example of this intermediate stage. They are outlawed by treaty and subjected to a measure of international policing. In certain cultures, they are treated with an official horror, but in others they are tolerated as a form of relaxation or as a vehicle for transcending religious experiences. Ambivalent patterns such as these may resolve themselves into either the first or third category or, given certain intercultural stimulations, cease to be treated as delictual.

[64] The Harvard Research on Treaties has noted a tendency to assimilate events generally stigmatized as crimes into an expanding category of *delicta juris gentium*.

effective public order systems without centralized sanctioning structures; sanctions may relate to roles, statuses, and functions and need not be associated with specialized organs.[65] But in more complex and geographically extensive societies and in intersocietal relations, it appears that effective public order cannot be consolidated without the delineation of some specialized authoritative sanctioning processes. As the range of sanction activities expands and as the complexity of the instruments comprising a sanction arsenal increases, specialized sanction processes become necessary to sustain expectations of effectiveness in a number of public order sectors. In large areas of civic order, decentralized patterns of sanctions may continue.

Both the League of Nations[66] and the United Nations[67] represent inclusive efforts to create a centralized enforcement process and, by its existence, to promote sanction expectations for essential constitutive and public order prescriptions. Although each organization has performed a number of useful functions relating to sanctions, neither can be considered wholly effective. In a case such as the *Rhodopian Forests* dispute,[68] the League may have performed an indirect enforcement function, by its mere presence, and individuals might have inferred therefrom a broader sanction potential. But the *Ethiopian* case[69] demonstrated that collective security was less a function of the League than of two or three crucial members. The case can be considered a severe erosion point for expectations of organizational sanction effectiveness.

The idea of an inclusive international organization as a sanction repository may not yet have recovered from the Ethiopian case. The United Nations was accorded a jurisdiction at least as broad as that of the League and, given contemporary international political tensions, has performed different types of enforcement roles in a surprisingly large number of situations.[70] Yet few thoughtful observers and probably fewer professional politicians and diplomats operate with sanction expectations associated with the United Nations. It is startling that

[65] Maine (fn. 2); Malinowski (fn. 9); Pospisil (fn. 2); Gluckman (fn. 9); Barkun (fn. 20).

[66] Covenant Articles 11-13, 16.

[67] Charter Articles 39-51.

[68] 15 *L.N.O.J.* 1417, 1432-33 (1934); see also *American Journal of International Law* 28 (1934), 760.

[69] For a comprehensive study of this case, see Albert E. Highley, *The Actions of the States Members of the League of Nations in Application of Sanctions Against Italy*, 1935/1936; same, *The First Sanctions Experiment* (A Study of League Procedures), 9 Geneva Studies (Geneva 1938).

[70] For surveys and evaluations, see Linda Miller, *World Order and Local Disorder: The United Nations Internal Conflicts* (Princeton 1967); for a recent review of the literature, consult David P. Forsythe, "United Nations Intervention in Conflict Situations Revisited: A Framework for Analysis," *International Organization* XXIII (1969), 115.

so many amateur promoters continue to invoke the United Nations as the panacea for crucial security policies, as though the Organization were a vast Deus ex Machina replete with a sheath of thunderbolts which it will unfortunately loose only upon plenipotentiary request. One can, of course, conceive of circumstances in which the objectives of political elites might move them to exploit this popular feeling and actually enfranchise the UN.

Sanction expectations are associated with a number of specialized agencies. The World Bank[71] and the regional banks for example have a real credit capacity; this represents teeth—if not incisors, at least molars—and a measure of what the economic agencies choose to term "international financial morality" is maintained by sanction expectations.[72] Other agencies have a comparable real or incipient sanction potential in their respective value areas.[73] Yet it appears that the greater part of international sanction expectations are associated with diplomatic and executive situations: implications of reciprocity and implied threats of retaliation for breach of community norms in which states perceive themselves as having a critical interest.[74] The undesirability of a deterrent or balance of terror system hardly requires expression. On the other hand, as Hinsley and others have argued,[75] it has provided a measure of minimum order for twenty-five years. Indirect sanctioning techniques, activating "world public opinion" bring many nonofficial arenas into operation and this trend may be expected to continue as the cultural premium on political participation rises. The emergence of effective centralized organs whose concern is minimum order and who can sustain sanction expectations sufficient to dispel the current gloom of insecurity appears still far off.

Base Values

Although sanctions may be and often are specified, they are essentially inchoate expectations of response to behavior deviating from group norms. The expectation may be autopunitive—internal sanctioning within the personality. Where group norms are not internalized as per-

---

[71] See pp. 312-14.

[72] See W. Michael Reisman, "The Role of the Economic Agencies in the Enforcement of International Judgments and Awards: A Functional Approach," *International Organization* XIX (1965), 929.

[73] See, for example, Articles 87 and 88 of the Convention on International Civil Aviation, *TIAS* No. 1591, 15 *U.N.T.S.* 295, 354.

[74] See Arthur Lenhoff, "Reciprocity in Function: A Problem of Conflict of Laws, Constitutional Law, and International Law," *University of Pittsburgh Law Review*, 15 (1953) 44; same, "Reciprocity: The Legal Aspect of a Perennial Idea," *Northwestern University Law Review* 49 (1954-55), 619, 752, McDougal and Feliciano (fn. 8), 296.

[75] F. H. Hinsley, *Power and the Pursuit of Peace* (Cambridge, Eng. 1963). But cf. John H. Herz, *International Politics in the Atomic Age* (New York 1959).

sonal demands, the effectiveness of public order and public sanctioning depends upon the extent to which desired values are perceived as
at the disposal of the inclusive community or, where sanction patterns
are bilateral and unofficial, so dispersed and interdependent among
participants that the feasibility of their consolidation and application
in an enforcement program is real. Where this expectation is low, sanction expectations are low and that sector of public order is relatively
unstable or weak. Hence a perusal of the bases of international sanctioning involves an examination of the degree to which crucial values
are at inclusive or exclusive disposal, on the one hand, or are so dispersed as to facilitate reciprocity and retaliation in support of authoritative prescriptions, on the other. Let us survey the allocation of a
number of values as they relate to international sanctions.

POWER

Although community prescriptions call for the concentration of
power within certain centralized organs for sanction and enforcement
purposes, power continues to be dispersed among nation-states rather
than monopolized by a formal authoritative process. The factual dispersal of power has created certain expectations about the support
which will be given to sustain a number of basic community prescriptions. Minimum order, for example, is widely perceived as dependent
upon a system of reciprocal deterrence, in which the strongest states
share a common interest in avoidance of escalation into high-level coercion. Regional security systems and bilateral and plurilateral mutual
aid agreements sustain other expectations about the continuation of
state and regional structures. As major states reconsider their policies
and commitments, many of these expectations are weakened and negotiations for new stable arrangements are undertaken. Insofar as some
power balance is achieved, new sanction expectations are consolidated.

WEALTH

The disposition of wealth about the globe gives a preponderant influence to states of the northern hemisphere and a higher effectiveness
to the policies and prescriptions to which they are committed. Insofar
as these states coordinate their wealth strategies through international
organizations, some measure of inclusive sanctioning is obtained. The
attempted oil embargo mounted by a number of OPEC members after
the Suez war of 1967[76] indicated, as did Iran's efforts more than a decade before,[77] that Northern need of Southern raw resources does not

[76] *New York Times*, June 16, 1967, p. 1 col. 8; *New York Times*, August 24, p. 51,
cols. 6-7.
[77] See, generally, Alan W. Ford, *The Anglo-Iranian Oil Dispute of 1951-52* (Berkeley 1954).

yet provide a potential sanction or a continuous parity in prescriptive participation.

Enlightenment and Skill

The enlightenment pool of any participant is obviously a key factor in formulating and assembling sanctions into an enforcement program; the assumption that a participant does or does not have such a pool is a component of an expectation of sanction effectiveness. A number of inclusive organizations do seem to have such enlightenment pools at their disposal, though they lack ready access to the other components necessary for assembling sanctions into enforcement. Enlightenment pools in national communities are dispersed unevenly about the globe; one can identify with little difficulty high and low enlightenment communities as well as chart trends of "brain draining" from the low to the high.

Respect and Rectitude

Respect, in the sense of views entertained by the self as to the image which it projects among others as well as the image of the collectivities with which it identifies as viewed by others and images entertained by the self about the self (there is, of course, reciprocal influencing between the two) is an important base of interaction and, in certain sanctioning contexts, may prove to be a point of high vulnerability. In many group situations, the primary thrust of a sanction may be the respect deprivation involved; other material deprivations are attendant upon the loss of respect, but it should be emphasized that the loss of respect itself may be severely dysphoric and that in many circumstances the sanction expectation of a respect deprivation may be the most decisive factor in securing group conformity. Where the ego is intensely identified with the group, group deprivation of respect may amount to a form of capital punishment.[78]

The effectiveness of a respect or rectitude sanction expectation depends, of course, upon a highly articulated identification with the

[78] "Some psychological sanctions, although of nonphysical nature, perform as strong a control as do physical sanctions. Ostracism, ridicule, avoidance, or a denial of favors—sanctions that are sometimes very subtle and informal—nevertheless may become more drastic than the corporal punishment to which we tend to attach over-importance even in our own culture. The Kapauku, for example, consider being shamed by a public reprimand, which sometimes lasts for several days, much worse than anything except capital punishment." Pospisil (fn. 2), 267-68. "From cross-cultural research and the above discussion, it follows that a legal sanction does not need to be corporal punishment or a deprivation of property. The form of a sanction is relative to the culture and to the subgroup in which it is used; it may be physical or psychological. We can define a legal sanction as either the negative behavior of withdrawing some rewards or favors that otherwise (if the law had not been violated) would have been granted, or the positive behavior of inflicting some painful experience, be it physical or psychological." Same.

group in question. Such identifications are not discrete but are influenced by contextual factors. In certain circumstances, for example, identifications with an inclusive community may be intense, and respect and rectitude sanction expectations may be effective deterrents. In other circumstances, however, identifications with an inclusive community may diminish as identifications with an exclusive group become more intense; here, the deterrent effect of the prospect of a respect deprivation by the inclusive community is considerably lessened.

Transnational respect communities do not necessarily follow the lines of authoritative constitutive structures. The United Nations, for example, may at a given time have a relatively low respect monopoly among a great number of participants. Yet functional respect communities following regional, class, or interest patterns may be effective. Among individuals, transnational respect communities may configure ethnic, religious, or skill groups that have achieved articulated transnational identifications. Individual scholars and scientists, for example, may demand certain action by their nation-states because they fear the loss of respect of colleagues abroad, attendant upon their acquiescence in policies which clash with those of their respect community.

Strategies

Sanction strategies, as opposed to enforcement strategies, are concerned with the inculcation of expectations of effective community commitment to the support of its prescriptions. Although sanction expectations may be derived from past deeds and from experience with successful enforcement programs, sanction strategies are, for the most part, anticipatory communications. On the level of municipal legislation, for example, a statutory instrument will set out a pattern of prescribed behavior and then indicate the range of deprivations which will be imposed upon those deviating from the norm. Where such an instrument is promulgated in a system of effective public order, a transference of expectations of effectiveness of general public order will be made to the prescription, and sanction expectations sufficient to support the prescription will be generated. Given expectations of effective public order, a specific indication of the type of sanction is not always necessary, though it may be desirable for other policy reasons. Consider the decalogue: a set of prescriptions of transempirical source are recited without specification of any sanctions. The only sanction indication is, interestingly, a promise of indulgence: in return for deference to the elders of the tribe and family, a long life is vouchsafed. But even in this formulatory pattern, it is probable that customary expectations of the sanctions to be imposed upon transgression of specific norms developed and were followed.

Effective sanction strategy involves a number of conditions. Of crucial importance is a personality system which, if it is not acculturated to respect for and conformity with authority, is at least sufficiently perceptive to appreciate its interdependence with others and the commitment of others to maintain stable structures of collaboration, including the sanctioning of deviant behavior. At the same time, there must be enough general community identification to render sanction expectations realistic. In addition, there must be a web of communication which is sufficiently articulated to reach the diverse members of the group in question and to inform them of both the prescription and its supporting sanction intention. Where the focus is upon intergroup as well as interpersonal relations each group structure must be sufficiently permeable to allow members to consolidate realistic perspectives and, in particular, to evolve identifications with an inclusive interest, encompassing all the interactive groups. Many of these conditions are imperfectly realized in many sectors of the international arena and, as a result, anticipatory sanction strategies are severely impeded.

International sanction strategies exhibit a wide diversity. A basic constitutive document, such as the Charter of the United Nations, inventories a broad range of possible measures which will be taken upon deviation from peremptory international norms, but does not specify which sanctions will actually be applied.[79] Considering the breadth of the policies involved and the possible diversity of the cases which may come before the United Nations, nonspecification introduces a useful flexibility. Were the UN itself perceived as an effective institution, such sanction generality would probably be a more effective strategy of sanction intention than would sanction specificity. As international prescriptions increase in their specificity, sanctions are often more specified. In the GATT, for example, there is frequently a clear indication of sanction countermeasures which will be taken upon the breach of certain provisions.[80] With less specificity, customary international law indicates under what general circumstances reprisals and retorsions may be undertaken,[81] but these terms have traditionally been more concerned with the volume and magnitude of response than with the specific type of response.

The most general international sanctions continue to be coarchical expectations of reciprocity and retaliation, of which reprisals and retorsion represent a partial legitimization. The effectiveness of this type of sanction strategy depends upon matter of fact assessments which participants are always making about the intentions of others and the potentialities or constraints of specific contexts. The literature

[79] Charter Articles 41 and 42.
[80] See Final Act, General Agreement on Tariffs and Trade, Articles 23, 25 and 27 in 1 GATT, *Basic Instruments and Selected Documents*, 1, 51-60.
[81] See, generally, O'Connell (fn. 35), 328-30.

of bargaining theory, as it applies to threats and deterrents, has begun to explore this field in detail;[82] its weakness, thus far, has been the tendency to focus upon individual cases, in terms of "win or lose" rather than upon a broad flow of interactions, in which the successful deviation from one prescription is related to countless other possibilities for retaliation. To have won a dispute at the cost of a general lowering of collaborative willingness *pro futuro* is hardly a net value gain.[83] It is in this respect that the basic coarchical sanction strategies of international law are considerably more successful than is pictured in the bargaining literature.

Outcomes

The outcomes of the process of international sanctioning are the stable features of the system of world public order. We have considered these earlier.

Toward International Sanction Expansion

International doctrinal literature is rich in laments over the sanction problem. A rather sizable group of international lawyers would probably accede to the Austinian view of the absence of sanctions and, indeed, of law in the international arena. The preceding discussion has shown that many international prescriptions are effectively supported by sanction expectations, although they tend to be associated with bilateral and plurilateral patterns of coarchy rather than with institutions of hierarchy. But the essential point, which is too often overlooked, is that sanctions cannot be considered as discrete phenomena; they are integral with public order and their expectations of effectiveness vary accordingly. The amelioration of a sanction system cannot be considered without indicating preferences for public order. Conversely, widely supported public order prescriptions either minimize the need for sanctions or generate sufficient support for conformity demands to supply their own sanction buttress.

From a developmental standpoint, then, one does not begin by suggesting how a sanction system can be created, but rather by indicating the contours of a world public order system, which is to be supported by sanctions. In an organized arena, authority may be concentrated in institutions. In a relatively unorganized arena, authority is concentrated on specific prescriptions. Before one supports or enforces a pre-

---

[82] See, for example, Thomas C. Schelling, *The Strategy of Conflict* (Cambridge; same 1960) *Arms and Influence* (New Haven 1966); Bernard Brodie, *Strategy in the Missile Age* (Princeton 1959); Henry A. Kissinger, *The Necessity for Choice* (New York 1961).

[83] See Karl W. Deutsch, *The Nerves of Government* (New York 1966). This flaw is further discussed in "Review": (W. Michael Reisman) *Arms and Influence*, by Thomas Schelling, *American Journal of International Law*, 6 (1967), 625-26.

scription, its content must be clarified. To the extent that the projected system is viewed as the realization of the demands of politically relevant strata about the globe, a common interest in support of that system will coalesce and the nonofficial sanctioning patterns which characterize societies without institutional development will be redirected to support the world public order system, or at least that part which is widely preferred. These sanction demands may carry over to the creation of necessary institutional arrangements.

Developing a model of a preferred world public order system must include ways of clarifying and consolidating the value demands of both elites and rank and file members in such a way that they put a premium upon norm-conforming behavior and are aroused to suppress illegitimate norm deviations. The content of the norms will be of crucial importance and diverse timetables may have to be developed as the world community moves to a higher approximation of a preferred public order. An element in this program will be the creation of predispositions for conformity. Unfortunately, the legal profession's "law habit" does not indicate how such a habit is developed, nor does the abundant anthropological and sociological literature on sanctions. This is a question which will require intensive interdisciplinary investigation. Heuristically, the problem of securing group conformity might be approached from the standpoint of the postulate of maximization: individuals act to maximize their perceived values. The extent of a convergence of value maximization and conformity, if any, with group norms will obviously vary with context; the same individual may, for example, perceive a value gain in conforming to the prescriptions of his religious group but not to the prescriptions of his national group and vice versa.

From a systematic standpoint, conformity to group norms may be activated by any and all value demands. Consider this brief survey. *Power*: An individual may conform to group norms either because of constraint or in order to secure or maintain acquired power. *Wealth*: An individual may conform to group norms because he anticipates a wealth gain or, more generally, because he believes that an extant system protects what he has already acquired. *Enlightenment*: Rational perceptions of common interest in orderly procedures may stimulate conformity. *Skill*: An individual may, as Piaget suggests, experience a value gain from the satisfaction of "knowing the rules" and being able to work with them.[84] *Respect*: Conformity may be valued for the respect it excites in others or for personal feelings of *rectitude* within the conforming personality. Each of these value possibilities may be considered negatively. For example, demands for power and wealth may lead to nonconforming behavior, if the individual perceives that con-

[84] Piaget (fn. 5), Chap. 7, passim.

formity will not satisfy these value demands. Enlightenment may force a recognition of tyranny and motivate resistance, and so on. In practice, values are agglutinative in the sense that conformity or deviation will often bring a complex of values. A severely sanctioned participant, for example, may lose civic rights (power), the right to practice his profession (enlightenment, skill, wealth, respect), his respect and rectitude status, and may undergo psychic and physical injury (well-being) because of his deprivation.

A survey such as this may provide a rough outline of why individuals conform to group prescriptions and may suggest a variety of techniques for formulating and applying international prescriptions in order to increase compliance and the predisposition to demand compliance of others. For the effectiveness of international sanctions is ultimately dependent upon the consolidation of the international community. This is the challenge.

II. Enforcement

Enforcement may be most economically understood as a purposive particularization of a public order sanctioning system: a specific assembly of sanction programs designed to realize, in value terms, an identifiable authoritative prescription.[85] In terms of the sequential decision functions which we have used elsewhere, sanction expectations are components of the prescriptive function and enforcement—the mobilization and application of sanctions—is a component of the application function.[86] In the philosophical ideal, prescriptions and their sanction buttresses will not require enforcement. As a practical matter, even the most intensely and widely demanded prescriptions—the *jura cogenta* of any community—may be challenged by dissident individuals. In times of rapid and cataclysmic change in which the organized community must redirect the behavior of large segments of the population into new courses, necessary prescriptions may require an even greater degree of enforcement. The capacity to enforce is a continuing restriction on the prescriptive or legislative goals of a community. Conversely, one factor in the range of flexibility of enforcement programs will be the overall efficaciousness of the total sanctioning system.

Because we are conditioned by our national experience to associate legal order with determinate forms of social organization, the question of international enforcement is particularly puzzling. There is no effective approximation of the sheriff—an authoritative and controlling

---

[85] An extensive consideration of this understanding of the process of enforcement is found in W. Michael Reisman, "The Enforcement of International Judgments," *American Journal of International Law*, 63 (1969), 1. See also pp. 326-33.

[86] McDougal, Lasswell, and Reisman (fn. 41), 253, 415ff.

institution specializing in enforcement—on the transnational plane. For that matter, there are only seminal beginnings of effective hierarchical institutions: the international arena is characterized by complex and contextually changing relations of hierarchy, coarchy, and subarchy among the diverse individual and composite actors. Yet, as we have observed in Part I of this chapter, there is an international public order system and it is sustained by a complex web of sanction expectations of varying degrees of intensity. The challenge to the student of configurative international law is not the creation of a system but, as Brierly put it, its organization.

> The real difference in this respect between municipal and international law is not that one is sanctioned and the other is not, but that in the one the sanctions are organized in a systematic procedure and that in the other they are left indeterminate. The true problem for consideration is therefore not whether we should try to *create* sanctions for international law, but whether we should try to organize them in a system.[87]

In the broadest sense, the problem is the creation and maintenance, through the world constitutive process, of viable enforcement procedures, as part of the global application function. In the specific sense, it is a matter of mobilizing sanctions in order to secure the enforcement of a particular authoritative decision.

A specific international enforcement problem can be most usefully approached in terms of problem solving: given an enforcement objective—the securing of a concrete value allocation decreed by an authoritative decision and/or deterrent, restorative, rehabilitative, or reconstructive consequences in world public order—how can one best exploit the environmental and predispositional components of the context. With a comprehensive frame of inquiry, the world social process presents myriad potentials of authority and control, which can be drafted to secure the realization of preferred policies. An appropriate map will also indicate such critical factors as optimum timetable, policy formulation, priority areas for investigation, and so on. But let us emphasize that enforceability is a matter of human choice. Environmental and predispositional factors may indicate a low probability of enforcement or enforcement only at an excessive value consumption.[88]

87 James L. Brierly, "Sanctions in International Law" in Sir Hersch Lauterpacht and Sir Humphrey Waldock, eds., *The Basis of Obligation in International Law and Other Papers of the Late James Leslie Brierly* (Oxford 1958), 212.

88 William T. Gossett, "The Law: Leader or Laggard in Our Society," *American Bar Association Journal* 51 (1965), 1131. The language of the United States Supreme Court in *Brown v. Board of Education*, 347 *U.S.* 483 (1954) indicates an appreciation of these problems. The court, it will be recalled, ordered school desegregation with "all deliberate speed," a phrase which was understood by local school boards and

This does not necessarily mean that preferred policies must be abandoned. It means rather that renewed negotiation for a prescriptive consensus may be called for, that the long range goal should be broken into a series of mediant objectives upon which attention can be usefully concentrated, that new strategies must be creatively investigated, and so on. If, for example, one cannot achieve total disarmament, one can seek mediant arms control, test bans, etc. If an atmosphere of mutual suspicion prevents effective policing, resources must be directed to technological devices which do not require physical intervention in the territory of a state. The appropriate targets for changes must be clearly identified. Radical systemic changes must begin with the realization that a system exists because effective elites believe that they maximize their immediate interests in that system. Hence change need not be directed at the stars, but more often at very accessible human beings who are attuned and responsive to political pressures. The point which must be emphasized is that the inability to secure immediate enforcement is not equivalent to fatalistic conclusions of eternal unenforceability.

A problem-solving approach to enforcement recognizes that specialized enforcement institutions, insofar as they exist, are only one strand in the intricate sanction web of the global social process and that a broad frame of inquiry may direct attention to a variety of subcontexts which can be turned to enforcement advantage.[89] In this respect, the

---

federal enforcement authorities as permitting them to take a variety of features such as school administration, community order, and so on into account in setting up desegregation timetables. The aftermath of the Brown case may represent an abuse of judicial consideration of the problems of actually applying an authoritative decision in a complex and varied social context. See, generally, Alexander M. Bickel, *Politics and the Warren Court* (New York 1965), 7-45. One point which must always be considered in the evaluation of projected environmental and predispositional impediments to enforcement is the new, additional factor of the compulsive authority of the decision itself; the extent to which generally held sanction expectations have attached to a process of decision predisposes participants to comply with that decision because of a combination of psychological and/or carefully considered political reasons. The point is that an authoritative decision, appropriately formulated to trigger inculcated predispositions, may tip the balance toward compliance.

[89] Why, for example, consider only the coercive powers of the executive in the public sector, when a variety of groups disposing of effective power in the civic sector can be drafted to participation in an enforcement program? In a business-oriented society, for example, economic groups can be positively involved in enforcement by drawing their attention to the advantages which they may derive from the innovative decision; alternately, extraneous inducements may be integrated within the decision to draft the support of wealth elites. In parliamentary democracies, the custom of "riders," though frequently abused, is a standard technique for expanding support for a program by joining to it other value promises which may have little or no material connection with the original prescriptive objective. Other value groups may also be involved. In every decision, application involves rectitude events. Hence formal rectitude groups' initial predisposition to support the decision and to lend their power to it can be expanded by comparable techniques.

international enforcer is a functionalist applying a functional system of enforcement. The functional system is based on the political and legal elements at play in an enforcement process: community authority and effective power. The relevant social context is scrutinized and combinations of authority and effective power, which can act functionally as a specific enforcement system, are arranged. From the spectrum of possible relationships, that combination which can enforce most economically, yet poses the least jeopardy to international peace, is chosen.

A functional system of enforcement in an arena of varying degrees of organization involves: (1) clarification of enforcement objectives; (2) identification of target; (3) delineation of the comprehensive enforcement context; (4) assembling an enforcement program; and (5) appraising the ongoing enforcement program.

Enforcement Objectives

It is in the area of enforcement rather than in sanctions that the problem of structure intervenes. While the existence of prescriptive structures may facilitate the inculcation of sanction-predispositions, sanctions need not be associated with authoritative and centralized structures. Indeed, there are a number of public order benefits to be derived from a dispersal of sanctions throughout the civic rather than public sector. But enforcement, representing as it does a concentration of public coercive power, is maximized and most easily controlled by a high degree of centralization. To characterize a predominantly coarchical system whose enforcement procedures frequently take the guise of self help as "primitive" is a somewhat misleading characterization. Self help procedures are available in so-called developed systems and, as a matter of policy, it may be desirable to leave certain areas to largely self-initiated and self-prosecuted enforcement.[90] But self help is less economical and less controllable and is obviously least desirable in enforcement programs requiring the greatest degree of coercion. This consideration has a very practical application to inter-

---

[90] The characterization "primitive system" involves no small amount of cultural and temporal parochialism when applied to folk cultures. I concede that I do not know what a primitive political system is. Considered within its plenary context, a so-called primitive system may be thoroughly adequate to the fulfillment of the diverse tasks which elites and/or rank and file may expect of it, while an advanced or developed system may be inadequate in this sense. It has often been noted that missionary activities have acted to destroy a culture by depriving individuals of the symbol and myth structure which they required within their milieu, and supplying them with one which was wholly unsuited to their conditions. The same point can be made in regard to political missionizing. If the word "primitive" has any designative justification in political systems, it is in regard to a system in which social goals have been clarified, but in which the techniques for their realization are still in the early stages of experimentation. There are, for example, no shortage of primitive political zones—hierarchically and coarchically—in American public order.

national enforcement programs: in an arena of relatively low organization, the objective of an enforcer can never restrict itself to the mere realization of a particular policy prescription. Of equal and at times significantly greater importance is the constitutive aspect of the problem: the creation of conditions facilitating voluntary compliance with and where necessary economic and expeditious enforcement of international decisions.[91]

Coordinate with the inevitable constitutive ramifications of each enforcement program is the continuing concern with the maintenance of minimum order. The high rectitude associations of compliance with the law and the possible severe inner repressions which are involved in the process of compliance frequently generate an intense public demand for harsh enforcement in cases of breach of group norms. Ambivalences toward the use of violence—official or otherwise—may contribute to a mechanical automatization of enforcement upon authoritative establishment of defections from demanded behavior. These characteristics are clearly reflected in John Austin's treatment of sanctions and they are implicit in the sonorous imprecations on the order of "fitting the punishment to the crime." But this approach to enforcement crumples under configurative appraisal. Enforcement is a procedure in defense of public order and no enforcement program should be undertaken unless it has been fashioned so as to advance this inclusive concern. This introduces a three-level requirement.

The first requirement, the constitutive ramification, has already been discussed. The second requirement is a concern for minimum order. It is obvious that one does not undertake an enforcement program that bodes a net public order loss, in terms of disruption, value consumption, and destabilization of requisite community authority structures. An enforcement program which threatens minimum public order—at any level of organization—is a contradiction in terms and must be abandoned or retooled to fulfill its proper function. In certain circumstances, there should be no enforcement. The possible need for a dramatic vindication of public authority by an enforcement program can be satisfied by largely symbolic activities. An enforcement program need not be effective in terms of realizing an authoritative allocation of values; it must, however, affect predispositions without detriment to public order.

The third requirement of an enforcement program is its conformity to specific community objectives: deterrence, restoration, rehabilitation, and reconstruction. Punitive deprivations or indulgences have no enforcement meaning if they are not planned as instrumental in achieving one of the above objectives.

[91] For a more detailed discussion, see Reisman (fn. 43), 13, 16.

There are a number of procedural principles which are crucial to rational enforcement programs. Lasswell and Arens have noted four policies: futurity, contextuality, economy, and realism.[92] For purposes of this chapter, attention will be directed specifically to the policy of contextuality.

Enforcement presupposes an authoritative decision. Ideally, the decision is delivered by a centralized institution, recognized by the community as monopolizing authority in the social sector in question; hence there will be little question of the authority of the decision. The decision may, however, emanate from unorganized and extremely diffuse processes and nevertheless enjoy wide acceptance as authoritative. Consider social sanctions for a gross breach of neighborhood etiquette. The culprit Jones is not subjected to a trial, nor is there collusion among the sanctioning neighbors. They all cease to associate with Jones and his family, however, and invitations to civic and religious activities are no longer extended. Jones and his family must ultimately move to another town. The neighbors know that Jones and his family have suffered enormously and perhaps permanently. A number of neighbors may feel some regret, but all are assured that they have acted properly.[93] We encounter here an example of an effective decision, taken in an extremely diffuse process whose authority is, nonetheless, not questioned by any of the participants.

Such authority is a critical component of lawful decision. The authority which attaches to a decision facilitates its enforcement, yet it may impede public order by the rigidity which it evokes. Authority has taken a stand and it must be vindicated; if not, the argument runs, no one will have respect for authority. Law expresses this in the doctrine of finality. Judgments are to be treated as irrevocably final because "interest reipublicae ut sit finis litium."[94] But the phenomenon

---

[92] Lasswell and Arens (fn. 8), 233; same "The Role of Sanctions in Conflict Resolution" (fn. 8), 27.

[93] Anthropological examples of this sort are discussed in Pospisil (fn. 2), and are noted by Malinowski (fn. 9), as part of the pattern of reciprocity, by which men exist in social groups. In the jurisprudential literature, Jeremy Bentham seems to have referred to this pattern of response as his "moral sanction" in his *Introduction to the Principles of Morals and Legislation* (fn. 8); Bentham sometimes referred to the moral sanction as the "popular sanction." A student of Bentham explains that "The moral sanction represents the punishment suffered from the want of neighborly assistance which has been withheld because of the misconduct or supposed misconduct of the sufferer. It is due to spontaneous disposition rather than to any settled rule." Rooney (fn. 7), 97. See also Beatrice B. Whiting, *Paiute Sorcery* (New York 1950). See also Epstein (fn. 9), 1, 4.

[94] "The common interest calls for the final resolution of disputes." This doctrine of *res judicata* or the finality of a judgment, like all basic legal doctrines, is manifested in a complementary set: on the condition that the judgment is valid. This complementarity permits decision-makers great flexibility in arriving at an authoritative decision in any case, but necessarily involves consideration of a broad context and a wide range of policies.

is found in other organized decision processes: the stubborn and ultimately self-defeating refusal of an administrator or corporation executive to change his decision, the obstinate refusal of a general to change
his strategy although thousands of lives are being needlessly sacrificed,
the concern with saving face in micro-group conflicts, and so on.

Social psychologists have inferred, from examples like these, that
there is a typical response involved: dissonance reduction.[95] If there
is such a response, it must be corrected by a focus of comprehensive
contextuality and continuous goal thinking in enforcement programs.
For the minimum objective of public order is not finality but stability,
without which no orderly progress toward concrete goals is possible.
Finality is one of a number of strategies for achieving stability and in
instances in which insistence on finality will destabilize public order,
alternate instruments must be sought. The process of mobilizing enforcement strategies is one of continuous reappraisal against a back-
drop of the most comprehensive focus of the most comprehensive
arena. It is only by this focus that maximum exploitation of authority
can be achieved and optimum public order consequences secured.

Enforcement considerations should not be initiated after a decision
has been taken and resistance has already been encountered. Consideration should begin in pre-arena phases, at the earliest point in social
interaction when a number of participants make conflicting claims to
a limited number of values. At this stage, prescriptive solutions may
mitigate conflicts, but it is utopian to imagine that they can prevent all
conflict. The community structures within which the conflict arises will
determine in great part the extent of the disputants' freedom in choosing decision procedures. In an unorganized arena, with relatively un-
refined institutional practices, the modalities by which participants
choose to reconcile claims and reach effective decisions are options
rather than predetermined patterns. It is at this stage that careful consideration must be given to postdecisional enforcement. Consider, as
one example, preadjudicative phases of a dispute which might be presented to an international tribunal:

> Enforcement consideration should begin in the preadjudicative
> phase, a negotiating or bargaining process. Words in the com-
> promis providing a reinforced finality are not an adequate acquittal
> of this demand. Bargaining theorists have demonstrated the range
> of possibilities in preagreement phases for structuring effective en-
> forcement procedures into the total agreement context. Some of
> these can be applied to the negotiation of a compromis or submis-

[95] Leon Festinger, "The Psychological Effects of Insufficient Reward," *American
Psychologist*, 16 (1961), 1.

sion. . . . The reluctance of one party to commit itself to such structuring is some indication of its probable reaction should it lose its case. Hence the initiating party might reformulate the content of the submission, undertake unilateral enforcement structuring, or turn to another modality of conflict resolution rather than adjudication.[96]

Similar considerations should be brought into play in the choice or structuring of other decision processes.

The formal decision phase, whether taken in a parliamentary, conference, adjudicative, diplomatic, or executive arena,[97] should be equally alive to the possibility of postdecision enforcement problems. A number of diplomats at the United Nations have noted that one takes those decision options which promise a degree of effectiveness and one eschews those which bode failure. On the same order, the International Court has refused to take jurisdiction in preliminary or later phases of a case, where the probabilities of compliance with, or coercive enforcement of, a judgment outcome were low.[98] These are rather primitive futuristic responses to enforcement problems. More creative responses involve integration within a decision of palatable and unpalatable elements such that the party considering repudiation of the decision will be deterred by the prospect of losing as much as it might gain. The possibilities of integrative solutions are broad and should constantly be investigated. In addition, the total value consequences of alternate decisions should be considered. The verbal formulation of a decision can at times soften a material loss; conversely, a bluntly worded judgment, though precipitating long-range prescriptive effects, may force a litigant to repudiate the decision. The crucial first step toward this phase of anterior enforcement requires decisionmakers to break free of the notion that they are mechanically applying the law; their total frame of decision reference must be sufficiently comprehensive to permit them to locate themselves as agents of enforcement at different decision sequences.

96 Reisman (fn. 91), 15-16.

97 McDougal, Lasswell, and Reisman (fn. 41), 111, 280-82.

98 These patterns are discussed in Alan H. Schechter, *Interpretation of Ambiguous Documents by International Administrative Tribunals* (London 1964), 130. See also Sir Hersch Lauterpacht, *The Development of International Law by the International Court* (London 1958), 91, 243. In the *Anglo-Iranian Oil Co. Case* (Preliminary Objections) [1952] *ICJ Reports* 93, for example, the United Kingdom sought to bring Iran before the Court on the basis of an Iranian declaration of adhesion under Article 36 of the Statute of the Court. By the most restrictive interpretation, the Court held itself without jurisdiction. Judge Read, dissenting, observed that some twenty days before the Court had confirmed its jurisdiction under a similar adhesion in the *Ambatielos Case* (Preliminary Objections) [1952] *ICJ Reports* 38. For a comparable judicial response, see *Case Concerning the Aerial Incident of 27 July 1955* (Preliminary Objections) [1959] *ICJ Reports* 98.

The conventional enforcement phase begins at the point at which there are widely shared perceptions of the authoritative application of prescriptions to a fact complex. The decision need not, as we have seen, be the product of an organized process, conventionally associated with decision authority, but may be the result of diffuse interactions. The crucial component is a shared subjective conclusion and this may be generated by no more than the interaction of demanded prescriptions and the common perception of a gross deviation from them. The hijacking of an El Al plane to Algeria is a good example of this type of decision phenomenon. No one required a formal decision by the Security Council to perceive that the coercive abduction of a civilian plane was, as both a single event and as a precedent, delictual and that transnational efforts would be made to secure restoration and deterrence. This decision cannot be located in an international institution; it was concluded at many different parts of the globe simultaneously. But it was nonetheless an authoritative response: a decision requiring and authorizing enforcement.

An enforcement program is not crystallized at one point in time, but is ideally under continuous appraisal; the effects of initiated strategies form a feedback flow in the light of which enforcers constantly review and reframe future strategies. It belabors the obvious to repeat that all things are in flux and that the introduction of a new vector of behavior —an enforcement program—creates new event complexes which may not have been foreseen. Rationality requires constant review. It is baffling that lawyers who have at last surrendered to the notion of changing law continue to cling to socially discrete and increasingly fictitious fact situations constructed at some point in the past and constantly imprinted on an ever-changing present, without reference to contemporary reality.

Target and Context

Attention may be focused on the context and its enforcement potentialities by means of a seven-phased model which concentrates on the full range of participants, their perspectives, relevant situations of interaction, the power bases of participants, the strategies by which the bases are manipulated, and the outcomes—conformity or deviation from the complex of enforcement objectives. Let us consider each phase *seriatim* and, in so doing, gain a general picture of the enforcement potentials offered in the contemporary system of international relations.

PARTICIPANTS

Participants may be most usefully considered in two categories; the target of enforcement and the enforcers.

TARGETS

Versailles and Nuremberg represent decisive steps away from the traditional notion that the actors in the international arena are or should be considered for decision purposes as monolithic state entities. The constitutive principle of responsibility requires that key causal actors be identified and that the target of enforcement be located at that point.[99] Collective guilt is essentially exonerative.[100] Moreover, imputations of responsibility to composite entities tend to solidify the resistance of all who may identify with that collective symbol and will press the enforcer inexorably to a Hamiltonian doctrine of ineluctable military enforcement.[101] Optimal strategy, then, requires careful identification of the target of enforcement. The mere act of identification may precipitate the following effects: (1) an immediate rectitude deprivation will be imposed upon the target; (2) established patterns of collaboration with other participants, which the target may inventory among his bases of power, will be disrupted, as individuals who feel that they are as yet not tainted withdraw from association; (3) identification of a definite rather than diffuse target will facilitate mobilizing bases and strategies and will encourage those who are dubious as to the efficacy of an enforcement program in the possibility of its success. Failure to identify specific targets may cause excessive value investment in enforcement, create ancillary, dysfunctional deprivations upon participants who are not responsible and, as a result, undermine confidence in the international enforcement system.

The identification of a target is far from simple, since considerations of effectiveness enter. The target may be one component of a power elite which is relatively immune to the projected effects of available

[99] Lasswell and Arens, "Toward a General Theory of Sanctions" (fn. 8), 229, 263-65.

[100] The point is made forcefully by Raul Hilberg, in his massive study, *The Destruction of the European Jews* (Chicago 1961). After World War II, a number of German theologians construed, in the Stuttgarter Erklärung, a general guilt of all humanity for the atrocities in the war. The Catholic Church protested this construction. Dr. Hans Asmussen replied: "Although every man is responsible for his own deeds, as certain that mankind is one kind is the certainty that this guilt is anchored forever in all mankind." Hilberg comments that Asmussen "transformed a collective guilt into a universal one. In his explanatory hands guilt became indistinguishable from life itself." Hilberg, 680.

As a general matter, the importance of the constitutive principle of responsibility cannot be overstated. Doctrines of limited bureaucratic responsibility, on the one hand, and of the universalization of responsibility for every act on the other, erode the very basis of ethical relations in any social organization. The principle of responsibility, it should be noted, does not import the automatic imposition of sanctions.

[101] "In any association where the general authority is confined to the collective bodies of the communities that compose it, every breach of the laws must involve a state of war; and military must become the only instrument of civil obedience." Alexander Hamilton, *The Federalist*, No. 15.

strategies. Hence another value elite with whom the target's power factors exist in a symbiotic relation may have to be sought. Or if the internal base of the target elite is a segment of the rank and file, enforcement endeavors may be directed to them. But the identification of a diffuse target and a shotgun enforcement approach should be avoided. Examples of international enforcement have frequently fallen below the desired standard in this regard.[102]

Once identified the target should not be considered a static entity. The target is not fixed but is moving. The enforcement process is always, as a minimum, dyadic, and the target may be expected to have as much political acumen as does the enforcer. Each enforcement step will elicit a counterenforcement step. Sound enforcement planning should seek to prevision insofar as possible the consequential event series attendant on any strategy move.

ENFORCERS

The range of international enforcers includes general international organizations, specialized agencies, regional organizations, nation-states acting jointly or severally, nonofficial groups, and individuals. In any given situation, different participants will manifest different capacities as potential enforcers; for enforcement is authoritative, mobilized influence, and influence is not an absolute arithmetical computation but in great measure a function of specific context. Thus, in a given context, a superpower may be relatively unable to mobilize its capacities to influence a particular target, while an Onassis or a civic protest group may. Creative enforcement will frequently involve the formation of entity combinations in order to secure maximum exploitation of available authority and power. For example, the enforcement power of a number of states may be augmented by formal authorization from a general international organization. The range of international enforcers may be briefly considered.

GENERAL INTERNATIONAL ORGANIZATIONS

Both the League of Nations[103] and the United Nations represent inclusive efforts to consolidate the enforcement function within one international organization. But the most attenuated conceptions of

---

[102] See, for example, Johan Galtung, "On the Effects of International Economic Sanctions." *World Politics*, XIX (1967), 378. Dr. Galtung assumes a holistic sanction program. Ideally, enforcement should identify pressure points in the target and seek to direct deprivations and/or indulgences at them.

[103] On the enforcement system of the League, see Jacques Nantet, *Les Sanctions dans le Pacte de la S.D.N.* (1936); D. N. Hadjiscos, *Les Sanctions Internationales de la Societé des Nations* (1920). The background of coercive sanction consideration in the drafting of the Covenant of the League of Nations is found in Camille V. E. Piccioni, *La Sanction Militaire des Decisions de la Societé des Nations* (1923).

common interest and elite suspicions of a genuinely effective international organization are clearly reflected. The United Nations is not a general enforcer but an enforcer *in extremis*.[104] One paradox of the Charter regime is that a state cannot activate the plenary enforcement powers of the Organization upon deprivation of a right guaranteed by international prescriptions unless the deprivation approaches crisis level or the plaintiff state is prepared to pursue a crisis diplomacy which can magnify the event to the level of a "threat to the peace." Any matter of international concern can, of course, be brought to the Security Council[105] or to the General Assembly[106] and, if pursued successfully, become a resolution with a degree of compulsive authority that will vary with the context of the case.[107] But the Charter restricted the plenary decisional competence of the Security Council and the application of coercive enforcement powers to predetermined crisis situations. These prescriptive factors, as well as the internal decision dynamics of the Council,[108] narrow severely the enforcement role of the United Nations. There are circumstances in which the Organization may act as an enforcer, for different crisis structures can alternately activate or decimate a relatively moribund set of institutional practices. In certain circumstances, the authority and potential control base of the United Nations can be impressive.

The ambivalences of Charter enforcement are reflected, in microcosm, in Article 94(2),[109] a provision, belatedly inserted, for enforce-

---

[104] Article 39 of the Charter sets out the criteria for application of the plenary powers of the Security Council: the Council cannot exercise these powers unless it makes a factual finding of a "threat to the peace, breach of the peace or act of aggression." The concept of "threat to the peace" was, of course, an intentionally flexible term of art.: "it was clearly within the expectations of both the framers and the general community that action by the Security Council might have to be anticipatory and was not required to await the full consummation of disaster. Thus, the competence accorded to the Council in Article 39 relates not merely to perfected 'breaches of the peace' and 'acts of aggression' but explicitly extends also to the prevention and removal of 'threats to the peace.'" McDougal and Reisman (fn. 39), 1, 7-8.

[105] Charter Articles 34 and 35.   [106] Charter Articles 11 (2), 11 (3), and 14.

[107] Monographic studies of the competence of the General Assembly are found in F. Blaine Sloan, "The Binding Force of a 'Recommendation' of the General Assembly of the United Nations," *British Yearbook of International Law*, 25 (1948-49), 1, and D.H.N. Johnson, "The Effect of Resolutions of the General Assembly of the United Nations," same, 32 (1955-56), 97. See also Richard A. Falk, "On the Quasi-Legislative Competence of the General Assembly," *American Journal of International Law*, 60 (1966), 782. It need hardly be added that the actual compulsive effect of any decision is not exclusively a function of documentary authority. A variety of contextual factors can effectuate a formally "advisory" or hortatory resolution or, on the other hand, drain a formally "binding" decision of all effectiveness.

[108] Charter Article 27.

[109] "If any party to a case fails to perform the obligations incumbent upon it under a judgment rendered by the Court, the other party may have recourse to the Security Council, which may, if it deems necessary, make recommendations or decide upon measures to be taken to give effect to the judgment."

ment of the judgments of the International Court of Justice.[110] The reinforced discretionary elements of the provision, which have been much criticized, need not concern us, for they merely express the implicit reality of contextual choice regarding whether and how to enforce a decision. But Article 94(2) is restricted to judgments of the ICJ and does not extend to the outcomes of any other transnational adjudicative or arbitral processes.[111] And there is no agreement as to whether Article 94(2) is an independent form of action or is dependent, for effective and perhaps coercive enforcement, upon establishment of an international crisis through a Council declaration of a "threat to the peace" under Article 39.[112]

Implicit in the circumscribed enforcement authority of the United Nations is a conception of legitimate coarchical enforcement of international rights and privileges in event complexes which do not comprise "threats to the peace." The range of modalities of enforcement extends from organization and state combinations to individual state action by self help. The controversy rages about the question of the degree of force which can be employed in such enforcement actions. Is Article 2(4) of the Charter an absolute prohibition, a prohibition limited to coercion directed at territorial integrity and political independence, a provision obsolesced by *rebus sic stantibus* and the frustration of Article 43 of the Charter, a policy statement whose application depends upon such factors as type of delict, the extent of specific authorization, and the minimum order features of the context?[113] Questions on this order require a comprehensive reexamination of the use of force in the contemporary world arena.

SPECIALIZED AGENCIES

The specialized agencies, exercising as they do higher degrees of supervision over specific patterns of transnational interaction, are in a proportionately better position to contribute to an enforcement program. Since they are closer to specific value flows, they are more capable of precipitating immediate indulgences and deprivations upon enforcement targets. Within certain sectors, for example, the IBRD and the IMF can refuse to extend credit and this may comprise a deprivation severe enough to persuade a participant to change a specific course of behavior.[114] The ICAO may announce termination of landing

[110] A brief recounting of the legislative history of this provision is found in Reisman (fn. 83), 1, 14.

[111] Compare, in this respect, the judgment and arbitral award enforcement provision of the Covenant of the League of Nations: Article 13 (4).

[112] For a survey of doctrinal views, see Reisman (fn. 83), 15 n.126.

[113] For a survey of different doctrinal positions on the construction of Article 2 (4) see pp. 332-33.

[114] It is difficult to document specific cases in which demands for internal changes in a recipient's public order system as a condition for receiving economic aid were

and overflight rights and may restrict or cancel other privileges.[115] The ILO and the FAO might terminate plans or even projects they had undertaken. Automatic imposition of such sanctions may, of course, be nugatory. They must be integrated within a total sanction program aimed at achieving a specific objective. Many of the Charters and Statutes of the specialized agencies spell out the enforcement procedures that they may undertake upon breach of their own norms.[116]

The specialized agencies are linked to the United Nations by a network of Special Agreements.[117] According to these, many of the agencies have committed themselves to assist the Security Council in the execution of Chapter VII of the Charter. Yet the commitment to assist is far from enthusiastic. The reluctance of many of the agencies to obligate themselves is evident in their extremely qualified duty to support as expressed in many of the Special Agreements.[118] In a number of instances, a directive from the Security Council is supposed to initiate automatic sanction implementation within the agency's operational arena;[119] but even this can be thwarted, as one recent case indicates.[120] The economic agencies which are particularly well tooled for rapid enforcement activities retain a discretion as to whether and by what means they will implement Security Council directives.

In addition to their higher degree of control over transnational value flows, the enforcement potential of specialized agencies is enhanced

---

successfully pressed by the international economic agencies. The agencies themselves are reticent in admitting such cases. It has, however, been reported that a condition of a World Bank Loan to Egypt was disengagement from Yemen, a condition made strictly upon financial considerations. The agencies' concern with "financial morality" has, apparently, been construed broadly and contextually. For a detailed treatment of these problems, see Reisman (fn. 72), 929.

115 8 *UNTS* 324, 330.

116 See, for example, Articles 5 and 6 of the Articles of Agreement of the International Bank for Reconstruction and Development, 2 *UNTS* 135, 160-86.

117 See Article 48 (2) of the United Nations Charter. A model and, in a number of ways, a high point in the negotiation of the special agreements, is that between the ICAO and the U.N. 8 *UNTS* 324. For background on the negotiation of the Agreements, see Walter R. Sharp, "The Specialized Agencies and the United Nations," *International Organization* 1 (1947) 460, 467; and same 2 (1948), 247. Some of the legal and in particular international constitutional problems raised by the Special Agreements regime are considered in Hans Aufricht, "Suppression of Treaties in International Law," *Cornell Law Quarterly*, 37 (1952), 691.

118 Thus, the Special Agreement with the IMF only obliges the Fund to take note of the obligations of its component members under Charter Article 48 (2) and continues that the Fund will "have due regard for decisions of the Security Council under Articles 41 and 42." Article 6 (1), Agreement between the United Nations and the International Monetary Fund, 16 *UNTS* (1948) 328, 332.

119 For example, Article 7 of the ICAO Special Agreement, 8 *UNTS* 324, 330. See also in this regard, the ICAO's constitutive document, The Convention on International Civil Aviation, Articles 87, 88, 15 *UNTS* 295, 394.

120 See U.N. Doc. A/6294 (April 1, 1966) from the Secretary-General of the ICAO to the U.N. asserting a conflict between the General Assembly's directive to *inter alia* the ICAO (Res. 2107 (XX)) and the Chicago Convention.

by the wide diversity of their internal decision dynamics leading to enforcement choices. The unique structure of the Security Council does not recur through the spectrum of functional agencies. The structures and dynamics of each agency differ and a de jure or de facto veto power in one potential enforcer may not exist in another.

REGIONAL ORGANIZATIONS

Formal regional organizations have an express dispute-resolving authority from the United Nations Charter, subject to conformity with the peremptory norms of that instrument,[121] and they can play important enforcement roles.[122] The crucial factor in regionalism, of course, is the political interdependence of adjacent states which makes each vulnerable to the concerted action of its neighbors. Hence a regional setting may promise a number of enforcement advantages. Effective regionalism may also deter global escalation of an enforcement action. Finally, there are certain practical and policy advantages to be gained by the localization of enforcement in the area in which the delict was originally committed.[123]

NATION-STATES

Nation-states, as the primary repositories of effective power, are the most promising candidates for enforcement roles. There is, of course, a marked disinclination to become involved in the affairs and problems of others, but counterbalancing this is the duty to aid in the enforcement of community decisions, an obligation deriving from "general principles."[124] The Treaty of Washington and the *Alabama*

[121] Charter Articles 52-54.

[122] In a number of recent conflicts, regional organizations played the dominant role in enforcement. In the Algerian-Moroccan boundary dispute, for example, the OAU was instrumental in the formation of an ad hoc arbitration commission. In the Honduras-Nicaraguan boundary dispute, the OAS pressed the parties to bring the matter to the International Court; after judgment, pressure from the organization was instrumental in securing acceptance of the judgment as a final resolution of the dispute. The Commonwealth is not, of course, a regional organization in the strict sense, but it did play a significant role in ending the Rann of Kutch war between India and Pakistan and in bringing the parties to submit their differences to arbitration.

[123] The most obvious advantage is, of course, a prevention of escalation and the involvement of the superpowers in a local confrontation. In addition, there are advantages to be gained from resolution of a dispute by parties most familiar with the idiosyncratic local conditions. In certain circumstances, hemispheric peacemakers may be more trusted. Finally, there are, I believe, educational advantages in insisting upon a general obligation to participate in the making and application of law.

[124] Article 38 (1), Statute of the International Court of Justice. Professor Pitman Potter has stated that, "There is the view or creed that holds the individual nation morally responsible for doing its share in effectively preserving international order. This requires a nation not merely to behave itself, and exhort others to be good also, but to share in action to restrain lawbreakers. Good will and good neighborliness are

award[125] are venerable precedents for the proposition that failure to prevent another's noncompliance with international law is itself a delict against the original victim and against the entire community.

A nation-state represents a complex set of institutions and practices, and optimum exploitation of a state in an enforcement program will require a rather detailed map of internal decision processes. Few states will step forward eagerly to participate in enforcement; different targets within a state must be identified and different strategies must be employed to draft them to an enforcement role. One influences the executive of a modern state with different procedures than those employed to persuade legislative action or those used to initiate the potential enforcement power of the courts. As a matter of policy, the automatic enforcement of a Security Council decision drawing upon the authority of Charter Article 25 in different national institutions requires no involved logical derivations.[126] In practice, however, courts, legislatures, and executives have and presumably will respond rather unevenly to an enforcement call.[127] Even where domestic enabling legislation exists,[128] the initiation and scope of its operation may require executive decree. Even a constitutional incorporation of international law in national law can be frustrated by such dubious distinctions as self-implementing and nonself-implementing international decisions.[129] The immediate allure of nation-states as participants in an enforcement program must be tempered

---

not enough unless embodied in co-operative security action." Pitman Potter, *Collective Security and Peaceful Change* (Chicago 1937), 14.

[125] John B. Moore, *International Adjudications*, II (New York 1936), 547.

[126] The following doctrinalists have supported this proposition: Shabtai Rosenne, *The International Court of Justice* 87-88 (Leyden 1957); Oscar Schachter, "The Enforcement of International Judicial and Arbitral Decisions," *American Journal of International Law*, 54 (1960) 1, 14; C. Wilfred Jenks, *The Prospects of International Adjudication* (London 1964), 709-10.

[127] The ragged treatment given to judgments of the International Court of Justice in municipal arenas is a good example. Consider the judgment of the Brussels Civil Tribunal in the *Socobelge v. Etat Hellenique* [1951] *International Law Reports* (1957), 3 in regard to the judgment of the Permanent Court of Justice in the *Societe Commerciale de Belgique Case*, PCIJ Series A/B, No. 78; the judgment of the Tribunal of Tangier in *Mackay Radio and Telegraph Co. v. Lal-la Fatma and others*, 21 *International Law Reports* (1954), 136, and the decision of the same court in *Administration des Habous v. Deal*, 19 *International Law Reports* (1952), 342 in an attempt to derive on the municipal-level rights decreed by the International Court of Justice in *Rights of United States Nationals in Morocco Case* [1952], *ICJ Reports* 176.

[128] See, for example, United Nations Participation Act, 1945, 59 *Statutes at Large* 619 (1945) Sec. 5, 620. See also 63 *Statutes at Large*, 735. American transactions involving Southern Rhodesia are regulated by Executive Order No. 11322, January 5, 1967, 4 *F.R.* 119; 22 *U.S.C.A.* § 287c; for the United Kingdom, see The United Nations Act, 1946, 9 and 10 Geo. 6 c. 45.

[129] For detailed comparative treatment, consult O'Connell (fn. 35), 37-88.

with the realization that these potential components may, themselves, have to be persuaded, indeed, forced, to participate in the international enforcement of a decision. A consideration of means of influencing policy formation within a modern nation-state goes far beyond this chapter. Some consideration of the roles of pressure and interest groups in this subsidiary program will be noted under subsequent headings.

PRESSURE AND INTEREST GROUPS

The role of nongovernmental organizations of national and transnational scope in all international decision functions remains relatively unexplored.[130] Yet it is clear that a large number of international and national institutions are "porous" and the motive force of their actions can be traced to the activities of diverse private groups seeking to secure the realization of their interests through organized authoritative processes.[131] International law knows its own mystical sacrament of transubstantiation, in which the special interests of a particular group suddenly burst forth as a vital national interest, and then all the symbolic and material resources of the state are marshalled.

Common to von Gierke,[132] Commons,[133] and Bentley[134] is the assumption that private groups necessarily pursue private or special interests. It would be more accurate to record that private groups coalesce and operate in order to realize highly cherished and intensely demanded values and that these values may well be expressive in the highest degree of the common interest. Peace groups, disarmament groups, and relief groups perform vital inclusive functions, even while they may militantly defend their nongovernmental status. It is a logical step for groups such as these and many others to extend their objectives to securing the enforcement of international decisions which conform to their own preferred value system. Whether diplomatic efforts are made to secure the purging of an institutional portfolio of securi-

130 See Ralph K. White, *International Non-Governmental Organizations* (New York 1951); J. J. Lador-Lederer, *International Non-Governmental Organizations and Economic Entities* (New York 1963).

131 Perhaps as a result of the pervasive fiction that only states are subjects of international law, international decision organs have been extremely reticent in identifying the actual parties in interest in major cases. A recent and heartening deviation from this trend is found in the Separate Opinion of Judge Jessup in the *North Sea Continental Shelf Cases* [1969] *ICJ Reports* 4, 67, and esp. 79, where the concrete interests and pressures of the petroleum industry are noted and the divergencies between the industry's interest and governmental interests are compared.

132 Otto Von Gierke, *Development of Political Theory*, Maitland trans. (New York 1900).

133 John R. Commons, *Proportional Representation* (New York 1907). See also his *The Economics of Collective Action* (Madison 1950).

134 Arthur F. Bentley, *The Process of Government* (Bloomington 1949).

ties invested in a delinquent state, or the extraterritorial premises of that state are disrupted by mass agitation, or pressure is brought directly on domestic decision-makers to change policy in regard to a delinquent, these activities comprise functional enforcement. There is no reason why such groups cannot be called into existence in democratic polities where they can be influential as part of an international enforcement program.

On the transnational plane, nongovernmental organizations may concern themselves exclusively with securing enforcement of international decisions. Note may be taken of the International Commission of Jurists, which examines alleged breaches and publishes the result in the hope that publicity will deter a delinquent government from continuing its defection from international norms. But private groups are by no means restricted to the ideological and diplomatic strategies. Funds may be collected for a victim (rehabilitation and reconstruction) and arms may be acquired and volunteer forces formed.[135]

INDIVIDUALS

A relatively small number of individuals may find themselves in a position of sufficient effective power to play an enforcement role in a particular case, either through direct value deprivations or through persuasive influence upon target personnel. A leading national intellectual or religious figure, for example, whose communications are carefully considered by the target elite may manifest a significant capacity to influence. Beyond this rather restricted circle, the automatic responses of individuals to an enforcement crisis may conceal a genuine sanction potential. Consider transnational wealth flows: expectations of stability upon which international economic interaction depends are shaken by a challenge to global authority. Transnational commerce tends to flee from instability. Thus, the effect of noncompliance may be an instinctive commercial and economic withdrawal, which imposes serious deprivations upon elements in the target state.

---

[135] Although the right to create, equip, and dispose armed forces is deemed an exclusive incident of sovereignty, a careful view of the world scene will show that the entrepreneurial formation and leasing of specialists in violence by no means ended with the Renaissance. Forces such as the Haganah, the IRA, and Al Fatah are examples of prestate and nonstate armies, funded through private efforts and across state lines. Private entrepreneurial armies, with and without special ideologies, have operated in the Far East and continue to do so in certain zones; mercenary forces with private funding have operated in Africa. From the local governmental standpoint, these groups may be characterized as bandits or insurrectionists, but from the standpoint of a disengaged observer, the phenomenon is simply one of nonstate entities claiming and effectively using strategies of high coercion through modalities of violence. The era of Pinkerton armies may no longer be fresh in American memory, but the municipal use of urban gangs to restrain violence in riot situations in return for respect, wealth, and power privileges certainly is.

Such private sanctions may be mobilized, intensified, and sustained by publicly communicating an intention to pursue enforcement action, part of which will be economic disruption.

Perspectives

We are concerned not only with a taxonomic listing of the potential participants in the enforcement process, but also with some grasp of their subjective patterns. Consider the enforcement target: the tooling of an enforcement program will be facilitated by knowledge of the target elite's personality, class, interest affiliation, and crisis experience. What are the identification patterns of the target and its coordinate expectations and demands? A comparable investigation must be conducted in regard to the range of enforcers in order to determine who may be influenced to contribute in greater or lesser quantity to an enforcement program. Perspective factors may require reshaping either enforcement objectives or specific strategy programs.

Perspectives are not, of course, static, but are responsive to a variety of stimuli. Type of delict, type of planned enforcement, identity of the target and past and future patterns of association with it, geographic range of enforcement operations, level of crisis, and other such factors will interact with stable perspectives and, in different circumstances, call forth different responses. But the effect of perspectives on enforcement cannot be underestimated. Consider the problem of stimuli intensifying latent interidentifications. In the Rhodesian case, for example, was the triadic pattern of two "white" governments and an unorganized black community a factor in the choice of low coercive enforcement instruments, even though such instruments promised little success and boded dysfunctional deprivations upon the black Rhodesian populace? Was the systematic trumpeting of loyalty to the Queen of the Smith government an effective counterstrategy, *within the United Kingdom*, to the British government's alleged attempts to forge an enforcement program? Was the Smith government's denunciations of internal and external Communism a technique of securing the identification and support of strata of Western states suffering from malignant Communophobia? Whether perspective factors are consciously planned, brilliantly intuited, or ignorantly bungled, they are, obviously, critical to an enforcement program.

Consider the influence of stimuli or coordinate expectations and demands. In the Italian case, M. Laval manifestly frustrated the possible effect of the League's sanction program, in which his government was a part, because the French elite expected a confrontation with Germany and demanded that Italy either ally itself with them or remain neutral. In World War II, President Roosevelt's belated announcement of the Allied intention of prosecuting all war criminals may have created an expectation throughout the vulnerable mid-elite of the Nazi government of inevitable conviction, and thus increased their determination to fight on.[136] Would a more selective imputation of responsibility have created different expectations and divided the Nazi hierarchy? To what extent does the American geopolitical view of world affairs cause it to take a course of excessive caution in enforcing United Nations decisions regarding the Republic of South Africa? To what extent does it condition our role in the formulation of enforcement programs against Rhodesia?

Considerations such as these relate to the perspective phase and, upon examination in a specific case, they may prove to be crucial. Enforcement strategists may undertake subsidiary strategies to create identity alignments, demand alignments, and so on. As a longer range goal, the world constitutive process must seek to foster the emergence of personalities in which demands for conformity with authoritative decision are intense and in which identifications are inclusive but can be specified to empathy with the victim of an international delict.

Situations

Under situations we may consider such factors as the geographical scope of the delict and the enforcement program, the degree of organization of the enforcement process, and temporal and crisis factors.

GEOGRAPHICAL FACTORS

Private international law has developed a limited terminology for describing the locus of delictual acts,[137] but it is patently inadequate when the aggregate value effects of any event are taken into consideration. A delict not only deprives the immediate victim of a complex of

---

[136] The Moscow Declaration of 1943 (International Conference on Military Trials 11-12), signed by Roosevelt, Churchill, and Stalin, in addition to its cynical omission of any mention of German atrocities practiced on the Jews of Europe, was strategically obtuse in that it was issued at least two years too late. Had it been issued at the first manifestation of Axis war crimes and atrocities, it might have deterred potential criminals. By the time it was issued, the ranks of the perpetrators and their accomplices were already enormous; the declaration drove home to these men that they had no alternative but to fight on for their very lives.

[137] A basic problem of the strict doctrine of *lex locus delicti* is that determination of locus of a crime is itself a legal conclusion varying with the law applied. From the standpoint of public interest, a state, formally assigned as the locus of the crime, may have no interest in its prosecution because it was totally unaffected by its consequences; the act may, moreover, have been lawful within that jurisdiction. On the other hand, if the effects of a crime are considered relevant in determining where it "took place," the crime may be found to have transpired in several states at one time. In *United States v. Marasco*, 275 F. Supp. 492 (S.D.N.Y. 1967), Judge Tyler commented that "I believe it unrealistic in the mid-Twentieth Century to try to assign a single place to the commission of multinational financial crimes such as those here charged by the Swiss government." Same, 495-96. The location of delict is inextricably concerned with sanctioning and enforcement policies and these are in urgent need of clarification.

values and in some cases partially or totally of all values, but it may precipitate great value changes upon many of the intersecting communities in which the victim is or was a member. Consider, for example, the assassination of Folke Bernadotte. His death not only deprived him but also his family of a source of wealth, affection, and respect; it deprived the Swedish communities of which he was a member and which may have made heavy investments in him of a highly productive citizen; it deprived the immediate parties in the Middle East of a mediator and may have raised the crisis level in that region even beyond the point of high tension which it had already reached; it deprived the United Nations of a skilled employee and, in this latter sense, it was a direct deprivation imposed upon the world community. Had the victim not been killed, but maimed or jarred into a catatonic state, the deprivation would have been continuing for a variety of different communities with which he was associated. The point is that the location of the actual act which effected the deprivation is an incomplete description, for the character of the delict is shaped by the full range of deprivations which it elicits. Some delicts are so awful and egregious in the responses that they arouse, that locus of the initial act fades into insignificance. Crimes against humanity, which, in the language of the General Assembly "shock[s] the conscience of mankind" are the extreme examples of such delicts.[138]

One advantage of localizing a delict is that maximum contributions to an enforcement program may come from those participants who are most outraged, and who suffer the greatest rectitude deprivation attendant upon deviation from a group norm: every breach of a group norm is, of course, a general rectitude deprivation for all other group members. Another advantage is that the ever-present problem of escalation in a divided and mutually suspicious arena is minimized. On the other hand, where the geographical locus of the delict is not of major significance, an enforcement program should seek to be as universally representative as possible.

There are obvious operational factors involved in predetermining the geographical scope of the enforcement arena. The cause of enforcement, the identity of the target, the bases which he can manipulate and the sectors in which he is vulnerable combine with the optimum bases which the enforcer can assemble to circumscribe the effective enforcement arena. But the ambit of potential choice of the enforcer should be recognized. He may structure his enforcement program so as to limit it to organized arenas, for example, the United Nations, the International Bank, and the IMF; he may concentrate upon

---

[138] Resolution 96 (I), December 11, 1946. See in this regard, the judgment of the Israel District Court in *Eichmann v. Attorney General*, Criminal Case No. 40/61, translated in *American Journal of International Law* 56 (1962), 805.

one value process, for example, the market of the target, without directing strategies to other internal arenas; he may employ selective strategies such as the deprivation of landing and overflight rights and port facilities, which restrict the enforcement program to a number of predetermined sectors and so on.

DEGREE OF ORGANIZATION

The mobilization of sanctions may be highly organized or it may, as we have seen, be the product of unplanned individual and uncoordinated group initiatives. In some circumstances, the enforcement program itself will predetermine the degree of organization; highly coercive strategies, for example, generally require organization, whereas severance of association patterns (as in the example of Jones and his neighbors) do not. Organized strategy programs present a countertarget to the target state, whereas diffuse sanctions do not. Varying degrees of organization are a matter of choice for the enforcer and he should assemble his enforcement program so as to maximize his own objectives and to minimize the possibilities of retaliation by the target.

TEMPORAL FACTORS

A number of the effects of a delictual event converge to foster a demand for rapid enforcement, both as a means of securing the appropriate value reallocation as well as demonstrating a vindication of authority. From an objective standpoint, this impatience for results is unrealistic, for the reallocation necessary to right the complex of a delict and its diverse and frequently wide value indulgences and deprivations will require a temporal span roughly proportionate to the objectives of the enforcement program. It is worth remembering that even a total and violent revolution is widely apocalyptic only in subjective senses; the realization of the value goals of the revolution may require 50 to 100 years, a period euphemistically referred to as "consolidation" during which the real objectives of the initiators are often thwarted. A realistic conception of the time element may, then, be a prerequisite to a realistic enforcement program and ultimately to an effective system of world public order. But such a conception must include content references to cultural and psychological understandings of time. Studies by Mischel and Staub[139] and Mischel and Grusec[140] confirm that varying time intervals between event and punish-

---

[139] Walter Mischel and Ervin Staub, "Effects of Expectancy on Waiting and Working for Larger Rewards," *Journal of Personality and Social Psychology*, 2 (1965), 625.

[140] Walter Mischel and Joan Grusec, "Waiting for Rewards and Punishment: Effects of Time and Probability on Choice," *Journal of Personality and Social Psychology*, 5 (1967), 24.

ment/reward are behaviorally significant and suggest that they may have longer term consequences regarding expectations of authority.

The time problem will be susceptible to rational treatment only when enforcers and all those who identify with them have acquired realistic conceptions of the complexities of social reconstruction and the time periods involved for securing goals within a framework of continuing minimum world order. Until then, strategy programs should seek to require public demands for rapid enforcement by symbolic rather than material activities in such a manner that support for the effective longer term enforcement program will be sustained. The dangers of promising quick enforcement when it is not achievable are readily apparent in our government's assurances of rapid progress and success in Vietnam and the Wilson government's fantastic promises of the effectiveness of economic sanctions in regard to Rhodesia. While public support could be drummed up with promises of speedy effectiveness, it dissolved and was transformed into disillusionment and hostility when the promised results were not forthcoming. In each case, the longer range effect was a widespread negative view of the effectiveness of authority in the international arena. In many respects, international law was in a more impoverished state than it would have been if no enforcement program had been undertaken.

CRISIS

Crisis is a situation in which intensely demanded values are perceived as at stake to a highly significant degree. Crisis is a matter of perception and need not be universally held. One state's impending crisis may, for example, be another state's windfall. Nor need a perceived crisis be an actual crisis, from the standpoint of an observer. On the other hand, one can make certain projections as to the probability of certain courses of action leading to crisis situations and the general effects of a rising crisis upon decision-making structures has been summarized.[141]

Given the overall structure of the contemporary global arena, inclusive policy favors crisis abatement and forms of crisis diplomacy should be considered unlawful. Where breach of an inclusive group norm precipitates a major crisis, the community enforcement goal is obviously the immediate lessening of the crisis level by means of appropriate enforcement strategies.[142] In such a case, the causal conjunc-

---

[141] Robert C. North and others, *Content Analysis: A Handbook with Applications for the Study of International Crisis* (Evanston 1963), 159ff.

[142] In respect to Article 39 of the United Nations Charter, we have noted that "when peace is threatened, the function of the United Nations is to restore peace and its necessary supporting conditions as quickly and as economically as possible. In this age of instant Armageddon, small solace could be gained from a realization that civilization was destroyed for 'good' and not 'evil' reasons. *Fiat justitia pereat*

tion of delict and crisis is felicitous, since it generates an impulse to enforcement and to the strengthening of community decision structures. Where, however, it is the reconstructive enforcement of a breach rather than the delictual event itself which promises to generate a crisis situation, enforcement objectives are neutralized by minimum order concerns. Total expectations of the effectiveness of authority may be significantly diminished.

The challenge to the enforcer is the formulation of an enforcement program which promises success and minimum order. Minimum order, it should be emphasized, includes sustaining the expectations of all politically relevant strata of the population as to the continuing intentions of authoritative decision. In this respect, symbolic enforcement, which does not affect the delinquent, but which nevertheless serves as a reaffirmation to enforce, may be a crucial, though infrequently used, weapon in the international enforcement arsenal.

Bases of Enforcement

Enforcement bases are comprised of authority and control. Each of these components is complex and contextually variable and merits separate treatment.

AUTHORITY

Authority is, of course, a crucial base of power in any interaction. In enforcement, authority also represents the most economical base and the enforcer will seek to monopolize and consolidate it in his enforcement program. In our discussion of participants, we considered the varying degrees of enforcement authority which attach to different participants.[143] It is useful to add that in a relatively unorganized arena which tolerates the institution of self help, authority may attach to functional roles rather than to specialized institutions. Where the precipitating events of self help are relatively unequivocal, the self helper may thus acquire a significant authority base by virtue of his self-assumed role.

---

mundus is not the principal underpinning of Article 39." McDougal and Reisman (fn. 39), 1, 8.

[143] See pp. 288-89. Consider, in this regard, Livingston: "So valuable a resource is scientific data, that states are becoming aware that denial of access to such information may serve as a potentially potent sanction or deterrent against those countries felt to be violating community norms. South Africa has already faced several attempts by the Afro-Asian bloc to exclude her from some of the U.N. Specialized Agencies, while at least one convention includes, in effect, a sanction of this type. This is the Nuclear Test-Ban Treaty of 1963, under which member states are not to participate in any way (presumably including the giving of aid to non-signatory countries) in the carrying out of nuclear explosions in any of the prohibited environments." Milton S. Livingston, "An International Law of Science: Order on Man's Expanding Frontiers," *Bulletin of Atomic Scientists* (December 1968), 6, 10.

Authority is not monolithic, but follows the intricate identification patterns of the individual. In a pluralistic society, each group in which the individual is a member makes loyalty claims. As a result, the authority system of any individual may have many levels, directed at many symbols, with varying degrees of intensity which may, in certain circumstances, change with the specific context of the case. In the international arena, loyalties owed to inclusive entities continue to be relatively weak, whereas the authority owed to nation-state symbols is most intense. Levels and divisions of authority must be recognized for formulation of an effective enforcement program. Thus, the identification of the multiple loyalties of potential enforcers can facilitate the amalgamation of these symbols in the enforcement program. Conversely, identification of the aggregate loyalties of the population within the target may aid in the optimum delineation of the formal target of enforcement. If, for example, one encounters a strong cultural pattern of loyalty to the "state," enforcers may publicly identify the culprits as individuals and carefully dissociate them from state symbols, thereby possibly diminishing the support which the target elite might ordinarily have called forth from their rank and file. A further step might be the recognition of a government in exile which would denounce the culprits and encourage the populace to support the inclusive community decision. Where the populace pays coordinate loyalties to external religious figures, the latter might be incorporated into an enforcement program.

CONTROL

The prominence of a variety of different values in enforcement scarcely requires comment. The extent to which the enforcer may assemble combinations of wealth, enlightenment, and skill in manipulatable combinations has obvious application. In a complex enforcement program, each of these values can be used indulgently or deprivationally in a wide variety of ways. They need not be directed solely at the target, but can also be used to induce other participants to involve themselves or lend their resources to a program, or to compensate peripheral participants who may be damaged by the side effects of enforcement.[144]

[144] A comprehensive frame of reference for an enforcement action will necessarily consider the aggregate of indulgences and deprivations which flow from the program. It is clear that enforcement will precipitate major changes in the established patterns of value exchange; the effects of the action may be felt far beyond the zone of application. Some participants may experience tremendous indulgences because of the change while others will face enormous deprivations. Hence enforcement planning must include consideration of equitable allocation of benefits and burdens created by the program; no participant should suffer unduly and no participant should gain an unwarranted windfall. In this respect, Charter Article 50 is, unfortunately, not framed in sufficiently positive terms to win the support of a state elite which perceives severe losses to its nationals should it participate in an en-

Special consideration must, however, be given to the role of respect and rectitude in international enforcement. These are preferable base values for enforcement for a number of reasons: they are economical, nonfungible and, like authority itself, they are augmented and extended by successful application. Yet, as the world community moves to a new level of global homogeneity, there has been a gnawing doubt as to the transcultural effects of rectitude and respect demands. Concededly, enormous cultural diversity persists, particularly if we understand culture to include the internal group dynamics by which loyalties are generated and reinforced in intergroup conflict. In certain circumstances cultural diversity can be so great that what is considered a serious deprivation in one cultural system may be relatively innocuous in another. In particular, respect deprivations from without an ethnocentric group will be relatively meaningless so long as a respect monopoly is centered within the group. If inclusive identifications have been imperfectly consolidated and the crisis level increases rapidly, there may be an abrupt retreat to primary group loyalties and the development of a quasi-gang mentality vis-à-vis other hostile groups, replete with conscious breaches of group morality to forge a *blutkit* as an ultimate and irredeemable confirmation of commitment.[145]

An appropriate framework of inquiry of the world social process attempts to identify trends over time rather than study a static cross sectional view at any one point in time. Such a framework indicates that in many sections of the globe there are stable transnational loyalties and shared perspectives of respect and rectitude. Factors such as class and interest group affiliation, the dispersion of ethnic groups, intermarriage, nuclear and extended family dispersal, and transnational religious institutions provide a focal point for respect and rectitude communities about the globe without regard to traditional nation-state boundaries. The enforcer must investigate alternate enforcement arenas in order to determine if any of them promise an ambit of operation for strategies employing shared respect and rectitude demands. Many will not. A public call from the Vatican to China, for example, may be an empty gesture, serving to consolidate only potential enforcement participants in Christian Europe and Latin America, but having no effect upon the enforcement target. On the other hand, a call from Peter's Throne to Germany, Poland, or Hungary, as targets of an enforcement program might have significant sanctioning effects. We

---

forcement program. A comparable reticence to engage in clear policy commitment is found in Article 16 of the Covenant of the League of Nations and it probably affected a number of smaller states in the Italian sanctions case. For discussion of this point, see David Mitrany, *The Problem of International Sanctions* 49-52 (London 1925).

145 F. Alexander, "War Crimes and their Motivation," *Journal of Criminal Law* 39 (1948), 298.

need hardly add that one does not measure the viability of a proposed enforcement strategy by its promise of total success or total failure, but by the extent to which it contributes to a compound enforcement program. The effects of respect and rectitude deprivations are particularly hard to measure, but they should not be dismissed out of hand. One obviously cannot conduct mass interviews in Rhodesia at the present time, but it is difficult to believe that the sense of isolation, of being an outlaw among all the states of the world has not, for all the whistling within that renegade state, taken its psychic toll, and that a form of ego diffusion not unlike that experienced by the Bantu in neighboring South Africa (who walks a street among whites who apparently do not recognize his existence) preys upon the white Rhodesian. Whether this psychic degeneration is in some sense determinative of outcomes and is functional or dysfunctional in terms of enforcement goals is, of course, another question.

The history of the jurisprudence of international law reveals that respect and rectitude are products of sustained group interaction.[146] With the increase of transnational interaction, transnational value groups may be expected to coalesce with increasing definition and to support special respect and rectitude systems, which may be amenable to incorporation in an enforcement program. Ruge and Galtung have noted the seminal development of such a system in the esprit de corps of a heterogeneous diplomatic group located in a foreign capital,[147] and Guetzkow and a number of other functionalists have considered the development of shared respect and rectitude as ancillary to the development of transnational skill group loyalties.[148] Physical and natural scientists who have, of late, suffered great pangs of conscience, are engaged in express codification of an ethical system which, it is hoped, will serve as a guide for all scientific inquirers.[149]

Strategies of Enforcement

The potential techniques by which an enforcement program is pursued cover a wide range; tragically, this remains an almost unexplored area of international law; the vast range of potential sanction strategies ac-

146 McDougal, Lasswell, and Reisman (fn. 2), 188, 289ff.

147 Friedrich Ruge and Johan Galtung, "Patterns of Diplomacy: A Study of Recruitment and Career Patterns in Norwegian Diplomacy," *Journal of Peace Research* II (1965), 101.

148 Harold Guetzkow, *Multiple Loyalties: Theoretical Approach to a Problem in International Organizations* (Princeton 1955).

149 Joseph de Rivera, "The Responsibilities of the Psychologist in World Affairs," *Journal of Social Issues* 25 (1969), 71; for a perspective on comparable anguishing in the physical sciences, see Don E. Kash, "Is Good Science Good Politics?" *Bulletin of Atomic Scientists* (March 1965), 34; Victor F. Weisskopf, "Why Pure Science?" *Bulletin of Atomic Scientists* (April 1965), 4; Walter Hirsch, "Knowledge for What?" *Bulletin of Atomic Scientists* (May 1965), 28; J. Gregory Dash, "Where Responsibility Lies," *Bulletin of Atomic Scientists* (January 1966) 35.

companying every constitutive and public order prescription continues in an almost paleolithic state. A number of students of legislation have noted the depressing fact that statutes expressing some of the most carefully and rigorously scientifically considered policies conclude with an enforcement clause on the order of: "violators will be sentenced to not more than 5 years in jail or $5000 or both." Nor are international prescriptive statements more advanced than this. The three enforcement clauses of the United Nations Charter range from confused casuistic formulation to virtual *petitio principii* of the very obligation of compliance to many types of international authoritative decisions.[150] International tribunals are notorious for their refusal to even consider contingent enforcement programs in case of non-compliance.[151]

An enforcement program may manipulate *any* values sought by the target, in varying degrees of indulgence or deprivation, with varying accompanying communications, and in diverse formulations of contingency. The degree of coercion with which the strategy is pursued may also be varied. It should be emphasized that the strategic phase involves the assembly of techniques for influencing the predispositions of the target and that forms of indulgence and deprivation are simply means toward that end. In different contexts, any value may be susceptible to manipulation as a means of influence; Dession's useful phrase "sanction equivalents" should be used to direct attention not only to the lateral dimension of value variation, but also to geographic and temporal dimensions of target expectations and value demands.[152]

A functional approach within a broad framework of contextual analysis is a prerequisite to the formulation of an optimum strategy program, since it offers the most comprehensive correlation of the relative capacities of the enforcers and the relative vulnerabilities of the target. A systematic treatment of enforcement strategies considers them in terms of target—diplomatic or ideological—and in terms of instrument—military or economic. An actual enforcement program, of course, amalgamates all strategies, by consideration and conscious inclusion or exclusion.

DIPLOMATIC

The advantages of enforcement strategies directed at elites are obvious. There can be an economy of communication, the target is finite and relatively fewer deprivations and/or indulgences need be

150 See pp. 310-12.

151 See, for example, *Case of the S.S. Wimbledon, PCIJ* (1923), Series A, No. 1, 32; Mavrommatis (Judgment No. 10—Jurisdiction) *PCIJ* (1927), Series A, No. 11, 4; Interpretation of Peace Treaties with Bulgaria, Hungary and Romania [1950] *ICJ Reports,* 229.

152 Dession (fn. 8), 22.

expended than would be required for influencing a broad heterogeneous audience. The identification of an elite group as the target to which responsibility for the delict is officially imputed may also fragment the solidity of that elite's broader popular support. This strategy will not avail where there is intense popular support for the elite's course of action or where the elite has persuaded the populace that compliance with the authoritative decision will bring disaster on the entire community: "we must hang together or we will hang separately." This is, of course, a common strategy and an almost automatic rhetorical device in interstate communication: "the great American people, dominated by an imperialist clique," "the great Russian people dominated by the Bolshevik gang," and so on.

The idea of affecting the predispositions of a target elite by promising indulgences should compliance be forthcoming is repugnant to Protestant notions of sin and punishment, but it is obviously an attractive and frequently more economical strategy than the imposition of deprivations. President Johnson's offer of a vast sum of money and the creation of a regional Mekong Delta project to the elite of North Vietnam[153] is a good, if unsuccessful example of this mode of persuasion. Yet the ambiguities inherent to this strategy should be recognized. The rectitude deprivation felt by all who perceive the breach of a group norm is in no way assuaged by seeing the culprit rewarded. The capitalization of compliance does open the way for even greater stakes in international blackmail. Yet there is no norm in international law which prohibits this variant strategy. The considerations which should govern the according of indulgences upon noncompliance will be considered in our discussion of the economic modality.

On the other hand, the lawfulness of the threat or actual imposition of deprivations upon elites in order to affect their behavior has given rise to some controversy in international legal circles. The Convention on the Law of Treaties expressly negates the validity of treaties secured by coercing through the diplomatic instrument.[154] This is an artificial and ultimately unworkable view, for the lawfulness of a coercive event or any other event is not determined by the coercion alone, but rather by the goals and policies involved, authoritative decision, minimum and maximum order goals, the features of the context, and so on. It should be patent that one characterization of law is a system of legitimate coercion and that, in conformity with relevant policies, coercion may be applied by or for the inclusive community. The

153 *New York Times*, March 26, 1965, p. 1, col. 1; *New York Times*, April 8, 1965, p. 1, col. 1.

154 Article 51, Vienna Convention on the Law of Treaties, A/Conf. 39/27 May 23, 1969; and see Julius Stone, "De Victoribus Victis: The International Law Commission and Imposed Treaties of Peace," *Virginia Journal of International Law* 8 (1968), 356.

Moscow coercion of the Czech leaders to surrender political independence was not a violation of international law because of the fact of coercion, but rather because the purpose of the coercion was one manifestly against the principles and purposes of the United Nations.

The traditional diplomatic enforcement strategies have included termination of diplomatic relations, nonrecognition,[155] recognition of a competing government, and exclusion or expulsion from international organizations. A number of these strategies are recognized as matters of national competence, which states apply individually as rather normal international bargaining tactics. Others such as exclusion or expulsion from an international organization are governed by international norms and require a high degree of collaboration among the enforcing states.[156] The technique of recognition of a competing elite as the authoritative government would ordinarily be considered as an act of gross intervention. There seems to be no reason, however, why it could not be undertaken by an international organization, such as the United Nations. The effectiveness of these strategies will depend upon the context of the case and the features of the total enforcement program.

IDEOLOGICAL

The ideological strategy, directed at broader groups, increases in complexity as the heterogeneity of the target group increases. Resource bases of enforcement must be constructed to affect the varying demands of the target and the symbolic counterparts must be made more complex so that they have meaning for each member of the target. And it must be recalled that the ideological identification of the target is, in many ways, a self-fulfilling prophecy; those identified with the target will often feel compelled to associate themselves with the fate of the target.

Despite these operational problems, the ideological modality is a regular component of a strategy program. Among composite enforcers, communication to the broad populace is necessary to secure an initial

---

[155] On the sanction of nonrecognition, see Sir John F. Williams, "La Doctrine de la Reconnaissance en Droit International et ses Développements Récents," *Hague Recueil* 44 (1933), 203, 240. A comprehensive study of nonrecognition as a technique of enforcement is given in Roland H. Sharp, "Duties of Non-Recognition in Practice 1775-1934," Geneva Special Studies 5, No. 4 (1934). This is an especially useful monograph because of its consideration of the Manchuko case and, in particular, its consideration of the effects of nonrecognition in a number of different arenas.

[156] Charter Articles 4, 6, 41 and 42. Expulsion has been deplored by a number of scholars as an inappropriate sanction: C. Wilfred Jenks, "Some Constitutional Problems of International Organizations," *British Yearbook of International Law,* 22 (1945), 1; Louis B. Sohn, "Expulsion or Forced Withdrawal from an International Organization," *Harvard Law Review* 77 (1964), 1381. Professor Friedmann has opined that these are appropriate sanctions; Friedmann (fn. 55), 88ff.

decision to engage in an enforcement program and thereafter to sustain willingness among the population to undergo a variety of deprivations incidental to the enforcement program. One response of the target may well be the propagandizing of the enforcer's rank and file. Propaganda, broadly understood, is never directed solely at one's adversary but continuously at one's own polity and it may be aimed not only at creating new predispositions, but supplying "facts" and evidence to sustain extant predispositions.[157] In regard to the target population, ideological communication need not impute culpability to all members of the target group. Propaganda regularly distinguishes between the "regime" and the "people" and may, while threatening the regime, offer assurances of the most restricted objectives in regard to the people. Such communications may be dysfunctional in the sense of forging all members of the target group into an even tighter unit. If the target capitulates, the ideological mode will become a requisite element in the program of its reconstruction.

The ideological mode may involve the imposition of resource deprivations upon an entire population and many strategy programs unwillingly degenerate into this. More useful is the promising of indulgences to the target and/or the enforcers. But the most valuable aspect of ideological enforcement is in anticipatory or futuristic use: the inculcation of perspectives in the broadest strata of the world community toward compliance with authoritative decision and contribution to enforcement programs.

ECONOMIC

The manipulation of wealth and related resources provides a range of extremely flexible policy instruments. Deprivatory uses, such as boycotting, export and import controls, license restriction currency dilution, dumping, and partial and total embargoes are obvious techniques which require relatively little comment.[158] Since everyone participates in the global market, the strategy may be employed by anyone. But the availability of these strategies is two-edged: in an interdependent world, each economic deprivation can be matched by a comparable re-

[157] W. Phillips Davison, *International Political Communication* (New York 1965); in this respect, the ideological modality is not one which is used solely as a target strategy. It must constantly be used to explain and inform the enforcer's rank and file of the reasons and progress of the enforcement program.

[158] See generally, Evans Clark, ed., *Boycotts and Peace: A Report by the Committee on Economic Sanctions* (1932) esp. 200-46; Highley (fn. 69), 36-44; Edouard Lambert, *Les Embargos sur L'importation ou L'exportation des Marchandise* (1936); Pierre Bartholin, *Les Consequences Economiques des Sanctions* (1939). Howard J. Taubenfeld and Rita F. Taubenfeld, "The Economic Weapon: The League and the United Nations," *1964 Proceedings of the American Society of International Law*, 183. Galtung (fn. 102). A rather comprehensive study of possibilities of international sanctions against South Africa is found in Ronald Segal, ed., *Sanctions Against South Africa* (London 1964).

sponse on the part of the target.[159] Hence, the easy availability of these strategies is balanced by the need for their extremely inventive employment.[160] The abstract legality of the use of many of these strategies continues to be controversial. Their lawfulness, as part of an authoritative enforcement program, will depend upon commensurance and conformity to minimum order requirements in the context of their application.

Considerations of economic strategies are usually premised on the continuation of basic market structures of the arena involved; the strategies operate within this structure. Enforcers should view such restrictions as matters of choice rather than constraint. Market structures may be consciously changed. The usual drag on preferred changes is the probable deprivation caused to ascendant elites or strata with vested interests in the status quo. Where, however, these elites are identical with the target of an enforcement program, enforcement may be made the simultaneous occasion of constitutive change and realization of authoritative decision. Consider, for example, the international liquidity problem and South Africa's continued defiance of United Nations' decisions. Were the world to abandon the gold standard for an IMF controlled credit system, an inclusive benefit would accrue and a crucial base of South African power might be attenuated.

Every economic strategy indulges some as it deprives others but some strategies do manifest a primary character of indulgence. Some of the problems attendant upon the employment of this strategy were noted above, and the question becomes under what conditions and for what purposes should purely indulgent strategies be tendered to a target which breaches and defies group norms? In view of the precedential impacts of an authoritative response of indulgence to a delictual activity, challenge and response may be viewed comprehensively as a termination or modification of an existing prescription and the accommodation of a new interest by a new authoritative prescription. Rather than enforcement of an old prescription, the claim, expressed by the behavior of the target, is legitimized in a new prescription. Viewed in these terms, it becomes clear that the strategy of economic indulgence

[159] Thus, in the cases of economic sanctions against Egypt and Cuba, each country responded by expropriating the property of nationals of the putative sanctioners. Such a response does not, it should be emphasized, necessarily balance out in terms of coercion upon future behavior. The deprivation of private property of a national is not equivalent, in aggregate effects, to the stemming of a vital resource such as oil to an enforcement target. With appropriate planning, the enforcer may be able to compensate his own deprived national and subrogate himself to private claims for settlement after the enforcement program has succeeded.

[160] Some of the insights afforded by studies of economic strategies and influence techniques on smaller entities may have direct or derivable application to economic techniques of enforcement. See for example, Martin Shubik, *Strategy and Market Structure* (New York 1959) 293-324; some general conclusions are drawn in Bruce M. Russett, *Economic Theories of International Politics* (New Haven 1968), 145-47.

should be employed only when the claimed new prescription is, it-self, more in conformity to community goals than is the preexisting prescription.

Indulgences may, however, be used in contingent sequences as part of a joint indulgent, deprivational program: deprivations are accompanied by a message that values will be reinstated in proportion to the increasing degree of compliance which the target tenders.

MILITARY

Crisis situations seem to generate an inexorable dynamic toward the use of the military instrument in modalities of high coercion. While the decision to employ the military instrument may temporarily dissipate high tensions, it fosters crisis and pushes it to a higher level. And even in symbolic uses, the military instrument is high in value consumption and minimal in value production. Wholly apart from moral considerations, this strategy instrument manifests features which would severely restrict its employment. But it is naive to assume that the military instrument will not and/or will not have to be used in enforcement action. In a system of power balancing or deterrence, the availability of a military capacity is a continuous communication that force will be met by counterforce. Hence, no matter what the individual distaste for this instrument, it must be recognized as a crucial modality of anticipatory enforcement. A reliance upon force on the ultimate operational level, is, of course, a choice. An arena of high coercion represents, in some senses, a collaboration between the disputants and the enforcer and should seek to retain the option of whether and to what extent an enforcement arena will be rendered an overt military arena.

The techniques by which the military instrument can be manipulated in order to secure preferred outcomes have been examined in a large literature and need not be treated here.[161] The more crucial problem of the legitimacy of the non-United Nations use of the military instrument for ostensible enforcement purposes has received equal attention but has secured considerably less agreement. The problem can be approached from the standpoint of the contemporary meaning of Charter Article 2(4), an apparently blanket proscription on the unilateral use of force, which had relevance, at least within the paper world of the Charter, when read in conjunction with the implementative programs of Chapter VII of that instrument.[162] Unfortunate-

161 See fn. 82.

162 An inventory of doctrinal views shows large variations in response to the realities of the international context. Sir Humphrey Waldock, "The Regulation of the Use of Force by Individual States in International Law," *Hague Recueil*, 81 (1962), 455, 492, and McDougal and Feliciano (fn. 8) 207-08, construe Article 2 (4) as an absolute prohibition on the use of force. Professor McDougal, has however, since

ly, the programs of Chapter VII were never realized. Hence, a continuing strict interpretation of Article 2(4) would be an invitation to lawbreakers who could anticipate a paralysis in the Security Council's decision dynamics; such an anticipation is by no means unrealistic. "The Charter," as Fitzmaurice has observed, "frowns on self-help without . . . having put anything in its place."[163]

A more realistic policy formulation would recognize the present inability of the world community to move to implementation of Chapter VII and would therefore accept the partial suspension of the full thrust of Article 2(4). High level coercion would then be legitimate, if its objective were lawful and if, in the context of the case, its application did not itself become delictual. The core of Article 2(4), that coercion not be used against the territorial integrity or political independence of the target, would continue in operation. More specifically, legitimate military enforcement would require satisfaction of four criteria: (1) exhaustion of all other modalities of enforcement; (2) use of force commensurate with the objective; (3) compliance with the laws of war; (4) a context of little likelihood of escalation.[164]

Outcomes

The outcomes of an enforcement program must be considered in three simultaneous senses. First, the degree to which the prescription in question was realized in terms of controlling value allocation. Second, the degree to which the enforcement program precipitated deterrent, restorative, corrective, or rehabilitative expectations *pro futuro*. Finally, the degree to which the enforcement program consolidated or failed to consolidate expectations of effectiveness in regard to enforcement on the constitutive level of world public order. Each of these dimensions of outcomes must be considered briefly.

In the most continuous and least visible sense, enforcement involves the continuous communication of a capacity to assemble and apply sanctions in order to realize the value allocations decreed by authori-

---

taken a more flexible view. Sir Hersch Lauterpacht and Lassa F. L. Oppenheim, *International Law*, 2 (New York 1952), 154, and Julius Stone, *Aggression and World Order* (Berkeley 1958), 95, construe the provision more broadly. From the standpoint of an observer employing a configurative theory of international law Article 2 (4) is seen as a communication between the elites of the nation-states of the world to refrain reciprocally from encroaching on their respective territorial bases of power. The observer, with his own clarified goal set, will consider this communication as only one factor in his recommendation of alternative decisions. There is a complementarity to all norms and it is useful to recall that, against a clarified goal set, the aspirations of specific elite groups may be illegitimate in terms of the observer's goals and/or the most general goals of the world community.

[163] Sir Gerald Fitzmaurice, "The Foundation of the Authority of International Law and the Problem of Enforcement," *Modern Law Review*, 19 (1956), 1, 5.

[164] For discussion of these criteria, see Reisman (fn. 43), 13, 20, 27-28.

tative prescriptions and decisions. One criterion of the effectiveness of an enforcement program is, then, the degree to which prescriptions are actually controlling in their effects; sensitivity to this criterion increases when an overt enforcement program is undertaken. To what extent does the enforcement program succeed in realizing the preferred value reallocation? To what extent does it succeed in so affecting the predispositions of the target that continuous force is not required to maintain the allocation? To what extent must the enforcement program become a continuing police operation?

Fundamental value allocations are struts of public order and their efficacy is not judged by haphazard survey at one point in time but rather over a time span. In precisely the same manner that a response to a norm breach has effects at a number of levels of public order, the norm breach itself may precipitate comparable multilevel effects. To what extent does an enforcement program contribute to future deterrence, correction, and restoration? It should be apparent that in a complex social process, simplified notions of causality cannot be applied. We cannot, for example, assume that because a norm deviation has been severely sanctioned, this event, in itself, will serve as an object lesson and future deterrent. The enforcement program itself must be constructed so as to consider these futuristic problems and to integrate within itself appropriate responses to their challenge.

To what extent does a particular enforcement program contribute to consolidation of the constitutive enforcement process? Every event precipitates a series of consequential expectations; does an enforcement program consolidate expectations of effective or ineffective constitutive decision? As we noted in the previous outcome dimension, simple causality must be avoided. A successful enforcement may create revulsion, or may involve such a large value consumption that participants become more rather than less reluctant to participate in future programs.

Toward the Future

The challenge of international law in the future is, I believe, less one of construction of a highly effective enforcement system than one involving the inculcation of a generally sanctioned system of public order prescriptions. Collective behavior has too often, in the past, been approached as a question of social pathology. But a sufficient concentricity of identifications, demands, and expectations to support non-coercive group life is, as Malinowski emphasized, a prerequisite of community. There are hopeful signs. It is increasingly difficult to gainsay the evolution of a global culture, with the resultant homogenization of many currently diverse perspective patterns. The process is being accelerated by a large body of international prescriptions which aim at the inculcation of certain standardized perspectives about the globe. There are, of course, countertrends, but if this major trend can be continued, much of the aggregate of international prescription may be internalized and supported by autopunitive sanctioning mechanisms within the personality rather than by heteronomic coercion. As the sanction component of international prescriptions becomes more effective, many of the apparently insoluble international enforcement problems will ease and, perhaps, be diminished.

The problem of enforcement will not, to be sure, wither away. A latent capacity to enforce must be developed and occasions in which enforcement is required will arise. But effective sanctioning lowers the need for highly effective and highly centralized enforcement. Policy advisers might well ponder this point. There is a mechanical attraction to a perfectly effective and automatic enforcement process, but such a system may not serve the genuine interests of a world public order of human dignity. Resistance to enforcement is resistance to a prescription. The appropriate response to such resistance is not automatic enforcement, but rather reconsideration of the prescription. Is its policy content correct? Does its thrust take due account of the idiosyncratic context? Is its timetable feasible and humane? Are the deprivations the prescription engenders compensated, and so on? When such a survey indicates that enforcement of that or an amended prescription is still necessary, there may be social advantages to retaining some ad hoc characteristics in the enforcement program. If "dirty work," as Hughes and Coser[165] have called it, is a necessary incident of order even in the ideal society, it is perhaps better that all citizens accept it with open eyes and shared responsibility.

[165] Everett C. Hughes, "Good People and Dirty Work," *Social Problems* 10 (1962), 3; Lewis A. Coser, "The Visibility of Evil," *Journal of Social Issues*, 25 (1969), 101.

CHAPTER 10

Arms Control and Disarmament

HAROLD FEIVESON

I. Our Past Failure

ARMS CONTROL,[1] as a strategy to lessen the costs and the dangers of the nuclear arms race, has had a pale and dismal history. Compared to the great opportunities foregone, even the very real achievements of arms control policy in the 1960's seem inconsequential. This is a deeply disheartening perspective, all the more so because the complex of factors which have impeded progress during the past quarter century persists today and in still more subtle forms.

The magnitude of our failure to secure even minimal control of the nuclear arms race is impressive. The pattern was set at the inception of the nuclear arms race when the great powers were unable to establish international controls over nuclear energy at a time when such controls could have been achieved at risks that now appear reasonable. An early nuclear test ban probably could have prevented the development of thermonuclear weapons, and a comprehensive test ban achieved in the late 1950's or early 1960's would almost certainly have prevented the development of MIRV's and sophisticated missile defense systems. In general, the movement from conventional to fission to thermonuclear weapons, the movement from bombers to missiles, and the hundredfold increase in the capacity of the world's nuclear arsenals during the second decade of the nuclear arms race all proceeded with no imposition of arms control prohibitions. Thus, entire classes of strategic weapon systems, which in theory might have been denied by arms control agreements, have been introduced at great cost and peril. The character and pace of these developments suggest a deep failure of arms control practice and understanding. Both sides have responded to nonexistent threats, thus in part creating them, and each

[1] "Arms control" is used here essentially in the manner of the classic Schelling-Halperin definition: "all forms of military cooperation between potential enemies in the interest of reducing the likelihood of war, its scope and violence if it occurs, and the political and economic costs of being prepared for it." The scope of the discussion here however is limited in two important respects: First, it is restricted for the most part to *strategic* arms control, cooperation between the nuclear superpowers in the interest of controlling the strategic nuclear arms race. Secondly, there is little discussion of various unilateral measures that nations may undertake to improve their command and control procedures, dispersal of missiles, etc., however reflective of a recognition of mutual interests among adversaries they may be. Thomas C. Schelling and Morton H. Halperin, *Strategy and Arms Control* (New York 1961), 2.

side has carelessly disregarded the impact of its strategic procurements on the adversary.

The story of course is not all sad. The limited nuclear test ban treaty; the Nonproliferation Treaty; the initial understandings on outer space, Antarctica, and the seabed; and the onset of U.S.-Soviet bilateral talks on strategic arms control have been especially encouraging and useful. Nevertheless, even these measures and concurrent unilateral actions to improve command and control procedures have not hitherto prevented either great power from undertaking or continuing strategic procurements already planned or under way. Neither great power has sought security through cooperative efforts with the adversary, and the strategic arms competition continues unabated.

II. Why We Failed

The reasons for this unhappy history are many: technical obstacles, strategic imperatives and asymmetries, conceptual confusions, and internal politics.

Technical Obstacles[2]

The technical problems, while never dominant, have nonetheless in the past contributed substantially to the lack of arms control progress. These problems have generally been of three kinds: how to verify an agreement, how to determine what constitutes a fair arms control measure and an improved strategic balance, and how to visualize and cope with drastic disarmament measures. Resolution of these questions has required technical analyses of considerable complexity, demanding some measure of consensus in each national security bureaucracy on technical issues which are inevitably imbued with substantial uncertainties.

Verification analyses require a sophisticated balancing of national intelligence capabilities against a parameterized set of adversary evasion techniques and levels of cheating, whose significance can be known only imperfectly. This balancing ensures that the technical analysis can never be altogether free from political and military judgments, since the level of prospective evasive effort and its significance are not simply narrow technical issues. Consequently, consensus even among technical experts is generally difficult to obtain. The seismic identification of underground nuclear tests provides an interesting illustration of this difficulty. Technical agreement can perhaps be

---

[2] Technical problems may be viewed as those most susceptible to expert technical and legal analysis and most subject (in theory) to empirical validation and to objective, value-free assessments. Except for highly detailed engineering issues, few significant problems relevant to arms control will be seen as a purely technical question, but some will clearly involve a considerable degree of objective analysis by technical experts. It is these which are here characterized as technical issues.

reached (albeit with considerable difficulty) on the number of un-identified seismic events *above a specified magnitude* which might be expected on the average in a given year. But there can be no un-equivocal technical answer to the questions of what magnitude is sig-nificant, what number of on-site inspections would be required to de-ter an attempted violation, or what number of violations would consti-tute a significant danger.[3]

Even were there complete confidence in the maintenance of an arms agreement, assessment of the strategic consequences of the agreement represents a very complicated problem. This remains true even, or perhaps especially, if these consequences are in the first instance sim-ply taken to be a series of paper calculations on the relative expected damage to the two superpowers under a variety of war outbreak con-tingencies. Such calculations inevitably depend on a very considerable number of parameters of highly uncertain value, given the necessarily abstract character of such nuclear exchange calculations and the ab-sence of much relevant experience and data.[4] Indeed, it is the begin-ning of wisdom to recognize that in any complicated military situa-tion, whether involving strategic exchanges, tactical nuclear warfare, or conventional battles, no confident and precise analysis and assess-ment of relative capabilities are yet possible.

The technical questions associated with efforts to analyze general and complete disarmament proposals are of a different kind, less nar-row and in a sense more real. It is doubtful that any nation would ever embark on disarmament schemes such as were outlined by the U.S. and Soviet draft GCD proposals of the early 1960's without a clear understanding of how its national interests could be forwarded by peaceful means, how disputes were to be settled, how international legislation would be effected, etc. Indeed, the lack of serious analysis of these kinds of questions attests to the frivolity of the GCD pro-posals, and suggests the great technical obstacles to substantial dis-armament that exist at present.[5]

---

[3] Leonard Rodberg, "Why No Underground Test Ban?" *War/Peace Report* (April 1969), 18, 19.

[4] See for example, statements of Secretary of Defense Robert S. McNamara on *The Fiscal Year 1968-72 Defense Program and 1968 Defense Budget*, January 1967. [Hereafter cited as *Posture Statement 1968*]; and *The Fiscal Year 1969-73 Defense Program and the 1969 Defense Budget*, January 1968. [Hereafter cited as *Posture Statement 1969*]; Statement by Secretary of Defense Clark M. Clifford on *The 1970 Defense Budget and Defense Program for Fiscal Years 1970-74*, January 1969. [Hereafter cited as *Posture Statement 1970*] Statement by Secretary of Defense Mel-vin R. Laird on *The Defense Program and Budget for Fiscal Year 1971*, February 20, 1970. [Hereafter cited as *Posture Statement 1971*]. Also Herbert F. York, "Military Technology and National Security," *Scientific American*, CCXXI, 2 (1969), 17-29.

[5] The draft GCD treaties may be found in *United Nations and Disarmament*, 241-89. Some analysis of the issues the treaties raise are cogently presented in Rich-ard A. Falk and Saul H. Mendlovitz, eds., *The Strategy of World Order, Disarma-*

Yet there is reason to believe that these technical complexities do not comprise the paramount obstacle to arms control. It is evident that verification questions turn ultimately on political rather than technical issues, and the same appears true for strategic calculations.[6]

Nevertheless, the technical issues continue to dominate our attitudes toward the strategic arms race and arms control. "Presidents and politburos . . . may not themselves be persuaded by the refined calculations of the nuclear gamesman—but they do not find it prudent to expose them for the political irrelevance they are. . . . In consequence, the internal politics of the strategic arms race has remained the prisoner of its technology."[7]

Strategic Obstacles

Apart from technical complexities, arms control has not always appeared consistent with the strategic objectives of the United States and Soviet Union. At various times, the search for improved deterrence, for extended deterrence, and for damage-limiting postures has impeded efforts to limit the strategic arms competition.

The most notable strategic obstacle to arms restraint during the past decade has been the very strong impulse in both the United States and Soviet Union to deploy invulnerable strategic offensive missile forces. Both sides have viewed the development of (their own) hardened dispersed land-based ballistic missiles, nuclear powered missile-carrying submarines, and perhaps MIRV's as well, as stabilizing, innovations to be courted, not prevented (even if possible). Such reactions reflected the widely held view that increases in invulnerability and second-strike retaliatory capacities were the sine qua non of the arms race.[8]

This stress on "assured destruction,[9] the touchstone of U.S. strategic

---

ment and Economic Development, IV 267-375; in articles by Hedley Bull, Marion McVitty, Klaus Knorr, and Richard Falk (Geneva Conference on Disarmament).

[6] See especially McGeorge Bundy, "To Cap the Volcano," Foreign Affairs, XLVIII, I (1969), 9-11. York (fn. 4).

[7] Bundy, same, 13.

[8] A clear statement of this view may be found, for example, in Posture Statement 1969 (fn. 4), 47-49.

[9] As defined by Secretary McNamara, "Assured Destruction" is the capability,

> To deter deliberate nuclear attack upon the United States and its allies by maintaining, continuously, a highly reliable ability to inflict an unacceptable degree of damage upon any single aggressor, or combination of aggressors, at any time during the course of a strategic nuclear exchange, even after absorbing a surprise first strike. . . .

> What kind and amount of destruction we would have to be able to inflict on an attacker to provide this deterrent cannot be answered precisely. However, it seems reasonable to assume that in the case of the Soviet Union, the destruction of, say, one-fifth to one-fourth of its population and one-half to two-thirds of its industrial capacity would mean its elimination as a major power for many years. Such a level of destruction would certainly represent intolerable punishment to

force doctrine and possibly now that of the Soviets' as well, and once a formidable concept used by those trying to impose restraint and rationality on strategic arms procurements, can be attributed to three mutually reinforcing factors: the apparent strategic importance of assured destruction, its utility in justifying or rationalizing strategic procurement decisions, and its quantifiability.

The strategic arguments are both simple and powerful. First, it is apparent almost by definition that a deliberate, carefully planned surprise nuclear attack on the U.S. would be altogether irrational if the U.S. maintained a capability for inflicting "unacceptable" damage on the attacker in retaliation—that is, if the U.S. maintained an assured destruction capability. Second, although we cannot know quite how nations will react in various crisis situations, maintenance of a credible assured destruction capability seems the one sure stabilizing factor in the maze of "double thinking" which would presumably take place during a crisis. To the extent that rationality plays a role in the crisis, the ability to destroy the adversary's society no matter what the adversary does, can, in the view of the assured destruction advocates, only improve the chances that he will not use nuclear weapons first, and that he will not be able effectively to threaten their use.

Quite apart from being a strategic objective, assured destruction has proven a useful notion in justifying and rationalizing strategic force procurement decisions, which, somewhat ironically, often have supported restraint in the strategic arms race.[10] During the past few years, a period in which the U.S. could in retaliation destroy well over one-half of the Soviet population and three-fourths of Soviet industry, stress on the saliency of an assured destruction capability meant that the U.S. has not had to increase its strategic forces. It is also true that in this period the U.S. missile force alone (indeed the sea-based missile force alone) has been capable of achieving assured destruction. Thus the arguments against new missile procurements and especially against an advanced manned bomber have been based primarily on their incrementally minuscule contribution to assured destruction. At the beginning of the period in which the U.S. developed its present large missile superiority, the assured destruction criterion was a useful tool

---

any industrialized nation and thus should serve as an effective deterrent to the deliberate initiation of a nuclear attack on the United States or its Allies.

As long as deterrence of a deliberate Soviet (or Red Chinese) nuclear attack upon the United States or its allies is the overriding objective of our strategic forces, the capability for *Assured Destruction must receive the first call on all of our resources and must be provided regardless of the costs and difficulties involved. . . .* (emphasis added)

Posture Statement 1968 (fn. 4), 38-39. The *1969 Posture Statement* in essence repeats this definition, though somewhat less succinctly.

[10] See, for example, *Posture Statement 1968* (fn. 4), 58-59.

for example in comparing the relative value of missiles and bombers. Similarly, at present, when the prospect of a future Soviet ABM is tempting the U.S. to new offensive procurements, the assured destruction criterion permits relatively easy analysis of various alternatives, such as between sea-based and land-based ballistic missiles. Comparison of weapon systems is always easiest if there is a single overriding objective which one is trying to achieve.

In addition to supplying a single salient objective, assured destruction is relatively easy to calculate, since unlike other strategic objectives (such as damage-limiting) it essentially reflects the outcome of a single contingency of war outbreak—a surprise adversary attack on the calculator's strategic forces using all his available ballistic missiles. Moreover, again unlike other strategic objectives, it is calculated on the basis of consistently conservative (or "worst case") assumptions. In addition, assured destruction has the inestimable advantage of being, after a fashion, quantifiable. That is, it is possible to say that under certain specified assumptions, the U.S. will be able to inflict some specified number of casualties on the Soviet Union (and conversely). The advantages of this kind of quantification are particularly apparent when assured destruction is compared to other plausible objectives: detente, lowering the probability of crises, reducing the risks of escalation during a crisis, etc. Decision-makers, especially those making procurement decisions under economic constraints, naturally grasp at those elements of the problems which are most readily measurable.

Notwithstanding these formidable arguments, the elevation of the assured destruction criterion to an essentially sine-qua-non condition for security in the nuclear age has proven a serious obstacle to arms control in recent years. It first of all has distorted our perspective and led on the one hand to an exaggerated reliance on an assured destruction capability, and on the other, to a disparagement of other strategic objectives. There are many analysts who appear to believe that if the U.S. (and, some would add, the Soviet Union) maintains an assured destruction capability, chances of a nuclear war would be negligible. These analysts leap from the perhaps justified belief that assured destruction is the most useful of the myriad of factors presumably affecting war outbreak, to the explicit or tacit belief that an assured destruction capability is sufficient to prevent war outbreak regardless of other considerations. They therefore look with unblinking favor on an unrestricted arms race if the primary tendency of the race appears to be toward improved assured destruction capabilities. A natural consequence of this view is indifference toward other objectives: detente, damage-limiting, constraining the arms race, nonproliferation, etc. To the assured destruction advocates, these objectives appear at best senseless if they do not contribute to an increase in invulnerable second-strike forces.[11] All this would be of little importance if a single-minded quest for improved assured destruction capabilities did not conflict with these other reasonable objectives. Unfortunately, it is very clear that it does conflict, due in the first instance to the not surprising fact that each side will always view the other side's strategic forces as a potential first strike threat; that is, the forces that comprise each side's assured destruction capability will simultaneously appear to the other side as a potential threat to its assured destruction. The result is an unrelenting arms competition of lesser or greater intensity depending on the actual extent to which the assured destruction forces are suited to a first-strike attack. In general, the persistent search for invulnerable second-strike forces may have unfortunate long-range dynamic effects, even if it is granted that the existence of such forces is stabilizing at a given moment.

These tendencies are greatly exacerbated by the extremely conservative interpretations given the assured destruction criterion by many officials and analysts. Such interpretations are conservative in three ways: they use a cascade of highly improbable worst-case assumptions to test whether the assured destruction capability could be maintained; they frequently insist, even after assuming a tissue of improbabilities, that each element of the nation's strategic forces separately must be capable of assured destruction; and they view matters almost exclusively from their own national viewpoint, not that of the adversary whom the assured destruction capability is designed to deter.[12]

The level of damage which will prove "unacceptable" to a potential aggressor, long a subject of controversy, also appears unnecessarily high. The current vogue in the U.S. to seek a 20 to 30 percent fatalities figure if it can be obtained by attacking the major Soviet cities, is hardly less arbitrary than any other.[13] It is based on that level of destruction which presumably will destroy the adversary's society; greater destruction would consequently be superfluous. In fact, however, the 20 to 30 percent level arises as much from cost-effective considerations as from its alleged effect on Soviet society. That is, diminishing returns operate very strongly after the 30 percent level is reached: 400 IMT warheads delivered on the Soviet Union could inflict approximately 30 percent fatalities; an additional 400 warheads would merely increase

---

[11] *Diplomatic and Strategic Impact of Multiple Warhead Missiles.* U.S. Congress, House, *Hearings before the Subcommittee on National Security Policy and Scientific Developments of the Committee on Foreign Affairs,* 91st Cong., 1st Sess., July 8, 9, 15, 17, 22, 24, 30, August 5, 1969, passim. [Hereafter cited as *MIRV Hearings.*]

[12] *Posture Statement 1970* (fn. 4), 49-52. Statement by the Director of Defense Research and Engineering, Dr. John S. Foster, Jr., *The Fiscal Year 1970 Defense Research Development Test and Evaluation Program 14 October 1969,* 1-5 to 1-10.

[13] *Posture Statement 1968* (fn. 4), 39.

fatalities a few percent.[14] Of course, since the relation between the level of threatened damage and deterrence is unknown, any attempt to set an assured destruction level is essentially meaningless. (For example, there is no reason to believe—as is implied by our interpretation of assured destruction—that deterrence depends on the best war outcome from the viewpoint of our adversary rather than the average or expected outcome, or for that matter the worst.) Certainly at the present time, deterrence does not depend on each side being able to inflict 40 to 80 million fatalities on the other. In times of crisis, the level of each side's assured destruction capability would probably be far less important than several other factors, which in the final analysis will depend on the peculiar psychology of the national leader or on the characteristics of a small executive committee operating under great pressure.

The quest for extended deterrence or, more plainly, for a nuclear capability sufficient to permit a first strike or the credible threat of such, has been a second major strategic goal impeding efforts to achieve strategic arms restraints. The U.S., at least, has for a long period maintained an ambiguous declaratory policy regarding the utility of strategic nuclear forces to deter and cope with aggressive actions other than nuclear attacks upon itself or its allies, notably a large-scale Soviet aggression into West Europe.[15] Since this utility derives ultimately from a credible threat to use such forces first, any policy or arms agreement which explicitly denied the U.S. such superiority seemed to embrace a severe political cost in terms of U.S. relations with its European allies. Today the belief in the saliency of an extended deterrence based on nuclear superiority appears to be waning. Even granted that a Soviet march across Europe remains today a plausible adventure, it is the simple presence of American forces in Europe and the attendant prospect that any large-scale use of force against NATO would set off an unpredictable and possibly disastrous sequence of escalation which provide the decisive American contribution to European security, not some elusive strategic superiority.[16]

Whatever the actual value of extended deterrence, the search for it now is doubtless a futile and illusory quest since no matter how few surviving missiles and bombers nuclear war models might credit to the adversary, it is highly unlikely that political leaders will ever be persuaded that a first strike is warranted.[17] However, as long as one or both sides maintain the illusion that a first-strike capability or some sort of nuclear superiority is attainable and desirable it will be impracticable to halt the arms race. For it is clear that the nuclear

---

[14] *Posture Statement 1969* (fn. 4), 57.

[15] See, for example, same, 80-82.

[16] Bundy (fn. 6), 17-18.   [17] Same, 13.

superiority which extended deterrence depends upon is not compatible with the assured retaliatory capacity both sides demand.[18] Thus a prerequisite to significant progress on arms limitations will be an explicit shedding of such illusions by both superpowers, and a concurrent willingness not to rely upon nuclear weapons other than to deter nuclear attack.

The strategic objective of extended deterrence itself reflects deeper national conceptions of foreign policy commitments and responsibilities which have in the past conflicted with arms control efforts. The United States, for example, has apparently adopted the view that extended deterrence against China is possible, and that given Chinese intransigence and American commitments in Asia, it is necessary. Thus, the search for a first-strike potential against China has presented one considerable pressure for deployment of a ballistic missile defense system.[19]

The search for extended deterrence is closely coupled with the wish to limit damage in the event of a nuclear war, the difference more one of intention than capability; extended deterrence supposes an explicit role for nuclear weapons whereas a damage-limiting capability connotes merely a prudential utility. The desire to limit damage, especially through the deployment of ballistic missile defense systems about urban areas, has obviously frustrated efforts to curb such deployment and has also helped discourage the completion of a comprehensive test ban. In recent years, the primary goal of further nuclear weapon testing has probably been the development of better warheads for ballistic missile defenses and for penetration of such defenses.

In addition to these past incompatibilities of strategic and arms control objectives, a certain asymmetry in U.S. and Soviet strategic doctrine has impeded progress in controlling the strategic arms competition. The capabilities and doctrines of the two superpowers were significantly out of balance until the late 1960's, with the Soviets lagging behind the United States in these respects by about five years. In the period from 1955 to 1960, the United States deterrent was based on strategic forces and a doctrine of massive retaliation, while the Soviets appeared to stress a European theater capability comprising both conventional and nuclear forces. During 1960-64, while the Americans were evolving a flexible response capability and were playing with complex theories of deterrence, controlled response, and damage limiting, the Soviets seemed to move toward a massive retaliation doctrine. During the next five years, the strategic outlooks of the two countries came closer together, though important conflicts remained, for exam-

[18] Harold Brown, "Security through Limitations," *Foreign Affairs*, XLVII, 3 (1969), 422-32.
[19] *Posture Statement 1971* (fn. 4).

ple regarding the interaction of strategic offensive and defensive systems. Finally, by 1970 there appeared for the first time a very evident parity of strategic capabilities and probably of doctrine as well.[20]

To the extent these asymmetries have been a significant barrier to arms control, as some observers believe,[21] this confluence of U.S. and Soviet strategic doctrine and capabilities may suggest renewed opportunities for arms control in the coming decade.

Conceptual Obstacles

Fundamental misconceptions have long plagued arms control considerations, ranging from simplistic and optimistic views regarding the feasibility of substantial disarmament to deeply unreasonable fears of even minimal arms limitation measures.

The idea of a formal comprehensive treaty which entailed very substantial reductions in nuclear arms and which would lead eventually to general disarmament played a significant role in arms control and disarmament discussions into the early 1960's, achieving its most dramatic manifestation with the general and complete disarmament treaty drafts introduced by the Soviet Union and United States in 1962.[22] Although these drafts themselves were probably not taken seriously by very many persons in either country, they were the outcome of a view toward arms control and disarmament which was then widely shared (even more widely in the preceding decade), and it is still held today by substantial if diminishing numbers of people. Such a view compounded several unquestioned assumptions: First, it held that formal treaties which would set out in detail phased disarmament programs were the only ways to secure a significant degree of arms control. Such programs moreover did not generally envision the nuclear arms race as a separable measure, but tended to tie nuclear arms control to concurrent reductions in conventional arms and to elaborate control mechanisms.[23] Second, the older view took for granted that reductions in armaments were desirable ends in themselves, that serious analyses of strategic stability and political dynamics in a disarming world were not of first importance. Third, and most seriously, the disarmament view tended to place an undue faith on the preeminence of

[20] Roman Kolkowicz (Project Leader), "Future Soviet Interests in Arms Control," ACDA/IR-151, II, 13-14. See also Kolkowicz, "Strategic Parity and Beyond: Soviet Perspectives," *World Politics* (April 1971), 431-51.

[21] Kolkowicz (fn. 20), 13-14.

[22] *The United Nations and Disarmament 1945-1965*, United Nations (New York), 91-98, 241-89.

[23] Something of this tendency lingers today in the view that strategic arms control ought to be linked to political settlements, although to be sure the basic assumptions of those who hold such a view and the earlier arms controllers are quite different, the former wedded to the idea that the dynamics and menace of the arms race merely reflect a more basic political antagonism. Same, 93-96..

technical and rational analysis of arms control problems, while seriously discounting the severe political and bureaucratic antagonisms to arms control that existed in each side's national security establishments.

Curiously, the rejection of this view by the arms controller of the 1960's led in at least one crucial respect to a similar kind of naiveté—an insufficient sensitivity to political and bureaucratic realities and a bounding faith in the ability of rational and systematic analysis to devise technical solutions to the menaces of the arms race. Hedley Bull has accurately described the character of the change in view:

> By contrast with both the traditional disarmament doctrine stemming from the pre-war period and the school of unilateral nuclear disarmament, which were inclined to regard defence and disarmament as opposed objectives of policy, and the influence of the military on disarmament policy as a sinister one, the "new thinking" insisted upon the unity of strategy and arms control, the continuing need for defensive measures under conditions of disarmament, the need for defence planners to take disarmament into account, and the subordination of both defence and disarmament to the objective of security. While this doctrine of the unity of strategy and arms control meant that traditional defence thinking, unrefined by the element of collaboration with the antagonist in military policy, was inadequate, it also carried the implication that arms control was not the preserve of radicals and rebels, but was a respectable pursuit that could be contemplated without alarm in the corridors of power. . . .
>
> It [suggested] that while the uncritical pursuit of disarmament implied the dismantling of the Soviet-American balance of terror, the proper object of arms-control policy was rather to preserve or perfect it. Arms-control policy should distinguish between those military developments which tended to stabilize the balance of terror, and those which tended to destabilize it; and while restricting the latter it should tolerate or even encourage the former. . . .
>
> The "new thinking" [possessed] a sense of being at the threshold of a new era in arms-control, reflected in proposals to expand governmental machinery for dealing with arms control, in hopes placed in the goal of what was called "stable deterrence," and above all in the confidence that was displayed in study and research as a means of improving the prospects of peace and security.[24]

Much of this "new thinking" also tended to employ, if not necessarily believe in, a rather narrow military and technical mode of analysis to

[24] Hedley Bull, "Arms Control: A Stocktaking and Prospectus," *Adelphi Papers,* LV (1969), 11-20.

evaluate arms control measures.[25] This kind of analysis grants a decisive reality to the technological balance, demanding that arms measures must not risk affecting it adversely. McGeorge Bundy has suggested the consequences of this view:

> If our domestic debates are necessarily carried in terms of technological pros and cons, what chance is there that we can base international negotiation on the cruder, simpler and less demanding realities of international political choice? If there is a real danger that this or that concession or limitation may affect the technological balance, if the technological balance has continuing importance in domestic political debate, and if suspicion and wariness on our side are easily outmatched on the other, then indeed the prospect seems unpromising.[26]

Despite such views, arms control might have looked more favorable in the past had our present conceptions of the arms race crystallized earlier. The central international political feature of the arms race, that it in fact resembles a race, a competition in which each side's strategic-force decisions force counteractions by the other, has not always been so apparent as it now seems. In the United States, there was a clear shift, reflected in the annual Posture Statements of the Secretary of Defense, from the belief that the two nuclear superpowers could seek quite asymmetric strategic objectives to the view that each side will do whatever it must to maintain a very substantial retaliatory capability.[27] Thus the posture statements trace the gradual relinquishment by the U.S. of any serious attempt to develop a damage-limiting capability that would diminish the Soviet deterrent, a shift explicitly based on the contention that the Soviets would respond to any such attempt.

The Soviets' growing awareness of the dynamics of the arms race is most dramatically exemplified by their apparent recognition of the dangers of bluffing. In a study of Soviet strategic behavior, Roman

[25] This tendency is reflected even in the work of the most committed advocates of arms control. See, for example, the several essays in Abram Chayes and Jerome B. Wiesner, eds., *ABM: An Evaluation of the Decision to Deploy an Antiballistic Missile System* (New York 1969).

[26] Bundy (fn. 6), 15-16.

[27] The early McNamara Posture Statements supposed the possibility of a United States damage-limiting capability that the Soviet Union would not necessarily react to. This idea is explicitly rejected in the Posture Statements of 1968 and 1969. The first posture statement of Secretary Laird, *Posture Statement 1971*, and the President's policy statement, *United States Foreign Policy for the 1970's: A New Strategy for Peace*, reprinted as a special section in the *New York Times*, February 19, 1970, hint something of a return to the earlier view where deterrence alone was not considered a sufficient strategic goal and asymmetric strategic objectives were believed possible.

Kolkowicz concluded that the Soviets have learned that "any excessive claims to fictitious or real strategic advantages over the United States tend to cause a disproportionate overreaction in Washington, which results in sizable programs which quickly cancel out any real or alleged advantage.[28] Khrushchev's strategic bluffs were condemned by his successors who rejected "certain kinds of bragging and irresponsible promises that are greatly inconsistent with actual possibilities."[29] In any event, it is clear that Soviet strategic bluffs, first with excessive missile claims and later with ballistic missile defense, have encouraged strong U.S. reactions.

The sharp emphasis on miscalculation and inadvertent escalation rather than on deliberate planned nuclear attacks as the central danger confronting the superpowers forms the second perspective on the arms race which has until recently been only imperfectly understood, and which is still not completely embraced by the national security community.[30] This new emphasis, arising from the trauma of the Cuban missile crisis,[31] from the waning of the U.S.-Soviet ideological conflict, and from the realization that any deliberate initial nuclear strike would be suicidal, places increased value on arms control understandings; its earlier deemphasis conversely tended to undervalue the achievement of arms control initiatives and to discount the value of strategic communication between the two superpowers.

No conceptual confusion has had as pernicious an effect as that concerning verification and inspection. Three sorts of misunderstandings have contributed to this confusion; one relating to the differences between verification and inspection, a second to the relationship between inspection and disarmament, and a third to each side's misperception of the other's position on inspection. Verification may be considered the ensemble of information gathered by a nation relevant to an adversary's adherence to an arms control agreement. It thus consists of three components: ordinary political reportage from journalists, diplomats, et al.; technical and political information derived from national intelligence efforts, satellite reconnaissance, espionage, etc.; and, finally, formal, agreed inspection procedures. The greater the information derived from the first two sources, the less the need for inspection —and, of course, all significant arms control agreements hitherto achieved (excluding the Nonproliferation Treaty) have been self-enforcing in the sense of not requiring any agreed inspection at all. The entire ensemble of information has three purposes: to detect and thereby to deter a *militarily significant* violation of the arms agreement, to establish confidence that the agreement is being maintained,

---

[28] Kolkowicz, "Future Soviet Interests in Arms Control," (fn. 20), 39.
[29] Same, 38.   [30] *MIRV Hearings*, 241-86.
[31] Arthur M. Schlesinger, Jr., *A Thousand Days* (Cambridge 1965), 93.

and to prepare for an appropriate response to any suspected or confirmed violation. The degree of verification required should therefore depend on the kind of agreement, and in particular on the scope of the violation (which would be significant). The role of verification, much less of inspection, is thus not to detect any minimal violation of an agreement, and it is unrealistic to demand that it do so.[32]

Although the character of the arms agreement will determine the kind of inspection required, it is a mistake to believe that the degree and obtrusiveness of inspection will necessarily increase in proportion to the scope of the arms limitation, or in proportion to the security sensitivity of a violation. It is very improbable that nations will ever rest their security on elaborate inspection systems if small undetected violations would jeopardize their national interests. That is, if a nation's security would be delicately sensitive to clandestine violations, the agreement could never be achieved in the first place. On the other hand, if the trust between the adherents were sufficient to obtain such agreement, substantial inspection would not be necessary. Inspection thus possesses something of the quality that "if you can get it, you don't need it; if you need it, you can't get it."[33]

Given the lack of conceptual clarity, it is not surprising that each nuclear power has had difficulty in understanding the position of the other. Many in the U.S. have considered Soviet acceptance of inspection on their soil as a test of whether they are to be trusted and their persistent reluctance as a sign that they are not to be. The Soviets appear by contrast to believe that the U.S. insistence on inspection is unwarranted, an indication that the U.S. is not fundamentally serious about arms control, and a ploy to gather information on Soviet forces. The deeper reason for Soviet opposition to inspection probably stems from a reluctance to accept a foreign government operating on Soviet territory with rights over Soviet citizens. It is no doubt also true that because of the relative openness of western societies, the Soviets probably believe they have less to gain through inspection than would the

[32] Richard J. Barnet, "Inspection: Shadow and Substance," 15-36, and "Violations of Disarmament Agreements," 157-77, in Richard A. Falk and Richard J. Barnet, eds., *Security in Disarmament* (Princeton 1965); "Verification of Reductions in the Number of Strategic Delivery Vehicles," Committee on Strategic Delivery Vehicles, Woods Hole Summer Study, 1962, in same, 51-68.

[33] Barnet, "Inspection," same. A simple algebraic whimsy, while not to be taken very seriously, may help to fix this idea. The amount of disarmament possible (D) must be proportional to the amount of trust (T) between nations. $D = aT$. The amount of inspection required (I) must be proportional to the amount of disarmament and inversely proportional to the amount of trust.

$$I = b \frac{D}{T}$$

$I = b \dfrac{D}{T} = b \dfrac{aT}{T} = ab = a$ constant. Hence the amount of required inspection would not change no matter how substantial the disarmament.

U.S. It is evident that these misconceptions must be swept away before there can be significant progress in arms control.

To a degree they already have been. The U.S. has recognized the sufficiency of unilateral intelligence to verify certain kinds of arms limitation measures, and in these instances has not insisted on agreed inspection procedures. The Soviet attitudes toward inspection are also perhaps changing. During the Nonproliferation Treaty negotiations, the Soviets moved from opposition to international inspection to a strong endorsement of such inspection (although to be sure only if it was confined to the nonnuclear countries).[34] The Soviets also offered, if only for a fleeting period, to accept on-site inspections on their territory in association with a comprehensive test ban. Nonetheless, the Soviets will have to be more forthcoming than they have been. Even in instances when agreed inspection procedures are not necessary, they could help to establish confidence in the agreement, particularly among American skeptics. The U.S. for its part will have to relax its sometime assumption that the Soviet Union will enter an arms agreement with the full intention of violating it if it can, and we will also have to realize that inspection even if obtained cannot accomplish all the goals we often expect of it. In this respect, the question of on-site inspections in connection with a comprehensive test ban is illuminating. The U.S. has insisted upon the right under a comprehensive test ban agreement to undertake a specified number of inspections at the sites of suspicious events to ascertain whether or not they were actually nuclear explosions, and it is this insistence coupled with a Soviet refusal to acquiesce to it that has in large part prevented progress toward a complete cessation of nuclear tests. The principal object of this insistence has been to devise a method of verification which could catch a violator red-handed. Yet, it is clear that this aim is illusory. Rather than permit an international inspection which would characterize it as having violated an agreement, any nation would instead risk the embarrassment of simply denying access to the site of the explosion. The U.S. would always have to rely on its own unilateral detection capabilities to protect itself from extensive violations.[35]

The widespread befuddlement over inspection and the confusions concerning other arms control issues probably have not in themselves substantially impeded arms restraint, but more importantly have permitted internal factions within both nuclear superpowers to develop effective intellectual rationales in opposition to arms control. Thus, for example, the inability of the U.S. and Soviet Union to achieve a comprehensive test ban doubtless stemmed less from verification conflicts

---

[34] See statement by Soviet Representative (Roschin) to the Eighteen Nation Disarmament Committee on March 12, 1968 in *Documents on Disarmament 1968*, 177-79.

[35] Rodberg (fn. 3), 19.

than from a reluctance by powerful bureaucracies in both countries to stop nuclear testing, though most of the rhetoric of the negotiation pointed to on-site inspection as the stumbling block.

Internal Obstacles

Although the debate over arms control uses the strategic and technical terms of international politics, it is evident that the internal politics of consent within each superpower play a central role in determining the pace of the strategic arms race. There are powerful internal pressures within both the U.S. and Soviet Union to develop, procure, and display new and sophisticated weapon systems irrespective of their strategic utility. These pressures arise from domestic political and economic factors, from competition among the military services, and more simply from the tendency of large technical bureaucracies to perpetuate themselves. The pressures reflect strong economic and political interests, and the pervasive beliefs that we should always be as technically sophisticated as possible, that prudence demands erring on the side of more rather than less, that extra weapons provide valuable insurance. As weapons technologies become increasingly complex, both the uncertainty in their performance and the length of time required to embed the new technology into operational systems increase. As a result each superpower must justify development and deployment of systems on the basis of hypothetical "greater than expected," threats five to ten years in the future, and threats, moreover, which could only be imperfectly gauged even were they already operational. The rationale for any weapon system is thus becoming increasingly divorced from any existing external threat.[36] As a consequence, one must look increasingly to the internal national security bureaucracies of the two sides to understand the strategic arms race.

Bureaucracies naturally seek their own goals, which may often not be in the national interest. The military bureaucracies of the nuclear powers have generally opposed arms control. To the professional military, arms control—that is, cooperation with the adversary on military matters—runs counter to all it has been taught about its own role and about the image of the enemy. The military doubtless believes its

---

[36] See, for example, John S. Foster, Jr. U.S. Congress, Senate, Preparedness Subcommittee, *Hearings on Status of United States Strategic Power*, SASC, 1968, Pt. I, 112. Quoted in Ralph Lapp, *Arms Beyond Doubt* (New York 1970), 4.

Most of the action the United States takes in the area of research and development has to do with one or two types of activities. Either we see from the field of science and technology some new possibilities, which we think we ought to exploit, or we see threats on the horizon, possible threats, usually not something the enemy has done but something we have thought ourselves that he might do, we must therefore be prepared for. These are the two forces that tend to drive our research and development activities.

proper role is always to recommend more arms and always to assume the worst of the opposition. Each military service and suborganization naturally seeks expansion of the weapons systems it controls. This bureaucratic disposition has been compounded in the United States, and no doubt in the Soviet Union as well, by the natural tendency of the defense establishment itself to undertake a large part of the analysis of arms control measures. The defense bureaucracies set the military requirements which must be met by any arms limitation agreement, and in several instances, most notably in support of seismic research and other verification studies, sponsor a large degree of the relevant research. To a large extent also the military has been permitted "to define the threats, and therefore the priorities, facing their country, and to determine the proper response to these threats."[37]

The uniformed military is joined in its special perspective by the aerospace industries, institutions with obvious interests in high levels of strategic arms competition, and to some extent by universities whose expansion during recent years has been due in large part to defense expenditures. Simply put, several powerful institutions in the U.S. tend to oppose arms control and there is no equivalent countervailing institutional pressure in its support.

The response by the military and by aerospace industry to the arms control challenge, while not forthcoming, has neither been unexpected nor unreasonable from their perspective. The peculiar character and influence of the defense establishment derives from unusal institutional and political norms supported or acquiesced in by the civilian leadership. This leadership itself, especially within the Department of Defense, is curiously exposed to serious conflicts of interest. Significant numbers of these national security managers come from milieus with substantial economic interests in high defense budgets. Their world view would thus be expected to comprise a set of attitudes hostile to arms control regardless of whether the individual bureaucrat might gain personally from such a hostility. A most significant part of the national security establishment with backgrounds in business, finance, and law has no association with the aerospace and associated industries. But they also tend to share a world view that stresses foreign and defense commitments over competing domestic demands for public monies.[38]

[37] Erwin Knoll and Judith Nies McFadden, eds., *American Militarism 1970* (New York 1969), 13. Report of the "Congressional Conference on the Military Budget and National Priorities" convened on Capitol Hill, March 28 and 29, 1969 under the sponsorship of members of the Senate and the House of Representatives. [Hereafter cited as *American Militarism 1970*.]

[38] See, for example: John Kenneth Galbraith, *How to Control the Military* (Garden City, 1969), Gabriel Kolko, *The Roots of American Foreign Policy* (Boston 1969), Richard Barnet, *The Economy of Death* (New York 1969). Robert Art, *The*

Most apparent, in the U.S. at least, the defense establishment has remained relatively free from the normal restraints of public and Congressional debate. Substantial sums of public funds are typically appropriated with little or no debate within or without Congress, much of the Congressional oversight being performed by a few powerful committees generally sympathetic to the executive departments they oversee.[39] This Congressional abdication is due to several factors. First there is a considerable paucity of information and technical expertise available to Congress, an especially serious matter given the mode of analysis developed by the Defense Department which tends to focus attention on the technical issues. Second, due in part to the committee structure, there is no real framework for a debate on defense procurement policies, and in particular on the relative priorities of defense and nondefense goals. Third, the introduction of modern techniques of systems analysis within the Defense Department and a concurrent compromise of rival requests by the several services before the defense requests reach Congress, have diminished Congress' ability to exercise its own judgment. Fourth, the security classification system permits the selected release of relevant information by the defense establishment to the public and even to Congress as a whole.[40] Finally, partly for ideological reasons and partly for more narrow economic interests, the political climate of the country seems to demand continued support for high-level defense expenditures—or so at least most Congressmen have concluded.[41]

There is certainly strong institutional resistance to arms control in the Soviet Union as well as in the U.S. This is clear from the occasional glimpses into the Soviet strategic debate sometimes possible, and from the times the Soviets have spent vast sums on weapon systems that do them no rational good.[42] It is also evident in the composition of the Soviet national security bureaucracy. Representatives of the military and the vital defense-industrial ministries hold powerful positions at the highest echelons of the Communist Party and Soviet government

---

TFX Decision (Boston 1968); Herbert York, *Race to Oblivion* (New York 1970); Lapp (fn. 36); Adam Yarmolinsky, *The Military Establishment* (New York, 1971); Alain Enthoven and K. Wayne Smith, *How Much Is Enough* (New York 1970); Seymour Melman, *Pentagon Capitalism* (New York 1970). It is evident that there exist very strong vested interests in weapons procurements and that these interests attempt to influence these procurement decisions in various ways. It is reasonably clear that in this endeavor they are partly successful. But a careful study of how such influence is manifested, both deliberately and inadvertently, remains to be documented and analyzed.

[39] Knoll and McFadden (fn. 37), 103-04.

[40] Same, 106-07. Also York (fn. 4), 17-29.   [41] Barnet (fn. 38), 125.

[42] Bundy (fn. 6), 15, 38. E. L. Warner, Princeton Center of International Studies (private communication).

where the crucial weapons procurement decisions are taken.[43] Roman Kolkowicz, after presenting some of the evidence, though finally hopeful that the Soviets are developing a genuine interest in arms control, nonetheless characterizes this resistance very strongly:

> Among the intractables and impediments on the road to arms control is the weight of history: The Soviet Union is one of the least likely partners in a proposed arms limitation agreement. Its ideological rhetoric, its verbal overkill, its revolutionary zeal, and its adherence to the might of arms all militate against its being a sincere partner in arms control. Indeed, it would seem foolhardy to suggest that the marshals, commisars, and Party *apparatchiki*, all raised on the value of power and with a deep distrust in the possibilities of human or political accommodation, would easily embrace the idea of self-denial of available arms.[44]

The institutional barriers to internal political consensus favorable to arms control are reinforced by the manner in which the relevant bureaucratic elements perceive and manipulate the previously discussed strategic and technical factors. Indeed, the overarching classes of obstacles—technical, strategic, conceptual, and bureaucratic—have always reinforced one another in complex ways, and are so intertwined that their analytic separation is merely an expository device. Their distillation occurs most pointedly in the ubiquitous concept of the "requirement," the requirement to develop a new missile, the requirement of on-site inspection, etc. Such requirements, reflecting in part specific bureaucratic interests, have defeated a variety of arms control initiatives. Advocates of arms control have never been able to devise their own set of requirements, which have always seemed either too vague (for example, reduce the risk of war) or not clearly desirable in themselves (for example, freeze missile production). The quintessential obstacle to arms control formed by defense requirements, moreover, permits no compelling response within the context of the present strategic debate. This is the tradition to plan militarily on the basis of a greater than expected threat; to hedge against unexpected developments, to buy new strategic systems as insurance, in short, to be prudent.[45] Advocacy of arms control is thus difficult within the bureaucracy. It requires either the questioning of widely accepted views of the enemy and security, or the adoption of a marginal analysis which adopts the prevailing wisdom. The first alternative is discouraged in any complex organization, and the second, while sometimes

[43] Warner (fn. 42).

[44] Kolkowicz, "Future Soviet Interests in Arms Control" (fn. 20), 39, 26-28.

[45] Bundy (fn. 6), 15; York (fn. 4); George W. Rathjens, "The Dynamics of the Arms Race," *Scientific American* (April 1969), 15-25.

effective, generally misses the main reasons one would wish to change the fundamentals of national security policy.[46]

This difficulty in obtaining support for arms restraint doubtless derives from still deeper causes reflecting political and psychological realities of the present international scene. The most evident of these factors is each side's fear of the adversary, which has reflected and fed the ideological and political conflicts of the past quarter century.

> The problem is essentially one of uncontrolled bureaucratic power which, in the manner of all bureaucracies, governs in its own interest and in accordance with its own parochial view of the world. . . .
>
> The principal instrument of power of this bureaucracy is fear. It is fear that gave it this enormous power and autonomy in the 1950s and early 1960s. This fear caused us to consolidate and delegate power. This power was born in an age of fear, [and] it will be curbed only as we resist fear, only as we look upon the world, Communist and non-Communist, with a certain calm intelligence.[47]

The counterpart of this fear and distrust has been a persistent sense, encouraged by political leaders in both countries and growing out of past experience with conventional forces, that in increasing numbers there is strength, that in ever-growing strength there is safety. To many, security has become synonymous with military strength, and arms control with weakness.

Since the justification for increased strategic forces rests on a fear of the enemy, there persists a strong reinforcing interaction between the arms race and the picture of the adversary on which it feeds. Consequently, any move toward arms control tends to set up a dissonance in the public's view of the enemy.[48] Partly for these reasons, and partly because political leaders must accept greater responsibility for trying to change the present drift than for accepting it, arms control measures are not always evaluated on a rational basis, the risks of arms control weighed more heavily than the risks of a continuing arms com-

---

[46] It appears likely that part of the opposition to arms control stems from an organizational rigidity, an inability to process information dissonant to the prevailing bureaucratic assumptions. An interesting theoretical study of such bureaucratic limitations has been done by Thomas H. Karas, "A Cybernetic Analysis of Organizational Limitations," Harvard University, March 1969, unpublished.

[47] John Kenneth Galbraith, quoted (fn. 38), 21-22.

[48] Ralph White, *Nobody Wanted War* (Garden City 1968). This very interesting study stresses several psychological factors which distort perceptions of national security. The tendency for nations under pressure to develop a black and white image of international conflict and to hold a "virile self-image" seem particularly pertinent to the arms control debate. Several other works, including Anthony Storr, *Human Aggression* (New York 1968), and Konrad Lorenz, *On Aggression* (New York 1963) also suggest that the obstacles to arms control may be reflective of very deep-seated concerns.

petition. A degree of security and verification is often demanded for arms control which could not otherwise be obtained even without arms limitations.

III. The Consequences of Failure

In our inability to secure control of the nuclear arms race, we have been led to our present condition—characterized by a precarious stability endangered by an expanding complex of uncertainties regarding the effectiveness of strategic nuclear forces and by a withering capability to control the spread of nuclear weapons. The present relatively secure balance derives in large measure from two fortuitous circumstances: the presence, on both sides, of invulnerable deterrent forces capable of inflicting levels of damage in a retaliatory strike which are both high and calculable with reasonable precision; and secondly the acceptance by both sides of a combination of attitudes and tacit doctrines that tend to discourage the first use of nuclear weapons. But these elements of stability may not persist if present trends in strategic weaponry proceed unimpeded by arms control understandings.[49]

Strategic Stability

At present, both the United States and Soviet Union can estimate their strategic capabilities and strategic force requirements with a modest degree of precision. Even so, the existing uncertainties encourage each side to deploy substantially greater forces than actually required for deterrence, and constantly give rise to alarums in one country or the other that the adversary will achieve an exploitable nuclear superiority. Unfortunately, the dominant characteristic of the next round of arms procurements will be a very marked increase in these uncertainties, most notably due to ballistic missile defenses, MIRV's, and improved accuracies of reentry vehicles. Widespread deployments of urban missile defenses alone would probably increase the uncertainties in estimation of force requirements by at least a factor of ten. If so, the forces required to produce any specified level of damage might then be known confidently only to within a factor of 50 or more.[50]

Ballistic missile defenses will possess the unfortunate characteristic of being at once inordinately more complex than any strategic weapon system hitherto deployed and essentially untestable. Yet to be at all effective such a defense will have to work virtually perfectly the first

---

[49] The character and consequences of the arms race have been described in several recent articles, of which the most interesting are Rathjens (fn. 45); *The Future of the Strategic Arms Race: Options for the 1970s,* Carnegie Endowment for International Peace (New York 1969); York (fn. 4); York (fn. 38). See also *Posture Statement 1970* (fn. 9).

[50] Rathjens (fn. 45).

time it is tested in combat. Thus it will doubtless always be the case that though a missile defense system may work very well, it will also stand a good chance of failing catastrophically. Secondly, beyond the sheer complexity of the system, the effectiveness of missile defenses will depend partly on several factors which would not be known to the offense, or to both. Neither side is likely to know how the other will allocate its missiles or interceptors, how vulnerable the defense radars are to blackout or the offense warheads to destruction, or how effectively the defense radars could sort out decoys and chaff. Finally, missile defenses would tear away the most compelling feature of the present balance—the certainty that if only a few warheads survived a first strike and were delivered over target in retaliation, the country attempting the first strike would suffer massive damage.[51]

Missile defenses have already given impetus to the development of MIRV's, a weapon system which could eventually increase the uncertainty in the number of deliverable warheads by each side by a rather large factor (from 2 to 3 on the low side to over 10 on the high), and remove both sides' confidence in the invulnerability of their fixed land-based missiles. Once MIRV systems are fully flight-tested, there appears no clear way to observe the extent to which they would actually be emplaced on already deployed missiles short of very intrusive inspection at the sites of the missiles and launchers themselves. The likely response to MIRV's, notably mobile missile systems, which will be difficult to observe and to count, will add still further uncertainties.

The prospect of improved accuracies of reentry vehicles, especially in association with MIRV's, appears equally disturbing. With no apparent physical obstacle to the achievement of accuracies as fine as 300 feet C.E.P. (though there would likely be severe engineering problems), even targets such as hardened missile silos could become threatened by warheads with yields as low as 100 kt, several of which could be clustered in a single MIRV package. The minuteman III MIRV, for example, now thought not to threaten Soviet missile sites, would in fact do so if reentry accuracies of 600 feet C.E.P. could be achieved.[52]

The uncertainties lead in the first instance to a somewhat paradoxical effect: under normal circumstances, tending to discourage a preemptive strike by either adversary, but nonetheless, encouraging each side to procure still greater strategic offensive and defensive

---

[51] Leonard Rodberg, "ABM Reliability," in Chayes and Wiesner (fn. 25), 107-17.

[52] York (fn. 4), 20. C.E.P. stands for circular probable error, the radius of a circle about the target which half the missiles would be expected to strike. If $d =$ distance at which an IMT explosion will destroy a certain hardened target, then the kill probability against that target is given by $P_k = 1 - 2^{-d2/a2}$ where $a =$ C.E.P./Y $1/3$, $Y =$ yield of explosion. A twofold increase in accuracy could offset a tenfold decrease in explosive yield.

forces. The reasons for this situation, essentially the current state-of-affairs, are apparent. The uncertainties are to a large measure shared by both sides, and consequently neither could be confident in the success of a first-strike which in any event could not be seriously entertained by any sane political leader. On the other hand, neither side could be sure that his opponent actually shared these uncertainties, nor confident that the opponent would not try in the future to develop a first-strike potential. Consequently, the clearest effect of uncertainties, especially when they combine with the normal prudential decision-making process, which postulates greater than expected threats, is to drive the arms race to high levels with resultant large expenditures of resources. The most serious potential impact of great uncertainty, however, derives from a danger that under circumstances of great pressure, those persons or small groups forced to make rapid and portentous decisions might well tend to behave in a fashion quite contrary to a more normal bureaucratic decision-making body, by gambling on the happiest outcome rather than the worst of the possibilities their decisions might effect. Land-based MIRV's and ballistic missile defense of cities, are in fact systems which favor the first use of nuclear weapons: MIRV deployments because they substantially increase the exchange ratios between fixed land-based missiles, and ballistic missile defenses because they appear much more effective against disorganized and scattered retaliatory attacks than against a deliberately conceived first strike.

Along with these threats to the stability of the U.S.-Soviet strategic confrontation, there is a substantial danger of a further spread of nuclear weapons. In a short time, several nations will possess sufficiently large civilian nuclear power programs to support significant nuclear weapon developments. While the connection between the bilateral strategic arms race and nuclear proliferation is indirect and not fully understood, it seems evident that the prospects for proliferation will increase so long as the two superpowers, by refusing to restrict the expansion of their nuclear arsenals, lend credence to the notion that nuclear weapons are valuable instruments of international politics.

Economic Considerations

Without significant arms limitations, and considering only programs now under way, the U.S. annual strategic budget will range between $12 billion and $25 billion in the early 1970's, probably much higher by the late 1970's. Soviet costs would be comparable.[53] These high levels of expenditure can have severe impact on the U.S. and Soviet economies. But the most worrisome economic aspect of the arms race is that because of the strong interactive effect of U.S. and Soviet weapon procurements, unless the current arms competition is drastically al-

[53] Rathjens (fn. 45), 30. Barnet (fn. 39).

tered through U.S.-Soviet agreements, it will rise at an ever-increasing pace. That is, we cannot expect strategic defense expenditures simply to level off as both sides achieve sufficient nuclear force levels. This situation is forcibly argued by the former Director of the Budget Bureau, Charles Schultze, who concludes that "if the [U.S.] military budget in the 1970's is not substantially lower than the level implied by our current policy, it will quite possibly grow well beyond that level in subsequent years. . . . Either decisions will be made to reduce those expenditures, or they may themselves create a situation in which further expenditure increases will occur." Defense expenditures will either be significantly reduced by new policies or significantly increased. "There may be no intermediate position."[54]

Strategic Doctrine

A continuing unconstrained arms competition would almost certainly undermine prospects for a U.S.-Soviet detente, and erode the complex of attitudes and doctrines which contribute decisively to strategic stability. Given the current relatively high degree of incredulity regarding nuclear weapon use, any significant change in present strategic doctrine would almost certainly be unfavorable. Thus, as nuclear weapons and delivery systems increase in sophistication, and new weapons are produced, it may be expected that entire new strategies will be devised, and new doctrines come into fashion.

Perhaps the clearest prospects of a decisive shift in doctrine and practice are that the current traditions against nuclear use and the use of chemical and biological weapons may fade. Nuclear weapons have not been used since 1945, nor has their use been threatened for coercive purposes. No country has seriously considered a very precise and selected use of nuclear weapons to accomplish a limited aim. This powerful taboo, however, could disappear if, for example, nuclear proliferation placed nuclear weapons in the hands of countries with strong regional ambitions or with fears that neighbors were soon to acquire a preponderance of conventional or nuclear power. Further, the selective use of strategic nuclear weapons, perhaps to show resolve in a crisis, may in time become part of the strategic doctrine, although the circumstances which could impel such a change cannot now easily be envisioned. An emerging interest in limited strategic nuclear war may indeed already be discerned. American policy statements in the early part of 1970 clearly hinted that deterrence, through an assured retaliatory capacity, may not be "sufficient," and that a capability to bargain in an intranuclear-war period may be required.[55] The military

[54] Charles L. Schultze, "Budget Alternatives after Vietnam," in Kermit Gordon, ed., *Agenda for the Nation* (Washington 1968), 13-48.

[55] See, for example, the President's foreign policy statement (fn. 27), William Beecher, *New York Times*, February 19, 1970, 28.

will no doubt be somewhat ambivalent about pursuing limited nuclear war doctrines. For while such doctrines could lend new justification to various strategic procurements (such as advanced manned aircraft) they would also imply increased civilian control over military operations. Nonetheless, the possible emergence of these doctrines is not a fanciful prospect, and is one which could strip away present illusions of security founded as they are on the clear irrationality of an all-out nuclear exchange.

Finally, any prolonged continuation of the arms race encompassing a massive escalation of offensive and defensive armaments, would almost certainly be accompanied by a significant rise in tension among the nuclear powers. Such an escalation, involving large missile defenses and eventually large shelter programs and possibly city evacuation procedures, would require the participation of the entire citizenry of the affected nations. This coupled with the necessity of the involved governments to justify very large defense expenditures at a time of rising expectations and demands among their citizens would doubtless lead to a significant degree of war propaganda. Nations would think more of war, seek nuclear security still more obsessively, and thereby create more dangers of crises and confrontations.[56]

The Relevance and Irrelevance of Strategic Forces

Recognition of the potential importance of strategic doctrine to stability helps resolve an apparent paradox inherent in the foregoing analysis. For without this realization, it would be inconsistent to argue on the one hand that the arms race has no political relevance and on the other that if continued it could lead to considerable peril. At the moment, there exist such powerful restraints among political leaders to the use of nuclear weapons, that calculations of assured destruction, comparative advantage after all-out nuclear exchanges, etc. indeed have little reality. But the persistence of these restraints is by no means assured under the pressure of an accelerated arms competition. The task of those responsible for national security is not so much to maintain massive retaliatory capacities, which are today hardly relevant to stability given current restraints, as to ensure that these restraints do not erode.

Difficulty of Control

In some ways the most worrisome aspect of the arms race is that it may now be passing beyond our capacity to control it. As our nuclear predicament thus becomes more complex and uncertain, it will also become increasingly difficult to control and transform through interna-

[56] Richard L. Garwin and Hans A. Bethe, "Anti-Ballistic-Missile Systems," *Scientific American* (March 1968).

tional agreement. The present moment may in this sense be one of perishing opportunity as well as eroding stability.

In the first place, verification of control agreements will become increasingly difficult. It is noteworthy that strategic arms control seems especially promising now partly because the strategic balance has entered a fortuituous phase where both sides know quite accurately the forces of the other but are unable to destroy those forces in a first strike. But this is a doubtless transient phase. The next cycle of new weapon systems will drastically diminish the visibility of strategic systems. Indeed this would be a major goal of both superpowers. In general, the search for invulnerable retaliatory forces, to the extent it is successful, will inexorably increase the problems of verification, for the characteristic which favors the first—"invisibility"—tends to thwart the second.

Beyond the verification problem, new complexity in the strategic balance will impede control efforts. At the moment, there is much confusion over the concept of "parity"—whether a lead by one country or the other in numbers of missiles is significant, and whether numbers of missiles (or warheads or total firepower, etc.) is a reasonable measure of strategic strength. The introduction of missile defenses and MIRV's will underscore such confusion by ensuring that any simple count of missiles as a basis of agreement would be relatively meaningless.[57] Shifts in strategic doctrine could also discourage arms control efforts. The present stress on deterrence through maintenance of retaliatory forces has the advantage of symmetry—both sides could achieve an assured deterrent simultaneously. If, however, one or both sides sought some superior bargaining posture, then no point in the strategic weapons competition would appear stable. The apparent adoption of a "sufficiency" rather than "superiority" doctrine by the United States in 1970 was thus helpful in breaking down barriers to arms control. But at the same time, the hints that sufficiency may be defined in such a way as to include some kind of bargaining superiority have suggested that parity may still not be a widely acceptable goal.

The prospect of proliferation of nuclear weapons and other weapon systems to countries other than the United States and the Soviet Union will further heighten the difficulty of achieving future arms restraint. Every facet of arms control negotiations would be rendered more complex. For some control measures, other countries than the two superpowers would have to participate in the negotiations. For other measures, where it still might be possible to conduct bilateral discussions, the negotiations would nonetheless be severely complicated by the degree to which other nation's forces would have to be considered.

[57] Rathjens (fn. 45), 38-39.

IV. Prospects for the Future

It is apparent that novel and unorthodox approaches to arms control will be required to overcome the obstacles which have impeded control efforts in the past. The character of these approaches and the emerging sensibility which they reflect are already discernible. The common thread to this sensibility is that the arms race and its control cannot be viewed simply in terms of the bilateral strategic balance, that one must both look beyond the arms race to note its interaction with other international political developments, and at the same time look within the arms competition at the national security establishments of the two superpowers.

Strategic Arms Control and the Spread of Nuclear Weapons

The time may be approaching when the single most powerful impulse to strategic arms limitations will be their impact on the spread of nuclear weapons. Most nations now being asked to sign and ratify the Nonproliferation Treaty have demanded that the treaty be followed as soon as possible by measures among the nuclear powers to halt the nuclear arms race and to reduce existing nuclear arsenals.[58] The Treaty itself declares the intention of the parties to achieve these demands.[59] The Treaty however merely underscores an association between the nuclear arms race and the prospect of nuclear proliferation that has long been evident, for it cannot be expected that large and economically powerful nations will indefinitely forego nuclear weapons if the United States and Soviet Union continue to act as if these weapons and associated systems are essential and decisive accoutrements to national prestige and security. Under such circumstances, claims of national equality, fears of a technological gap, a sense that the nuclear powers betrayed the Nonproliferation Treaty obligations would all press toward decisions by these nations to develop nuclear forces.

On the other hand, it seems within the capacities of the United States and Soviet Union to establish quite the contrary pressures. The two nuclear superpowers are very powerful legislators of international convention. If through measures to control the nuclear arms race, they gradually impose a degree of illegitimacy on nuclear weapons (much as international conventions and practices have illegitimized lethal

[58] See, for example, *Final Document of the Conference of Non-Nuclear Weapon States*, October 1, 1968. *Documents on Disarmament 1968*, 668-87.

[59] Same, 461-65. Art. VI states: "Each of the Parties to the Treaty undertakes to pursue negotiations in good faith on effective measures relating to cessation of the nuclear arms race at an early date and to nuclear disarmament, and on a treaty on general and complete disarmament under strict and effective international control."

chemical and biological weapons)[60] and recognize limits on sovereign discretion in the disposition of nuclear forces, nations such as Germany, Japan, and India will find it increasingly difficult and unattractive to develop their own nuclear forces.[61] This is so partly because such development would be jointly opposed by the United States and the Soviet Union, whose willingness to place pressure on prospective nuclear powers would be strengthened by their own willingness to accept arms limitations. Although it may be somewhat fanciful to attribute qualities of conscience to nations, it cannot be doubted that concepts of sovereign equality and fairness of obligation are powerful shapers of international behavior. Thus, having conducted atmospheric nuclear tests over almost two decades, the United States, United Kingdom, and Soviet Union could not plausibly rally opposition even within their own countries to French and Chinese nuclear testing at the time of the limited test ban agreement. Conversely, nothing would so fortify the United States and Soviet willingness and capability to impose constraints on other countries than a general recognition that such constraints were shared at least in some measure by the two superpowers.

Prospective nuclear powers would face technical difficulties as well

[60] An interesting analogy between chemical and biological weapons and nuclear weapons is made by Frederic J. Brown, *Chemical Warfare* (Princeton 1968), 290-316.

[61] It has occasionally been argued that since American and Soviet ballistic missile defense deployments would afford the two superpowers some protection against nuclear attack by prospective nuclear powers, the latter would be further discouraged from mounting a nuclear weapon program. However, with few if any exceptions, the dominant incentives for the development of national nuclear forces have little to do with the capabilities of these prospective nuclear states to inflict damage on the United States or the Soviet Union. A related argument has frequently been asserted that American missile defenses, by reducing our vulnerability to nuclear attack from China, would enhance the credibility of our security assurance to India, Japan, and other Asian countries, who would otherwise demand their own nuclear forces as a deterrent to China. This argument as well remains unconvincing primarily because China's willingness to use or threaten to use nuclear weapons against Asian neighbors is not likely to depend on whether or not the United States has a missile defense, and is likely to remain very small in any case. Instead, by further widening the disparity between the two superpowers and other nations, American and Soviet missile defense deployments could create entirely new problems. These new problems will be of two kinds, those due to the reactions of allies to the American and Soviet missile defenses and those that will be raised if the United States (or the Soviet Union) attempts to assist or provide other nations with missile defenses. The first set of problems will arise from contradictory fears among non-nuclear countries and minor nuclear powers that their major nuclear ally, by virtue of a relatively greater degree of invulnerability, will on the one hand retreat to a neoisolationist position or on the other hand engage in a too risky foreign policy. If, alternatively, the United States or the Soviet Union attempted to alleviate such trends through provision of missile defenses for allies (utilizing nuclear weapons, as present and foreseeable technology demands), this may severely undermine the nuclear control policies of the nuclear powers, and in general provide a way station in the countries assisted to national nuclear forces.

if curtailment of the arms race permitted the achievement of a comprehensive test ban and a gradual strengthening of an international safeguard system. The value of a test ban is that it imposes symmetric obligations on nuclear and nonnuclear states, thereby making abrogation by a prospective nuclear power difficult to justify, while at the same time imposing very harsh practical constraints to the development of nuclear weapons if nations adhere to it. Although it is conceivable that a comprehensive test ban could be achieved without other notable restrictions on the arms race, it seems unlikely that either nuclear power would wish in such circumstances to forego nuclear weapons testing altogether. Indeed deployment of ballistic missile defense systems in particular will provide strong pressures on both nuclear powers not only to continue to conduct underground nuclear tests but eventually to resume nuclear weapons tests in the atmosphere as well.

While the connection between the arms race and the long-term effectiveness of nuclear safeguards is more subtle than in the instance of the test ban, it is likely to be more important. It is already commonplace that the production of nuclear material in peaceful nuclear power programs after the next decade will be sufficient to support the production of thousands of nuclear weapons *annually*. Since even a small fraction of this material could provide the basis of a moderate national nuclear weapons program or of the program of subnational terroristic groups, it is evident that a strong safeguard system to ensure against diversion of nuclear material from peaceful to weapons programs is required. A commitment among nonnuclear states to accept verification by the International Atomic Energy Agency, as is called for by the Nonproliferation Treaty, would be a valuable first step. But ultimately, an adequate safeguard system would almost certainly have to include some degree of interpenetration of national nuclear power programs and a gradual internationalization of parts of the peaceful nuclear industry. Otherwise a safeguard system would appear too fragile, too susceptible to abrogation by one or more parties, and too vulnerable to a massive defection from the system once a small breach had been made. However, development of a more stringent safeguard system and indeed even the full implementation of the procedures called for in the Nonproliferation Treaty, probably will depend on the ultimate willingness of the principal nuclear powers to halt further production of nuclear material for weapons purposes. Such a measure would not be acceptable to the nuclear powers in the context of an unconstrained arms race, particularly one that featured large missile defense systems and extensive multiple warhead deployments.

More important however than the technical constraints which U.S.-Soviet arms control agreements could impose on nonnuclear states would be their potential to strengthen the tradition that nuclear weapons could not be used to achieve normal political goals. Such could be accomplished indirectly through limitations on strategic arms and a concurrent recognition by both superpowers that any quest for nuclear superiority is both futile and dangerous. The tradition could be more directly reinforced by an explicit agreement among the nuclear powers, arising from the strategic limitations and the assumptions that must underlay them, not to use nuclear weapons first.[62] It also seems clear that if retardation of the arms race promised still further nuclear disarmament, the expectations of the nonnuclear states would be fundamentally altered. It is one thing to decide to initiate a nuclear weapons development at a time when there is widespread belief that nuclear proliferation is inevitable and prospects for nuclear disarmament very dim, and another to do so when these expectations are reversed.

This widened perspective of arms control, not merely as a set of technical agreements but rather as part of a strategy of developing an international legal order to minimize violence, could have consequences transcending the nuclear proliferation issue. Restraints on unilateral discretion to employ force and on nuclear threats, for example, would appear valuable ways to reduce the risk of war. The new sensibility will have to recognize the importance of developing international norms of permissible military behavior, and recognize as well the role of arms control measures in establishing such norms. Such recognition would, however, imply a broadening of strategic arms control discussions to include international actors other than the two nuclear powers. The demand incorporated in the Nonproliferation Treaty for nuclear arms control may thus be merely a prelude to a more extensive international insistence that the U.S.-Soviet strategic arms competition is not the concern of the two nuclear superpowers only.

Internal Politics

The preceding analysis has insisted on the difficulties of obtaining internal consensus in favor of arms control within each side's national security establishment. It is likely that much of the style of arms control negotiations during the coming years will reflect this central fact.

In the U.S., this new style will first be manifest in a greater public role in strategic force procurement policy. The enduring consequences of the debate over missile defense will probably be some form of institutionalization of the citizen forums which sprang up about the coun-

[62] Richard A. Falk, *Legal Order in a Violent World* (Princeton 1968), 414-40.

try in 1969, and renewed attempts by Congressmen to develop procedures which would permit serious review of the Defense Budget.[63] However, for such review to be possible there will have to be a general recognition that the central issues pertinent to arms control are not technical but rather political and moral. If the impact of arms limitation measures on the technological balance remains the decisive focus of debate, the issues will probably prove too esoteric for Congress and the public to challenge the defense bureaucracy. The debate over ballistic missile defense has obscured this point, for even the opponents of missile defense have argued essentially in technical terms: that missile defenses would not work, that the Soviet Union did not have a first-strike potential, etc. They have not seriously raised the critical question of whether the balance of terror ought to remain the chief bulwark of international security and whether the elaborate calculations of strategic advantage have any political relevance.[64]

The matter has been put in one of its strongest forms by McGeorge Bundy:

> The neglected truth about the present strategic arms race between the United States and the Soviet Union is that in terms of international political behavior that race has now become almost completely irrelevant.
>
> There is an enormous gulf between what political leaders really think about nuclear weapons and what is assumed in complex calculations of relative "advantage" in simulated strategic warfare. Think-tank analysts can set levels of "acceptable" damage well up in the tens of millions of lives. They can assume that the loss of dozens of great cities is somehow a real choice for sane men. They are in an unreal world. In the real world of real political leaders—whether here or in the Soviet Union—a decision that would bring even one hydrogen bomb on one city of one's own country would be recognized in advance as a catastrophic blunder; ten bombs on ten cities would be a disaster beyond history, and a hundred bombs on a hundred cities are unthinkable. Yet this unthinkable level of human incineration is the least that could be expected by either side in response to any first strike in the next ten years, *no matter what happens to weapons systems in the meantime.*
>
> The basic consequence of considering this matter politically and not technically is the conclusion that beyond a point long since passed the escalation of the strategic nuclear race makes no sense for either the Soviet Union or the United States.[65]

[63] Knoll and McFadden (fn. 38), 101-31.
[64] Wiesner and Chayes (fn. 25). See, also, Bull (fn. 24), 20.
[65] Bundy (fn. 6), 9-11.

The importance of the internal debate within each country is underscored by the nature of modern weapons technology. For it appears that arms control, if it is achieved in the coming decade, will have to be marked by a significant degree of national self-restraint. Advances in technology have made it increasingly difficult to design international agreements which could not be circumvented or rendered unworkable by technical developments not touched by the original understandings. We now are confronted with a highly ramified technology which cannot easily be controlled all at once through explicit international agreement. As a consequence, arms restraint will probably have to initiate from unilateral national decisions not to deploy destabilizing new weapons. This would be perhaps the surest way to halt the spiral of both sides responding to potential greater than expected threats rather than to systems that have already entered the alert forces.[66]

In general, such restraint could not be expected to encompass military research and development. Military R & D has wide support from even the strongest arms control advocates who believe that the R & D not only provides a valuable hedge against breakthroughs by the adversary, but more significantly tends to reassure each side that such breakthroughs are not actually occurring. Nevertheless, in certain instances, such as with lethal chemical and biological weapons, a unilateral suspension of development activities may be politically feasible and strategically wise, perhaps the best way to ensure that such weapons do not proliferate to nonnuclear countries where their possession could be highly dangerous.

The realities of internal politics and military technology also combine in support of informal arms control understandings. The large phased reductions of strategic weapons sought in the formal treaty proposals of the past do not now appear politically feasible, and are no longer of clear value in reducing the level of destruction in a nuclear war. Thus, with damage reduction a diminishingly feasible arms control goal, the main goal must now be to diminish each side's image of the other as an implacable nuclear threat, and to encourage a more rational security debate within each nation. These goals could probably be best pursued through informal understandings and communications that would provide the occasion for exchanges of information about strategic forces, strategic plans, and strategic concepts.[67]

There could be considerable variety to such informal understandings: simple strategic dialogues in which no explicit commitment on actual deployment patterns are made, exchanges of strategic procurement plans (such as the U.S. makes publicly available in any event each year), and moratoriums on deployment or testing all appear feasi-

66 Rodberg (fn. 51).   67 Bundy (fn. 6), 15.

ble and potentially valuable.[68] To be sure, not all areas of arms competition will be conducive to such modalities. In particular, the control of ambivalent technologies, those enterprises that possess the ambivalent quality of being useful for both peaceful and military purposes (such as space exploration, weather modification, and nuclear power), will probably require more formal methods of control. Nevertheless, the scope of activity which could be subsumed under informal arrangements seems very substantial. Indeed, there appear significant technical reasons to support an emphasis on informal understandings. First, the development of sophisticated satellite observations systems has narrowed the range of arms limitation measures that seem to require formal inspection.[69] Second, the character of advancing technology demands flexible agreements which can be modified as new weapon potentials are perceived or realized. Although such flexibility can perhaps be achieved in carefully drafted treaties, it can probably be most easily effected by more informal arrangements.[70]

A final reason to believe that informal agreements will appear increasingly attractive to both sides is the uncertain role of China's nuclear force in the next decades. Although China could not hope to achieve a first strike capability against either superpower in the foreseeable future, regardless of virtually any kind of arms-control measure the U.S. and Soviet Union could devise, they might be able to achieve a reasonable retaliatory capacity. An attempt to prevent this has occasionally been one of the objects of the U.S. ballistic missile defense program, and conceivably could explain some of the Soviet interest in missile defenses as well. In any event, it may be expected that the two nuclear superpowers will be reluctant to enter treaty arrangements that did not include China, even if, as would appear to be the case, China's nuclear force is virtually irrelevant to U.S.-Soviet decisions to curtail the arms race.[71]

CONCLUSION—RADICAL VERSUS REFORMIST PERSPECTIVES

Two crucial issues dominate the future of arms control. The first is the extent to which old ideas and institutions must be altered as a prelude to substantial arms control. It is clear that the critical arenas of arms control debate will increasingly be within each side's defense es-

[68] Jerome Kahan, "Informal Arrangements for Controlling the Strategic Arms Race," Brookings, Informal Paper (September 1969).

[69] Jeremy J. Stone, "Can the Communists Deceive US?" Chayes and Wiesner (fn. 25), 193-98.

[70] For an excellent discussion of how formal agreements could be rendered more flexible, see George Bunn, "Missile Limitations by Treaty or Otherwise?" *Columbia Law Review*, 70 (January 1970), 1-47.

[71] Rathjens (fn. 45), 21-24; *Posture Statement 1970* (fn. 4), 45-46; Allan S. Whiting, "The Chinese Nuclear Threat," in Chayes and Wiesner (fn. 25), 160-70.

tablishments; that arms control will be preeminently decided by a double negotiation between the arms control "hawks" and "doves" in each country. What remains uncertain however is how radical a transformation in thinking and in institutional structures and procedures will be required for the arms control advocates to prevail in such debate.

Beyond this question is a still deeper one: whether even substantial arms control could decisively achieve international stability if it is not soon followed by a radical change in international politics and eventually in the nation-state system itself. Arms control may prove a very unstable regime, founded as it is on a curiously ambivalent view of the adversary, in which a balance of terror resting fundamentally on threats of mutual vengeance coexists with strong motives to cooperate with the potential enemy. This ambivalence probably must ultimately become resolved either by a move toward some minimal world order and an international system more compatible with our shared humane values than is our present condition, or by a return to the belief in the enduring primacy of the nation-state in a world of nuclear weapons.

CHAPTER 11

Toward the Control of International Violence: The Limits and Possibilities of Law

RICHARD J. BARNET

I. THE PROBLEM OF LAW OBEDIENCE

IT IS familiar rhetoric at disarmament conferences that the control of violence demands the growth of law. The United States has presented plan after plan for arms reduction in which international legal institutions play an integral role. According to the American approach, the present crude system for maintaining peace through national military forces must be replaced by another system for promoting world order and stability. That system, while having elements of force in it, should be rooted in law. Legal institutions, including forums for determining disputes among nations and police forces to impose sanctions, must expand their authority as the stockpiles of arms are reduced. Only if governments develop confidence in alternatives to war for resolving differences among nations will they be willing to put away their weapons. The Soviet Union, while skeptical of international institutions with independent authority, especially international military forces, also rests its disarmament program on traditional principles of international law, such as coexistence and nonintervention.

Scholars and publicists too have stressed the urgency of moving from a world under arms to a world under law. It is sometimes noted that what is most needed in the international community are habits of law obedience which would encourage nations to observe legal restraints on their freedom of action. But despite the speeches national statesmen make about the interdependence of the modern world and the new limitations on national sovereignty made necessary by the perils of the nuclear age, powerful states are in fact claiming for themselves the legal right to make a greater number of decisions—and more far-reaching ones—than at any time in the last 400 years. The United States has claimed the right to bomb countries without a declaration of war, to undermine governments it considers hostile, and to threaten nuclear war in order to force the redeployment of missiles it considered a threat to its security. The Soviet Union have claimed the right to invade Hungary and Czechoslovakia at will. The nuclear powers have arrogated to themselves a competence to make unilateral decisions affecting the politics and economics of other states on an unprecedented scale. Such extravagant claims for the right of self-judgment of course undermine the basis for a climate of law obedience.

In a rational world nations would come to see that ultimately their individual self-interest depends upon the establishment of a system of world order and that no single nation is powerful or wise enough to create or maintain that order. In such a world the reinforcement of habits of law obedience would be explicit national goals. Nations would weigh the effect of individual foreign policy decisions on the prospects for an effective world legal system. A national government would at least raise the issue whether the pursuit of a particular objective through particular means is likely to make it more or less difficult to encourage other individuals working for other governments to obey the law in similar cases. In such an international society someone would have the responsibility of confronting the national leader with the choice between pursuing a foreign policy objective through means which, from a world order standpoint ought to be considered illegal, or foregoing an immediate advantage in the interest of building a secure international community.

Yet the experience of nations suggests that national leaders do not make individual policy decisions with world order criteria in mind. For example, in the rational system we have been imagining, the Legal Advisor of the State Department would counsel the President not to intervene unilaterally in internal wars. Instead, on the most pressing questions of foreign policy the Legal Advisor, like his colleagues in other foreign ministries around the world, devotes his efforts to putting together a legal case for what his government wants to do. Law is not a restraint on policy but an instrument of policy.

It is hardly surprising that legal advisors give the sort of advice they do. For one thing, lawyers, especially "house counsel," customarily stretch the law as far as possible to satisfy their clients, and there is a good deal of elasticity in many of the norms of international law. But, more important, neither the lawyer nor the client has much faith in the legal system. Neither believes that the acceptance of restraints on foreign policy objectives and methods will be reciprocated by rival states. The risks in obeying the law are thus considered too great. When a litigant has his "day in court," he normally does not envisage history ending when the judge enters an unfavorable verdict. But a political leader acting for a nation does not dare to take the same detached view of any particular crisis because he believes that his nation, no matter how great its power, is always in a precarious position simply because the world is hostile and irrational. In defending United States policy in Vietnam the President told the Congress in his 1966 State of the Union message that military intervention is made necessary by the "madness" rampant in the world. Those who believe they face desperate adversaries reject limitations on their freedom of action as self-defeating. It matters little what the letter and spirit of international obligations require.

Because the leaders of the postwar world have often had this image of the world, they have not seriously contemplated disarmament. While they are persuaded that a major nuclear war will destroy their nations, they continue to believe that the manipulation of the nuclear threat is the sole effective means of survival. The Legal Advisor ought to point out that his client's individual decisions affect his adversaries' views of the world. He can make the adversary feel that the world is either more or less rational, more or less hostile, by what he does. His actions can encourage or discourage restraint in others. But this is the way detached observers of the international scene may think; it is not the way political leaders think in times of crisis.

The development of a living law for guiding and restraining the behavior of states is a political prerequisite for disarmament but it will not come about through exhortation. Some have suggested that it could come about only as a consequence of "consensus." Their argument goes something like this: Nations will not accept the restraints of government and join together to form a community until they reach some agreement on common ends and values. Thus governments must narrow their differences on ideology, values, and world views before they can form a community under law. Merely to settle the major existing disputes will not usher in the "rule of law." The cold war, they point out, has witnessed the disappearance, if not the settlement, of many critical conflicts which raised the risk of war, but the disposition of these crises did not create a framework for the legal control of international violence. Iran, Greece, Cuba, and Quemoy have faded from the headlines, but the distrust that dissolves community remains. To get the world legal order needed for disarmament nations must first agree on common goals and values. There must be some degree of consensus on what constitutes a just world order. Indeed, a bare consensus on the need to eliminate or restrict international violence is not enough. If nations feel that their power, wealth, or values are threatened by others, they will be tempted to violence no matter how suicidal that impulse may be. Those who are moved by this argument are greatly encouraged by the introduction of the profit motive into Soviet economics and the extension of the welfare state in the United States. For them, these developments are small steps in an evolution toward homogeneity which could be the basis of a world community under law.

The problem with talking about consensus as a precondition for a world legal order, however, is that it tells us nothing about either the process or the time scale for the development of law. We have very few ideas on which goals or values there is a need for consensus to establish a climate of law obedience. We have little basis for predicting how long such a consensus may take to develop, although it must surely proceed at a slower rate than some other processes of change in the world, such as upheaval in underdeveloped societies, technological growth, and the population explosion, which are likely to exacerbate conflict.

Moreover, the assumption that the impulse to violence in nations is rooted in ideological differences may be quite wrong. The governments of Imperial Germany and Czarist Russia did not fundamentally differ in the way they viewed the state and the international system. Indeed, one might rather argue that two nations which have the same goals and value systems and have organized their societies in approximately the same way are more likely in a world of scarcity to come into conflict with each other than with a nation committed to a different life style, just as the man who wants to be a corporation president is apt to find himself pitted against someone with a similar ambition rather than against a religious mystic or a symphony orchestra conductor. No doubt differing ideologies and traditions complicate the process of resolving conflict, but the primary sources of conflict are concrete issues relating to the distribution of economic and political power. On these issues, which are constantly shifting as social conditions change, no lasting consensus is possible.

It is not difficult to understand the primary reasons why governments in the present world do not accept legal restraints. Nor is it particularly hard to conceive of a number of plausible visions of an ideal world in which they would. But we are acutely aware that we lack a program for moving from a present reality to a less self-destructive future. We sense that an international society in which the nation or some successor political form will accept legal restraints on its behavior and abandon its reliance on arms will come about as the consequence of a "system change" in international relations. By "system change" I mean another of those periodic leaps of history at the end of which values, social structures, and rhetoric are transformed, and the earth is easily recognizable as a different place from what it was. The fall of the Roman Empire, the Industrial Revolution, the rise of the European nation-state are examples. It appears that we are now in the midst of a "system change" of similar, probably greater, magnitude. The principal forces we can see that are propelling us toward a revolution in the international system are the transformation of war through atomic energy, the entry of the nonindustrialized areas into the world economy, the rapidity of social change in virtually all internal societies, and the growth of the technology of biological, psychological, and political manipulation.

Neither the "habit of law obedience" nor the "consensus" formulations of the problem adequately take account of this process; they describe a radically new end result but do not suggest how it might come about. In speculating on the future the task of the international lawyer is to explore specific ways in which law might be used to promote a "system change" without precipitating disaster. Discussions of world order and disarmament often treat law itself as a mystical goal. In the American eschatology the end is a *World under Law*. We have set aside a Law Day to celebrate this vision. The global struggle is portrayed as conflict between revolution and violence on the one hand, and law and order, on the other. But law is a neutral instrument. Even those who accept the idea of natural law and believe in the possibility of inherently good or universally valid statutes and principles recognize that laws enacted by human societies fall far short of this ideal. Law has been used as an instrument of oppression as well as an instrument of justice since men formed the first polity. Principles of international law have been invoked without serious challenge by all major powers in support of a variety of predatory behavior. Law can be a powerful instrument of social control for the development of international society. It can be used to promote both physical survival and justice, or it can be used to legitimize an oppressive or dangerous status quo. How law works is mysterious; but it should be viewed not as a mystique but as a workaday tool for solving specific problems. The purpose of this chapter is to sketch some of the functions international law might serve for transforming the present international environment into a warless world.

II. The Role of Law in Controlling Expectations: A Look at Two Treaties

Probably the greatest obstacle to the acceptance of disarmament by national governments is the universal expectation that violence is bound to recur on the international scene and the deep-seated belief that there is no way to deal with this prospect other than to keep their weapons ready. Politicians of this century have grown up in an atmosphere of continued violence. The prospect of a world in which weapons are not needed seems unreal. As Haas and Whiting have observed:

> Precisely because national communities expect further international violence, they seem to have resigned themselves to the recurrence of war. . . . Thus the expectation of future violence is part and parcel of political consciousness. As long as this fatalistic mode of

thought continues, no demonstration of interdependence can be expected to change national loyalties to devotion to a global system of values. Anticipation of violence seems to breed continued acceptance of national values and interests and not a desire to transcend them.[1]

The expectation of violence as an inevitable fact of life is the heart of the soldier's ideology. Eight months before the end of World War II, H. H. Arnold, Chief of Staff of the U.S. Army Air Corps, warned publicly of the next war and declared that in such a war the United States would be bombed from the air.[2] The man who was Commanding General of the Strategic Air Command for six years, General Thomas Powers, has predicted that the United States faces an endless sequence of enemies, including the possibility of an "African Hitler" who will arise to take the place of the Communists once they are defeated.[3] It is true that soldiers have special psychological and professional reasons for believing in the inevitability of violence, but their views are shared in great measure by their civilian superiors.

These are hardly unreasonable expectations for they seem to be supported by a good deal of history. But if these expectations form the basic premise on which policy is built, there is little prospect for building an international order that is not based on the national control of the means of violence. It is sometimes argued that the very expectation of violence, particularly when it threatens to reach catastrophic proportions, will prompt national leaders to put the weapons of war beyond their reach. There is impressive evidence, however, that the fear of violence causes nations to grasp ever more tightly to the symbols and rhetoric of parochialism and, especially, to their own instruments of violence. When the United States faced the prospect of nuclear war in the Cuban missile crisis of 1962, those participating in the decisions could fit comfortably on the couch in the President's office. Allies were informed, not consulted. Within the country, neither Congress nor the foreign policy bureaucracy played a role. Diplomatic alternatives to an "eyeball to eyeball" confrontation were given scant consideration. It is true that when the crisis passed, there was a surge of interest in finding less risky alternatives for dealing with international conflict. But as the memory of the terrifying week faded, and new international problems arose, the sudden impulse toward reform of the international system which the crisis had generated, spent itself. The futility and perils of war are widely appreciated, but we are still operating within the war system.

[1] Ernst Haas and Allen Whiting, *Dynamics of International Relations* (New York 1956), 18-19.

[2] *New York Times*, February 8, 1945.

[3] Thomas Powers, *Design for Survival* (New York 1964), 212.

Does law have a role to play in tempering self-fulfilling prophecies of violence? Another way of asking the question is to consider whether by agreeing to place legal limits on the unilateral right to resort to violence, national governments can restructure each other's expectations. The answer appears to depend upon the type of commitment. Let us look at two examples from recent history.

The Kellogg-Briand Pact which "outlawed" war as an instrument of national policy never substantially changed expectations. There were good reasons for this. The wording of the treaty was vague. It was so limited by its own exceptions as to be virtually meaningless. It provided for the right to self-defense and let each signatory decide for itself when it was committing illegal aggression or lawful defense. The Senate made it clear that whatever the United States determined was essential to the enforcement of the Monroe Doctrine would be considered self-defense. The French and British made similar reservations. An observer of the time commented that the Pact of Paris was the most comprehensive treaty for legalizing war ever enacted. For all these reasons it was not taken seriously except by a small group. The Treaty passed the U.S. Senate 85 to 1, but the view of Senator Carter Glass was typical of the prevailing opinion in the chamber and in the country. "I am not willing that anybody in Virginia shall think that I am simple enough to suppose that it is worth a postage stamp in the direction of accomplishing permanent peace. . . . But I am going to be simple enough, along with the balance of you, to vote for the ratification of this worthless, but perfectly harmless peace treaty."[4] John Dewey favored the treaty because he believed that "the moral conviction of the world" was the only effective restraint on the nations' impulse to war. But the Treaty, which is often held up to show the worthlessness of declaratory rules of conduct not backed by specific sanctions, never represented a moral consensus.

The limited Nuclear Test Ban, on the other hand, did change expectations in a limited way. There is a widespread belief in the world that the nations which signed that treaty will, as a result, limit their actions in certain specific respects. Even the nonobligatory moratorium on nuclear tests changed perceptions of the international environment enough to produce surprise and shock when the Soviet Union resumed testing in the Fall of 1961. When the Test Ban was signed, it was widely expected that the signatories would comply with it and that their compliance would make some difference in international affairs. Why was this? First, unlike the Kellogg-Briand Pact, it addressed a series of specific commands and prohibitions to national governments. A responsible government official could read the text and know what he was allowed to do and what was forbidden. The area of conduct to be

[4] Selig Adler, *The Isolationist Impulse* (New York 1957), 218.

regulated under the Treaty clearly fell within the competence of national governments.

Second, the circumstances under which the Test Ban was negotiated and ratified in the United States and the Soviet Union suggested that the signatories had made a political commitment to the obligations of the treaty. In the United States the Kennedy Administration mounted a nationwide campaign enlisting business leaders and former heads of the military establishment to persuade the country to support it. The Administration risked a major political battle with the substantial group in the Senate who opposed making agreements with the Soviet Union. In the year before a presidential election the decision to push for an arms agreement with the Soviet Union, however limited, showed a serious purpose.

The leaders of the Soviet Union took even greater political risks in negotiating the Test Ban. For them, signing the treaty meant not only reversing long-held diplomatic positions against a ban which still permitted underground testing, but, more important, precipitating and exposing to the world a bitter ideological dispute with their principal ally, China. It cost the Soviet leadership something to press for the Test Ban and this fact was not lost on the United States and the other parties to the agreement. It was reasonable to assume that if the Soviet leadership were willing to fight the internal battles within the Communist world to get support for the Treaty, they probably meant to keep it.

Third, the Treaty prescribed rules of conduct which the signatories considered to be in their interest provided they were also observed by others. The Treaty did not impose obligations fundamentally at variance with emerging policies. Indeed, there have been more nuclear tests underground since the Treaty than were conducted in all the years preceding it. Both the United States and the Soviet Union had concluded that the risks of fallout and accelerated proliferation outweighed the inconvenience of shifting to underground testing. Much of the widespread confidence in the Treaty was thus based on the belief that the test ban registered a consensus on a relatively narrow issue.

National leaders in the United States and the Soviet Union took care not to exaggerate the significance of the limited test ban. They pointed out that it was the limitations in the Treaty that made its survival possible. Nonetheless, the world began to look different once the Treaty went into effect. If it was possible to conclude one agreement, people asked, could not additional areas of agreement be found? Expectations concerning the prospects for law obedience and for the introduction of more law were raised. Indeed, it was widely predicted that the Treaty of Moscow would produce major shifts in perception. Several witnesses of the Administration testifying in favor of the Treaty warned that this rather minimal arms control agreement could bring with it a dangerous "euphoria." Governments, and particularly their populations, might drastically downgrade their expectations of violence.

Indeed, this happened to a great extent. In the wake of the Test Ban, governments of Western Europe and the United States concluded that the risk of a Soviet invasion of Europe was over. The U.S. image of "monolithic communism" began to change. The Soviet armies were still in East Germany in strength. A thousand nuclear rockets were still aimed at the great cities of the continent. But the perception of the threat was altered. It is true that the perception of the threat had been changing for some time and that this reassessment was itself partly responsible for the political climate which made the test ban possible. But the signing of the agreement considerably hastened the process.

III. The Quality of Legitimacy

Can we identify the process by which law operates in the international environment to change expectations? One obvious way is to increase the likelihood of a specific response to specific conduct. When Bernard Baruch proposed a system of sanctions for meting out "swift, sure, and condign punishment" to any nation which violated any nuclear disarmament obligations, he reasoned that would-be violators would be deterred from breaking the law and that, therefore, all the rest would feel safe enough to comply with the law. The prospect of effective sanctions under a law specific enough to let officials of national states know what they must not do would increase the faith of all states in the stability and safety of the international order and remove the temptation of self-help. This is the simplest and most common image of the way law functions in society. It is the image of the policeman keeping order in the small town or perhaps more appropriately, the sheriff bringing law to the wild West. This image of how law changes perceptions in a social system is the inspiration for the Austinian definition of law: A command backed by a threat of punishment. In all official American schemes and proposals for far-reaching disarmament since the Baruch Plan the prospect of punishment has been the prime technique for manipulating the expectations of the international community.

The current U.S. disarmament draft provides for a United Nations Peace Force with "sufficient armed forces and armaments so that no state could challenge it." It is intended as a plausible vision of the control of violence in a world of national states. When subjected to analysis however, the vision proves quite implausible. It assumes the continuance of independent sovereign states and gives no clue as to why such states should agree to submit to punishment by an international army. Much of the pessimism about disarmament is traceable to this dilemma: Violence by states cannot be controlled, it is asserted, without an independent agency capable of punishing national governments for violations of the laws which are to govern a disarmed world. But no powerful government will permit itself to be put into a position where either an international police force or a coalition of other governments would have the legal right to destroy it. Since it seems so unlikely that national governments will accept an all-powerful international policeman, the official promotion of this vision has a negative effect on expectations. One can imagine a defense minister advising his chief, "If this is the only prospect for the effective legal control of international violence, then we had better look to our defenses. I would advise taking a chance on our wits and weapons rather than on some unknown police authority who, more likely than not, will turn out to be the tool of our rivals."

But law can change expectations other than by serving as a trigger for punishment. "Conduct, especially social conduct," Max Weber points out, "can be oriented on the part of the actors towards their *idea* of *legitimate order*."[5] The existence of an order or a rule of conduct can change the perceptions of those to whom it speaks in a variety of ways. The introduction of law into a social system can change expectations of violence. People walk or refuse to walk alone on city streets depending upon whether they think they will find law and order there. These expectations have very little to do with the number of policemen on duty. Characteristically, the "unsafe" centers of our big cities, where citizens correctly sense a breakdown of law and order, abound in police and police dogs. The citizen senses the absence of effective law because the rules of conduct have ceased to be acceptable to a significant number of individuals who live, work, or roam in the areas. The law has lost legitimacy.

The term "legitimacy" is commonly used to describe the quality of a legal rule which elicits acceptance or obedience from those to whom it is meant to apply. Legitimacy is offered as an explanation for the observable distinction between rules of law, on the one hand, and customs, traditions, arbitrary commands, or morals, on the other. The term is a convenient label for characterizing certain processes of social chemistry which anthropologists and historians have noted throughout the story of man. It does not tell us much about those processes except to suggest that there is an element of magic in it. There is a profound mystery that takes place in infants as well as in societies when a rule is perceived not merely as the expression of power but as a source of

[5] Max Rheinstein, ed., et al., *Max Weber on Law in Economy and Society* (Cambridge 1954), 8.

obligation. When a child says to himself "I ought not to do that" rather than "My parents will spank me if I do that," psychologists say he has "internalized" the rule and made it a part of his personality. He has begun to be his own policeman. When this process takes place he no longer looks at the outside world in quite the same way as he did before. However, to persuade an older child, or a leader of a national government, that rules "ought" to be obeyed, not merely, that there are no physical alternatives to compliance, it is usually necessary to convince him that the same obligations apply to others as well. The sense of obligation is based on ideas of fairness and mutuality. There is a premise that others in the society are also bound. When a man accepts an obligation, he assumes that a relevant group is undertaking a correlative obligation. The commitment itself represents expectations about how the rest of the group will behave. In a successful system of tax administration, for example, a taxpayer considers the assessment of taxes legitimate not only because he accepts as a principle the right of the government to collect revenues, but because he believes that others are paying their fair share. Where he doesn't think so, as in many tax systems around the world, he does not pay, despite the risk of stringent criminal penalties.

IV. The Process of Legitimation and the Control of International Violence

How can a rule of law for the control of international violence acquire similar legitimacy? Max Weber has described four ways in which rules of conduct become legitimate. It would be unwise to assume that the processes that have been commonly observed on the basis of examination of the way law has developed in many different societies throughout history are to be repeated at the international level, but the possible application of this experience is a reasonable starting place for an examination.

A. TRADITION

The first factor in human society encouraging legitimacy, according to Weber, is tradition. "Valid is that which has always been."[6] There is no doubt that tradition has played a decisive role in the development of international law. Customs and established practices relating to territorial waters, for example, have been elevated to the status of law. Countless rules on such questions command acceptance throughout the world. But in the area of war and peace, tradition has lost its hold as a source of legitimacy. Former Secretary of State Dean Acheson has put more candidly what politicians and bureaucrats represent-

---

[6] Max Rheinstein (fn. 5), 8.

ing great powers generally believe and act upon. International law, is "neither an aid nor an impediment in determining military policy."[7] In the modern state critics who question decisions of foreign policy on grounds of illegality are apt to be regarded as quaint.

There are several reasons for the failure of tradition in the international law of war and peace. International law rules for controlling the conduct of states grew up at a time when the character of international society was profoundly different from what it is today. In the formative period of international law the active participants were "a small club of European nations, joined in the nineteenth century by the newly emerging nations of the American Continent."[8] The rules of conduct for regulating the members of this club related almost exclusively to formal, external relations. The law regulating the coexistence of sovereignties was for the most part a collection of negative injunctions. The international system was expected to function smoothly if states avoided certain prohibited behavior much of which could be characterized as "interference in domestic affairs." In Wolfgang Friedmann's words, "International relations did not purport to penetrate beyond the shell of diplomatic intercourse into the economic and social aspects of the polities that dealt with each other as units."[9]

The entry into the world political arena of almost a hundred new nations that, formerly, were objects rather than subjects of international diplomacy has destroyed the "club" aspects of international life. A sovereign can no longer count on dealing with the head of another state who is a relative or a schoolmate. Indeed, he is very likely to find that the ambassador or prime minister with whom he must deal has spent much of his early life in jail, and has quite different ideas about taste, style, and philosophy. What may look like a fine tradition to the head of an old established state is apt to strike the leader of a revolutionary society as a vestige of an ugly past. The common language of the older law and diplomacy is in many cases no longer understood.

The traditions undergirding the international law of the European state system, a period stretching roughly 350 years, seem peculiarly anachronistic in an era of passionate ideological and political differences, for these traditions depended upon ignoring differences or religion, philosophy, or political system within states. The notion that international law and politics had no concern with what people within national boundaries believed or did was solemnized in the famous Latin formula "cujus regio, ejus religo" in the Treaty of Westphalia of 1648. In an international society composed primarily of European

[7] Dean Acheson, *Power and Diplomacy* (New York 1958), 42.

[8] Wolfgang Friedmann, *The Changing Structure of International Law* (New York 1964), 4.

[9] Same, 5.

monarchies no national government had much incentive to disturb this dogma of noninterference. But the tradition was weakened in the mid-nineteenth century by the campaign of the Holy Alliance against liberal revolutions. In the twentieth century the tradition has been all but destroyed. States with global ideologies have devoted energy to the encouragement of worldwide revolution or the suppression of revolutionary movements. Indeed, all major powers now regard it as their right or even duty to help transform the economy and social structure of other states. International institutions also claim jurisdiction over matters of human rights, economic development, and health within national boundaries. The formulas on noninterference in domestic affairs remain in the U.N. Charter, but the political, military, and economic techniques of penetration into foreign societies are so well developed and so widely used that the tradition of Westphalia does not speak to the modern world. Thus the old rules of nonintervention seem so at odds with universal practice that despite their long history and continued reaffirmation, they do not elicit wide acceptance.

B. "REVEALED TRUTH"

A second basis of legitimacy, according to the Weberian formulation, is "affectual, especially emotional, faith." In early societies the acceptability of a body of law proceeded from the belief in the sacredness of the prophet who promulgated it. Hammurabi, Moses, and the other great lawgivers of history demanded obedience because of mystical powers or mystical experiences. Even in the modern democratic state the leader can create or rewrite rules of conduct having the force of law by virtue of his personal authority. Thus, the President of the United States can legitimate conduct which appears to contravene written law, such as a massive military operation without U.N. authorization or declaration of war, by clothing it in the aura of the Presidency. But personal charisma is not a likely basis for legitimating international law rules. In the first place, there is no individual with the responsibility for promoting international law who possesses this sort of personal authority. The closest we have had to a prophet of international law was Dag Hammarskjold who attempted to use his office to create law for the international control of violence. His efforts evoked a reaction from the Soviet Union so strong as to threaten the existence of the United Nations as a cold-war arbiter or forum. The personal lawgiver, from Moses to the President of the United States, can obtain popular acceptance for particular utterances because his jurisdiction is unquestioned. The Hammarskjold experience indicates that no one individual has been accorded that jurisdiction for making international law. The history of the World Court also shows how limited is the lawgiving power of an international tribunal.

Although faith is an important source of legitimacy in the contemporary world, the most powerful faith is patriotism. Thus the "revealed truth" of which Weber speaks has the effect of reinforcing the independence and freedom of action of national governments rather than limiting them. The most effective justification offered for acts of violence is that the interests of the "nation" demand it. This is revealed truth, for the interests of a nation cannot usually be demonstrated or logically deduced. In a large, complex society, there are many conflicting interests on which a particular question of foreign policy may touch. Fighting a war or overthrowing a particular government may discernibly advance some of these interests, but not others. Seldom do the various private interests of all groups within a nation clearly coincide. Occasionally of course, there are wars when the issue of national survival is unambiguously posed, as in the Battle of Britain of 1940. But these are exceptional crises. Usually it is a matter of debate whether the "national interest" requires a particular policy. Yet despite the absence of personal stakes in a particular decision it is usually possible to get a national consensus on foreign policy by making an appeal to patriotism and national honor. In every country the citizens send their sons to war, and risk their own death and financial ruin for objectives that seem to have no relevance to their private interests because people accept what their government does on faith. If we are to have a world where nations are subject to rules limiting their use of violence, revealed truth must become an instrument for legitimating acts of the international community, not just the nation-state. But such a body of revealed truth is likely to be the outgrowth, not the source of new legal institutions.

C. RULE OF NECESSITY

An order may be treated as legitimate, Weber observes, "by virtue of value-rational faith." Thus people accept a rule of conduct because it has been "deduced as absolutely demanded."[10] The early writers on modern international law, such as Gentili, Grotius, and Pufendorf, attempted to derive the basic rules for regulating the conduct of states from natural law principles. These were "self-evident" propositions such as the obligations of states to keep promises to each other, to respect each other's property, and to pay for the damage they do to one another. Without the acceptance of such principles, it was agreed, no international society could exist, and, indeed, while states continually quarreled over their application to particular cases, the principles were widely accepted. In the contemporary world it is hard to find a body of rules that all nations will accept as valid simply because they

10 Rheinstein (fn. 5), 8.

strike everyone as logically essential. A blanket prohibition on the first use of nuclear weapons would seem to come as close to a universal precept grounded in necessity as one could envisage. The explosion of even a single nuclear weapon poisons the atmosphere which the people of all nations breathe and threatens to set off the ultimate, consuming fire. Yet it has been impossible to reach agreement on such a prohibition, and, indeed, both sides in the cold war have threatened to use nuclear weapons for diplomatic objectives which did not involve national survival.

The appeal to necessity fails because there is no agreement on what constitutes necessity. When the actors in international society were a few more or less monolithic states who could speak for whole societies, it was much easier to reach a consensus on "value-rational validity." Now that there is such a variety of perspectives and traditions on the international scene, there are few questions where this is possible. For example, if we look at the traditional natural law view of property which forbids expropriation without just compensation, we find that the decolonizing nations do not agree that these principles are riveted in the nature of things.

D. POSITIVE ENACTMENT

The final basis of legitimacy, in Weber's analysis, and by far the most important in the modern state, is "positive enactment." A rule of conduct is accepted because it has been adopted in accordance with procedures which themselves are deemed legitimate. In international society, treaties and other express enactments by states have become the dominant source of law. States will, for the most part, accept as legitimate only those rules to which they have expressly given assent. This is the dilemma that frustrates efforts at legal control of international violence: States will feel bound only when they have given their word, and they will be exceedingly chary about accepting obligations that limit their future freedom.

Let us retrace our steps a moment. We started by observing that states would not disarm as long as they lived with the expectation that others would resort to violence. The physical disappearance of weapons by itself is hardly convincing enough to bring about a radical change in such expectations. Similarly, international law rules regulating the use of violence frequently do not change expectations and hence do not reduce the likelihood of violence because they have lost or have never had legitimacy. When we examined the classic sources of legitimacy described by Max Weber, we found that three of them, tradition, revelation, and rationally deduced necessity, did not look like promising avenues for strengthening the role of law in international society. International law for the control of violence is not regarded as legitimate either by governments or their populations unless it is expressedly legitimated and even then the record of law obedience is uneven. Since there is neither a world legislature nor other institutions for prescribing the rules of peaceful change, governments themselves decide sometimes unilaterally, sometimes in concert, when they want to change the rules or make old rules legitimate. Thus the critical question turns on the motivation of national governments: How can they be encouraged to accept rules restricting their own freedom to resort to violence and to obey them even where it appears inimical to their immediately perceived interests?

V. NATIONAL SECURITY BUREAUCRACIES AND THE RULE OF LAW

The analysis of the process by which governments might come to accept legal limits on their discretion to use violence requires a close look at the actual operations of the modern government, particularly how national leaders define the national interest and the relationship of the nation to the world community. Nations defend individual decisions and policies in terms of the national interest and treat it, as we suggested, as "revealed truth." But these decisions and policies are in fact the product of a composite of the guesses, fears, prejudices, and the ambitions of a specific group of individuals who are charged with defining the "national interest" and carrying it out. They look at each threat and opportunity in the international environment through the filter of their particular world view. If law is to have an impact on the way nations behave, it must relate directly to the perceptions of national leaders who define the national interest. For they have the power by their acts and words either to promote the process of legitimacy or to undermine it. Nations will obey the law only when national leaders in the daily operation of government come to see compelling political reasons for observing legal limits in their personal discretion.

In order to examine how this might happen, it is important to look at a national government not as a monolithic unit but as a coalition of bureaucracies. Those most responsible for defining the issues and setting the tone of a nation's foreign policy are bureaucrats with a professional stake in a particular view of the world. How a nation relates to the world depends greatly on the character of these bureaucracies and this in turn depends upon the distribution of power and rewards within a society. Where, for example, military bureaucracies are dominant, international issues tend to be defined as military problems. Where bureaucracies with a stake in expanding trade or other sets of relationships have a major voice, the definition of national interest is usually quite different.

Max Weber points out that the characteristic feature of a "guaranteed" legal order is a staff or a bureaucracy to carry out rules. The very existence of such a staff shapes people's expectations; if there is a group of individuals with a professional stake in enforcing certain rules, the rules are likely to be carried out. This idea has been elevated to the status of a presumption in the Anglo-American law of evidence. Where an official has a duty to perform a certain act, the act is presumed done.

Traditional national security bureaucracies ordinarily oppose restrictions on the right to use violence because the power struggle view of the world has been a central organizing idea for the national state. According to this view, there is a limited supply of goods in the world, including prestige and deference, and all nations make generous estimates of their fair share. Therefore, the only safe course for even a rich and powerful nation is to keep acquiring more. The rise of other nations to power and influence necessarily threatens your own. In the language of strategy, life is a zero-sum game.

The more hostile the international environment, the more articulate becomes the power-struggle premise for all international decisions. The major crises of the postwar world can be best understood as symbolic episodes in a massive power struggle. The Berlin crisis and the Cuban missile affair were regarded literally as matters of life and death, not because they raised the issue of national survival or enslavement for either of the great power contenders, but because they were thought to involve the appearance of a radical shift of power from one side to another. Each side rejects the disarmament proposals of the other for the same reason. In the power-struggle model, the primary questions of international politics are jurisdictional, not problem-oriented (who should have power over the problem?, not, what should be done to solve the problem?). The complex substantive issues that confront the planet such as food scarcity, overpopulation, and the violation of human rights are simplified and subsumed under the competition for power. Governments view the issues more as weapons in political struggles than as primary concerns. They continually strive to put themselves in an ever better position to do what they want, but the purposes for which they accumulate power are in flux and often remain obscure. Governments run by traditional national security bureaucracies are far more accomplished at getting power than in using it for purposes other than acquiring more.

It is hardly surprising that the manipulation of violence has been the principal organizing idea for these officials; defense has been the raison d'être of the nation. Until the relatively recent advent of the welfare state, the only commitment a government made to its people was to defend them against outside attack. By its nature the defense task is peculiarly difficult to fit into an international framework. The

recent history of NATO is but the latest confirmation of the imperma-
nence of alliances.

The national security bureaucracies have enjoyed a spectacular
growth in power during the past century in almost all countries. In
Britain, Japan, Germany, the Soviet Union, China, and the United
States, the governments have been dominated by those committed
more to national self-sufficiency than to interdependence, more to
nationalism than to internationalism. The embryonic international society that existed before the turn of the century in which individuals
moved freely across national boundaries without passports and governments moderated their political conflicts to preserve needed commercial relations, has given way to the century of total war. Whether
the changed conditions of international life were responsible for the
growth of the bureaucracies or the bureaucracies helped create the
conditions is not important for our purposes. The result has been that
the governments of the most powerful states are in the hands of those
who by tradition and professional experience see the pursuit of power
by national states as the ultimate reality of international life.

VI. The Growth of New Bureaucracies and the Redefinition of National Security

Brierly may have overstated the contrast when he observed twenty
years ago that "individuals, by and large have the same basic interests,
personal and proprietary, whereas the interests of states are almost infinitely diverse. In a sense in which no individual is, every state is
unique."[11] But he is correct in suggesting that there are more long-
term common interests transcending national boundaries to be found
among individuals, corporations, labor groups, professional societies,
agronomists, and nonmilitary bureaucracies than among such traditional spokesmen for the national interest as foreign ministers or chiefs
of staff.

Such functional relationships which are centered on problems of
common interest form the basis of a transnational society. According
to Wolfgang Friedmann:

> Transnational society is represented by the increasing volume and
> scope of international co-operation in matters of common concern.
> The principal agents of these transnational relations are the states,
> using the instrumentalities of multilateral or bilateral international
> conventions, in such fields as international transport and communi-
> cations, health, conservation of fisheries, meteorological standards
> and the like. An important proportion of these transnational rela-
> tions is, however, carried and promoted by semi-public and private

[11] James L. Brierly, *The Outlook for International Law* (London 1944), 40-41.

groups dealing directly with each other. The activities carried on by these non-governmental international organizations range over the whole spectrum of relations, cultural, scientific, political, social and economic activities. They include such quasi-official bodies as the International Red Cross, or the World Council of Churches, various rival international organizations of Labour, the International Chamber of Commerce, the International Rubber Research Board, the International Tea Committee, the International Air Transport Association or the International Institute of Administrative Science. While the hundreds of non-governmental international organizations and associations vary greatly in importance and influence, they are clearly representative of the vast number of transnational activities in virtually all fields of human endeavour.[12]

Friedmann points out that some private groups already exercise what Karl Renner calls a "delegated power of command." By virtue of a particular economic position or expertise they make law. They act in what was formerly a legal vacuum and by acting they create new relationships. National governments must now take into account the views of new actors on the international scene, who derive their power from transnational relationships and from their capacity to solve pressing international problems.

The chief significance of the development of these new transnational actors is that they undermine the monopoly on foreign relations formerly held by the national security bureaucracies. New bureaucracies are claiming a share in decisions on international affairs that were once the exclusive province of generals and diplomats. Their presence on the international scene thus hedges the traditional exercise of sovereignty. The transnational corporation, for example, such as Standard Oil or Shell with assets, shareholders, and management from many countries, is a new actor with a critical role in making decisions on international affairs, particularly in Western Europe. The bureaucracies that run transnational corporations are subject to a set of loyalties and interests that transcend the nation-state. It appears that these new factors in world politics will become more and more influential. The direction of that influence is still not clear, but it will be dictated far more by concrete interests of the corporations than by traditional national security concerns. These bureaucracies see their own interests served by the development of cooperative transnational relationships rather than by the manipulation of violence. Thus they tend to see the national interest in less chauvinistic terms than the traditional national security bureaucracies.

The new problem-oriented bureaucracies should gain in power as

[12] Friedmann (fn. 8), 37-38.

the traditional national security bureaucracies increasingly fail—either to define adequately or to achieve national objectives through military means. For example, the tasks of rural reconstruction or population control of backward societies have little chance of success, as the Vietnam experience indicates, if they are an adjunct of the military effort of a great power. The more closely development projects are identified with a political confrontation, the more motivation someone will have to sabotage the effort. It is not fear of war that will loosen the grip of the older national bureaucracies and will make room for new ones, so much as repeated demonstrations of the impracticability of war. The more powerless the national security establishment of the modern state is shown to be in solving crucial problems, the more bureaucracies not closely tied to the confrontation model, whether in national governments, international agencies, or private organizations, will have opportunity to act. Such transnational bureaucracies may deal with a range of concrete problems from the international movement of capital to the control of food production.

One can predict that as nondefense bureaucracies of national governments, supranational institutions, and private groups assume a larger role and become accepted as part of the legitimate international order, their very existence will restrict the freedom of choice of national governments to define and pursue the national interest in traditional ways. Because of their skills and the importance of their tasks, such groups will enjoy increasing political power within their own societies. They are likely to claim increased legitimacy as rule-making authorities as the essential nature of their tasks becomes increasingly accepted.

Bureaucracies with concrete transnational connections and the need for a legal framework within which to operate are thus a promising stimulus for international legislation. For example, literacy programs, water resources programs, development authorities for particular regions, and common markets can become new sources of law. As bureaucracies devoted to such substantive tasks act on the international stage, their activities will be increasingly rationalized into an international legal structure. Because they are professionally committed to the solution of substantive transnational problems requiring cooperation they are likely to have alternative models of world politics, and, particularly, different conceptions of power. Bureaucracies, such as the Peace Corps or the Public Health Service, tend to define the national interest as the solution of practical problems. They do not deny the existence or importance of power in international life, but they are prone to seek ways to channel it to specific, constructive ends. They are likely to be more committed to international decision-making because most nondefense questions in international politics are difficult to resolve by individual nations acting alone. They are apt to be unsympathetic to the rhetoric of nation-to-nation confrontation which is frequently used to justify violations of international law rules limiting violence.

The body of law which these new sources of "positive enactment" are likely to develop conforms more to what H.L.A. Hart calls "facilities for realizing wishes" than a "collection of dont's." These new actors on the international scene are interested in law as a necessary regulator of advantageous relationships. But to protect these relationships they will also have a strong interest in persuading their political leaders to observe rules limiting the resort to violence. Where various influential constituencies within the nation have a personal stake in foreign policy it is no longer so easy to sacrifice these concrete interests to the abstract and mystical goals for which nations customarily resort to violence.

There are no satisfactory answers in the context of either the nation-state system or any of the alternative models for world government yet advanced, to the problem of a safe and equitable distribution of military power in the world. Some arrangements for the control of national military forces and international police forces will have to be made, but this is, in all likelihood, not the issue around which a warless world can be organized. The proliferation of problem-solving bureaucracies, however, may make it possible to avoid or postpone confronting directly the problem of managing violence while men turn their energies to more easily solvable problems.

VII. The Clash of the Bureaucracies

The growth of the problem-centered bureaucracies holds out some prospect of surrounding and taming these traditional national leaders who see the abstract concept of "national security" as the highest goal of policy and who believe that where the survival of their particular nation-state is threatened, legal restraints on violence must be abandoned. But this hopeful trend coexists with another trend with quite opposite implications. Since World War II, particularly, the national security establishments of the modern state have tried to arrest the process of decentralization of decision-making in international affairs by extending their own jurisdiction to what was formerly the "private sector." It has recently come to light that in the United States the Central Intelligence Agency has financed and exercised control over students, journalists, private foundations, labor unions, businessmen, and intellectuals in connection with their ostensibly independent international activities.[13] Even tourists have been encouraged to perform in-

---

[13] *New York Times*, February 19, 1967.

telligence functions. In the Soviet Union such groups are also subject to direction of the central government. In both countries the purpose has been the same. The national security bureaucracies have tried to establish a monopolistic control of international contacts so that the special interests of particular persons may be subordinated to the "national interest" as the national security establishment defines it. National security bureaucracies infiltrate and seek to control independent actors on the international scene because these new bureaucracies threaten to undermine the power of the old.

These bureaucracies are thus in conflict over fundamental questions of identity and function. The Peace Corps, for example, has gone to great lengths, including a recently revealed secret agreement with the C.I.A.,[14] to remain free of penetration by intelligence and military bureaucracies. The result has been that in the Dominican Republic, for example, Peace Corps volunteers took a position independent of the American Embassy, the military forces, or the C.I.A., and publicly criticized the U.S. intervention.[15] From their perspective, the landing of military forces destroyed the relationship they were trying to build. Precisely because of their independence the volunteers were a thorn in the flesh of the American ambassador.

Whether the new bureaucracies will be able to withstand the pressure toward monopolization of foreign relations will ultimately depend upon the development of supporting constituencies within the nation-state. One reason why national security bureaucracies have had such freedom to define the national interest for the rest of the population is that all but a very few citizens have any immediate or personal interest in international transactions. Since they have no personal knowledge or experience, they are content to leave the matter to experts, i.e., those who traditionally define the national interest. As more citizens become personally involved in international affairs because of the development of communications, commerce, and new transnational careers, the problem-centered bureaucracies should acquire new power to redefine the national interest. As an instrument for controlling human expectations and influencing behavior, law can play an important role in this process.

[14] *Washington Post*, March 13, 1967.
[15] *New York Times*, May 7, 1965.

Index

BOOKS WRITTEN
UNDER THE AUSPICES OF THE
CENTER OF INTERNATIONAL STUDIES
PRINCETON UNIVERSITY

Gabriel A. Almond, *The Appeals of Communism* (Princeton University Press 1954)

William W. Kaufmann, ed., *Military Policy and National Security* (Princeton University Press 1956)

Klaus Knorr, *The War Potential of Nations* (Princeton University Press 1956)

Lucian W. Pye, *Guerrilla Communism in Malaya* (Princeton University Press 1956)

Charles De Visscher, *Theory and Reality in Public International Law*, trans. by P. E. Corbett (Princeton University Press 1957; rev. ed. 1968)

Bernard C. Cohen, *The Political Process and Foreign Policy: The Making of the Japanese Peace Settlement* (Princeton University Press 1959)

Myron Weiner, *Party Politics in India: The Development of a Multi-Party System* (Princeton University Press 1957)

Percy E. Corbett, *Law in Diplomacy* (Princeton University Press 1959)

Rolf Sannwald and Jacques Stohler, *Economic Integration: Theoretical Assumptions and Consequences of European Unification*, trans. by Herman Karreman (Princeton University Press 1959)

Klaus Knorr, ed., *NATO and American Security* (Princeton University Press 1959)

Gabriel A. Almond and James S. Coleman, eds., *The Politics of the Developing Areas* (Princeton University Press 1960)

Herman Kahn, *On Thermonuclear War* (Princeton University Press 1960)

Sidney Verba, *Small Groups and Political Behavior: A Study of Leadership* (Princeton University Press 1961)

Robert J. C. Butow, *Tojo and the Coming of the War* (Princeton University Press 1961)

Glenn H. Snyder, *Deterrence and Defense: Toward a Theory of National Security* (Princeton University Press 1961)

Klaus Knorr and Sidney Verba, eds., *The International System: Theoretical Essays* (Princeton University Press 1961)

Peter Paret and John W. Shy, *Guerrillas in the 1960's* (Praeger 1962)

George Modelski, *A Theory of Foreign Policy* (Praeger 1962)

Klaus Knorr and Thornton Read, eds., *Limited Strategic War* (Praeger 1963)

Frederick S. Dunn, *Peace-Making and the Settlement with Japan* (Princeton University Press 1963)

Arthur L. Burns and Nina Heathcote, *Peace-Keeping by United Nations Forces* (Praeger 1963)

Richard A. Falk, *Law, Morality, and War in the Contemporary World* (Praeger 1963)

James N. Rosenau, *National Leadership and Foreign Policy: A Case Study in the Mobilization of Public Support* (Princeton University Press 1963)

Gabriel A. Almond and Sidney Verba, *The Civic Culture: Political Attitudes and Democracy in Five Nations* (Princeton University Press 1963)

Bernard C. Cohen, *The Press and Foreign Policy* (Princeton University Press 1963)

Richard L. Sklar, *Nigerian Political Parties: Power in an Emergent African Nation* (Princeton University Press 1963)

Peter Paret, *French Revolutionary Warfare from Indochina to Algeria: The Analysis of a Political and Military Doctrine* (Praeger 1964)

Harry Eckstein, ed., *Internal War: Problems and Approaches* (Free Press 1964)

Cyril E. Black and Thomas P. Thornton, eds., *Communism and Revolution: The Strategic Uses of Political Violence* (Princeton University Press 1964)

Miriam Camps, *Britain and the European Community 1955-1963* (Princeton University Press 1964)

Thomas P. Thornton, ed., *The Third World in Soviet Perspective: Studies by Soviet Writers on the Developing Areas* (Princeton University Press 1964)

James N. Rosenau, ed., *International Aspects of Civil Strife* (Princeton University Press 1964)

Sidney I. Ploss, *Conflict and Decision-Making in Soviet Russia: A Case Study of Agricultural Policy, 1953-1963* (Princeton University Press 1965)

Richard A. Falk and Richard J. Barnet, eds., *Security in Disarmament* (Princeton University Press 1965)

Karl von Vorys, *Political Development in Pakistan* (Princeton University Press 1965)

Harold and Margaret Sprout, *The Ecological Perspective on Human Affairs, With Special Reference to International Politics* (Princeton University Press 1965)

Klaus Knorr, *On the Uses of Military Power in the Nuclear Age* (Princeton University Press 1966)

Harry Eckstein, *Division and Cohesion in Democracy: A Study of Norway* (Princeton University Press 1966)

Cyril E. Black, *The Dynamics of Modernization: A Study in Comparative History* (Harper and Row 1966)

Peter Kunstadter, ed., *Southeast Asian Tribes, Minorities, and Nations* (Princeton University Press 1967)

E. Victor Wolfenstein, *The Revolutionary Personality: Lenin, Trotsky, Gandhi* (Princeton University Press 1967)

Leon Gordenker, *The UN Secretary-General and the Maintenance of Peace* (Columbia University Press 1967)

Oran R. Young, *The Intermediaries: Third Parties in International Crises* (Princeton University Press 1967)

James N. Rosenau, ed., *Domestic Sources of Foreign Policy* (Free Press 1967)

Richard F. Hamilton, *Affluence and the French Worker in the Fourth Republic* (Princeton University Press 1967)

Linda B. Miller, *World Order and Local Disorder: The United Nations and Internal Conflicts* (Princeton University Press 1967)

Wolfram F. Hanrieder, *West German Foreign Policy, 1949-1963: International Pressures and Domestic Response* (Stanford University Press 1967)

Richard H. Ullman, *Britain and the Russian Civil War: November 1918-February 1920* (Princeton University Press 1968)

Robert Gilpin, *France in the Age of the Scientific State* (Princeton University Press 1968)

William B. Bader, *The United States and the Spread of Nuclear Weapons* (Pegasus 1968)

Richard A. Falk, *Legal Order in a Violent World* (Princeton University Press 1968)

Cyril E. Black, Richard A. Falk, Klaus Knorr, and Oran R. Young, *Neutralization and World Politics* (Princeton University Press 1968)

Oran R. Young, *The Politics of Force: Bargaining During International Crises* (Princeton University Press 1969)

Klaus Knorr and James N. Rosenau, eds., *Contending Approaches to International Politics* (Princeton University Press 1969)

James N. Rosenau, ed., *Linkage Politics: Essays on the Convergence of National and International Systems* (Free Press 1969)

John T. McAlister, Jr., *Viet Nam: The Origins of Revolution* (Knopf 1969)

Jean Edward Smith, *Germany Beyond the Wall: People, Politics and Prosperity* (Little, Brown 1969)

James Barros, *Betrayal from Within: Joseph Avenol, Secretary-General of the League of Nations, 1933-1940* (Yale University Press 1969)

Charles Hermann, *Crises in Foreign Policy: A Simulation Analysis* (Bobbs-Merrill 1969)

Robert C. Tucker, *The Marxian Revolutionary Idea: Essays on Marxist Thought and Its Impact on Radical Movements* (W. W. Norton 1969)

Harvey Waterman, *Political Change in Contemporary France: The Politics of an Industrial Democracy* (Charles E. Merrill 1969)

Richard A. Falk and Cyril E. Black, eds., *The Future of the International Legal Order*, Vol. I, *Trends and Patterns* (Princeton University Press 1969)

Ted Robert Gurr, *Why Men Rebel* (Princeton University Press 1969)

C. S. Whitaker, Jr., *The Politics of Tradition: Continuity and Change in Northern Nigeria, 1946-1966* (Princeton University Press 1970)

Richard A. Falk, *The Status of Law in International Society* (Princeton University Press 1970)

Henry Bienen, *Tanzania: Party Transformation and Economic Development* (Princeton University Press 1967, rev. edn., 1970)

Klaus Knorr, *Military Power and Potential* (D. C. Heath 1970)

Richard A. Falk and Cyril E. Black, eds., *The Future of the International Legal Order*, Vol. II, *Wealth and Resources* (Princeton University Press 1970)

Leon Gordenker, ed., *The United Nations and International Politics* (Princeton University Press 1971)

Cyril E. Black and Richard A. Falk, eds., *The Future of the International Legal Order*, Vol. III, *Conflict Management* (Princeton University Press 1971)

Harold and Margaret Sprout, *Toward a Politics of the Planet Earth* (Van Nostrand Reinhold Co. 1971)